Tokyo

Chris Rowthorn
Chris Taylor

東京東京東京東京東京東京東京東京東

KU-680-605

東京東京東京東京東京東京東京東京東京東京東京東京東京東京東京東京

Tokyo

3rd edition

Published by
Lonely Planet Publications
Head Office: 90 Maribyrnong St, Footscray, Victoria 3011, Australia
Branches: 150 Linden St, Oakland, CA 94607, USA
10a Spring Place, London NW5 3BH, UK
1 rue du Dahomey, 75011 Paris, France

Printed by
Colorcraft Ltd, Hong Kong

Script Typeset by
Atsushi Takagi, Australia

Photographs by

Glenn Beanland	Japan National Tourist	Chris Rowthorn
Thomas Daniell	Organization (JNTO)	Chris Taylor
Charlotte Hindle	Matthias Ley	Tony Wheeler
Richard I'Anson	Martin Moos	

Front cover: Tokyo Metropolitan Government Offices (Fish-eye view), Grant V Faint, The Image Bank

First Published
March 1993

This Edition
September 1998

Although the authors and publisher have tried to make the information as accurate as possible, they accept no responsibility for any loss, injury or inconvenience sustained by any person using this book.

National Library of Australia Cataloguing in Publication Data

Rowthorn, Chris.
Tokyo.

3rd ed.
Includes index.
ISBN 0 86442 567 8.

1. Tokyo (Japan) – Guidebooks. I. Title.

915.21350449

text & maps © Lonely Planet 1998
Tokyo Subway Network reproduced by kind permission of Teito Rapid Transit Authority
photos © photographers as indicated 1998

All rights reserved. No part of this publication may be reproduced, stored in a retrieval system or transmitted in any form by any means, electronic, mechanical, photocopying, recording or otherwise, except brief extracts for the purpose of review, without the written permission of the publisher and copyright owner.

Chris Rowthorn

Chris was born in England and grew up in the USA. After graduating from college in 1989, he worked as a guacamole chef in a brew pub in Berkeley, California. Tiring of over-ripe avocadoes, he worked for a while in an environmental chemistry laboratory back east. He moved to Japan in 1992 and, after a stint as an English teacher, became a regional correspondent for the *Japan Times*. He took time off from newspaper writing to co-author the 6th edition of the Lonely Planet guide to *Japan*. Chris currently lives in Kyoto and travels whenever possible in Asia.

From the Author

Chris would like thank Hiroko Kimura of the Japan National Tourist Organization for her tireless efforts. He would also like to thank Kisaburo Minato and the entire Minato family for their kindness. Special thanks are also due to Chiori Matsunaga for her excellent and accurate work with kanji. Thanks also to Ralph Saunders, Nozomi Oishi, Shigehisa Yamashita, Elizabeth Shea, Tom Daniell, Gordon Maclaren, John Gorman, Robert Schwartz, Lucy Dewar, Neil Garscadden, Brian Eisenburger, Hendrien Broens, Naoki Shoji, Marius Serrao and Yu Xin Zhang.

This Book

The 1st edition of *Tokyo* was written by Chris Taylor, who also researched and updated the 2nd edition. Chris Taylor's work has been expanded and updated by Chris Rowthorn for this 3rd edition.

From the Publisher

This edition of *Tokyo* was edited by Russell Kerr. It was proofed by Anne Mulvaney and Greg Alford. Maps were drawn by Verity Campbell and Chris Thomas, with valuable colour mapping assistance from Leanne Peake.

While Max stood guard, Verity designed the book and took it through the wee hours of layout. The flash cover was designed by Margie Jung.

Thanks to Quentin Frayne for his patient assistance with the occasionally recalcitrant language section, Atsushi Takagi for his expert work with the Japanese script, Megan Fraser for her general interest in the book and last-minute assistance, and Kerrie Williams for doing the hard work on the index.

We'd also like to acknowledge Geoff Stringer, Kristin Odijk, Chris Love, Katrina Browning, Nick Tapp, Adam McCrow and Sharan Kaur for trying to keep the trains running on time. Hats off to Mick Weldon for his original *manga* artwork.

Thanks

Many thanks to the travellers who used the last edition and wrote to us with helpful hints, useful advice and interesting anecdotes. The many to whom we are grateful include:

Kaori Akahane, Paul Bakker, Artur Correia, Doug Fischer, Manuel Gonzalez, Jill Hannah, Miyuki Ishii, Paul Lufkin, Iris Lun, Alfred MacRae, Linda Nagy, Jane Perkins, PS Ranjan, Tom Riddle, Yves Rosiers, Connie Schmollinger, Kumiko Tasaki, Kees Verloop, Peggy Weymouth.

Warning & Request

Things change – prices go up, schedules change, good places go bad and bad places go bankrupt – nothing stays the same. So, if you find things better or worse, recently opened or long since closed, please tell us and help make the next edition even more accurate and useful.

We value all of the feedback we receive from travellers. Julie Young coordinates a small but hardworking team who read and acknowledge every letter, postcard and email, and ensure that every morsel of information finds its way to the appropriate authors, editors and publishers.

Everyone who writes to us will find their name in the next edition of the appropriate guide and will also receive a free subscription to our quarterly newsletter, *Planet Talk*. The very best contributions will be rewarded with a free Lonely Planet guide.

Excerpts from your correspondence may appear in new editions of this guide; in *Planet Talk*; or on our Web site – please let us know if you don't want your letter published or your name acknowledged.

Contents

Introduction

Tokyo is such a huge city that you could spend a lifetime exploring it. At first glance, it may look like a nondescript labyrinth of concrete housing estates and office blocks traversed by overhead expressways and railway lines. But it doesn't take long to realise that, like all great cities, Tokyo is a conundrum, a riddle of contradictions that springs from tensions between large-scale ugliness and meticulous detail, the frantic rhythms of 20th century consumer culture and the still, quiet moments that are the legacy of other, older traditions.

Tokyo is the nesting place of both Japan Inc and the lineages of the old town of Edo. Reposing by fashionable Ginza and administrative Nihombashi is the Imperial Palace, with its gardens and photogenic views. In the heart of Akasaka, surrounded by world-class hotels, trendy boutiques and eateries, is Hie-jinja Shrine. The central areas of Ueno and Asakusa are home to splendid museums and to bustling Sensō-ji Temple, possibly Japan's liveliest Buddhist temple. And just two hours from Tokyo by train are the historic towns of Kamakura and Nikkō, and the scenic regions of Hakone and Mt Fuji.

While Tokyo sports some of the world's biggest and most lavish department stores, the average Tokyo suburb hasn't fallen prey to supermarket culture – the streets are lined with tiny specialist shops and restaurants, most of which stay open late into the night. Near soaring office blocks are entertainment quarters – mazes of narrow alleys that blaze with neon by night and offer intoxicating escape from the work regimen that is the lot of Tokyo's surging crowds of office workers. And in the shadow of the overhead expressways exist pockets of another Tokyo – an old wooden house, a Japanese inn, an old lady in kimono and *geta* slippers sweeping the pavement outside her home with a straw broom.

What confronts the visitor above all is Tokyo's sheer level of energy. On the busy train lines, even late on a Monday night, it's standing room only. The crowds carry you through an auditory assault, from ghostly train announcements and sing-song instructions on escalators to blasting shop jingles and the digitised melodies of traffic lights and vending machines, not to mention the politicians in cars fitted with loudspeakers, thanking constituents for having voted for them in the last election.

Some of the best sights Tokyo offers jump out at you unexpectedly on a crowded street – the woman dressed in kimono buying a hamburger at McDonald's or the Buddhist monk with an alms bowl, poised serenely in the midst of jostling shoppers in Ginza. Tokyo is a living city. It may offer the visitor some splendid sights, but it is less a collection of sights than an experience.

Facts about Tokyo

HISTORY

When the first European visitors, Portuguese traders, came to Japan in the 16th century, Tokyo was an unlikely destination. The area then known as Edo was a sizeable fishing town and even had an abandoned castle, but there was little to indicate that Edo would one day grow to become the capital of Japan and one of the world's major cities. Strangely enough, however, the Portuguese visitors were instrumental in the events that led to Edo usurping Kyoto as Japan's traditional seat of imperial power and becoming Tokyo. Some three centuries after the first western influx, when Commodore Matthew Perry of the US Navy showed up with demands that the country open its doors to commerce with the outside world, it was to the erstwhile fishing town of Edo that he came.

Before Edo

Shintō, Japan's native religion, had its origin in the Yayoi period (300 BC to 300 AD). But the most important event in the early history of Japan was the arrival of Buddhism in the 6th century via China and Korea.

Buddhism brought a highly evolved system of metaphysics, codes of law and the Chinese writing system, a conduit for the principles of Confucian statecraft. By the 8th century, however, the Buddhist clerical bureaucracy had become vast, threatening the authority of the imperial administration. The emperor responded by relocating the capital from Nara and establishing a new seat of imperial power at Heian (modern-day Kyoto). Kyoto was, by and large, to serve as the imperial capital until the Meiji Restoration and Tokyo's foundation as Japan's capital. The one interruption came when Minamoto Yoritomo defeated the ruling Taira clan and established the first shōgunate in Kamakura in 1180. He ruled a military government there until 1333, when he was toppled by a rebellion and official power reverted to Kyoto.

Even from Kyoto's early days, a warrior *samurai* class in the employ of feudal lords (*daimyō*) was emerging. Much of Japan's subsequent history was a record of struggles for power among the daimyō while the emperor mostly watched impotently from the haven of Kyoto's Imperial Palace.

By the time the Portuguese arrived in 1543, Japan was a divided realm of feudal fiefs. One of the most powerful daimyō, Oda Nobunaga, was quick to see how the Portuguese might have a part to play in his own ambitious plans. He saw Christianity as a potential weapon against the power of the Buddhist clergy and made ample use of another import brought by the God-fearing Portuguese – firearms. By the time he was assassinated in 1581, Nobunaga had united much of central Japan. He was succeeded by Toyotomi Hideyoshi, who continued unification but looked less favourably on the growing Christian movement, subjecting it to systematic persecution.

Hideyoshi's power was briefly contested by Tokugawa Ieyasu, son of a minor lord who had been allied to Nobunaga. After a brief struggle for power, Ieyasu agreed to a truce with Hideyoshi; in return, Hideyoshi granted him eight provinces of eastern Japan, including all of the Kantō region. While Hideyoshi intended this as a move to weaken Ieyasu by separating him from his ancestral homeland, the young Ieyasu looked upon the gift of land as an opportunity to strengthen his power. He set about reclaiming his homeland and turning Edo into a real city.

When Hideyoshi died in 1598, power passed to his son, Hideyori. However, Ieyasu had been busily scheming to secure the shōgunate himself and soon went to war against those loyal to Hideyori. He finally defeated them at the Battle of Sekigahara in 1600, leaving Ieyasu in a position of supreme power. He chose Edo as his permanent base and thus began 250 years of Tokugawa rule.

Tokugawa Edo

Tokugawa Ieyasu was appointed *shōgun* (military administrator) in 1603 by the emperor. One of the most important acts of the Tokugawa regime in its quest to achieve total control of the country was to implement the *sankin kōtai* system. This demanded that all daimyō throughout Japan spend at least one year out of two in Edo. Their wives and children were to remain in Edo. This dislocating ransom policy made it difficult for ambitious daimyō to usurp the Tokugawas.

Society was made rigidly hierarchical, comprising (in descending order of importance) the nobility, who had nominal power; the daimyō and their samurai; the farmers; and finally the artisans and merchants. Class dress, living quarters and even manner of speech were all strictly codified, and interclass movement prohibited.

When Ieyasu died in 1616, his ashes were briefly laid to rest in Chūbu before being moved to Nikkō. Generations of Tokugawas improved upon his shrine, transforming it into one of the grandest in all Japan.

In 1638, concerned that missionaries were gaining too much power, Ieyasu's grandson, Tokugawa Iemitsu, massacred a number of Kyūshū Christians and closed the country to almost all foreign trade. This radical isolation policy, known as *sakoku*, was to remove Japan from the world stage for nearly three centuries.

These sudden changes led to the rapid growth of the small town of Edo. By the early 17th century the population had grown to more than one million, making it the largest city in the world. Meanwhile, the caste-like society imposed by Tokugawa rule divided Edo into a high city (Yamanote) region and a low city (Shitamachi) region. The higher Yamanote (literally hand of the mountains) area was home to daimyō and their samurai, while the lower orders of Edo society were forced into the low-lying Shitamachi area.

Shitamachi residents lived in squalid conditions, usually in flimsy wooden structures with earthen floors. Great conflagrations often swept across these shantytowns. These fires were known to locals as *Edo no hana*, or flowers of Edo. The cocky bravura of the expression sums up the spirit of Shitamachi – living under circumstances of great privation and in accordance with a social order set by the Tokugawa regime, Shitamachi produced a flourishing culture that thumbed its nose at social hardships and the strictures of the shōgunate. Today, *ukiyo-e* prints give us glimpses into this world, where money meant more than rank, actors and artists were the arbiters of style and prostitutes elevated their accomplishments to a level matching those of the ladies of nobility.

Another feature of Edo that has left its mark on today's Tokyo was the division of the city into towns *(machi)* according to profession. Even today it is possible to stumble across small enclaves that specialise in particular wares. Most famous are Jimbōchō, the bookshop area; Kappabashi, with its plastic food and kitchen supplies; Asakusabashi, with its toy shops; and Akihabara, which now specialises in electronics, but which has been a bicycle retailing area, an area specialising in domestic household goods and a freight yard.

Tokyo Rising

The turning point for the city of Edo, indeed for all of Japan, was the arrival of Commodore Matthew Perry's armada of 'black ships' at Edo (Tokyo) Bay in 1853. Perry's US Navy expedition demanded that Japan open to foreign trade. Other western powers were quick to follow the USA in demanding the Japanese open treaty ports and end the isolation policy. The coming of westerners heralded a far-reaching social revolution against which the antiquated Tokugawa regime was powerless. In 1867-8, faced with wide-scale antigovernment feeling and accusations that the regime had failed to prepare Japan for the threat of the west, the last Tokugawa shōgun resigned and power reverted to Emperor Meiji.

The Meiji Restoration was not an entirely peaceful handover of power. In Edo some 2000 Tokugawa loyalists put up a futile last-ditch resistance to the imperial forces in the brief Battle of Ueno. The struggle took place around Kanei-ji Temple, which, along with Zōjō-ji Temple, was one of Edo's two mortuary temples for the Tokugawa shōgunate.

In 1868 the emperor moved the seat of imperial power from Kyoto to Edo, renaming the city Tokyo (Eastern Capital) in the process. In some ways it was less a restoration than a revolution. A crash course in industrialisation and militarisation began, and by 1889 Japan had instituted a western-style constitution. In remarkably little time Japan achieved military victories over China (1894-5) and Russia (1904-5) and embarked on modern, western-style empire building, from annexation of Taiwan (1895) to Korea (1910) and Micronesia (1914).

Nationalists were also transforming Shintō into a jingoistic state religion. Seen as a corrupting foreign influence, Buddhism suffered badly – many valuable artefacts and temples were destroyed, and the common people were urged to place their faith in the pure religion of 'State Shintō'.

During the Meiji period, changes that were taking place all over Japan could be seen most prominently in the country's new capital city. Tokyo's rapid industrialisation, uniting around the nascent *zaibatsu* (huge industrial and trading combines), drew job seekers from around Japan, causing the population to grow rapidly. Western-style buildings began to spring up in fashionable areas such as Ginza, and in the 1880s electric lighting was introduced. However, if the Meiji Restoration sounded the death knell for old Edo, there were two more events that were to erase most traces of the old city.

Tokyo Disasters

The Great Kantō Earthquake struck at noon on 1 September 1923. It was less the earthquake itself than the subsequent fires, lasting some 40 hours, that laid waste to the city. A quarter of the quake's 142,000 fatalities occurred in one savage firestorm that swept through a clothing depot.

In true Edo style, reconstruction began almost immediately. The spirit in which this was undertaken is perhaps best summed up by Edward Seidensticker. He observed that it was popular wisdom that any business which did not resume trading within three days of being burnt out did not have a future. Opportunities were lost in reconstructing the city – streets might have been widened and the capital might have been transformed into something more of a showcase. As it was, Tokyoites were given a second opportunity.

From the accession of Emperor Hirohito and the initiation of the Shōwa period in 1926, Japanese society was marked by a quickening tide of nationalist fervour. In 1931 the Japanese invaded Manchuria, and in 1937 embarked on full-scale hostilities with China. By 1940 a tripartite pact with Germany and Italy had been signed and a new order for all of Asia formulated: the 'Greater Asia Co-Prosperity Sphere'. On 7 September 1941 the Japanese attacked Pearl Harbor and thus the USA, their principle rival in the Asia-Pacific region.

Despite initial successes, the war was disastrous for Japan. The earliest bombing raids on Tokyo took place on 18 April 1942, when B-25 bombers carried out a bombing and strafing raid on the city, with 364 casualties. Much worse was to come. Incendiary bombing commenced in March 1944, notably on the nights of the 9th and 10th, when some two-fifths of the city, mainly in the Shitamachi area, went up in smoke and some 70,000 to 80,000 lives were lost. The same raids destroyed Asakusa's Sensō-ji Temple, and later raids destroyed Meiji-jingū Shrine. By the time Emperor Hirohito made his famous address to the Japanese people on 15 August 1945, much of Tokyo had been decimated and sections of it almost completely depopulated as surely as if it had shared the same fate (atomic-bomb explosions) as Hiroshima and Nagasaki.

Postwar Years

Tokyo's phoenix-like rise from the ashes of WWII and its emergence as a major global city is something of a miracle. Once again, Tokyoites did not take the devastation as an opportunity to redesign their city, but rebuilt where the old had once stood.

During the US occupation in the early postwar years, Tokyo was something of a honky-tonk town. Now-respectable areas such as Yūrakuchō were the haunt of the so-called *pan-pan* girls, and areas such as Ikebukuro and Ueno had thriving black-market zones. The remains of Ueno's black market can be seen in the Ameyoko Arcade, which is still a lively market, though there is no longer anything very black about it.

By 1951, with a boom in Japanese profits arising from the Korean War, Tokyo, especially the central business district, was being rapidly rebuilt, and the subway began to take on its present form. The city has never looked back. From the postwar years to the present, Tokyo has continually reconstructed itself.

During the 1960s and 70s, Tokyo re-emerged as one of the centres of growing Asian nationalism (the first phase was in the 1910s and 20s). Increasing numbers of Asian students have come to Tokyo, taking home with them new ideas about Asia's role in the postwar world.

One of Tokyo's proudest moments came when it hosted the 1964 summer Olympics, and in preparation the city embarked on a frenzy of construction unequalled in its history. Many Japanese see this time as a turning point in the nation's history, the moment Japan finally recovered from the devastation of WWII to emerge as a major player in the modern world economy.

Construction and modernisation continued at a breakneck pace through the 70s, with the interruption of two Middle East oil crises, to reach a peak in the late 80s, when wildly inflated real estate prices and stock speculation fuelled what is now known as the 'bubble economy'. When the bubble burst in 1989, the economy went into a slump, one from which it has not fully recovered.

In March 1995, members of the Aum Shinrikyō cult released sarin nerve gas on a crowded Tokyo commuter train, killing 12 and injuring 5000. This, together with the Kōbe earthquake of the same year, signalled the end of Japan's feeling of omnipotence, born of the unlimited successes of the 80s.

Now, the city is working to get over its crisis of confidence and shake the seemingly intractable recession.

Having survived mad cults and the burst of the bubble, Tokyo continues to forge ahead. Vast areas of Tokyo Bay have been reclaimed and are now home to international conference centres and business parks, and work is under way to overhaul the already excellent subway system. The city is also attempting a modest 'green revolution'.

Tokyo is above all a singular expression of Japanese modernity, with a concentration of industry, business, higher education, the arts and a sheer diversity rarely found in capital cities around the globe.

東京 東京 東京 東京 東京 東京 東京 東京 東

The Uyoku

Since the end of WWII, right-wing and nationalist sentiments have generally taken a back seat to moderate political views or outright apathy. However, there remain pockets of right-wing sentiment. These are most visible to the visitor in the form of sinister black buses and vans which ply the streets of big cities blaring patriotic Japanese songs at ear-splitting volume. These vehicles represent the propaganda arm of the *uyoku*, far-right political parties and organisations.

While rather alarming at first sight, uyoku buses and their occupants pose no threat to tourists. Rather, their target is the Japanese public. When not playing music, speakers deliver lengthy diatribes against Japanese politicians or a litany of nationalist sentiments shot through with a fierce devotion to the emperor.

Uyoku groups have limited appeal these days – Japanese pedestrians studiously ignore black buses blaring 100 decibels of noise. When regular citizens pay them any notice at all, it's usually to dismiss them as cranks.

There is a dark side to the uyoku: they act as a volunteer police force for right and right-leaning politicians, effectively prohibiting criticism of the emperor. This is done by intimidating would-be critics with threats of violence, which are occasionally carried out.

As long as Japan maintains a stable and healthy economy, the uyoku will likely remain a fringe element with little political clout. If, however, things change, it is conceivable that their status will too. In the meantime, the black buses remain a sobering echo of a darker time in Japanese history. ■

東京 東京 東京 東京 東京 東京 東京 東京 東

GEOGRAPHY

Tokyo is situated on the Kantō Plain, on the eastern seaboard of Honshū island, the largest of Japan's four principal islands.

Administratively, Japan is made up of 47 prefectures (usually *ken*). Tokyo Metropolitan Prefecture itself comprises 23 wards *(ku)*, 27 cities *(shi)*, one county *(gun)* and four island administrative districts *(shi-chō)*, a total area of 2168 sq km. Tokyo Metropolitan Prefecture is bordered by Saitama Prefecture to the north, Chiba Prefecture to the northeast, Tokyo Bay to the south-east, Yamanashi Prefecture to the west and Kanagawa Prefecture to the south-west.

The western Yamanote wards lie on the Musashino Plateau, a deposit of volcanic ash from the Fuji-Hakone mountain range. Parts of the eastern Shitamachi area lie beneath sea level and other areas have been built up on reclaimed land in the Tokyo Bay area.

CLIMATE & WHEN TO GO

Like the rest of Japan, the best time to visit Tokyo is spring, from March to May. From early April is the cherry blossom season, when even Tokyo can seem quite beautiful.

It's a lively time too, with hordes of revellers heading off to the parks for *hanami* (cherry

1 Nerima-ku 練馬区	13 Chiyoda-ku 千代田区
2 Itabashi-ku 板橋区	14 Taitō-ku 台東区
3 Kita-ku 北区	15 Sumida-ku 墨田区
4 Adachi-ku 足立区	16 Edogawa-ku 江戸川区
5 Katsushika-ku 葛飾区	17 Kōtō-ku 江藤区
6 Arakawa-ku 荒川区	18 Chūō-ku 中央区
7 Bunkyō-ku 文京区	19 Minato-ku 港区
8 Toshima-ku 豊島区	20 Setagaya-ku 世田谷区
9 Nakano-ku 中野区	21 Meguro-ku 目黒区
10 Suginami-ku 杉並区	22 Shinagawa-ku 品川区
11 Shibuya-ku 渋谷区	23 Ōta-ku 大田区
12 Shinjuku-ku 新宿区	

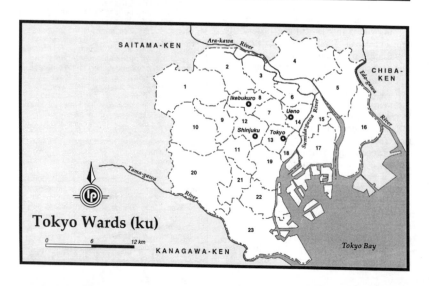

Tokyo Wards (ku)

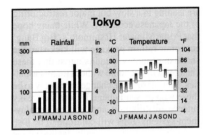

blossom viewing) parties. Summer is hot and muggy, a time when the overcrowded trains are at their most unbearable. The monsoon season *(tsuyu)*, which usually falls at the beginning of summer in June, can mean four or five days of torrential rain that can play havoc with a tight travel itinerary.

Autumn (September to November) is the next best time to be in Tokyo. Areas like Kamakura and Nikkō are especially beautiful at this time of year. The weather is cool and there's a high proportion of clear days – perfect sightseeing weather. Temperatures occasionally drop below 0°C in winter, but most of the time it's just heavy overcoat weather. Tokyo generally gets a couple of snowfalls every winter, but they're usually over fairly quickly. Depending on your preferences, the quiet winter can be a better time to be in Tokyo than the height of summer.

On the whole, it's probably a good idea to avoid visiting Japan during major holidays, in particular Golden Week (29 April to 5 May) and the mid-August O-bon festival. Things close down over New Year as well. However, holidays can be a good time to do some sightseeing in Tokyo, as most of the locals are away and the city becomes a ghost town (well, almost). If your trip includes other parts of Japan, however, try and reschedule it around these national holidays.

ECOLOGY & ENVIRONMENT
Tokyo is one of the cleanest cities in Asia. This was not always the case. Back in the years of helter-skelter economic growth following WWII, Japan was one of the most polluted countries in the world. From 1967, when Japan's first anti-pollution laws were passed, things have improved immensely.

However, water pollution is still a problem in the rivers of Tokyo and in Tokyo Bay, and air pollution often exceeds government-set levels. Nevertheless, pollution is not a deterrent to exploring the city, as it can be in other Asian metropolises.

The main environmental concern for residents is the shortage of greenery and parks. The average Tokyo resident enjoys a living space of less than 20 sq metres, streets and transport facilities are crowded, and it is often a long haul to a real park. Most suburban 'parks' consist of a tiny patch of bare earth with a couple of swings.

There is currently something of a 'green movement' in Japan, centring on recycling, co-op movements, organic food, proper waste-disposal and citizen action groups. Recent changes in recycling laws have also led to decreases in solid waste dumped into already overloaded landfills. Japan still lags far behind other industrial democracies, but there is hope that the country will continue to work toward increasing environmental awareness.

FLORA & FAUNA
Flora
The flora of the Kantō Plain resembles that of some parts of Korea and China. Much of the plain was originally marshland, while areas of higher ground were heavily forested. In today's Tokyo, you will see little evidence of either zone, since both are mostly buried under concrete. Parks are heavily manicured and do not reflect the original flora. Many of them are beautiful, however.

Within easy reach of Tokyo are a number of national parks which give you a better chance to appreciate the natural beauty of Japan. These include Nikkō National Park and Fuji-Hakone-Izu National Park (see the Excursions chapter). Further afield, Minami-Alps National Park presents the visitor with some of Japan's most stunning mountain scenery.

Fauna

You will see little evidence of Japan's wild-life in Tokyo, where pigeons and domestic animals hold sway. However, national parks are home to some wilder species, including the endemic Japanese macaque (better known as the snow monkey).

In the city, even family pets are routinely treated poorly, often tied to stakes and left to bark at passers-by. Pets are also regularly abandoned and left to be destroyed by the city authorities. At zoos in Tokyo and else-where, the cages and display areas of animals are often cramped and dirty. This does not go unnoticed by the Japanese, who are starting to band together to fight such mistreatment. Contact the Japan Environmental Exchange (☎ 03-5434-9456) for more information.

ECONOMY

Japan's postwar success story has led to certain exaggerated perceptions. While exports are highly visible, they still account for less than 10% of the nation's GNP. Japanese investment in the USA is still on a far smaller scale than similar investment by countries such as Britain and Canada.

In just 50 years, Japan has gone from being a defeated empire to the world's largest creditor nation. This can largely be attributed to industriousness, reinvestment in research and development, far-sighted management and production strategies, the export orientation of the economy, controls on imports and the shifting fortunes of the yen.

A major reason for Japan's much vaunted trade surpluses has been the low level of its imports. For a long time, Japanese imports could be largely accounted for by its energy requirements, of which it imports more than 80%. This has been changing over the last few years. The high yen and consumer dis-satisfaction with exorbitant retail prices have made cheap foreign products irresistibly at-tractive to discount outfits which buy in bulk overseas and bypass Japan's complicated, value-adding retail distribution network.

Then there's the recession which came in the wake of the much-vaunted 'bubble eco-nomy' of the late 80s. All these developments are leading to a slow but major restructuring of the Japanese economy. While many hope that Prime Minister Hashimoto's 'Big Bang' economic reform package will kick-start the sluggish economy, pundits agree that these changes will not come without many casual-ties. Victims of these changes are likely to be those who presently benefit from the creaky finance, distribution and lifetime employ-ment systems. Jobs will continue to be lost, and the jobs crisis currently facing young graduates will extend further into the ranks of Japan's mid-career workers.

Tokyo's role in these changes has been central; the rest of Japan tends to have to catch up. Thus, while the rest of the country is still getting used to the idea of multiple careers in one lifetime, loyalty to one's self over one's company, and life online during the Internet 'revolution', in trend-setting Tokyo these are accepted as givens.

POPULATION & PEOPLE

According to mythology, the origins of the Japanese people stretch back to a time when the world was the pristine playground of the gods. The Japanese are, according to this scheme, divine in origin, the issue of the sun goddess, Amaterasu Ōmikami.

In more secular terms, Japanese people belong to the Mongoloid group, like Koreans and Han Chinese. Evidence points to Japan as the terminus for waves of immigration from other parts of Asia, Europe, Siberia and even the Polynesian islands of the Pacific.

Around 11.8 million of Japan's more than 123 million people live in metropolitan Tokyo. The city's daytime population is actually much higher – more than 22 million people use Tokyo's transport system every day. The high cost of land and lack of resi-dential space has pushed many Tokyo commuters beyond the suburbs into other cities like Yokohama, Tachikawa and Chiba.

Like the rest of Japan, the population of Tokyo is extremely homogeneous. Recent years have seen a large influx of foreign workers, but nothing to match the scale of immigration found in many major cities around the world. More importantly, foreigners, or *gaikokujin* (literally, outside country person, usually contracted to *gaijin*), in Tokyo are for the most part there temporarily, and the laws conspire to keep it that way.

The largest group of non-Japanese permanent residents in Tokyo are Koreans, who are for outsiders, and for the Japanese, largely an invisible minority. Nonetheless, Koreans who are as 'Japanese' as possible still face discrimination in the workplace and in other aspects of their daily lives.

There are also sizeable populations of Chinese, Filipinos and Iranians in Tokyo, mostly used to fill jobs which socially mobile Japanese are unwilling to do, like construction and factory work. Many of these immigrants, fluent in Japanese, are finding more lucrative employment and some have opened their own businesses, braving the hardships of the long-standing recession.

The Ainu, among the earliest inhabitants of Japan, have been reduced to very small numbers and are today found almost only in communities on Hokkaidō. You're certainly not likely to run into any Ainu in Tokyo, and if you do, the chances are they will have well and truly integrated into the Japanese mainstream.

You will also come across a surprisingly large homeless population in Tokyo, as well as large numbers of urban poor left behind by the postwar economic boom and bust. Many of these people come from Japan's once 'untouchable class', the *burakumin*, a group that performed labour which the higher classes refused to do, like slaughterhouse work and leather work. While discrimination against those of burakumin ancestry is now illegal, it persists. It is still considered perfectly normal to hire a detective to ferret out any possible traces of burakumin blood in a potential spouse's family tree.

In addition to these disenfranchised classes, there are huge numbers of affluent young people in Tokyo who are so different from their predecessors as to merit the title *shinjinrui* (literally, new human type). The existence of these 'Japanese yuppies' is deeply troubling to older Japanese, who see them as the death knell of traditional ways.

Within Japan, Tokyoites themselves are considered almost a separate species. Many Japanese say that they are aloof, even condescending, but in practice this is rarely the case. To a foreign resident, they are by far the most cosmopolitan of all Japanese, hardly noticing foreigners who in other parts of the country are cause to gape and giggle.

ARTS

The wealth of modern Japan is partly founded on the ability to absorb influences from the outside world and use them to create something distinctly Japanese. The extraordinarily rich art of Japan is founded on very much the same ability. In essence, Japanese art is the result of this ability coupled with a tremendous native technical facility and aesthetic sensitivity.

Until the last century, the main influences on Japanese art came from nearby China and Korea; indeed, the artists themselves were often itinerant artisans from these countries.

Japan also absorbed influences from such distant places as Persia, Afghanistan and even ancient Rome, since China maintained an active trade with these places along the Silk Road. Perhaps the most important influence came from India, via China, in the form of Buddhism.

From the Meiji Restoration in 1868, the west also began to exert a powerful influence on Japanese arts. Modern art galleries in Tokyo display influences of major western movements from expressionism to postmodernism.

The artistic traffic has not been all one-way, however. *Ukiyo-e* (pictures from the floating world) prints owe something to Chinese innovations such as multicolour wood-block printing, but are distinctively Japanese in their execution and subject matter. Ukiyo-e caused a sensation among artists in late 19th century Europe, and were much admired and subtley imitated by major artists like Manet, Gauguin, Van Gogh and Toulouse-Lautrec.

continued on page 20

Tokyo Architecture

Much of Tokyo may resemble the set of an old Godzilla movie, but if you know where to look, the city offers some amazing architectural experiments. Some work, some don't, but they're all worth a look.

The architecture of Tokyo can be loosely divided into three periods: surviving Edo structures, buildings of the Meiji era (1868-1945) and modern architecture. Almost nothing of Edo architecture has survived the calamities of the 20th century. The Imperial Palace is a reconstruction on the site of the old Edo-jō Castle. Very few Edo-style wooden homes still exist, though occasionally they pop up (the area between Nippori and Ueno is a good place to look), sandwiched between 'mansion' apartment blocks. The best place to seek out traditional temples and shrines is not Tokyo itself but the areas of Kamakura and Nikkō. In Tokyo, however, it is worth visiting some of the old Edo gardens such as Hama Rikyū Detached Palace Garden, Koishikawa Kōraku-en Garden and Rikugi-en Garden for their beautifully restored grounds and traditional teahouses.

The Meiji Restoration saw a large-scale invasion of western architectural forms. Examples can be seen in buildings such as the Akasaka Detached Palace and the 'imperial-style' Tokyo station. An early (somewhat over-stated) example of a mixed Japanese-western style can be seen in the Kabuki-za Theatre in Ginza.

CHRIS ROWTHORN

Box: Happily there's more to the cityscape than western-derived 'New International Style' buildings and rooftop boxes (photograph by Martin Moos).

Right: A bird's-eye view of the city captures the haphazard array of commercial box tops, whose over-worked inhabitants spill out nightly onto the neon alleys, arcades and plazas below.

Shrines

Shrines are the places of worship in Shintō. The first shrines were simply places of natural significance, like waterfalls and mountains, delineated with a special rope called a *shimenawa*. From this rope evolved the use of fences and eventually special gates *(torii)* which remain today as the most obvious feature of shrines.

Shrine buildings themselves probably evolved from rice storehouses used in pre-Buddhist Japan, and many of their now ornamental features were once functional. The main building of the shrine is the *honden*, which enshrines the *kami* (god) of the shrine. This can never be entered by laymen and only occasionally by Shintō priests. In front of the honden is the *haiden*, or hall of worship, which is used for worship and offertory. In smaller shrines, these two are often joined together under one roof.

CHRIS TAYLOR
MARTIN MOOS

MARTIN MOOS

Top: In traditional architecture, doors and windows provide a graceful intermediary space, not a sharp boundary, between inside and outside. The inside may be a simple room (left) or a more spiritual space, as in this window on Dai-mon Gate, Zōjō-ji Temple (right).

Bottom: The red lions of Taiyūin-byō Shrine at Nikkō watch over proceedings below. The opulence and regular upkeep of the shrines around Tokugawa Ieyasu's tomb served in part to prevent feudal lords (who were ordered to pay for repairs) from financing rebellions against the shōgunate.

CHRIS ROWTHORN

Top: An intriguing monument to Asahi's brewing success and known to local expats as 'the golden turd', Asakusa's Super Dry Hall is topped by Philippe Starck's La Flamme d'Or (The Golden Flame).

Bottom: The Glass Hall of the Tokyo International Forum may be the world's biggest ode to puttering hobbyists – it looks like a giant ship constructed inside a glass case. On the other hand, gazing at its white-boned ribs, you may feel like Jonah, swallowed by a whale. Whatever the hall was designed to invoke, it's a design and engineering marvel. For the record, the atrium is 60m high and the hall is 208m long.

CHRIS ROWTHORN

Between Jinja & Ji The oldest shrines were built in a purely Japanese style, but after the introduction of Buddhism, shrine buildings started to incorporate elements of temple architecture – and vice versa, eg some temple precincts have torii to mark the site's guardian kami. Also, a shrine may have what appears to be a *sanmon* or *niōmon* (a heavy gateway, of a kind more often found at the entrance to a temple, with tiled roof and two *niō* figures). As open centres of spiritual power coexisting in a syncretic culture, it's not surprising shrines and temples exchange many features.

CHRIS ROWTHORN

While politicians still make controversial visits to Yasukuni-jinja Shrine, they now have to reach into their own pockets to feed the collection box – in 1997 Japan's Supreme Court ruled that ritual offerings of public money were unconstitutional.

Temples

Along with the religion itself, Japan imported from Korea and China the architecture used in Buddhist temples. While some differences exist between the temples of Japan's various schools of Buddhism, most temple compounds contain the following basic structures:

Pagoda This is a tower-like structure based on the Indian stupa, which is believed to house a relic of the historical Buddha. While these were the focal point of early Japanese temples, in later temples they are often relegated to the periphery.

Kondō or Hondō This is the main hall of the temple and is often found at the centre of the compound. Housed within this structure are the main images of the Buddha as well as other elements of a Buddhist altar. This is where worship takes place, and lay people are sometimes excluded from entry on all but special occasions.

Kōdō This is the lecture hall where monks gather to study and recite scriptures. It is often beside the main hall.

Mon This means gate and refers to both the large outer gate of the temple *(daimon)* and the smaller inner gate *(chūmon)*. Housed within these gates you will sometimes find two niō, whose role it is to fend off evil and remind visitors to enter with a pure mind.

Kyōzō This is the sutra repository, which is used to store the sacred scriptures of the temple. Often built in the shape of a log cabin on stilts, this structure is designed to maintain a constant internal temperature to guard the sutras against decay.

Other Structures On the periphery of the compound you will also find the monks' daily living areas, like the dining hall and the dormitory. Of course, now that many temples are operated as business concerns, you will also find a temple office.

Modern Architecture

Shrines and temples the city may more or less preserve, but in Tokyo real value has always reposed in land, not buildings: architecture tends to be utilitarian, designed to be replaced after a couple of decades of use, but there are some fabulous structures scattered across town.

The overwhelming architectural feature of the city is the Tokyo Metropolitan Expressway – 220km of it girds the city. As Tajima Noriyuki points out in his wonderful pocket guide *Tokyo – A Guide to Recent Architecture*, 'The scale and monumentality, weight and strength of the expressway – like ancient Roman city walls – easily overwhelms any of the city's buildings, and striking contrasts are formed against its backdrop'. Take a look at how the expressway interacts with street scenes in central Tokyo (particularly Yūrakuchō and Nihombashi) and you'll see what he means.

The most famous of Japan's home-grown architects is Tange Kenzō. His Tokyo Metropolitan Government Offices in Shinjuku may look sinister (and have been criticised as totalitarian), but they are a remarkable achievement and pull in large numbers of visitors daily (around 6000). Those with an interest in Tange's work should also look out for the United Nations University, close to Omotesandō subway station.

The Tokyo Metropolitan Government Offices dominate the west Shinjuku skyline. Prominent architect Kurokawa Kisho has criticised the design as an anachronism, 'A Notre Dame-like symbol of the age when God still ruled the world'.

CHRIS ROWTHORN

Peter Eisenman has made some avant-garde contributions to Tokyo's urban landscape. The NC building is perhaps the most interesting. It embodies the movement of tectonic plates and the transient nature of Tokyo architecture. The result is a structure caught in the moment of collapse, all angles at odds with each other, as if someone had given a child a felt-tip pen and asked them to design a building. The NC building is close to Shin-Koiwa station on the JR Sōbu line.

In central Tokyo, the Tokyo International Forum was the product of an international competition. The result is a glass and steel ocean liner with a miracle of a hall – pedestrian walkways are planned to link Yūrakuchō and Tokyo stations via the forum. The new Edo-Tokyo Museum in Ryōgoku is a bizarre structure that you can't help but marvel at, particularly as you stand in the sprawling plaza that surrounds it – the Star Wars connotations seem to strike everyone.

Visitors to Asakusa in search of 'lost Japan' might pause and take a look at the Super Dry Hall, an eccentric Philippe Starck design that celebrates Asahi beer. This upside-down building has what looks to be a golden turd on its bottom (head) – the 'golden flame' represents the frothy head of a beer. The interior is as remarkable as the exterior.

In recent years, the Tokyo Bay/Daiba areas have seen a boom in experimental architecture. Buildings like the Fuji Television Broadcast Center and the Tokyo Big Sight international conference hall are examples of architectural exuberance given free reign; both are must-sees. Crowded Tokyo has also seen a small revolution in the use of interior space. The Metropolitan Art Space and Toyota Amlux buildings in Ikebukuro and the Spiral building in Aoyama are all good examples. Shibuya is a good area to scout for architectural highlights, notably the Bunkamura, Humax Pavilion and the Beam building.

THOMAS DANIELL

MARTIN MOOS

CHRIS ROWTHORN

With its overtones of a marital arts practice hall, a futuristic temple in Kamiyacho (upper right) ironically exemplifies the eclectic approach of old Edo-era architecture.

Across Rainbow Bridge in Tokyo Bay is the Odaiba megaproject, with Tokyo 'Big Sight' (upper left) and Tange Kenzō's Fuji Television building (bottom). If Disney ever built a Blade Runner Land, it might look like this.

continued from page 15

Aesthetics

Outside influences notwithstanding, there is something called 'Japanese aesthetics', however elusive it might be. The Walkman may be as 'essentially Japanese' in its conception and design as tea ceremony: the purpose of both is to create an 'empty', contemplative space.

This artistic focus on space is exemplified in the creation of miniature landscapes, as in the meditative arts of *bonsai, bonkei* and *ikebana*. Bonsai miniaturises trees through careful pruning, while bonkei achieves the same with an entire landscape. Ikebana is promoted as a requisite skill for the cultivated 'young lady', but again it has a stress on contemplation.

Chanoyu, or tea ceremony, expresses all these peculiarly Japanese qualities. Sen-no-Rikyū (1522-91) transformed tea ceremony into an art form. He believed that using rough and irregular settings and utensils (many of which were from Korea) reflected the asymmetry of an egoless natural world. This was in stark contrast to the delicate designs and stylised perfection of Chinese ceramics.

If the Japanese themselves had to define their aesthetic principles, two words from the Zen art of tea would inevitably be used: *wabi* and *sabi*. Sometimes claimed to be beyond the grasp of non-Japanese, these words refer to a kind of rustic simplicity, a sublime quality and understated beauty prized in their art. Japanese also admire art which they describe as *shibui*. This word translates roughly as restrained, quiet and cultivated. Taken together, these three words suggest what the Japanese call beautiful.

But there are also grand public displays that contradict the logic of many 'Japanese' qualities. Nikkō's shrines, for example, are far from understated. They are decorated in a riot of colour, and the deliberate 'mistakes' were not due to an aesthetic of imperfection, but to a fear that the works' perfection would arouse the envy of the gods. But these *are* public displays, often owing much to Chinese influences, and are in a different category to most Japanese art forms.

Gardens

The Japanese are fond of saying that they love nature. It is perhaps more accurate to say that they love a well-tended, 'humanised' nature. Nowhere is this more evident than in the Japanese garden, which may at first glance look like raw nature, but is in fact reflectively and meticulously planned down to the last pebble.

There are a few main features which set Japanese gardens apart from those in Europe. Notable among these is a lack of flowers, water fountains and flowing rivers. More importantly, in Japan, every effort is made to harmonise the garden with the living space, as opposed to the European garden, which tends to stretch away from the house and exist very much as a space unto itself.

Fine Arts

Painting The techniques and materials used in the early stages of Japanese painting owed much to Chinese influence. Buddhism also provided Japanese painting with a role as a medium for religious instruction.

Towards the end of the Heian period (794-1185) the emphasis on religious themes painted according to Chinese conventions gave way to a purely Japanese style, *yamato-e*, which covered indigenous subjects, and was frequently used in scroll paintings and on screens.

Ink paintings *(suiboku* or *sumi-e)* made by Chinese Zen artists were introduced to Japan during the Muromachi period (1333-1576) and copied by Japanese artists who produced hanging pictures *(kakemono)*, scrolls *(emaki)*, decorated screens and sliding doors.

During the Momoyama period (1576-1600), the ruling classes demonstrated their opulence and prestige by commissioning artists to use flamboyant colours and copious gold leaf. The most popular themes were those depicting Japanese nature (plants, trees and seasons) or characters from Chinese legends.

Western techniques of painting, including the use of oils, were introduced during the 16th century by the Jesuits.

The Edo period was marked by earnest patronage of a wide range of painting styles. The earlier Kanō school continued to be in demand for the depiction of subjects related to Confucianism, mythical Chinese creatures, or scenes from nature. The Tosa school, whose members followed the yamato-e style of painting, was kept busy with commissions from the nobility to paint scenes from the ancient classics of Japanese literature.

The Rimpa school not only absorbed the style of other schools (Chinese, Kanō and Tosa), but went beyond them to produce strikingly original decorative painting. The Rimpa school art produced by Tawaraya Sōtatsu, Honami Kōetsu and Ogata Kōrin ranks among the finest of this period.

Calligraphy Known as *shodō* (the way of writing) in Japanese, this is one of Japan's most vital and valued arts, cultivated by nobles, priests and samurai alike, and still studied by Japanese schoolchildren as *shūji*.

Like Japanese writing, the art of shodō was imported from China. In the Heian period, a distinctly Japanese style of shodō evolved called *wayō*. This is more fluid and curved than the purely Chinese style (called *karayō*). The Chinese style remained very popular in Japan even after the Heian period among Zen priests and the literati.

In both Chinese and Japanese shodō there are three types of script. The most common is called *kaisho*, or block-style script. Due to its clarity, this style is favoured in the media and in applications where readability is a must. The second is *gyōsho*, or running hand. Often used in informal correspondence, it is half-cursive and somewhat more difficult to read. The third type is called *sōsho*, or grass hand, and is a truly cursive style. Sōsho abbreviates and links the characters together to create a graceful, flowing effect.

Ukiyo-e If there is one art that westerners instantly associate with Japan, this is it. The name, 'pictures of the floating world', refers to a Buddhist metaphor for the transience of the human world. The subjects chosen by ukiyo-e artists were characters and scenes from the 'floating world' of the pleasure quarters of Edo, Kyoto and Osaka.

In Europe, the vivid colours, novel composition and flowing lines of these prints sparked a vogue which a French critic dubbed 'Japonisme'. Among the Japanese, however, the prints were hardly given more than passing consideration – millions were produced annually in Edo, often thrown away or used as wrapping paper for pottery.

The reputed founder of ukiyo-e was Iwa Matabei. The genre was later developed by Hishikawa Moronobu, who rose to fame with his illustrations for erotic tales. His wood-block prints of scenes from the entertainment district of Yoshiwara introduced the theme of *bijin-e* (paintings of beautiful women), which later became a standard subject. Early themes also covered scenes from the theatre and the erotic *shunga*. Kitagawa Utamarō is also famed for his

Geisha were favoured subjects for the practice of *katachi* – infusing the artistic form with life energy.

bijin-e, which emphasise the erotic and sensual beauty of his subjects. All that is known about Tōshūsai Sharaku is that he produced 145 superb portraits of kabuki actors between 1794 and 1795.

Toward the end of the Edo period, two painters produced outstanding works in this art genre. Katsushika Hokusai was a prolific artist who observed his fellow Edo inhabitants with a keen sense of humour. His most famous works include *manga* (cartoons), *Fugaku Sanjūrokkei* (Thirty-Six Views of Mt Fuji) and *Fugaku Hyakukei* (One Hundred Views of Mt Fuji).

Andō Hiroshige followed the lead of Hokusai and specialised in landscapes, although he also created splendid prints of plants and birds. Hiroshige's most celebrated art includes *Tōkaidō Gojūsan-tsugi* (Fifty-Three Stations of the Tōkaidō); *Meisho Edo Hyakukei* (One Hundred Views of Famous Places in Edo); and *Omi Hakkei* (Eight Views of Omi) – Omi is now known as Lake Biwa-ko.

Manga With design, cinema and architecture, cartoons are probably the most recognised of Japan's modern arts. Manga is a catch-all word covering cartoons, magazine and newspaper comic strips, and the comic books seen everywhere – even high art ukiyo-e prints were once a form of manga, evolving with *kibyōshi* (yellow cover) wood blocks used to create adult story books. The great woodblock artist Hokusai coined the word 'manga' by combining the characters for 'frivolous' and 'picture'.

The father of modern manga was Tezuka Osamu, who in the late 1940s began working cinematic effects based on European movies into his cartoons. His adventurous stories quickly became movie-length comic strips – films drawn on paper. What Tezuka started took off in a big way once weekly magazines realised they could boost sales by including manga in their pages.

As a result of Tezuka's innovations, Japanese comics are rarely slim affairs (weekly comics as thick as phone directories are not unusual). Manga's multipanel movements,

perspectives bringing the reader into the action, close-ups and curious angles have been belatedly picked up by US comics; many manga also spin off into popular, cutting-edge animation films *(anime)* that can make Disney's look like goofy doodling (to say nothing of the soundtracks). Oshii Mamoro's 1995 anime version of the Masamune Shirow manga *Ghost in the Shell* is a good example; the *Macross* series is another.

Manga text is in Japanese, but there's usually an English subtitle on the cover announcing whether it's a 'Lady's Comic', a 'Comic for Business Boys' or even an 'Exciting Comic for Men' (for 'exciting' read 'soft porn'). Japanese censors may cover the pubic hair in imported porn, but it all hangs out in comic books – peer over a shoulder on the train and you may catch a schoolgirl quietly following the progress of a 2km-long penis as it ravages Tokyo. Even the 'Lady's Comics' can contain a fair bit of sex (check out *Comic Amour*). But manga also tackle straight subjects: *jitsuma manga* (practical comics) and *benkyō manga* (study comics) teach everything from high school subjects to ikebana and international finance.

Crafts
Craft workers have always enjoyed the same esteem accorded artists and their works are prized as highly as fine art. Indeed, the distinction between art and craft is artificial in Japan, as many crafts are produced purely as works of art (lacquerware) and many works of art are made to be used in daily life (painted screens).

Ceramics & Pottery Ceramic art in Japan is usually said to have begun with the introduction of Chinese techniques and the founding of a kiln in 1242 at Seto (Aichi Prefecture) by Tōshirō. The Japanese term for pottery and porcelain, *setomono* (literally, things from Seto), even derives from this ceramic centre, which is still thriving.

The popularity of tea ceremony in the 16th century stimulated developments in ceramics.

The great tea masters Furuta Oribe and Sen-no-Rikyū promoted production of exquisite Oribe and Shino wares in Gifu Prefecture. Hideyoshi allowed the master potter Chōjiro to embellish the tea bowls he created with the character *raku* (enjoyment), the beginning of Kyoto's famous *raku-yaki* style of pottery. Tea bowls became highly prized objects commanding stupendous prices. Even today, connoisseurs happily shell out as much as US$30,000 for the right tea bowl.

There are more than 100 pottery centres in Japan, producing everything from exclusive tea utensils to souvenir badges *(tanuki)*. Department stores regularly organise exhibitions of ceramics. Master potters are revered – the finest are designated 'Living National Treasures'.

Lacquerware Known in Japan as *shikki*, lacquerware is made using sap from the lacquer tree *(urushi)*. Once it is hardened, lacquer becomes inert and extraordinarily durable. The most common colour of lacquer is amber or brown, but additives have been used to produce violet, blue and even white lacquer.

Japanese artisans have devised various ways to further enhance the beauty of lacquer. The most common method is called *maki-e*, which was developed in the 8th century. Here, silver and gold powders are sprinkled onto the liquid lacquer to form a picture. After the lacquer dries, another coat of lacquer is applied to seal the picture. The final effect is often dazzling and some of the better pieces of maki-e lacquerware are now 'National Treasures'.

Washi In the Heian era, handmade paper *(washi)* was highly prized by the Kyoto court for writing poetry and diaries. Colours were added to produce patterns – even silver and gold leaf were used to create highlights. Paper was sometimes made specially to accentuate the sentiments of a particular poem. Washi continued to be made in large quantities until the introduction of western paper in the 1870s. Recently, washi has enjoyed a revival, and a large variety of colourful, patterned paper is available in speciality stores.

Textiles Textiles have always played an important role in Japan, since the fabric of one's kimono was a ready indication of one's place in the social order. Until the introduction of cotton in the 16th century, Japanese textiles were made mostly of bast fibres or silk. Of all textiles, intricately embroidered brocades have always been the most highly prized, but sumptuary laws imposed on the merchant class in the Edo period prohibited the wearing of such kimonos. To circumvent these laws, new techniques of kimono decoration were devised, most importantly *yūzen* dyeing. Here, rice paste is applied to the fabric like a stencil to prevent a colour from bleeding onto other areas of the fabric. By repeatedly changing the pattern of the rice paste, complex designs can be achieved.

Carpentry It has been said that jade is the perfect medium for the expression of the Chinese artistic genius. Likewise, wood may be the perfect medium for Japanese artistry. Perhaps nowhere else has the art of joinery been lifted to such levels as it has in Japan.

This genius translates well into the art of cabinet-making. Particularly prized by collectors of Japanese antiques are chests called *tansu*. Perhaps the most prized of these is the *kaidan dansu*, so named because it resembles a flight of stairs (kaidan means stairs). These are becoming increasingly difficult to find – determined hunting at flea markets and antique stores will still yield a few good pieces, but don't expect any bargains.

Dolls Two festivals celebrate Japan's long love affair with dolls: Hina Matsuri (Doll Festival), when girls display *hina ningyō* dolls; and Children's Day, when boys and girls show special dolls.

Some common dolls are *daruma*, which are based on the figure of Bodhidharma, who brought Buddhism to China from India; *gosho ningyō*, chubby plaster dolls sometimes dressed as figures in nō dramas; *Kyō ningyō*, elaborate dolls made in Kyoto, dressed in fine brocade fabrics; *kiku ningyō*, large dolls covered in real chrysanthemum flowers; and *ishō ningyō*, a general term for elaborately costumed dolls, sometimes based on kabuki characters.

Kites Japanese kites were originally linked to Shintō rites and flown with messages to the gods and spirits. Historically, kites also have a military connection in Japan as bearers of signals.

With the emergence of Edo as a major city, kite-flying gained a popular appeal. Wood-block prints from the Edo period often depict the Edo skyline jostling with swooping paper kites. The Edo period established a repertoire of kite designs that are still popular.

The most popular depicts a warrior hero from Japanese history or legend. Also popular is a daruma design, based on the spherical dolls of the same name. Other designs depict birds or insects, especially the cicada.

Bamboo Crafts Japanese bamboo baskets are among the finest in the world and are amazing in their complexity and delicacy (as well as their price). Ladles and whisks used in tea ceremony are also made of bamboo, and make attractive souvenirs. Be careful when buying bamboo crafts in Japan, as many are not Japanese at all, but cheap imitations imported from China.

Bonsai & Bonkei A skill imported from China during the Kamakura era (1185-1333), bonsai is the dwarfing of trees or the miniaturisation of nature. Some bonsai have been handed down over generations and are extremely valuable. Bonkei is the art of reproducing nature on a small tray using moss, clay, sand etc.

Flower Arrangement Ikebana, the art of flower arranging, stems from the 15th century, and can be grouped into four main styles: *rikka* (standing flowers); *nageire* (throwing-in); *shōkai* (living); and *moribana* (heaped). There are several thousand different schools at present, the top three of which

Bonsai (meaning planted in a container) is a Meiji word, though the practice came from China during the Heian period.

are Ikenobō, Ōhara and Sōgetsu, but they share one aim: to arrange flowers to represent heaven, earth and humanity. Ikebana displays were first used as part of tea ceremony, but can now be found in homes – in *tokonoma* (the alcove for displays) – and even in large hotels.

Ikebana is also a lucrative business – its schools have millions of students, including many young women who view proficiency in the art as a means to improve their marriage prospects.

Tea Ceremony
Known as chanoyu or *chadō* (the way of tea), the ritual drinking of tea dates back to the Nara period (710-94), when it was used by meditating Buddhist monks to promote alertness. By the 14th century, it had developed into a highly elaborate and expensive pursuit for the aristocracy.

The turning point took place in the 16th century, when Sen-no-Rikyū eschewed opulence and established a more elemental aesthetic. Other tea masters took different approaches, and today tea ceremony can be divided into three major schools.

Girls' Comics

Unlike in the west, Japanese comics are far from a male preserve: *shōjo manga*, or 'girls' comics', are hugely popular. Since the mid-60s, these comics have been mainly created by women. Artists like Ikeda Riyoko, Hagio Moto and Takemiya Keiko were pioneers in the art of gender ambiguity, taking on 'male' themes with characters far from stereotypical. Later shōjo manga developed highly influential subgenres defined by (and defining) age groups and outlooks (eg female expectations in Tokyo and in small cities).

Amateur manga is another area where women are prominent in Japan. The two day, semi-annual Komikku Māketto (Comic Market) in Tokyo attracts thousands of young women to displays of amateur work by female artists. The theme is mainly brief homoerotic encounters between boys, an interesting twist on popular boys' manga of the mid-80s. These cut-up tales of eroticised violence typify the so-called *yaoi* creed: 'no climax, no purpose, no solutions'.

The appeal for girls of liaisons between boys (lesbian encounters in the genre are rare) is hard to work out: maybe it's the broken taboo or the displaced purity of fated attraction that sells. Certainly the purity is unsullied by politics. Some gay activists have criticised the absence of social messages in yaoi manga – which, defenders insist, is exactly the point.

Those interested in manga can join the crowds perusing recent issues in bookshops. Many smaller hotels, hostels and ryokan have stacks of old issues for their guests' amusement. *Dreamland Japan – Writings on Modern Manga* by Frederik Schodt (1996) is a good introduction; the Internet offers hundreds of additional resources.

Amateur manga is booming in Japan, not least because the stock characters can be adapted to nearly any story and setting you'd care to create. Ilustrations by Mick Weldon.

CHRIS TAYLOR

MARTIN MOOS

CHRIS TAYLOR

CHRIS ROWTHORN

Calligraphy (shodō) is a high art with everyday applications in Japan: (clockwise from top left) ice cream is for sale beneath these banners; inscribed paper fortunes tied for luck to temple offerings; lanterns in the breeze at Yasukuni-jinja Shrine; the characters for Japan (Nihon) read from right to left.

The traditional setting is a thatched tea-house set in a landscaped garden. Tea preparation and drinking follows a highly stylised etiquette, and the mental discipline involved was once essential to the training of a samurai. Novices tend to find it fatiguing, and connoisseurs maintain that full appreciation of the art takes years of reflection.

Performing Arts

The two most famous Japanese theatrical traditions are *kabuki* and *nō*. Both are fascinating, but without a great deal of prior study, don't expect to understand much of the proceedings. This is not a major problem, as both forms work well as spectacle; in any case, even native Japanese speakers have difficulties understanding the archaic Japanese used in traditional theatre. Fortunately, some theatres in Tokyo have programmes with a synopsis of the play in English, and headphones are sometimes available for a commentary in English.

Kabuki is a blend of music, dance, mime, and spectacular staging and costuming.

Kabuki The origins of kabuki lie in the early 17th century, when it was known as *kabuki odori* (loosely, avant-garde dance). Its first exponent was a maiden of Izumo Taisha Shrine who led a troupe of women dancers to raise funds for the shrine. It quickly caught on and was soon being performed with prostitutes in the lead roles. With performances plumbing ever greater depths of lewdness, the Tokugawa regime banned women from kabuki. They were promptly replaced with attractive young men of no less availability. The exasperated authorities issued another decree, this time commanding that kabuki roles be taken by older men.

This move had a profound effect on kabuki. The roles played by these older male actors required greater artistry to be brought off credibly. The result was that, while remaining a popular art form expressing popular themes, kabuki became a serious art, with its more famous practitioners becoming the stuff of which legends are made.

Kabuki is a theatre of spectacle, of larger-than-life gestures, and as such employs opulent sets, a boom-crash orchestra and a ramp through the audience that allows important actors to get the most mileage out of their melodramatic entrances and exits. Kabuki mostly deals with feudal tragedies of divided loyalties and of the struggle between duty and inner feelings (eg love suicides).

Unlike conventional western theatre, the playwright is not the applauded champion in kabuki. The play is merely a vehicle for the performance of the actor; he is remembered long after the writer who put the words in his mouth is forgotten.

Nō Nō is older than kabuki, dating back some 600 years. It seems to have evolved as a cross between Shintō-related dance and mime traditions, and dance forms from elsewhere in Asia. It was adopted as a courtly performing art, and underwent numerous refinements. Unlike the spectacle of kabuki, the power of nō lies in understatement – subtle masks and the stark emptiness of the sets direct all attention to the performers.

Two performers alone are vital to nō presentation – the one who watches *(waki)* and the one who acts *(shite)*. As nō is a theatre of masks, it is the role of the one who watches to, as it were, unmask the one who acts. The shite is not who he or she seems, but is usually a ghost whose spirit has lingered on because of a past tragedy. The unmasking gives way to the second act, in which the shite dances a re-enactment of the tragedy, and reveals his or her true identity.

Whether this is a liberation from, or a sorrowful celebration of, the lingering pain of the tragedy partly depends on whether the story is a happy one or not. It also depends on how you interpret the sometimes quite bizarre but nevertheless spell-binding proceedings of the nō performance.

Kyōgen This comic drama evolved hand in hand with nō. It first served as an interlude, but came to stand on its own and is now more often performed between two different nō plays. Unlike the heavily symbolic nō, kyōgen draws on the everyday world for its subjects and is acted in colloquial Japanese. The subjects of its satire are often samurai, depraved priests and faithless women. Performers are without masks and a chorus or chants is used.

Rakugo *Rakugo* (the dropped word) is a comic narrative dating back to the late 16th century.

It is delivered by a solitary performer seated on a cushion in the centre of a propless stage, with rare musical flourishes provided by offstage drums, *shamisen* or flute. Like kabuki, where the performer reigns supreme, the prestige of rakugo artists lies not with the stories they tell but how they tell them.

Bunraku Developed in the Edo period, *bunraku* is Japan's unique puppet theatre, using puppets that are a half to two-thirds life-size, operated by three puppeteers, who remain visible to the audience. A narrator tells the story and provides the voices for characters; music comes from the shamisen.

Butō This experimental dance was born in the 60s and has received a fair amount of international attention and acclaim. Butō dancers perform nearly nude, with loincloths and body paint. Movement is slow, drawn-out and occasionally grotesque, intended to express emotions in the most elemental, direct way possible.

Music
Ancient Music *Gagaku* is the 'elegant' music of the imperial court. It flourished between the 8th and 12th centuries, then fell out of favour until the renewed interest in 'national' traditions during the Meiji period.

Nowadays, a gagaku ensemble usually consists of 16 players performing on drums, stringed instruments such as the *biwa* (lute) and *koto* (plucked zither), and wind instruments like the *hichiriki* (Japanese oboe) and various types of flute.

Traditional Japanese Instruments The shamisen is a three-stringed instrument resembling a banjo with an extended neck. It was very popular during the Edo period, and is still used as formal accompaniment in Japanese theatre (kabuki and bunraku). The ability to perform on the shamisen remains one of the essential skills of a geisha.

The koto is a type of plucked zither based on a Chinese instrument. The koto gradually increased the number of strings from five to 13. Koto schools still operate, often catering to young women.

The biwa, which resembles a lute, was played by travelling musicians, often blind, who recited Buddhist sutras to the accompaniment of the instrument. Although biwa ballads came into vogue during the 16th century, the instrument later fell out of favour. More recently, composer Takemitsu Tōru has found a new niche for the biwa in a western orchestra.

The *shakuhachi* is a wind instrument imported from China in the 7th century. It was popularised by wandering Komosō monks in the 16th and 17th centuries, who played it as they walked alone through the woods. Even today, the sound of the shaku-

The *koto* is still an essential geisha accessory.

hachi conjures for the Japanese an image of lonely monks and dark forests.

Taiko refers to any of a number of large Japanese drums often played at festivals or in parades. The drummers who perform this music train year-round to endure the rigours of playing these enormous drums.

Modern Music Japan has the second largest domestic record market in the world, and you can meet fans of everything and everybody from Bach fugues to acid jazz, from Ry Cooder to Marilyn Manson. Even if you don't speak any Japanese, you can at least sit around with young Japanese and swap the names of bands you like.

The local scene is dominated by the *aidoru*, or idol singer. Generally untalented, idols enjoy a popularity generated largely through media appearances and is centred on a cute, girl-next-door image. Idols are so interchangeable that a completely computer-generated aidoru made the charts in 1997.

Almost every western musical form and trend has produced Japanese imitators, but not much Japanese music makes the western big-time. Exceptions are artists like Kitarō and Sakamoto Ryūichi, a former member of Yellow Magic Orchestra. Though little known in his own country, one musician held in high esteem by many western musicians is Kina Shōkichi, a major force in the popularisation of indigenous Okinawan music. His electric-traditional crossovers make for fascinating, often haunting listening.

Literature

Japan's first real literary works, the *Kojiki* (Records of Ancient Matters) and *Nihon Shoki* (Chronicle of Japan), were written in the 8th century in emulation of Chinese historical accounts. It was only during times of relative isolation from the mainland that Japanese literature developed its own voice.

Much of what became Japanese literature was first written by women, since men wrote in Chinese characters, while women wrote in the once lowly Japanese script *(hiragana)*. Among these early authors is Lady Murasaki Shikibu, who wrote one of Japan's classics: *The Tale of Genji*. This lengthy novel documents the intrigues and romances of early Japanese court life.

The Narrow Road to the Deep North is a travel gem by the revered poet Matsuo Bashō. *Kokoro*, by Natsume Sōseki, is an early modern classic depicting the conflict between old and new Japan.

Tanizaki Junichirō's *The Makioka Sisters* (1957) is a famous family chronicle that has been likened to a modern-day *The Tale of Genji*. Ibuse Masuji's *Black Rain* (1969) is a response to Japan's defeat in WWII.

Snow Country, by Kawabata Yasunari, is a famous story set in Japan's north. Mishima Yukio's *The Golden Pavilion* (one-fourth of a brilliant tetralogy) uses the burning of Kyoto's Kinkaku-ji Temple in 1950 as an occasion for a meditation on philosophy, sexuality and nihilism. Abe Kōbō's *Woman in the Dunes* is a haunting tale by one of Japan's best avant-garde writers.

Murakami Ryū's *Almost Transparent Blue* is strictly sex and drugs and was a block-buster in the 70s. Murakami Haruki is the bestselling author of nonconformist works like *A Wild Sheep Chase* and *The Wind-Up Bird Chronicle*.

Nobel laureate Oe Kenzaburo's *A Personal Matter* is a good introduction to the modern literary scene.

Film

Motion pictures were first imported in 1896 and, characteristically, Japan was making its own by 1899. Until the advent of talkies, dialogue and general explanation of what was going on was provided by the *benshi*, a live commentator. As in live Japanese theatre, the benshi performance quickly became as important a part of the cinematic experience as the film itself.

Japanese films were initially cinematic versions of traditional theatre, but the 1923 earthquake prompted a split between period films, or *jidaigeki*, and new *gendaigeki* films, which followed modern themes. The more realistic storylines of the new films soon influenced traditional ones, hence the *shin jidaigeki*, or new period films. During this era, samurai themes became an enduring staple of Japanese cinema.

The 50s are generally considered the golden age of Japanese cinema. Directors like Kurosawa Akira led Japanese cinema onto the world stage when his *Rashōmon* (1950) took top prize at the Venice Film Festival in 1951. Kurosawa soon emerged as Japan's most influential director. His classic 1954 film *Shichinin-no-Samurai* (Seven Samurai) gained the ultimate accolade when it was shamelessly ripped off by the Hollywood blockbuster *The Magnificent Seven*. Other Kurosawa classics include *Yōjimbō* (1961), the tale of a masterless samurai who single-handedly cleans up a small town bedevilled by two warring gangs, and *Ran* (1985), a gorgeous epic historical film. Kurosawa's recent work, like 1990's *Yume* (Dreams) and *Madadoyo* (1993), has not been as well received in the west.

Itami Jūzō's *Tampopo* (1985) is a wonderful comedy about sex and food – 'Zen and the art of noodle making', as one critic described it. In the 70s and 80s Japanese cinema retreated before the onslaught of international movie making, but some independent Japanese films have had recent art house success abroad.

Sumō

Sumō was originally performed in Shintō shrines as a form of divination, but was already popular as a sport in the 6th century. The rules are simple: the victor causes any part of his opponent's body other than his feet to touch the ground inside the ring *(dōyo)*, or pushes him outside the ring. There are no rounds – often it is all over in a matter of seconds – and there are no weight classes: they are all *big*.

Sumō's origins remain in the shrine-like roof over the ring and in the brightly attired wizard-like figure of the referee, or *gyōji*. The gyōji comes complete with a dagger which he once might have used to commit ritual suicide if he made a bad decision. Another Shintō feature is the purifying scattering of salt into the ring.

Although sumō wrestlers look like enormous flabby infants, their physiques are actually the products of long and intensive training. Part of this is eating big. *Chanko-nabe*, a special stew with weight-accruing properties, is a staple of the sumō diet. But the rest of the training is very physical, and all that flab conceals a lot of muscle.

Apart from upholding Shintō values, a successful sumō, particularly one who joins the top 50 in *sekitori* status, will have fame and a very comfortable living. Those who reach grand champion, or *yokozuna*, status are made for life and often achieve a kind of cult status during their careers. And for those who don't succeed? Well, it's off to weight watchers and perhaps a career as a furniture removalist.

Take careful note of the warm-ups: in sumō, the battle is often over before it's begun.

SOCIETY & CONDUCT

While Japan is quick to adopt technical innovations from abroad, the country is quite reluctant to abandon its traditional ways of doing things. For the visitor, this means that some things may come as quite a surprise, and others may appear quite puzzling, even downright incomprehensible.

The Group

One of the most widely disseminated ideas regarding the Japanese is the priority of the group over the individual. Loyal workers bellowing the company anthem and attending collective exercise sessions have become a motif almost as powerful as Mt Fuji in calling to mind the Land of the Rising Sun.

It's easy to see the business-suited crowds jostling on train platforms as so many ant-like members of a collectivised society that has rigorously suppressed individuality. If this starts to happen, remember that in some senses the Japanese are no less individual than their western counterparts. The difference is that while individual concerns have a place in the lives of the Japanese, their principal orientation remains that of the group, without which the individual has no meaning.

There is a creative, sometimes tragic, tension between *honne*, personal views, and *tatemae*, the views demanded by one's position in the group. The group emphasis gives rise to the important *uchi* (inside) and *soto* (outside) distinction. All things are either inside or outside. Relationships, for example, are generally restricted to those inside the groups to which they belong.

The inside-outside distinction is hardly unique to Japan; it's just that in Japan being inside a group makes such special demands on the individual. Perhaps foreigners who have spent many years in Japan learning the language and who finally throw up their hands in despair, complaining 'you just can't get inside this culture', should remember that to be 'inside' in Japan is to surrender the self to the priorities of the group – and not many outsiders are willing or able to do that.

Men & Women

Japan may be a modern society in many respects, but don't look for the same level of equality between the genders that you may expect in your own country. As with nearly everything else in Japan, male-female roles and social relationships are strictly codified. Although this is changing, it's definitely doing so at a much slower pace than in the west. Part of the reason is that 'feminism' is a western import and in a Japanese context tends to have a different resonance than it does in its culture of origin.

Japanese women, like women in other parts of the world, are subordinate to men in public life. However, both sexes have their spheres of influence, domains in which they wield power. Basically women are *uchi-no* (of the inside) and men are *soto-no* (of the outside). Woman's domain is the home, and here she will take care of all decisions related to the daily running of domestic affairs. In the public world it is principally the role of women to listen, to cater to male needs and often to serve as vents for male frustrations – 'uchi' is the place for emotions, too.

The codification of men's and women's roles translates over to the marriage market, which has an impact on women's career options – it is widely perceived that they should be married by their mid-20s, and married women are expected to resign from their work. However, there's been a rise in the number of women willing to cast aside expectations, travel and pursue a career, even if it jeopardises their chances for marriage. Indeed, the present generation has been called *mukekkon* (no-marriage), because so many people are simply not getting married or are putting it off until much later than before.

However, Japan still has a long way to go before any real gender equality exists in terms of equal pay, job promotion and representation in management and government.

Meeting the Japanese

The Japanese have a reputation as being hard to get to know, but even on a short visit to Tokyo there are opportunities to meet them.

Perhaps the easiest are those in a more formal setting, such as the conversation lounge or via the home visit system (see the Home Visit System entry in the Facts for the Visitor chapter). Alternatively, just going out for a drink somewhere usually gives you an opportunity to meet locals in a more relaxed setting. Generally all it takes is a smile and a nod to be brought into a conversation.

The Japanese are generally a shy people (unless they've been drinking), relatively unused to mixing with foreigners and fearful of upsetting situational harmony with embarrassing mistakes. Especially when asking directions, try to appear calm and relaxed, and smile as you do so.

Etiquette

In rule-bound Japan social interaction is cluttered with a wide range of dos and don'ts. The good news is that with a bit of sensitivity most of it is easy to pick up and Japanese are generally very tolerant when it comes to foreigners. The times are also changing in Japan, and young people tend to be a lot less scrupulous about traditional rules – among themselves and with foreigners at least.

Bowing Most young people and businessmen are accustomed to shaking hands, but the bow is still the traditional mark of respect for greetings and leave takings. The depth of a bow is an index of status: when bowing with your boss, for example, your bow should be the deeper of two. As a visiting foreigner, an inclination of the waist and a bob of the head will do the trick.

Business Cards *Meishi* (business cards) carry much more weight in Japan than they do in the west. Information about a person's status can be obtained from a business card, and they are ritually exchanged on first meetings. It's good form to accept cards with both hands and examine them before tucking them away into your purse or wallet. Don't write on a card that someone has given you, at least not in their presence.

Direct Speech Unlike most westerners, the Japanese do not make a virtue of being direct. People tend to feel their way around problems and sound out things in ways that to many foreigners seem impossibly vague, but actually aim to preserve harmony and avoid 'loss of face' – for you as much as for them. Thus, forceful and contrary opinions will be seen as embarrassingly vulgar and will more likely elicit a nervous giggle than a candid exchange of views.

Giving & Taking Debt and obligation *(giri)* are a social currency in Japan and incurring either should not be done lightly by the visitor. What may strike you as a simple request or favour may assume far greater significance in the eyes of your Japanese counterpart. Nowhere is this more apparent than in the almost sacred ritual of gift giving. Gifts in Japan are used as thanks for favours done, a means to get things done, guarantees of continued favour and as just plain gifts.

A gift given demands at some point one in return. Keep this in mind when making visits of any kind, particularly to a Japanese home. If you need to pick up a gift at the last minute, there are plenty of stores in the bigger train stations just for this purpose. Also, if you are offered a gift by Japanese, it is polite to put up a brief resistance.

At Home It is usual to sit on the floor at home. Japanese sit with their feet tucked under them in a slouched-back kneeling position, and unless you've had a lifetime of training, it quickly becomes excruciating. Stretching out your legs discreetly is OK, but be careful not to point your feet at anyone.

Before you step into a Japanese home, slip off your shoes and exchange them for a pair of the slippers provided. This also applies at some public buildings, temples, shrines and traditional restaurants. These slippers can be worn everywhere inside except the bathroom, where you will have to switch to the special bathroom slippers. In any room where there is a *tatami* (straw mat) floor, it is usual to go barefoot or in socks.

In Public When outdoors it is bad form to stroll around eating (the exception is ice cream, which as everyone knows is an ambulatory foodstuff). Blowing your nose in public is definitely out. The done thing is a stoic and noisy sniffle maintained until you find somewhere private to do your business. Urinating in public (for men at least), on the other hand, is socially acceptable provided you have been drinking. In fact, drinking in general seems to provide a ticket to freedom from much Japanese social etiquette.

RELIGION

The term religion can be misleading when it is applied to Japan. In Christian and Islamic cultures, religion is connected to the idea of an exclusive faith. However, religions in Japan tend to mingle and find expression in different facets of daily life – Shintō, Buddhism, Confucianism and even Christianity (eg in wedding ceremonies) all play a role in Japanese society.

Shintō

Shintō is an indigenous religion that gained its name, 'the way of the gods', to distinguish it from Buddhism, a later arrival. It grew out of an awe of nature, including the sun, water, rock formations, trees and even sound. These were believed to have their god *(kami)*, giving rise to a complex pantheon of gods and a rich mythology, including an account of the nation's birth from the land of the gods. Certain sites were particularly sacred, and on these shrines were erected. Purification with water (to bring one closer to the kami) before entering such sacred domains is an important Shintō ritual.

Shintō shrines are generally far more serene places than Buddhist temples, though you will often find both almost next door to each other. Compare the solemnity of Meiji-jingū and Yasukuni-jinja shrines with the bawdy carnival atmosphere that prevails at the Buddhist Sensō-ji Temple in Asakusa.

In daily life, Shintō functions less as a religion and more as a custom, with visits to a shrine used to mark important days in the Japanese calendar. At midnight on New Year's eve and on the following morning, families head to the local shrine to pray for good luck in the coming year in a custom known as *hatsumōde* (first shrine visit). A visit to a shrine is also used to mark coming of age, the birth of a baby or the union of marriage. In a sense, the Japanese view Shintō, and Shintō shrines, as insurance – a touchstone to insure safe passage through the world. They see Buddhism as more intimately related to the soul and their passage into the next world. Thus, Japanese people often remark, 'Shintō is for when you're born, Buddhism is for when you die'.

The postwar separation of religion and state has been challenged by the controversial Yasukuni-jinja, which enshrines Japan's war dead and is regularly visited by politicians. As far as most people are concerned, however, there appears to be little regret that Shintō has reverted to its previous role as a guarantor of safe passage through daily life.

Buddhism

Siddhartha Gautama, the Indian prince who became the Buddha, based his teaching largely on karma (*innen* in Japanese), a radical conception of cause and effect. Buddha observed that life is 'suffering' (*duhkha* in Sanskrit, a sort of background discontent made comfortable by the illusions of ego), and that the cause of this suffering is desire. Desire exists because of an illusory split between the self and the world – we chase after a unity that the very concepts 'I' and 'we' deny.

Thus, desire expresses itself in more than simply the sensual; indeed, the totality of what we call existence is desire. The concept of nirvana, or enlightenment, then, is not a blissful paradise but an extinction of desire, an exit from *samsara* (a Sanskrit term), the wheel of suffering.

Buddhism in Japan, as in China, belongs to the Mahayana (Greater Vehicle) school, and has fissured into a great number of smaller schools of thought, the most famous of which in the outside world is Zen. Zen takes its name from the Chinese Ch'an, which is in turn from the Sanskrit *dhyana*,

Visiting a Temple or Shrine

Visitors to Japan are often nervous about committing some dreadful faux pas at a temple or shrine. Relax – as with most other aspects of their lives, the Japanese are not particularly rigid in these matters and certainly wouldn't judge a foreign visitor for not adhering to ritual patterns. As with nearly everything else, if you simply adhere to what would be good manners in your own country, you will almost never commit offence.

Shrines

Just past the *torii* (gate) is a trough of water *(chōzuya)* with long-handled ladles perched on a rack *(hishaku)* above. This is for purifying yourself before entering the sacred precincts of the shrine. Some Japanese do forego this ritual and head directly for the main hall. If you choose to purify yourself, however, take a ladle, fill it with fresh water from the spigot, pour some over one hand, transfer the spoon and pour water over the other hand, then pour a little water into a cupped hand and rinse your mouth, spitting the water onto the ground beside the trough (not into the trough).

Once you've purified yourself, head to the *haiden* (hall of worship), which sits in front of the *honden* (main hall) enshrining the god of the shrine *(kami)*. Here you'll find a thick rope hanging from a gong, in front of which is an offerings box. Toss a coin into the box, ring the gong by pulling on the rope (to summon the deity), pray, then clap your hands twice, bow and then back away from the shrine. Some Japanese believe that a ¥5 coin is the best for an offering at a temple or shrine, and that the luck engendered by the offering of a ¥10 coin will come further in the future (since 10 can be pronounced 'tō' in Japanese, which also means 'far').

Amulets are sold, usually for ¥100 or ¥200, at the shrine office near the worship hall. Finally, if photography is forbidden at a shrine, it will be posted as such; otherwise, it is permitted and you should simply use your discretion when taking pictures so as not to interfere with other visitors.

Temples

Unless the temple contains a shrine, you will not have to purify yourself before entry. The place of worship in a temple is in the *hondō*, which usually contains a Buddhist altar and one or more Buddha images. Entry is usually free; otherwise admission is around ¥300. The standard practice is to toss some change into the offerings box which sits in front of the altar, step back, place one's hands together, pray, then bow to the altar before backing away.

Most temples sell *omikuji* (fortunes written on little slips of paper). These usually cost ¥100. You either pay an attendant or place the money in an honour-system box. Fortunes are dispensed randomly from a special box containing sticks with different numbers written on their ends. Shake the box until one stick drops out of a hole in its top. Take this to the attendant and you will be given a fortune matching the number on the stick. This will be written in Japanese under one of four general headings: *dai-kitchi* (big luck), *kitchi* (luck), *sho-kitchi* (small luck) and *kyō* (bad luck). You can always ask a Japanese to read your fortune for you. If you don't like the fortune you've got, don't worry, just do what the Japanese do: fold the fortune and tie it to a nearby tree branch so that the wind can disperse the bad luck (there's always a tree nearby festooned with white fortunes).

You can also purchase amulets called *omamori* at temples. These usually cost a few hundred yen and come in a variety of shapes and sizes, the most common of which is a piece of fabric bearing the temple's name enclosed in a plastic case. Some temples have omamori for specific things like traffic safety, good health and academic success.

Finally, photography is usually permitted inside small, local temples, but not in larger, fee-charging places.

CHRIS TAYLOR

CHRIS ROWTHORN

CHRIS ROWTHORN

Top: The giant red lantern at Asakusa's Sensō-ji Temple is claimed to be a reproduction of a scene in one of Hiroshige's ukiyo-e (wood-block) prints.

Left: If your temple fortune (omikuji) is unlucky, let the wind disperse its effects by tying it outside.

Right: A chōzuya (water trough) with ladles for purifying yourself before entering a shrine.

CHRIS TAYOR

MARTIN MOOS

MARTIN MOOS

CHRIS ROWTHORN

CHRIS ROWTHORN

TONY WHEELER

MARTIN MOOS

Prayers are offered and amulets are bought in a variety of forms at temples and shrines. Prayers and fortunes written on paper and wood (including hollow gourds, bamboo sticks and painted plaques) make good souvenirs – though you may want to find out what the fortune is before you pass it on.

meaning meditation. Two major Zen schools are Rinzai and Sōtō; both stress meditation, but Rinzai also employs *koan* (illogical riddles) to break the mind's dependence on fixed structures of thought.

Buddhism's relations with Shintō have produced a distinctive result – Buddhism has become a salvation religion of sorts. Traditionally the soul *(tama)* left the body at death, but continued to watch over the fortunes of the family. *Hotoke*, the word for a departed soul, also happens to mean a Buddha or enlightened being; thus, Buddhism in Japan has become associated with 'life after death'. In the popular mind, Buddhist 'saints' (usually Bodhisattvas – those who have postponed enlightenment in order to help others along the same path) have also become figures to be appealed to for help in this life.

Add to this the popularity of Pure Land Buddhism (which uses invocation of Amida Buddha's name as a salvation device) and the result is that Buddhism, with some crucial differences, provides spiritual help for the average person in much the same way popular Christianity does in the west. This is perhaps best embodied by the most popular Japanese Bodhisattva, Jizō, who looks after travellers and children. Stone Jizō statues can be found all over Japan, and many temples have row upon row of them.

Confucianism

Confucianism began in China and made its way to Japan via Korea in the 5th century. However, its principles have had much less effect on Japan than on either neighbour. Central to Confucius' thought is the harmony of 'heaven, earth and humanity', an ideal reflected in the Japanese art of ikebana. These can best be harmonised by the 'upright man' (*Chunzi* in Chinese), who upholds the patriarchal 'five relations'.

Quotes from the *Analects* (the collected sayings of Confucius) are sometimes used in formal speeches, and remnants of Confucianism can be seen in such things as the rigidly hierarchical structure of Japanese companies, respect for elders and strictures to care for one's parents in their old age. The close family structure and tight web of social obligations all reflect a Confucian influence, though few Japanese would mention Confucianism as a guiding principle in their lives.

Christianity

The first Christian missionary to reach Japan was the Jesuit Francis Xavier in 1549. Others followed briskly in his footsteps and by the turn of the 16th century there were some 300,000 Japanese converts – Franciscans and Jesuits came into conflict several times over the rights to these souls.

After suppression during the Tokugawa era, Christianity enjoyed a resurgence during the Meiji Restoration, but was again officially discouraged during WWII. Today there are about 1.1 million Japanese Christians, slightly less than 1% of the total population. Protestants slightly outnumber Catholics.

Religious Services

The following places of worship offer services in English. Catholic services are held at St Anselm's Benedictine Church (☎ 03-3491-6966) in Meguro and at St Ignatius Church (☎ 03-3263-4584) in Kōjimachi. St Alban's (☎ 03-3431-8534) in Kamiyachō has Anglican services on Sunday, as do the Tokyo Baptist Church (☎ 03-3461-8425) in Shibuya and the Tokyo Union Church (☎ 03-3400-0047) in Omote-sandō.

The Islamic Center of Japan (☎ 03-3404-6411) has Friday prayer at its Arabic Islamic Institute in Setagaya. The Japan Islamic Congress Majid (☎ 03-3205-1313) has call to prayer five times daily at the congress's centre in Shinjuku.

Other religious groups in Tokyo include the Jewish Community of Japan (☎ 03-3400-2559) and the Tokyo Bahai'i Center (☎ 03-3209-7521).

For general Buddhist services in English, Hongan-ji Temple in Tsukiji has a sermon in English on the second and fourth Sunday of every month at 5 pm. For more on Zen lectures and meditation sessions, see the Activities section in the Things to See & Do chapter.

LANGUAGE

Visitors to Tokyo shouldn't have too many language problems. Lots of people speak English, and there are quite a few English signs. The main issue is the writing system, which uses three different scripts. The most difficult of these is *kanji*, the ideographic script developed by the Chinese. Some 2000 kanji are in daily use.

If you want to get into the written language before arriving, it would make more sense to learn *hiragana* and *katakana*. There are 48 characters in each, the former being used for native Japanese words and for verb endings, and the latter for foreign loan words such as *kōhi* (coffee) and *kēki* (cake).

The *romaji* used in this book follows the Hepburn system of romanisation/transliteration, with macrons (bars over vowels) used to indicate long vowels. Most place names use both romaji and English – the romaji suffix is usually separated from the proper name by a hyphen and followed by its English translation, eg Hongan-ji Temple (*ji* is the romaji word for temple).

Happily, Japanese is not tonal and pronunciation is fairly easy to master.

Traditionally, only close friends and children call each other by their first names, so a new Japanese acquaintance will normally just tell you their surname. Surnames come before given names, not after, as in the west. (However, famous Japanese names are usually westernised in English texts.) When addressing a person, follow their surname with *san*, equivalent to Mr, Mrs, Miss or Ms, eg Ms Suzuki becomes *Suzuki san*.

The following Japanese phrases should cover most everyday situations, but for a more comprehensive guide, get Lonely Planet's *Japanese phrasebook* or *Japanese audio pack*.

Pronunciation

a	as in 'father'
e	as in 'get'
i	as in 'hit'
o	as in 'lot'
u	as in 'put'

Vowels that have a bar (macron) over them (ā, ē, ō, ū) are pronounced the same as standard vowels except that the sound is held twice as long.

The vowel **u** is not always pronounced, eg when it occurs between **k** and **s** (eg *gakusei*, 'student', sounds like *gaksei*); and in verb endings *-desu* and *-masu* (for example, *ii desu*, 'It's good', sounds like *ii des*).

Consonants are generally pronounced as in English, with these exceptions:

f	purse the lips and blow lightly
g	as the 'g' in 'goal' at the start of a word; as the 'ng' in 'sing' in the middle of a word
r	more like an 'l' than an 'r'

Greetings & Civilities

Good morning.
  ohayō gozaimasu
  おはようございます。
Good afternoon.
  konnichi wa
  こんにちは。
Good evening.
  konban wa
  こんばんは。
How are you?
  o-genki desu ka?
  お元気ですか。
Fine. (appropriate response)
  ē, okagesamade
  ええ、おかげさまで。
Goodbye.
  sayōnara
  さようなら。
See you later.
  dewa, mata
  では、また。
Excuse me.
  sumimasen
  すみません。
I'm sorry.
  gomen nasai/sumimasen
  ごめんなさい／すみません。

Excuse me. (when entering a room)
   o-jama shimasu/shitsurei shimasu
   おじゃまします／失礼します。
Thank you.
   arigatō gozaimasu
   ありがとうございます。
It's a pleasure.
   dō itashimashite
   どういたしまして。
No, thank you.
   iie, kekkō desu
   いいえ、結構です。
Thanks for having me.
  (when leaving)
   o-sewa ni narimashita
   お世話になりました。
Please. (when offering something)
   dōzo
   どうぞ。
Please. (when asking for something)
   onegai shimasu
   お願いします。
OK.
   daijōbu (desu)/ōke
   大丈夫（です）／オーケー。
Yes.
   hai
   はい。
No.
   iie
   いいえ。
No. (for indicating disagreement)
   chigaimasu
   ちがいます。
No. (for indicating disagreement;
  less emphatic)
   chotto chigaimasu
   ちょっとちがいます。

Small Talk

Do you understand (English/Japanese)?
   (ei-go)/(nihon-go)
   wa wakarimasu ka?
   （英語）／（日本語）
      はわかりますか。
I don't understand.
   wakarimasen
   わかりません。

Please say it again more slowly.
   mō ichidō, yukkuri itte kudasai
   もう一度、ゆっくり言ってく
      ださい。
What is this called?
   kore wa nan to iimasu ka?
   これは何といいますか。
My name is ...
   watashi wa ... desu
   私は、 ... です。
What's your name?
   o-namae wa nan desu ka?
   お名前はなんですか。
This is Mr/Mrs/Ms (Smith).
   kochira wa (Sumisu) san desu
   こちらは（スミス）
      さんです。
Pleased to meet you.
   dōzo yoroshiku
   どうぞよろしく。
Pleased to meet you too
   hajimemashite, kochira koso dōzo
   yoroshiku
   はじめまして、
      こちらこそどうぞよろしく。
Sorry to keep you waiting.
   taihen o-matase shimashita
   大変お待たせしました。
It's been a long time since I last
  saw you.
   o-hisashi buri desu
   お久しぶりです。
Please (also) give my regards to
  Mr/Mrs/Ms Suzuki.
   Suzuki san ni (mo) yoroshiku
   o-tsutae kudasai
   鈴木さんに（も）
      よろしくお伝えください。
It's up to you. (when asked to make
  a choice)
   o-makase shimasu
   おまかせします。
Is it OK to take a photo?
   shashin o totte mo ii desu ka?
   写真を撮ってもいいですか。

Requests

Please give me this/that.
   (kore)/(sore) o kudasai
   （これ）／（それ）をください。

Please give me a (cup of tea).
   (o-cha) o kudasai
   （お茶）をください。
Please wait (a while).
   (shōshō) o-machi kudasai
   （少々）お待ちください。
Please show me (the ticket).
   (kippu o) misete kudasai
   （切符を）見せてください。

Getting Around

I want to go to ...
   ... ni ikitai desu
   ... に行きたいです。
Where is the ... ?
   ... wa dochira desu ka?
   ... はどちらですか。
How much is the fare to ...?
   ... made ikura desu ka?
   ... までいくらですか。
Does this (train, bus, etc) go to ...?
   kore wa ... e ikimasu ka?
   これは ... へ行き
   ますか。
Is the next station ...?
   tsugi no eki wa ... desu ka?
   次の駅は ... ですか。
Please tell me when we get to ...
   ... ni tsuitara oshiete kudasai
   ... に着いたら教え
   てください。
Where is the ... exit?
   ... deguchi wa doko desu ka?
   ... 出口はどこですか。
How far is it to walk?
   aruite dono kurai kakarimasu ka?
   歩いてどのくらいかか
   りますか。
Where is this address please?
   kono jūsho wa doko desu ka?
   この住所はどこですか。
Could you write down the address
  for me?
   jūsho o kaite itadakemasen ka?
   住所を書いていただけ
   ませんか。
east/west/north/south
   higashi/nishi/kita/minami
   東／西／北／南

Accommodation

I'd like a ... (hotel/inn).
   ... (hoteru)/(ryokan)
   o sagashiteimasu
   ... （ホテル）／（旅館）
   を探しています。
Do you have any vacancies?
   aita heya wa arimasu ka?
   空いた部屋はありますか。
I don't have a reservation
   yoyaku wa shiteimasen
   予約はしていません。
a single room
   shinguru rūmu
   シングルルーム
a double room
   daburu rūmu
   ダブルルーム
a Japanese-style room
   washitsu
   和室
a room with a bath
   basu tsuki no heya
   バス付きの部屋

Food

Do you have an English menu?
   eigo no menyū wa arimasu ka?
   英語のメニュー
   はありますか。
I'm a vegetarian.
   watashi wa bejitarian
   desu
   私はベジタリアンです。
Do you have any vegetarian meals?
   bejitarian no ryōri wa
   arimasu ka?
   ベジタリアンの料理は
   ありますか。
I'd like the set menu please.
   setto menyū o o-negai shimasu
   セット・メニュー
   をお願いします。
What do you recommend?
   o-susume wa nan desu ka?
   お勧めは何ですか。
Please bring the bill.
   o-kanjō onegai shimasu
   お勘定お願いします。

Shopping

How much is this?
kore wa ikura desu ka?
これはいくらですか。

It's too expensive.
taka-sugimasu
高すぎます。

I'll take this one.
kore o itadakimasu
これを頂きます。

Can I have a receipt?
ryōshūsho o itadakemasen ka?
領収書をいただけませんか。

I'm just looking.
miteiru dake desu
見ているだけです。

Numbers

0	*zero/rei*	○
1	*ichi*	一
2	*ni*	二
3	*san*	三
4	*yon/shi*	四
5	*go*	五
6	*roku*	六
7	*nana/shichi*	七
8	*hachi*	八
9	*kyū/ku*	九
10	*jū*	十
11	*jūichi*	十一
12	*jūni*	十二
13	*jūsan*	十三
14	*jūyon*	十四
20	*nijū*	二十
21	*nijūichi*	二十一
30	*sanjū*	三十
100	*hyaku*	百
200	*nihyaku*	二百
1000	*sen*	千
5000	*gosen*	五千
10,000	*ichiman*	一万
20,000	*niman*	二万
100,000	*jūman*	十万
one million	*hyakuman*	百万

Health

How do you feel?
kibun wa ikaga desu ka?
気分はいかがですか。

I don't feel well.
kibun ga warui desu
気分が悪いです。

It hurts here.
koko ga itai desu
ここが痛いです。

I have asthma.
watashi wa zensoku-mochi desu
私は喘息持ちです。

I have diarrhoea.
geri o shiteimasu
下痢をしています。

I have a toothache.
ha ga itamimasu
歯が痛みます。

I'm allergic to antibiotics/penicillin.
*kōsei busshitsu/penishirin ni
arerugii ga arimasu*
抗生物質／ペニシリン
にアレルギーがあります。

I need a doctor.
o-isha san ni mite moraitai desu
お医者さんにみて
もらいたいです。

Emergencies

Help me!
tasukete!
助けて。

Watch out!
ki o tsukete!
気をつけて。

Call the police!
keisatsu o yonde kudasai!
警察を呼んでください。

Call a doctor!
isha o yonde kudasai!
医者を呼んでください。

Facts for the Visitor

ORIENTATION

Tokyo is a vast conurbation spreading out across the Kantō Plain from Tokyo Bay. Nevertheless, for visitors nearly everything of interest lies either on or within the Japan Railways (JR) Yamanote line, the rail loop that circles central Tokyo. In Edo times, Yamanote referred to Tokyo's 'high city', the estates and residences of feudal barons, the military aristocracy and other members of the elite of Edo society in the hilly regions of Edo. Shitamachi, or 'low city', was home to the working classes, merchants and artisans.

The high/low distinction persists, though Shitamachi now generally refers to the slightly down-at-the-heels atmosphere that lingers in the markets and backstreets of Ueno and Asakusa, while Yamanote is basically any place which doesn't fit this description, meaning most of modern Tokyo.

One confusing aspect of Tokyo is its lack of a main centre. While most cities are built around a central area which gradually tapers off to distant suburbs, Tokyo has several large urban hubs, most of which are located on the Yamanote line. The main financial and commercial districts can be found in the areas around Tokyo station. Nearby, the Imperial Palace is perhaps the spiritual centre of Tokyo and sits in the middle of the rough circle formed by the Yamanote loop line. Government buildings can be found to the west of these areas in Kasumigaseki and Akasaka, while the city government offices are located still further west in Shinjuku. Shopping districts are spread all over the city, and each major stop on the Yamanote line is surrounded by a booming mercantile zone.

Essential for finding your way around Tokyo is a good map. One complication is the lack of street names; the few large ones that are named end in *dōri* (avenue or road). If you're going to do any exploring, you're going to be riding the city's subways and the JR rail system, both of which are excellent. The JR Yamanote line does an above-ground loop that takes you through most of the important centres of the city. Being a loop, the trip can be done very cheaply, because buying a ticket to the next station for ¥130 doesn't stop you going the long way around, taking in the central city on the way.

Surrounding central Tokyo are sprawling, uninteresting urban zones made up mostly of homes, small businesses and factories. Once you pass through these areas, you finally reach the pleasant greenery of Saitama, Gunma and Yamanashi prefectures.

To the south, the bay-side city of Yokohama has been working hard to escape its image as just another Tokyo suburb. It is now home to large international conference halls and the headquarters of some of Japan's large businesses. The city's pleasantly cosmopolitan atmosphere also makes it popular with many of the area's expats, who live there to escape the crush and cost of central Tokyo.

MARTIN MOOS

The cityscape that inspired *Godzilla*.

東京東京東京東京東京東京東京東京東

Japanese Addresses

In Tokyo, as in the rest of Japan, finding a place from its address can be a near impossibility, even for the Japanese. The usual process is to ask directions (even taxi drivers often have to do this). Businesses often include a small map in their advertisements or on their business cards to show their location. Having the address written in Japanese is also a great help.

Off the main roads, there are very few streets with names. Addresses work by narrowing down the location of a building to a number within an area of a few blocks. Unlike English addresses, they work from top to bottom. Thus, Tokyo would be indicated first, followed by the *ku* (ward), then the *chō* or *machi* (loosely, suburb) and then the *chōme*, which is an area of just a couple of blocks. Numbers for the building and chōme are frequently condensed into two or three numbers, as in 1-10-5 Akasaka, where 1 is the chōme and 10-5 indicate the location of the building. But beware: this can also be written in a different order – 10-5 Akasaka, 1 chōme – and mean exactly the same. It can all be awfully frustrating at times.

One good way the Japanese avoid these complicated addresses is to refer to major landmarks, often railway stations. People will often ask you which train line and station you will take, then they'll tell you which station exit *(deguchi)* to use. From here, they'll give you directions based on local landmarks like police boxes, parks, stores and the number of streets you must cross.

Thus, before going to an unfamiliar address, see if you can get a map drawn for you. If all else fails, try 'Mukai ni kite itadakemasu ka?', which means 'Can you come meet me?'. ∎

東京東京東京東京東京東京東京東京東

MAPS

Visitors to Tokyo should get a copy of the *Tourist Map of Tokyo*, available from either the Tourist Information Center (TIC) near Tokyo station or in Narita airport. This excellent, free map provides a good overall view of the city. More detailed, but slightly out of date, Kodansha's *New Tokyo Bilingual Atlas* is available at Tokyo's larger bookshops. You can also pick up a free copy of the TRTA subway authority's *Subways in Tokyo* map, which also has explanations on buying tickets and special deals. For a more comprehensive guide to Tokyo's transportation system, see Kodansha's *Rail and Road Atlas*. Bus maps of the city are also available (see the Bus section in the Getting Around chapter).

If you read Japanese, Shobunsha maps and Rurubu guides are probably the best and are available at most of Tokyo's bookshops. For detailed maps of Tokyo's train lines and stations, *Chikatetsu Benri Gaido* is a handy resource, and would be a good idea for anyone moving to the city.

There is very little in the way of mapping for Japanese cities available outside Japan; the above-mentioned *New Tokyo Bilingual Atlas* is probably the best bet.

TOURIST OFFICES

The Japan National Tourist Organization (JNTO), with both Japanese and overseas offices, is the government agency dealing with tourism promotion and travel inquiries about Tokyo and the rest of Japan. It also produces a great deal of literature.

Tourist Information Center (TIC)

JNTO operates two Tourist Information Centers (TIC) in the Tokyo area – on the 1st floor of Terminal 2, Narita airport (☎ 0476-34-6251) and in the basement of the Tokyo International Forum (Map 3) near Tokyo station (☎ 03-3201-3331). TIC offices will make accommodation reservations, but only for hotels and *ryokan* (traditional Japanese inns) that are members of the Welcome Inn group.

The Tokyo TIC offers Teletourist (☎ 03-3201-2911), which is a round-the-clock taped information service on current events in town. JNTO also runs Goodwill Guides, a volunteer programme with some 30,000 members who wear a blue and white badge with a dove and globe logo.

The Tokyo TIC address is B1F, Tokyo International Forum, 3-5-1 Marunouchi, Chiyoda-ku, Tokyo 100. To get there from Tokyo station, exit the Marunouchi side of the station, cross the street towards the Tokyo central post office, turn left in front of the post office and walk parallel to the JR tracks for about 200m. You'll see a large glass building shaped like a ship. This is the Tokyo International Forum building; the TIC is in the basement to the right of the escalator.

FACTS FOR THE VISITOR

The office has huge stocks of material – as a starter, pick up copies of the *Tourist Map of Tokyo* and magazines such as *Tokyo City Guide*, *City Life* or *Nippon View*. The latter have good listings of shows, expositions and sales around town. For more specialised interests, the TIC has pamphlets on everything from ikebana clubs to factory tours. All you have to do is ask.

The Tokyo TIC is open from 9 am to 5 pm weekdays, until noon Saturday, closed Sunday and national holidays. The Narita airport office is open from 9 am to 8 pm daily.

Telephone Services

JNTO operates a Japan Travel-Phone service for visitors to the Tokyo region. English-speaking travel experts can be contacted from 9 am to 5 pm daily on ☎ 03-3201-3331, or toll-free outside Tokyo on ☎ 0088-224-800 or ☎ 0120-444-800 from any green or grey public phone. Another excellent service, Japan Hotline, is provided by Dial Service (☎ 03-3586-0110). It can be contacted from 10 am to 4 pm, Monday to Friday.

Other Information Offices

The Tokyo city government operates three English information offices: one (Map 2) on the Yaesu (east) side of Tokyo station inside the main JR ticket office, another (Map 6) on the east side of JR Shinjuku station (ground floor near the My City exit) and the third (Map 6) on the same station's west side to the right of the Keiō line entrance. Offices are open from 9 am to 6 pm, closed Sunday and public holidays.

CHRIS ROWTHORN

Information counters are easy to spot.

The major tourist sights around Tokyo also have information offices *(annai-jo)* in prominent locations. Generally they have brochures and maps, and are able to help with finding accommodation. These are not dedicated English information offices, however, and the staff may not always speak good English. If you would like a licensed, professional tourist guide, ask at the TIC, or phone the Japan Guide Association in Tokyo on ☎ 03-3213-2706.

For information on JR services, see the Train section in the Getting There & Away chapter.

JNTO Offices Overseas

JNTO offices overseas include:

Australia
   (☎ 02-9232-4522) Level 33, Chifley Tower, 2 Chifley Square, Sydney, NSW 2000
Canada
   (☎ 416-366-7140) 165 University Ave, Toronto, Ontario M5H 3B8
France
   (☎ 01 42 96 20 29) 4-8 rue Sainte-Anne, 75001 Paris
Germany
   (☎ 069-20353) Kaiserstrasse 11, 60311 Frankfurt am Main 1
Hong Kong
   (☎ 2968-5688) Suite 3704-05, 37/F, Dorset House, Taikoo Place, Quarry Bay, Hong Kong
South Korea
   (☎ 02-732-7252) 10th Floor, Press Center Building, 25 Taepyongno 1-ga, Chung-gu, Seoul
Switzerland
   (☎ 022-731-81-40) 13 rue de Berne, 1201 Geneva
Thailand
   (☎ 02-233-5108) Wall Street Tower Building, 33/61, Suriwong Rd, Bangkok 10500
UK
   (☎ 0171-734-9638) 20 Saville Row, London
USA
   Chicago: (☎ 312-222-0874) Suite 770, 401 North Michigan Ave, IL 60611
   Dallas: (☎ 214-754-1820) Suite 980, 2121 San Jacinto St, TX 75201
   Los Angeles: (☎ 213-623-1952) Suite 1611, 624 South Grand Ave, CA 90017
   New York: (☎ 212-757-5640) Suite 1250, One Rockefeller Plaza, NY 10020
   San Francisco: (☎ 415-989-7140) Suite 601, 360 Post St, CA 94108

DOCUMENTS
Visas
Tourists and business visitors of many nationalities who are not planning to engage in any remunerative activities while in Japan are exempt from obtaining visas, if staying in Japan for less than 90 days. Stays of up to six months are permitted for citizens of Austria, Germany, Ireland, Mexico, Switzerland and the UK. Nationals of these countries will usually be issued the standard 90 day visa and will have to apply for a 90 day extension, if they want to stay for another 90 days (see Visa Extensions). Stays of up to three months are permitted for citizens of Argentina, Belgium, Canada, Denmark, Finland, France, Iceland, Israel, Italy, Malaysia, Netherlands, New Zealand, Norway, Singapore, Spain, Sweden, the USA and a number of other countries.

Australians and South Africans are among those nationals requiring a visa. This is usually issued free, but passport photographs are required, and a return or onward ticket must be shown. Visas are valid for 90 days.

Working Holiday Visas Australians, Canadians and New Zealanders between the ages of 18 and 25 (the age limit can be pushed up to 30) can apply for a working holiday visa. This visa allows a six month stay and two six-month extensions. Its aim is to enable young people to travel extensively during their stay, so employment is supposed to be part-time or temporary, although in practice many people work full time.

A working holiday visa is much easier to obtain than a working visa and is popular with Japanese employers, as it can save them a lot of inconvenience. Applicants must apply for the visa in their own countries and have the equivalent of A$4000 in funds and an onward ticket.

Working Visas Requirements are a lot stricter these days: legal employment categories specify standards of experience and qualifications. In theory, working visas must be arranged outside Japan, but some people *do* manage to arrange them in Japan, then pick them up outside the country (they are not issued in Japan). If you can find an employer to sponsor you and have all your paperwork in order, you will be issued a Certificate of Eligibility. Once you get this, it is necessary to leave the country with the certificate and apply for a working visa at a foreign visa office.

Visa Extensions It has become quite difficult to extend visas. With the exception of nationals of the few countries whose reciprocal visa exemptions allow for stays of six months, 90 days is the limit for most people. Those who do apply should provide two copies of an Application for Extension of Stay (available at the Tokyo Immigration Bureau), a letter stating reasons for the extension, supporting documentation and your passport. There is a processing fee of ¥4000.

Many long-term visitors to Japan get around the extension problem by briefly leaving, usually going to Hong Kong, Seoul or Bangkok, then re-entering the country on a new tourist visa issued at the airport. However, this is risky and immigration officials know that such people are probably working illegally in Japan. It is not unusual for individuals who attempt this to be detained at the airport and sent home on the next available plane – after buying a very expensive one way ticket.

The Tokyo Immigration Bureau (Map 2) has a visa information line (☎ 03-3213-8523/7) where questions about visas can be answered in English. The service operates Monday to Friday from 9.30 am to noon and 1 to 4 pm. The bureau is best reached from Ōtemachi subway station on the Chiyoda line. Take the C2 exit, cross the street at the corner and turn left. Walk past the Japan Development building; the immigration bureau is the next building on your right.

Alien Registration Card
Anyone, including tourists, who stays more than 90 days must get an Alien Registration Card *(gaikokujin toroku shomeisho)*. The card can be obtained at the municipal office of the city, town or ward in which you're

FACTS FOR THE VISITOR

living, but moving to another area requires that you re-register within 14 days. To register, you need your passport, an application form and two passport-size photographs.

You must carry your Alien Registration Card at all times, as the police can stop you and ask to see it. If you don't have it, you will be taken to the station and will have to wait there until someone fetches it for you.

Travel Insurance
A travel insurance policy to cover theft, property loss and medical problems is a wise idea. With such a wide variety of policies available, it may be best to consult your travel agent. Some policies offer a choice of lower and higher medical expense options; choose the high-cost option for Japan. The international student travel policies handled by STA Travel or other student travel organisations are usually good value.

When you buy your policy, always read the fine print. Some policies exclude 'dangerous activities' such as scuba diving and motorcycling. If you plan on motorcycling in Japan, check that your policy covers you. Also, keep all documentation of any medical treatment that you receive, as these will be required when making a claim later on.

Driving Licence
Those planning on driving in Tokyo (really not recommended) should come prepared with an International Driving Permit (with your regular licence as a backup). If you have this, renting a car is no problem – finding somewhere to park is another matter.

Hostelling International Card
You can organise international youth hostel membership before you leave home or do it in Tokyo. Contact Japan Youth Hostels Inc (☎ 03-3269-5831) for more information. There are offices scattered around Tokyo, eg in the basement of Sogo department store (Map 3) near the Tokyo TIC.

Student & Youth Cards
A valid international student card will win you discounts on entry fees to some sights in

Tokyo and sometimes discounted prices on long-distance train travel, but that's about it.

EMBASSIES & CONSULATES
Japanese Embassies Abroad
Australia
> Embassy: (☎ 02-6273-3244) 112 Empire Circuit, Yarralumla, Canberra, ACT 2600
> Consulates:
> Brisbane (☎ 07-3221-5188)
> Melbourne (☎ 03-9639-3244)
> Perth (☎ 08-9321-7816)
> Sydney (☎ 02-9231-3455)

Canada
> Embassy: (☎ 613-241-8541) 255 Sussex Drive, Ottawa, Ontario K1N 9E6
> Consulates:
> Edmonton (☎ 403-422-3752)
> Montreal (☎ 514-866-3429)
> Toronto (☎ 416-363-7038)
> Vancouver (☎ 604-684-5868)

China
> (☎ 2522-1184) 47th Floor, One Exchange Square, 8 Connaught Place, Central, Hong Kong

France
> (☎ 01 48 88 62 00) 7 Ave Hoche, 75008 Paris

Germany
> (☎ 0228-81910) Godesberger Allee 102-104, 53175 Bonn

Ireland
> (☎ 1-269-4033) Nutley Building, Merrion Centre, Nutley Lane, Dublin 4

Israel
> (☎ 695-7292) Asia House, 4 Weizman St, 64 239 Tel Aviv

Netherlands
> (☎ 346-9544) Tobias Asserlaan 2, The Hague 2517KC

New Zealand
> Embassy: (☎ 04-473-1540) 7th Floor, Norwich Insurance House, 3-11 Hunter St, Wellington 1
> Consulate: Auckland (☎ 09-303-4106)

Singapore
> (☎ 235-8855) 16 Nassim Rd, Singapore 258390

Thailand
> (☎ 02-252-6151) 1674 New Petchburi Rd, Bangkok 10320

UK
> (☎ 0171-465-6500) 101-104, Piccadilly, London W1V 9FN

USA
> Embassy: (☎ 202-238-6700) 2520 Massachusetts Ave NW, Washington, DC 20008-2869
> Consulates:
> Anchorage (☎ 907-279-8428)
> Atlanta (☎ 404-892-2700)
> Boston (☎ 617-973-9772)
> Chicago (☎ 312-280-0400)

Honolulu (☎ 808-536-2226)
Houston (☎ 713-652-2977)
Kansas City (☎ 816-471-0111)
Los Angeles (☎ 213-617-6700)
New Orleans (☎ 504-529-2101)
New York (☎ 212-371-8222)
Portland (☎ 503-221-1811)
San Francisco (☎ 415-777-3533)

Foreign Embassies in Tokyo
Most countries have embassies in Tokyo. Visas are generally more expensive in Japan than in neighbouring countries, however. It's best to call the visa office first to confirm opening times.

Australia (Map 1)
 (☎ 03-5232-4111) 2-1-14 Mita, Minato-ku
Canada (Map 7)
 (☎ 03-3408-2101) 7-3-38 Akasaka, Minato-ku
China
 (☎ 03-3403-3380) 3-4-33 Moto-Azabu, Minato-ku
France (Map 1)
 (☎ 03-5420-8800) 4-11-44 Minami-Azabu, Minato-ku
Germany (Map 1)
 (☎ 03-3473-0151) 4-5-10 Minami-Azabu, Minato-ku
India (Map 2)
 (☎ 03-3262-2391) 2-2-11 Kudan-Minami, Chiyoda-ku
Indonesia
 (☎ 03-3441-4201) 5-2-9 Higashi-Gotanda, Shinagawa-ku
Ireland (Map 2)
 (☎ 03-3263-0695) 2-10-7 Kōjimachi, Chiyoda-ku
Israel
 (☎ 03-3264-0911) 3 Nibanchō, Chiyoda-ku
Malaysia (Map 1)
 (☎ 03-3476-3840) 20-16 Nampeidaichō, Shibuya-ku
Netherlands (Map 3)
 (☎ 5401-0411) 3-6-3 Shiba-kōen, Minato-ku
New Zealand (Map 1)
 (☎ 03-3467-2271) 20-40 Kamiyamachō, Shibuya-ku
Pakistan
 (☎ 03-3454-4861) 2-14-9 Moto-Azabu, Minato-ku
Philippines
 (☎ 03-3496-2731) 11-24 Nanpeidaichō, Shibuya-ku
Russia
 (☎ 03-3583-4224) 2-1-1 Azabudai, Minato-ku
Singapore (Map 7)
 (☎ 03-3586-9111) 5-12-3 Roppongi, Minato-ku

South Korea (Map 1)
 (☎ 03-3452-7611) 1-2-5 Minami-Azabu, Minato-ku
Sri Lanka
 (☎ 03-3585-7431) 1-14-1 Akasaka, Minato-ku
Taiwan (Association of East Asian Relations)
 (☎ 03-3280-7811) 5-20-2 Shirogane-dai, Minato-ku
Thailand
 (☎ 03-3441-1386) 3-14-6 Kami-Osaki, Shinagawa-ku
UK (Map 2)
 (☎ 03-3265-5511) 1 Ichibanchō, Chiyoda-ku
USA (Map 3)
 (☎ 03-3224-5000) 1-10-5 Akasaka, Minato-ku

CUSTOMS
Customs allowances include the usual tobacco products, three 760ml bottles of alcohol, 57g of perfume, and gifts and souvenirs up to a value of ¥200,000. Liquor is not cheap in Japan, so it's worth bringing some for yourself or as a gift; there is no possibility of reselling it for profit. It is likely that anything slightly pornographic will be confiscated at Customs. Be warned that the penalties for importing drugs are very severe.

There are no limits on the import of foreign or Japanese currency. Export of foreign currency is also unlimited, but there is a ¥5 million limit for Japanese currency.

MONEY
Costs
Tokyo is the most expensive city in Asia, if not the world, but this isn't an insuperable barrier to an enjoyable trip. There are always cheaper options in Tokyo – it's just a matter of seeking them out. A cup of coffee can indeed cost ¥600 or more, but the many chain outfits charge ¥170. If you want coffee, not a break in a coffee shop, it's ¥110 from an ever-present vending machine.

A rock-bottom daily budget – ¥3200 for a dorm bed, ¥2000 for modest meals, ¥1500 for transport, ¥2000 for incidentals – means you're looking at nearly ¥9000 a day. You may well spend more – a budget business hotel is ¥7000 to ¥10,000 a night.

Food costs can be kept down by taking set meals. 'Morning service' *(mōningu sābisu* or *setto)* in most coffee shops is around ¥400. Set meals at lunch *(teishoku)* are ¥800; cheap noodles are ¥500 and *bentō* (boxed lunch) cost around ¥600. For dinner, a set course or a single order is about ¥900. An evening meal and beer in an *izakaya*, or traditional pub, is around ¥3000. Youth hostels charge around ¥450 for a Japanese breakfast and ¥800 for dinner.

Other prices include: museum admission (¥400 to ¥1000), movie ticket (¥1600 to ¥2000), foreign magazines (¥800 to ¥1200), local English newspapers (¥120 to ¥160), 36 exposure colour film, no processing (¥420), orange juice at a coffee shop (¥450), average cocktail (¥800 to ¥1000), shirt dry-cleaning (¥200) and cigarettes (¥230 to ¥300).

Transport can be expensive. Transport passes are available (see the Getting Around chapter), but a Japan Rail Pass isn't worthwhile unless you are travelling to other parts of Japan. For *shinkansen* (bullet train) trips and domestic flights, discounted tickets are available at some theatre ticketing outlets (see the Travel Agents section in the Getting There & Away chapter). Only use taxis as a last resort.

Carrying Money

The Japanese are used to a safe society and often carry around wads of cash. You can too, but take the usual precautions. Travellers cheques are the safest and most practical way to carry large amounts of money.

Cash

Cold hard yen is the way to pay in Japan. While credit cards are becoming more common in Tokyo, cash is still much more widely used, and travellers cheques are rarely accepted as payment.

Travellers Cheques

US dollar cheques are preferable; other major currencies are acceptable. Travellers cheques can be changed at almost any bank, at many department stores and at some hotels (middle and top-end hotels will usually change them, small business hotels usually will not). Do not expect to pay with them in restaurants, stores or hotels (there are some exceptions to this, usually at top-end places).

You can also buy travellers cheques in Japan, with cash at almost any major bank, and with credit cards at the offices listed in the Credit Cards entry of this section.

ATMs

Do not expect your foreign cash or credit card to be accepted by most regular cash machines; you're going to have to find one which is specially made to accept foreign-issued cards, of which the two most useful are Visa and MasterCard. There are 'Global ATM' machines which accept most foreign-issued cards. These are distinguished by the wide range of accepted credit cards pictured next to their operating instructions. Look for these in the lobbies of bigger department stores and banks. In Shinjuku, try the Global ATM on the 7th floor of Keiō department store (Map 6); in Ginza, look outside the Yūrakuchō Mullion building (Map 3) (next to Sumitomo bank). You need your PIN number to get a cash advance with a credit or cash card. Also, note that most Sumitomo bank offices will give cash advances to Visa card holders. For more information on ATMs which accept your cards, call the Tokyo offices directly at the numbers listed below.

Most of the ATMs designed to accept foreign-issued cards have English instructions. On standard Japanese machines, you will have to be able to read some Japanese or ask someone for assistance.

Credit Cards

MasterCard and Visa are the most widely accepted, followed by American Express and Diners Club. Almost all top-end and some middle-range hotels accept credit cards, but most cheaper hotels, youth hostels and ryokan do not. Mid-range and top-end restaurants catering to foreigners generally accept credit cards. The big department stores and pricier small stores usually accept cards, but most regular shops do not. JR and private train lines don't take them. Never assume that a place accepts credit cards; check beforehand. In general, it is better to carry plenty of cash in Japan than to be reliant on credit cards.

The main card offices in Tokyo are:

American Express
(☎ 03-3220-6100; 0120-020-120 toll-free, 24 hours) Ogikubo Head Office, American Express Tower, 4-30-16 Ogikubo, Suginami-ku
Diners Club
(☎ 03-3499-1311; 3797-7311 in an emergency; 3499-1181 after hours) Senshu Building, 1-13-7 Shibuya, Shibuya-ku
JCB Card
(☎ 03-3294-8111) 1-6 Kanda Suragadai, Chiyoda-ku
MasterCard
(☎ 03-5350-8051; emergency service for foreign visitors ☎ 0031-11-3886) Dai Tokyo Kasai Shinjuku Building, 16F, 3-25-3, Yoyogi, Shibuya-ku
Visa
(☎ 03-5251-0633; 0120-133-173 in an emergency) Imperial Tower, 11F, 1-1-1 Uchisaiwaichō, Chiyoda-ku

Currency

The currency in Japan is the yen (¥). Banknotes and coins are easily identifiable; there are ¥1, ¥5, ¥10, ¥50, ¥100 and ¥500 coins; and ¥1000, ¥5000 and ¥10,000 notes. The ¥1 coin is of lightweight aluminium; ¥5 and ¥50 coins have a hole in the middle.

Exchange Rates

As this book went to production, exchange rates were:

Australia	A$1	=	¥85
Canada	C$1	=	¥92
Germany	DM1	=	¥73
Hong Kong	HK$1	=	¥17
New Zealand	NZ$1	=	¥74
Singapore	S$1	=	¥83
UK	UK£1	=	¥220
USA	US$1	=	¥130

Changing Money

You can change cash or travellers cheques at an 'Authorised Foreign Exchange Bank' (signs will always be displayed in English) or at some large hotels and stores. Some post offices now exchange money – look for the 'Authorised Foreign Exchange' sign. Although Korean and Taiwanese currency have recently become easier to change, it is still

wise to change them into US dollars or yen before you arrive in Japan.

Banking Hours

Banks are open Monday to Friday from 9 am to 3 pm, closed on weekends and national holidays. Procedures can be time-consuming at some banks. If you're caught cashless outside regular banking hours, you can try a large department store or major hotel. The Shinjuku branches of Isetan and Keiō department stores (Map 6), as well as Ikebukuro's Seibu (Map 5) (on the 7th floor), will change travellers cheques. The Bank of Tokyo's Shibuya branch (☎ 03-3610-7000) also has an after-hours exchange service until 6 pm daily; it's on Meiji-dōri.

Money Transfers

If you are having money sent to a bank in Japan, make sure you know *exactly* where the funds are going: the bank, branch and location. Telex or telegraphic transfers are much faster, though more expensive, than mail transfers A credit-card cash advance is a worthwhile alternative.

Bank & Post Office Accounts

If you open a savings account at one of the major banks, you'll receive a savings book and a cash card which allows you to draw cash at any branch or from an ATM. Just say 'futsū chokin' (general deposit), and this should get the ball rolling.

An easy option is to open a post office savings account *(yūbin chokin)* at the Tokyo central post office; this allows you to withdraw funds from any post office. A general account with the post office yields slightly higher interest rates than at banks. A general postal savings account is *tsūjō chokin*.

No matter what kind of account you open, you will not receive much interest on your money – interest in Japan averages less than 1%. For a US dollar account, higher interest rates and 24 hour ATM service, contact Citibank (☎ 0120-223-773), which has several branches in Tokyo.

Tipping & Bargaining

The absence of tipping does reduce costs a little; nobody expects a tip so it's best to keep it that way. But if your maid at a ryokan has given fairy godmother service, you can leave her a small present. If you give cash, the polite way is to place it in an envelope.

Fixed prices prevail in Japan. Akihabara's 'Electric Town' is one exception – most big electronics stores there will give 10% discounts. Don't haggle; a polite request is all that is required. Some flea market vendors are open to bargaining, some won't even consider it; just ask politely.

Taxes & Refunds

Japan has a 5% consumer tax. If you eat at expensive restaurants and sleep in luxury, you will also encounter a service charge which varies from 10% to 15%. A local tax of 3% is added for restaurant bills exceeding ¥5000 or for hotel bills over ¥10,000 (you can ask for separate bills to avoid this). At *onsen* (hot-spring) resorts, a separate onsen tax applies. This is usually 3% and applies at cheap accommodation, even youth hostels.

Those on a tourist visa can avoid the 5% consumption tax on purchases at major department stores and at duty-free stores like Laox in Akihabara. For a refund on general purchases, check first that the department store has a service desk for tax refunds. Take the purchase, receipt and your passport to the service desk for an immediate refund.

DOING BUSINESS

Those who come to Tokyo to do business will find a wide range of support services available. With deregulation plans and the Japanese consumer trend away from overpriced goods marketed by domestic giants, things may improve for foreign businesses.

Business Services

Whether you want a good serviced office to kick-start operations in Tokyo or a printing firm to run off a few extra *meishi* (business cards), you'll find plenty of suppliers.

If you're on a tight schedule, however, it's best to make some inquiries before you depart, particularly if you want to prepare some translated materials or require interpreting. Consult the Japan desk of your government's trade organisation or an overseas office of the Japan External Trade Organization (JETRO), the import promotion agency of the Japanese government.

Once in Japan, your main allies are your national chamber of commerce and JETRO. The Tokyo JETRO Business Support Center (☎ 03-5562-3131; fax 5562-3100) is in the Akasaka Twin Tower building (Map 3) at 2-17-22 Akasaka, Minato-ku, Tokyo 107. It offers free office space and meeting rooms, free consultancy and a good library of English-language information about doing business in Japan. In order to use JETRO's services, your company must be registered in your home country and you must apply through the JETRO office in that country. Businesses of any size are welcome, but JETRO does not provide services to PR firms, service industries, banks or newspapers. There are also JETRO Business Support Centers in Yokohama (☎ 045-451-9071), Osaka (☎ 06-614-8910) and Kōbe (☎ 078-857-7221).

Kimi Information Center (Map 5) (☎ 03-3986-1604) in Ikebukuro offers a range of business services. Larger hotels also offer business support services, even to non-guests.

Some foreign chambers of commerce in Tokyo are:

American Chamber of Commerce
 (☎ 03-3436-1446) Bridgestone Building, 3-25-2 Toranomon, Minato-ku 105
Australian & New Zealand Chamber of Commerce
 (☎ 03-3201-2592) CPO Box 1096, 100-91
British Chamber of Commerce in Japan
 (☎ 03-3267-1903) Kenkyusha Eigo Center Building, 1-2 Kagurazaka, Shinjuku-ku 162
Canadian Chamber of Commerce
 (☎ 03-3224-7825) Shelzrene Building, 7-4-7 Akasaka, Minato-ku 107
French Chamber of Commerce and Industry in Japan
 (☎ 03-3288-9558) Iida Building, 5-5 Rokuban-chō, Chiyoda-ku 102
German Chamber of Commerce and Industry in Japan
 (☎ 03-5276-8733) KS Building, 2 Banchi Sanban-chō, Chiyoda-ku 102

Helpful Japanese and Tokyo government organisations include:

Foreign Investment in Japan Development Corp
(☎ 03-3224-1203) Akasaka Twin Tower Building, 2-17-22 Akasaka, Minato-ku 107
Industrial Structure Improvement Fund, Import and Investment Promotion Division
(☎ 03-3241-6283) Kaigin Building, 1-9-1 Ōtemachi, Chiyoda-ku 100
Japan Chamber of Commerce and Industry, International Division
(☎ 03-3216-6497) Tosho Building, 3-2-2 Marunouchi, Chiyoda-ku 100
Ministry of International Trade and Industry, International Business Affairs Division
(☎ 03-3501-6623) 1-3-1 Kasumigaseki, Chiyoda-ku 100

第一生命館内
郵便局
POST OFFICE

CHRIS ROWTHORN

Luckily, the Japanese postal service can decipher those mysterious addresses.

There are no trade banks as such in Japan, but the bigger Japanese banks have international sections. Some larger Japanese bank head offices are:

Bank of Tokyo
(☎ 03-3245-1111) 1-3-2 Nihombashi, Chūō-ku
Fuji Bank
(☎ 03-3216-2211) 1-5-5 Ōtemachi, Chiyoda-ku
Mitsubishi Bank
(☎ 03-3240-1111) 2-7-1 Marunouchi, Chiyoda-ku
Sumitomo Bank
(☎ 06-206-8111) 4-6-5 Kitahama, Chūō-ku, Osaka

POST & COMMUNICATIONS
Post

The symbol for post offices is a white and red 'T' with a bar across the top. Red mailboxes are for ordinary mail and blue ones are special delivery. The Japanese postal system is reliable and efficient.

The airmail rate for postcards is ¥70 to any overseas destination; aerograms cost ¥90. Letters under 25g are ¥90 to other countries within Asia; ¥110 to North America, Europe or Oceania (including Australia and New Zealand); and ¥120 to Africa and South America.

Sending parcels overseas from Japan can be as much as 30% cheaper than airmail with Surface Airlift (SAL), and only takes a week longer. Note that post offices conveniently sell different sized cardboard boxes, which allows you to pack and send on the spot. The larger department stores also can arrange international postage when you purchase major items.

District post offices in and around Tokyo (the main post office in a ward, or *ku*) are normally open from 9 am to 7 pm on weekdays, to 3 pm on Saturday, closed on Sunday and public holidays (some larger district offices are open to 12.30 pm on Sunday and public holidays). Local post offices are open from 9 am to 5 pm on weekdays, closed weekends and public holidays. There are after-hours windows at some district offices; the one at Tokyo's central post office is open 24 hours a day.

Tokyo central post office (Map 2) (☎ 03-3284-9539) is on the Marunouchi side of Tokyo station, across the street slightly south of the main station building. The Yokohama central post office (☎ 045-461-1385) is on the south-east side of Yokohama station, across from the JR East offices.

For sending and receiving international mail, see the Tokyo international post office information in the following Receiving Mail section.

Mail can be sent to Japan, from Japan or within Japan when addressed in roman script (*romaji*) but it should, of course, be written as clearly as possible.

Receiving Mail In Tokyo, have your mail sent to the main international post office, as this office is familiar with the concept of poste restante. Have it addressed as follows:

SURNAME, First Name, Poste Restante, Tokyo International Post Office, 2-3-3 Ōtemachi, Chiyoda-ku, Tokyo

To get to the Tokyo international post office (Map 2) (☎ 03-3241-4891), take the A4 exit of Ōtemachi subway station. The post office will hold mail for 30 days. Hours are 9 am to 7 pm weekdays, to 5 pm Saturday, to noon Sunday and national holidays.

American Express will hold mail for its card holders or users of American Express travellers cheques. Normally, mail will be held for 30 days only unless marked 'Please hold for arrival'.

Some embassies will hold mail for their nationals – check before you depart. Hotels and youth hostels are another possibility.

Courier Services International couriers operate in Japan, but you can also use the EMS service *(kokusai ekisupuresu)* available at all post offices, though you need an EMS number to access it. EMS is usually as cheap as, and can be faster than, international shippers like Federal Express (☎ 0120-003-200), Nippon Express (☎ 03-3572-4305) and the Overseas Courier Service (☎ 03-5476-8106).

Japan also has an excellent system of private domestic carriers, such as Yamato Takyūbin (☎ 03-3798-5131), which can deliver documents and parcels door-to-door around the country, usually overnight. Bring your package to a convenience store like Lawson's and send it from there (the clerks can help you fill out the forms and explain payment). It's cheap, often less than ¥1500 for a small package.

Telephone
The Japanese public telephone system is very well developed and there are many public phones (rarely vandalised). Services within Japan are principally handled by

東京 東京 東京 東京 東京 東京 東京 東京 東

Japan Area Codes
The country code for Japan is 81. Tokyo's area code is 03 (not used if dialling a Tokyo number from within the same area code). Below are area codes for some main cities and tourist areas. You do not dial the first 0 in these codes if dialling from overseas:

Fukuoka	092
Hakone	0460
Hiroshima	082
Kamakura	0467
Kyoto	075
Matsuyama	0899
Nagasaki	0958
Nagoya	052
Narita	0476
Nikkō	0288
Osaka	06
Sapporo	011
Sendai	022
Shimoda	0588
Yokohama	045

東京 東京 東京 東京 東京 東京 東京 東京 東

Nippon Telegraph and Telephone Corporation (NTT).

Local calls cost ¥10 for three minutes; long-distance or overseas calls require a handful of coins. Unused ¥10 coins are returned after a call, but change is *not* given for ¥100 coins. Most pay phones will also accept prepaid phone cards *(terefon kādo)* in denominations of ¥500 and ¥1000. The cards are readily available from vending machines and convenience stores.

International Calls Rates have become more competitive, as Kokusai Denshin Denwa (KDD) now operates alongside the newer International Telecom Japan (ITJ) and International Digital Communication (IDC).

Paid and reverse-charge (collect) overseas calls can be made from grey ISDN phones and green phones which have a gold metal plate around the buttons. These are usually found in phone booths marked 'International & Domestic Card/Coin Phone'. Due to the proliferation of counterfeit telephone cards, it is no longer possible to make international calls from green phones (though you can make operator-assisted calls from these

Tokyo Blossoms

Tokyo isn't the greenest city in the world, but there are quite a few parks and gardens scattered around, and even a few tree-lined streets.

Autumn Foliage

Tokyo's trees are particularly beautiful during the autumn foliage season (*koyō*), which runs from about mid-October to early November. Look for the maple, which goes through a minor spectrum of yellows and oranges before climaxing in a fiery red. Here are the best spots to observe the changing colours:

Koishikawa Kōraku-en – (Map 1) Bunkyō-ku – With its lovely pond and surrounding gardens, this may be Tokyo's best foliage spot.

Ueno-kōen – (Map 4) Taitō-ku – Famous for its cherry blossoms in spring, this park is also a fine foliage spot.

Kitanomaru-kōen – (Map 2) Chiyoda-ku – Just north of the Imperial Palace, this pleasant park is a great place for an autumn stroll or picnic.

Omote-sandō Promenade – (Map 7) Shibuya-ku – One of Tokyo's few tree-lined avenues, this is most pleasant on Sunday, when the street is closed to motorised traffic.

CHRIS ROWTHORN

Shinjuku-gyoen – (Map 6) Shinjuku-ku – This spacious garden contains many fine foliage spots, particularly in the western-style garden.

Yoyogi-kōen – (Map 7) Shibuya-ku – With ginko, zelvoka and cherry trees, this is a lovely place for an autumn stroll.

Yasukuni-jinja – (Map 2) Chiyoda-ku – The tree-lined approach to the shrine is beautiful when the foliage is at its peak.

Plum Blossom Viewing

Although overshadowed by their more famous cousins, the cherry blossoms, plum blossoms are still dearly loved by the Japanese as early harbingers of spring. These pink and white blossoms usually start to bud in February and bloom from late February to early March. If it's cold, a stroll under the blossoms will suffice, but if it's warm, bring a blanket and have a blossom party! These are Tokyo's better known plum blossom spots:

Upper Box: Maple foliage (Photograph by Chris Rowthorn)

Middle: Harajuku's Omote-sandō Promenade is at its best on any Sunday in autumn; the seasonal colours of leaves care little for the prevailing winds of fashion.

Bottom Box: Plum Blossoms (Photograph by Chris Rowthorn)

Shinjuku-gyoen – (Map 6) Shinjuku-ku – One of Tokyo's best plum blossom spots. The majority of blossoms are located in the Japanese-style garden, but there are other trees scattered around the other gardens.

Imperial Palace East Garden – (Map 2) Chiyoda-ku – A small collection of red and white plum trees well complemented by the rest of the garden.

Koishikawa Kōraku-en – (Map 1) Bunkyō-ku – A stroll garden with both red and white plum trees and a lovely pond.

Koishikawa Botanical Gardens – (Map 1) Bunkyō-ku – The plum garden has a collection of 50 red and white plum trees.

Hama Rikyū Detached Palace Garden – (Map 3) Chūō-ku – About 50 red and white trees located on the east side of the garden.

Hibiya-kōen – (Map 3) Chiyoda-ku – A pleasant, accessible park with a small collection of plum trees.

Hanami

The climax of spring and perhaps the most celebrated moment of the Japanese year is the arrival of the cherry blossoms. This generally occurs some time in April, and the entire nation erupts in cherry blossom mania.

Hanami (cherry blossom viewing) parties continue through the roughly week-long season, from the earliest buds to the last clinging blossoms. Both daytime parties and moonlit soirees are popular. Sake plays an important role, as do singing and dancing (portable karaoke machines often appear).

At popular hanami spots the best sites are often taken by people who have camped out overnight for them. But there is always somewhere left to sit, and a stroll in a Tokyo park on a clear spring day through a riot of pink blossoms and boisterous parties is unforgettable.

With over 1000 trees of several varieties, Ueno-kōen (Map 4) is the hanami capital of Japan. A stroll through the frenzied grounds is a chance to see the Japanese at their most uninhibited. Here are some other spots which may yield a little more breathing room:

Shinjuku-gyoen – (Map 6) Shinjuku-ku – A prime hanami attraction with several varieties of cherry trees, including *yaezakura*, double-blossoming cherries.

Yasukuni-jinja – (Map 2) Chūō-ku – More than 1000 cherry trees in the shrine grounds; also check out the cherry trees lining the nearby Imperial Palace moat.

Yoyogi-kōen – (Map 7) Shibuya-ku – Plenty of space here to admire the park's 500 or so cherry trees.

Hama Rikyū Detached Palace Garden – (Map 3) Chūō-ku – About 100 cherry trees here, including wild cherry trees. An admission fee keeps the crowds at bay and the rest of the garden is pleasant as well.

Sumida-kōen – (Map 4) Taitō-ku and Sumida-ku – There's lots of trees on both banks of the Sumida-gawa River near Asakusa.

Shiba-kōen /Zōjō-ji – (Map 3) Minato-ku – About 100 trees with the temple for a backdrop.

Box: Cherry Blossoms (Photograph by Chris Taylor)

Sakura-doki (cherry blossum time) is an old word for spring in Japan, a brief time when hanami parties wistfully celebrate the falling of soft petals in the gentle breeze – or a chance to get blotto in a park along with several thousand of your closest karaoke-crazed friends.

MATTHIAS LEY

phones). In hotel lobbies and airports, you will also find KDD 'Credit Phones' which allow you to make international calls with credit cards issued outside Japan. In some youth hostels and 'gaijin houses', you will also find pink coin-only phones from which you cannot make international calls (though you can receive them).

Calls are charged by the unit (no three minute minimum), each of which is six seconds, so if you've not got much to say you could phone home for just ¥100.

You save money by dialling late at night. Economy rates with a discount of 20% apply from 7 to 11 pm, Monday to Friday, and all day to 11 pm on weekends and holidays. From 11 pm to 8 am a discount rate brings the price of international calls down by 40%. Note that it is also cheaper to make domestic calls by dialling outside the standard hours.

To place an international call through the operator, dial ☎ 0051 – international operators all seem to speak English. To make the call yourself, dial ☎ 001 (KDD), ☎ 0041 (ITJ) or ☎ 0061 (IDC) – there's very little difference in their rates – then the international country code, the local code and the number.

Another option is to dial ☎ 0039 for home country direct, which takes you straight through to a local operator in the country dialled (your home country direct code can be found in phone books or by calling ☎ 0051). You can then make a reverse-charge call or a credit-card call with a telephone credit card valid in that country. In some hotels or other tourist locations, you may find a home country direct phone where you simply press the button labelled USA, UK, Canada etc, to be put through to your operator. You need to arrange the home country direct service with your home telephone company before you leave for Japan.

Directory Assistance Dial ☎ 104 for local directory assistance, or for assistance in English ring ☎ 0120-364-463 (9 am to 5 pm weekdays). For international directory assistance dial ☎ 0057. An English telephone directory is available in *City Source*. It is free, available at any NTT office or the Tokyo TIC. To place a domestic collect call, dial ☎ 106. For orders and inquiries about having a phone installed, ring the NTT English Service Section on ☎ 0120-364-463, toll-free.

Fax, Telegraph & Email

Fax An economic miracle Japan may be, but getting access to fax services in Tokyo can be difficult. If you're staying in a major hotel, you should have no problem. For those in more downmarket digs, the branches of KDD in Shinjuku (Map 6) (☎ 03-3347-5000) and Ōtemachi (☎ 03-3275-4343) can receive and send international faxes from 9 am to 5 pm, Monday to Friday (closed on holidays). The Shinjuku branch is on the station's west side; the Ōtemachi branch is next to the C1 exit of Ōtemachi subway station. Sending faxes is easier than receiving them at KDD. The Ōtemachi branch requires an annual membership fee (¥5000). There is also a branch out at Narita airport (☎ 0476-3347-8730) in the Passenger Terminal Central building (4th floor), which is open from 9 am to 8 pm weekdays, to 6 pm weekends and holidays.

Alpha Corporation, on the 1st floor of Shinjuku's Tokyo Hilton International hotel (Map 6) (☎ 03-3343-2575) and in the Akasaka Tōkyū Hotel (Map 3) (☎ 03-3580-1991), offers fax services. Kimi Information Center (Map 5) (☎ 03-3986-1604) in Ikebukuro will both receive and send faxes.

Telegrams For international information, ring ☎ 03-3344-5151 (some English is spoken) or go to the KDD offices mentioned above. Prices are pretty steep for international telegrams, and they aren't quick. For domestic telegrams in English, you can also go to any major NTT office, eg the Marunouchi head office (☎ 03-5001-3300).

Email Compuserve, America Online and IBM subscribers can pick up their email via local numbers in Japan. Check with your server before coming to Japan for local access numbers. Phone jacks in Japan are the

FACTS FOR THE VISITOR

same seven pin type used in America. Many of the grey IDD public telephones in Japan have a jack that will allow you to log on.

INTERNET RESOURCES

Though the Internet was slow in coming to Japan, the country is scrambling to catch up, and there is currently a wealth of information on Japan available online. Check out JNTO's homepage (www.jnto.go.jp).

TELLNET (www.majic.co.jp), put up by the folks at Tokyo English Lifeline, is a site which provides 1200 pages of free information on living in Japan. Tokyo Q is a large, inventive and useful Tokyo entertainment resource (www.so-net.or.jp/tokyoq).

See the Gay & Lesbian Travellers entry in this chapter for some gay-friendly Web sites.

Lonely Planet Online

While you're holding a copy of Lonely Planet's latest 'treeware' for Tokyo, check

東京 東京 東京 東京 東京 東京 東京 東京 東

Tokyo's Internet Cafes

Internet cafes haven't taken Tokyo by storm, but there are a good number of them about. The trend – a healthy one – is less towards the fully fledged Internet cafe than to real cafes which contain a couple of computers.

Good examples of this user-friendly trend include Cafe des Près (Map 7) (☎ 03-5411-3721), on Omote-sandō in Harajuku, which has a couple of IBMs (¥500 for 30 minutes). Las Chicas (Map 7) (☎ 03-3407-6863), in Aoyama, has a single Mac which diners can use for free, as does Kiss (Map 7) (☎ 03-3401-8165).

Pulse Point (☎ 03-3289-0132), on the 4th floor of Ginza's Sony building (Map 3), has bagels with Macs or IBMs – the cost is ¥500 for 30 minutes.

Cyberia (☎ 03-3423-0318), in Nishi-Azabu, has IBMs (¥500 for 30 minutes) and offers lessons. You can receive email here, and cappuccino is on tap. If you can find the Yoshida building in Roppongi, the IAC Internet Surf Shop (☎ 03-5561-9339) has the same rates – and serves beer.

YuMeDi Akihabara (☎ 03-5296-5581) has more than 100 Macs and 30 IBMs, and charges ¥1500 for the day. Unfortunately, you can only send email here, not receive it. ■

東京 東京 東京 東京 東京 東京 東京 東京 東

out the latest travel news, views, updates and more to destinations in Japan, the rest of Asia and the globe at LP's award-winning Web site (www.lonelyplanet.com). Features include photo galleries, cyber-postcards, travel literature and a lively bulletin board.

BOOKS

Tokyo has a number of bookshops with excellent selections of books. Most of the following books should be available in Tokyo, usually in paperback.

Lonely Planet

For trips further afield in Japan and the region, Lonely Planet's *Japan*, *Kyoto* and *North-East Asia* guides contain all the travel detail you'll need.

Alex Kerr's recent *Lost Japan* recounts both the dangers facing modern Japan and the author's fascinating experiences in the country.

Guidebooks

Guidebooks to Tokyo come and go quickly, but a few specialised guidebooks are good supplements to the book you have in your hands. Gourmets should look for the *Tokyo Restaurant Guide* by John Kennerdell.

Serious nightlife addicts could seek the *Tokyo Nightlife Guide* by the folks at *Tokyo Journal*.

Tokyo Museums – A Complete Guide by Thomas & Ellen Flannigan is what its title suggests. *Tokyo for Free*, by Susan Pompian, lists hundreds of no-cost activities in the city.

Old Tokyo – Walks in the City of the Shogun by Enbutsu Sumiko is a helpful walking guide to Tokyo's lingering past. Her *The Sumida Crisscross – Tokyo River Walks* is excellent.

Gary Walters' *Day Walks Near Tokyo* covers 25 accessible countryside trails. John Carroll's *Trails of Two Cities* outlines walks around Yokohama and Kamakura.

Culture & Society

Look for the brilliant *Outnation – A Search for the Soul of Japan* by Jonathan Rauch. *In the Realm of the Dying Emperor* by Norma

Field is a thoughtful and beautifully written assault on views of Japanese society as both monolithic and de-individualising. Karl Taro Greenfield attempts the same in his racy *Speed Tribes – Children of the Japanese Bubble*.

Max Danger – The Adventures of an Ex-Pat in Tokyo commands a loyal following.

Another light but illuminating read is *You Gotta Have Wa* by Robert Whiting.

Recently updated, *The Japanese Today* by Edwin O Reischauer has long been a standard textbook and is a must-read. *Appreciations of Japanese Culture* by Donald Keane is an eclectic collection of essays by a renowned scholar of Japanese culture.

東京 東京 東京 東京 東京 東京 東京 東京 東京 東京 東京 東京 東京 東京 東京 東京 東京

Tokyo's Bookshops

The English-language sections of several of the larger Tokyo bookshops would put entire bookshops in many English-speaking cities to shame.

The main bookshop area in Tokyo is Jimbōchō (Map 2), and although most of the bookshops there cater only to those who read Japanese, there are a couple of foreign-language bookshops. The best among these is Kitazawa Shoten (☎ 03-3263-0011), which has an excellent academic selection on the ground floor and second-hand books on the 2nd floor. For a decent selection of English books, many of them titles on Japan, Asia and arts and culture, take a look in Tuttle Books (☎ 03-3291-7071) and Issei-dō (☎ 03-3292-0071). For the best selection of used English paperbacks in the neighbourhood, check out the small Wonderland Books (☎ 03-3233-2507).

One of Japan's better bookshops chains, Kinokuniya has two branches in Shinjuku (Map 6). The old branch on Shinjuku-dōri (☎ 03-3354-0131) has a good selection of English-language fiction and general titles on the 3rd floor, including an extensive selection of books and other aids for learning Japanese. It's closed on the third Wednesday of the month. The new Kinokuniya branch (☎ 03-5361-3301) in the annex of the Takashimaya Times Square Complex has one of the largest selections of English-language books in Tokyo on the 6th floor.

Maruzen (☎ 03-3272-7211) in Nihombashi (Map 2) near Ginza has a collection of books almost equal to Kinokuniya's, and it is always a lot quieter. This is Japan's oldest western bookshop, established in 1869. English-language books are on the 2nd floor. It also has a limited selection of French-language magazines, books and newspapers. It's closed on Sunday.

The 3rd floor of Jena (Map 3) (☎ 03-3571-2980) in Ginza doesn't have the range of some other foreign-language bookshops, but it does have a good selection of fiction and art books, and it stocks a large number of newspapers and magazines. It's closed on public holidays.

Just to the south of Tokyo station, Yaesu Book Centre (Map 3) (☎ 03-3281-1811) has a good selection of English-language books as well as some French and German titles.

The best selection of used English-language books is probably in Ebisu (Map 8) at Good Day Books (☎ 03-5421-0957). In addition to a wide range of paperbacks, there are some hardcover books and magazines. It also accepts books for exchange, and (very) occasionally will purchase used books. It's closed Tuesday.

For business reading, you can try the bookshops at JETRO (☎ 03-3582-5522) in Toronomon and the Keizai Kōhō Center (☎ 03-3201-1415) in Ōtemachi. The Government Publication Service Center (☎ 03-3504-3885) in Kasumigaseki also sells Japanese and bilingual official publications. There's also a branch in Ōtemachi.

Bojinsha (☎ 03-3239-8673), a small but well-stocked bookshop on the 2nd floor of the Kōjimachi New Yahiko building near Yotsuya JR and subway stations, is an excellent place to pick up texts or AV tools for anyone wanting to learn or teach the Japanese language. ■

CHRIS ROWTHORN

Shelf space is also at a premium in Tokyo.

東京 東京 東京 東京 東京 東京 東京 東京 東京 東京 東京 東京 東京 東京 東京 東京 東京

History

For a fascinating history of Tokyo from 1867 to 1923, look for Edward Seidensticker's *Low City, High City*. His *Tokyo Rising – The City Since the Great Earthquake* continues the story.

Lafcadio Hearn lived in Meiji Tokyo and wrote many books and essays. Hearn's *Writings from Japan* includes some of his best work. Paul Waley's *Tokyo – City of Stories* is a contemporary attempt at Hearn.

Religion

Good primers include *Japanese Religion – A Cultural Perspective* by Robert S Elwood & Richard Pilgrim and *Religions of Japan – Many Traditions within One Sacred Way* by H Byron Earhart.

Probably the best introduction to Zen is *Zen and Japanese Culture* by Daisetzu T Suzuki. Peter Matthiessen gives a personal account of his Zen experiences in *Nine Headed Dragon River*.

Business

There is a mountain of tomes purporting to unlock the secrets of Japanese business. *The Art of Japanese Management – Applications for American Executives* has been around for a while, but is still a good introduction.

For nuts and bolts information there's the *Japan Company Handbook* (Toyo Keizai) detailing listed companies. *Nippon* (JETRO) is an annual statistical publication. Other annual publications include *Survey of Japanese Corporations Overseas* (Toyo Keizai), *Japan Trade Directory* (JETRO), *Japan Economic Alamanac* (The Nikkei Weekly) and *Japan: An International Comparison* (Keizai Kōhō Center, or Japan Institute for Social and Economic Affairs).

Practical guides include *Setting Up an Office in Japan* (American Chamber of Commerce in Japan, 1993), *Setting Up and Operating a Business in Japan* by Helene Thian (Tuttle, 1990) and *Setting Up Enterprises in Japan – Guidelines on Investment, Taxation and Legal Regulations* (JETRO, 1993). JETRO's *Investment Japan – A Directory of Institutions and Firms Offering Assistance to People Seeking to Set Up a Business in Japan* is a comprehensive listing of useful contacts across all industries. The *Japan Yellow Pages* is published by Japan Yellow Pages Ltd (☎ 03-3239-3501).

Language

One of the best colloquial textbooks is *An Introduction to Modern Japanese*, available with an expensive set of tapes. *Japanese for Busy People* comes in several volumes and is also a popular textbook and tape series.

You can impress your Japanese friends with little gems culled from books as diverse as *How to Sound Intelligent in Japanese* by Charles de Wolf and *Japanese Street Slang* by Peter Constantine. Of course, it would be sensible to get the basics of Japanese grammar down before you try quoting Sartre to the local convenience store worker.

For a guide to street-wise *kanji*, a copy of *Reading Japanese Signs* is indispensable. For a more systematic approach to kanji, one of the best books around is *Kanji in Context*. If you want a reference book, Hadaminsky & Spahn's *Kanji & Kana* is without peer for clarity and ease of use.

Fiction

See the Arts section of the Facts about Tokyo chapter for accessible examples of Japan's rich literary heritage.

NEWSPAPERS & MAGAZINES

Newspapers

There are four good, widely available local English newspapers: the *Japan Times*, *Mainichi Daily News*, *Yomiuri Daily* and *Asahi Evening News*. The *Japan Times* is popular for its classified section – Monday is the day to check for employment. The *Yomiuri Daily* has a 'View from Europe' section culled from Britain's *Independent* and a 'World Report' from the *Los Angeles Times*. For business news, try *Business Tokyo* and *Nikkei Weekly*. Overseas papers and magazines are available at major foreign-language bookshops.

Magazines

Tokyo has several English-language magazines covering local events, entertainment and cultural listings. The *Tokyo Journal* is the best; the Cityscope section alone is worth the ¥600 a month for its listings of movies, plays, concerts, art exhibitions and unclassifiable 'events'. Its classified ads are very useful if you're staying for some time. The *Tokyo Journal* is available at bookshops with English-language sections.

Tokyo Classified is a free weekly magazine with classifieds and some news of restaurants, bars and upcoming events. It can be found at record stores like Virgin and Tower, and some bigger bookshops. More widely available is *Pia*, a Japanese-language 'what's-on' publication.

Free information magazines are available at hotels, TIC offices and Narita airport. These include *Tokyo Classified*, *City Life News Tokyo* and *The Nippon View*. The weekly *Tokyo Weekender* is similar.

If you're studying Japanese, articles in the *Hiragana Times* are in English and Japanese, and the kanji includes *furigana* (script used to give pronunciation for kanji) readings.

RADIO & TV
Radio

InterFM on 76.1 FM was created in 1996 to serve the needs of Tokyo's large foreign population. The station broadcasts news and daily-life information mainly in English, but also in seven other languages, including Spanish and Chinese. The music is more cosmopolitan than most other stations, too. You can also tune into the US armed services' Far East Network (FEN; 810 kHz).

TV

Unlike radio (where DJs often throw in some English), most TV is Japanese-only. In any case, it's mostly inane variety shows. It's worth watching a bit as a window into the culture, but you're unlikely to get addicted.

TVs can be fitted with an adaptor so that certain English-language programmes and movies can be received in either Japanese or English. The Japan Broadcasting Corporation (NHK) has a nightly bilingual news report, though it is rarely very informative. The better hotels do have English-language satellite services, including BBC and CNN.

PHOTOGRAPHY & VIDEO
Film & Equipment

The Japanese are a nation of photographers – no social occasion is complete without a few snaps and an exchange of the photos, so photographic gear is easy to come by.

A 36 exposure Kodachrome 64 slide film costs about ¥950 without processing. Disposable cameras are even sold from vending machines (¥1500 to ¥2000); more expensive ones have a built-in flash.

You can also pick up disposable 3D cameras in Japan. The effect is more jarring than pleasing, but pictures taken with such cameras make interesting souvenirs.

Japan uses the American NTSC standard for video. If you are using PAL or SECAM, bring your own video cartridges with you. It is possible to buy video cameras in Tokyo that switch between the standards.

Processing

Processing print film is fast and economical in Tokyo, although the standards vary. Prices range from ¥1000 to ¥2000 for a 36 exposure roll of film, depending upon the shop and the brand of film (Japanese Fuji film is usually the cheapest). One photo chain to look out for is Yellow Camera, which offers 90 minute processing. When you hand in the film, you will be asked 'O-isogi desu ka?' ('Are you in a hurry?'); if you can wait overnight (the cheaper option) a simple 'no' will suffice.

Kodachrome slide film can only be processed by the Imagica Kodak depot in Ginza. The processing is fast (24 hours) and the results are good. There is no problem honouring prepaid Kodachrome film.

Photo Etiquette

When taking pictures of the Japanese, be aware that they are generally self-conscious people and some may not welcome the attention. Asking 'Photo OK?' is an appropriate way to be sure that you won't cause offence. A long lens is another way around potential problems. Hip youth in places like Harajuku are generally amenable to being photographed and some may even welcome the attention. One group to be distinctly wary of are those you even remotely suspect of being *yakuza* gangsters. These types are *very* camera shy and have been known to 'confiscate' or destroy cameras of imprudent photographers.

TIME

Japan is in one time zone, nine hours ahead of Greenwich Mean Time (GMT). Daylight-saving time is not used in Japan.

In train stations, bus stations and airports, a 24 hour clock is used, eg 5 pm is 17.00 and midnight is 24.00.

ELECTRICITY

The Japanese electric current is 100V AC, an odd voltage found almost nowhere else in the world. Furthermore, Tokyo and eastern Japan are on 50 cycles, and western Japan (including Nagoya, Kyoto and Osaka) is on 60 cycles. Most North American electrical items, designed to run on 117V, will function reasonably well on Japanese current. The plugs are flat two pin, identical to US and Canadian plugs.

LAUNDRY

Most hotels, mid-range and up, have laundry services. Or there's the coin laundry, something of an institution in suburban Japan, but nonexistent in central Tokyo. If you are at a budget ryokan, ask the staff for the nearest laundromat *(koin randorii)*. Costs range from ¥200 to ¥300 for a load (some places have extra-large machines for ¥500) and ¥100 for 10 minutes of drying time. Note that some washing machines in koin randorii automatically add detergent, a feature which may or may not be indicated in English. You can always ask someone, 'Sekken irimasu ka?' ('Is soap necessary?'). If you need soap, there are usually on-site machines selling small bags for ¥100 (some of these also make change of ¥1000 notes).

Dry cleaners *(kuriningu-yasan)* are in almost every neighbourhood. The standards are high and some offer rush service. It's about ¥200 for your basic business shirt. You may be asked, 'Norizuke shiage shimashō ka?' ('Do you want it starched?').

Hotel laundry service is available, though not surprisingly, it costs significantly more than doing it yourself.

WEIGHTS & MEASURES

Japan uses the metric system. One exception is the unit used for the size of rooms, which are measured in *jō*, or *tatami* mats. In Tokyo (the size differs across Japan) a tatami measures 1.76m by 0.88m.

HEALTH

Travel health depends on your pre-departure preparations, your day-to-day health care and how you handle any medical problem or emergency that develops. However, looking after your health in Tokyo should pose few problems, since hygiene standards are high and medical facilities are widely available, though expensive.

No immunisations are required for Japan, but it's wise to keep up to date with tetanus, diphtheria and polio shots (boosters are recommended every 10 years). Tap water is safe to drink and the food is almost uniformly prepared with high standards of hygiene. It is advisable to take out some health insurance – see the Documents section earlier in this chapter.

Those who would like an in-depth look at health issues in Japan and advice on what to do if you get sick in the country may want to pick up a copy of Meredith Maruyama's *Japan Health Handbook* (December Books, 1997).

A small medical kit is a good thing to carry, even though most items will usually be readily available in Japan. If you wear glasses it's a good idea to bring a spare pair and your prescription. If you require a particular medication take an adequate supply as it may not be available locally. Take the prescription with the generic rather than the brand name, which may be unavailable, as it will make getting replacements easier. It's wise to have the prescription with you to show you legally use the medication.

Pharmacies *(kusuriya* or *yakkyoku)* have a good selection of drugs, both western and Chinese herbal *(kanpō yaku)*. You can usually spot a pharmacy by the stacks of medicinal products in the windows and the American pharmacy symbol. Most are open standard business hours, though some in nightlife districts and big train stations may stay open until midnight.

Be warned – most pharmacy products are labelled in Japanese. Those who want to know exactly what they're taking should go to the American Pharmacy in Ginza (see Medical Assistance below).

Although oral contraceptives are available from clinics specialising in medical care for foreigners, it is preferable to bring adequate supplies with you. Condoms are widely available, but visitors are advised to bring their own or buy a foreign brand from the American Pharmacy.

Medical Assistance

The TIC has lists of English-speaking hospitals and doctors in Tokyo. Dental care is widely available at steep prices. If you need a medicine not readily available in local pharmacies, try the American Pharmacy (Map 3) (☎ 03-3271-4034) close to the TIC. Oddly, most drugs in Japan are supplied not by pharmacies but by doctors. Critics say that as a result, doctors are prone to over-prescribe and choose the most expensive drugs.

You may want to call the Tokyo Medical Information Service (☎ 03-5285-8181) for advice about which hospital or clinic can best address your needs. The information service also provides telephone interpretation if a language barrier would prevent you from receiving emergency care. The service operates for non-emergency cases on weekdays from 9 am to 8 pm. For emergency cases, you can call weekdays from 7 am to 10 pm, on weekends from 9 am to 10 pm. In addition to English, there are also staff on hand who can speak Spanish, Thai, Korean and Chinese.

The Association of Medical Doctors for Asia International Medical Information Center (☎ 03-5285-8088) is a similar service, open from 9 am to 5 pm, Monday to Friday, closed weekends and public holidays.

If you need medical help in English, the Tokyo Medical and Surgical Clinic (☎ 03-3436-3028) in Kamiyachō on the Hibiya subway line has foreign doctors. Appointments can be made Monday to Friday from 9 am to 4.45 pm and until 1 pm on Saturday. The International Clinic (☎ 03-3583-7831) in Roppongi also provides services in English. It is open from 9 am to 5 pm Monday to Friday, and from 9 am to noon on Saturday. When making your appointment, be sure to ask for exact directions to get to the clinics. Both clinics are closed Sunday and holidays.

Some other clinics include:

Hibiya Clinic
(☎ 03-3502-2681) open Monday to Friday, 9.30 am to noon and 1 to 5 pm; close to Hibiya Park
King Clinic
(☎ 03-3409-0764) open 9 am to 4.45 pm, closed Saturday and Wednesday afternoon; Harajuku
Ojima Dental Clinic
(☎ 03-3268-8818) open Monday to Friday, 10 am to 1 pm and 2 to 6 pm; emergency calls also accepted; Shinjuku
Totsuka MT Clinic
(☎ 045-862-0050) open 9 am to 7 pm (to 4 pm Sunday); obstetrics, gynaecology, paediatrics; Yokohama

MARTIN MOOS

Tooth in advertising?

FACTS FOR THE VISITOR

Emergencies

Emergency services will usually only react quickly if you speak Japanese. You can dial ☎ 110 for police or ☎ 119 for a fire or an ambulance, though English may not be spoken.

For information on your nearest medical treatment centre, ring the information desk of the Tokyo Fire Department (☎ 03-3212-2323); English is spoken. There's also the Tokyo English Lifeline, or TELL (☎ 03-5721-4347), and Japan Helpline (☎ 0120-461-997), a 24 hour a day emergency number. Don't clog the line unless you really do have an emergency.

You can also go to a *kōban* (police box) for help in an emergency. These are neighbourhood police stations which can be found on street corners and near railway stations. Kōban have a glass front and a door which is usually left open to the street. You may see some police officers inside; other times they are hidden in the back. Don't visit a kōban unless you have a real problem, as many police look at a visit from a foreigner as a good chance to check their documents, generally waste their time and possibly even to collar a scapegoat.

Counselling & Advice

Adjusting to life in Japan can be tough, but there are several places to turn for help. The TELL phone service (☎ 03-5721-4347) offers confidential and anonymous help. Tokyo Tapes (☎ 03-3262-0224) has a wide variety of tapes to help you deal with problems. For longer-term residents, there is also the Foreign Residents Advisory Center (☎ 03-5320-7744), which is operated by the Tokyo metropolitan government, open Monday to Friday.

TOILETS & PUBLIC BATHS

In Japan you will come across both western-style and Asian squat toilets. At the latter, when squatting the correct position is facing the hood. Make sure the contents of your pockets don't spill out. Toilet paper isn't always provided, so carry tissues. In homes and ryokan, separate toilet slippers are often provided just inside the door.

Public toilets are almost always free in Japan. The kanji for 'toilet' is 手洗い ; for 'men' it is 男 ; and for 'women' it is 女 .

WOMEN TRAVELLERS

By international standards Tokyo is an extremely safe city for women travellers. However, there is a well publicised type of molester known as a *chikan* (masher), who travels packed trains in order to touch female travellers in the close confines of rush-hour traffic. While Japanese women seem to put up with this or simply move away if possible, another option is to grab the offending hand and shout 'Chikan!'.

Note that some public toilets are not sex-segregated. While this does not usually result in any problems, if you prefer, there's usually a sex-segregated toilet somewhere nearby.

Also, it is not a good idea to walk in certain areas alone at night. These areas are basically those which any solitary traveller would avoid at night – dark alleys, bar districts and the like. If it looks dangerous, go another way. Hitchhiking is a definite no-go for the solitary female traveller.

GAY & LESBIAN TRAVELLERS

For the traveller, Tokyo is more hip and westernised than its Asian counterparts when it comes to the gay and lesbian scenes. This doesn't mean it's necessarily easy to break into the local scene – foreigners will find some bars unfriendly – but there is an active international scene that includes clubs, bars, newsletters, support groups etc.

The magazine *Outrageous Tokyo*, which lists gay-friendly associations, clubs and events, is a good starting point. It should be available at HMV in Shibuya and Shinjuku, and at Shinjuku's Virgin Megastore (Map 6).

International (Gay) Friends (☎ 03-5693-4569; English is spoken) has meetings every third Saturday of the month. You can write International (Gay) Friends for more information at IF Passport, CPO Box 180, Tokyo 100-91.

These Web sites may be of help in planning your trip:

HyperStag
    www.gavie.or.jp/jp/hpstag/index.html
Gaynet Japan
    www.gnj.or.jp/gaynet/
OutRageous Tokyo
    shrine.cyber.ad.jp/darrell/outr/home/
    outr-home.html
Planet Rainbow
    www.kt.rim.or.jp/rainbow/

DISABLED TRAVELLERS

Many new buildings have access ramps, traffic lights have speakers playing melodies when it is safe to cross, train platforms have raised dots and lines to provide guidance, but there is much in Tokyo that is downright dangerous, depending on your disability.

Tokyo's congested rail system is bad enough if you are nimble on your feet. If you are going to travel on a train and need assistance, ask one of the station workers as you enter the station. There are cars on most lines which have areas set aside for those in wheelchairs. Those with other physical disabilities can use one of the seats set aside near the train exits, called *yūsen-zaseki*.

One indispensable guide is *Accessible Tokyo* put out by the Japanese Red Cross. You can write them for a copy at Japanese Red Cross Language Service Volunteers c/o Volunteers Division, Japanese Red Cross Society, 1-1-3 Shiba Daimon, Minato-ku, Tokyo 105, Japan (☎ 03-3438-1311; fax 3432-5507).

Three travel-information sources for the mobility-impaired are Mobility USA (☎ 1-541-343-1284), PO Box 1076, Eugene, OR 97440, USA; Access Foundation (☎ 1-516-887-5798), PO Box 356, Malverne, NY 11565, USA; and Society for the Advancement of Travel for the Handicapped (SATH) (☎ 1-718-858-5483), 26 Court St, Brooklyn, NY 11242, USA.

SENIOR TRAVELLERS

Japan is an excellent place for senior travellers, and Japanese seniors themselves are among the most active travellers in the world. To qualify for widely available senior discounts, you have to be over 60 or 65, depending upon the place/company. One interesting deal offered by JR for senior couples travelling together is the 'Full Moon Green Pass' which costs (for two people) ¥79,000 for five days, ¥98,000 for a week and ¥122,000 for 12 days. These are on sale at major JR stations from 1 September to 31 May and can be used on consecutive days from 1 October to 31 May, excluding 28 December to 6 January, 21 March to 5 April and 27 April to 6 May (Japanese peak travel periods). These are valid on all JR lines in Japan, including most shinkansen, and entitle you to unlimited travel in Green (1st class) reserved seats and sleeping berths, and the Narita express. To qualify, you must be a married couple whose combined age exceeds 88 (passports can prove this). A ¥5000 discount applies to those over 70.

Japanese domestic airlines (JAS, JAL and ANA) offer senior discounts of about 25% on some flights. For more information, contact the airlines (see the Airlines entry in the Getting There & Away chapter).

In addition to travel discounts, you can get discounts on entry fees at most temples, museums and movie theatres.

TOKYO FOR CHILDREN

Tokyo is a relatively easy and safe place to travel with children. One of the few difficulties is the constant attention paid to small children. Otherwise, you will find lots of services, including nappy-changing tables in newer public bathrooms and trains, free child minding at big department stores and widely available discounts for children.

There are a myriad of ways to keep them amused, and a lot of children's entertainment in Tokyo is so lavish and ingenious that it's fun for accompanying adults too.

For ideas, see the Tokyo with Children boxed text in the Things to See & Do chapter and the Kids' Stuff entry in the Shopping chapter (for some amazing toy shops).

For general advice on travel with children, pick up Lonely Planet's *Travel with Children* by Maureen Wheeler.

USEFUL ORGANISATIONS
Clubs & Associations
No matter what your interest, there is probably a club or association for it in Tokyo.

English-language telephone directories, *City Source* and *Japan Yellow Pages* are valuable initial resources. Paul Ferguson's *Networking in Tokyo: A Guide to English Speaking Clubs and Societies* and the American Chamber of Commerce in Japan's *Living in Japan* are useful lifestyle guides.

Embassies and chambers of commerce, along with a myriad of international sister-city and friendship societies, stage activities open to visitors and residents in Tokyo. Also check the *Tokyo Journal* – there's everything from the Breakfast Toastmasters Club to the Japan Tropical Forest Action Network.

Conversation Lounges
Special clubs have been formed to give Japanese the opportunity to meet foreigners (English-speaking ones at least). Activities generally centre around a lounge or coffee shop, entry to which costs foreigners little or nothing – it is the Japanese who pay.

Mickey House (Map 5) (☎ 03-3209-9686) is an 'English bar' that offers free tea and coffee, and reasonably priced beer and food. It is a good place to meet young Japanese as well as long-term gaijin residents. Take the Big Box exit of Takadanobaba station and walk straight ahead. Mickey House is on the 4th floor of a building on the left, just after a subway entrance.

A similar club worth a look is the Corn Popper Club (☎ 03-3715-4473) in Ebisu.

Home Visit System
The home visit system is publicised in JNTO pamphlets and provides visitors to Tokyo with a chance to spend time with a Japanese family. Visits take place in the evening, and while dinner is not usually served, the hosts will often provide tea and sweets. It is polite to bring a small gift with you.

Home visits can be organised by the Tokyo branch of the Home Visit Service (☎ 03-3502-1461). There is also a branch in Yokohama (☎ 045-641-5824).

LIBRARIES
Tokyo has quite a few libraries with material in European languages. The British Council (Map 2) (☎ 03-3235-8031) in Iidabashi has a good collection of books and magazines. It's open from 10 am to 8 pm, closed weekends. The American Center (☎ 03-3436-0901) has a library in the Shiba-kōen area (Map 3). It's open from 10.30 am to 6.30 pm, closed weekends.

The Japan Foundation Library (Map 1) (☎03-3263-4504) in Kioichō is open only to foreigners and holds some 30,000 English books. It's open from 10 am to 5 pm, closed Sunday and Monday.

The most extensive library in Tokyo is the National Diet Library (Map 3) (☎ 03-3581-2331), close to Nagatachō subway station (with a branch in Ueno). It has more than 1.3 million books in western languages. It's open from 9.30 am to 5 pm, closed Sunday.

For the World Magazine Gallery, see the Ginza section of the Things to See & Do chapter.

The Bibliotheque de la Maison Franco-Japonaise (☎ 03-3291-1144) is close to Ochanomizu station; open from 10 am to noon and 1 to 6 pm, closed Saturday. The Goethe Institut Tokyo Bibliotek (☎ 03-3583-7280) is open from noon to 6 pm (8 pm on Friday), closed on weekends. It's close to Aoyama-itchōme subway station on the Ginza line.

JETRO's head office (Map 3) (☎ 03-3582-5522) in Toronomon also has an excellent reading library. There are also libraries operated by the Keizai Kōhō Center (☎ 03-3201-1415) in Ōtemachi, chambers of commerce and embassies.

Other libraries include:

Asia-Africa Library
 (☎ 0422-44-4640) 5-14-16 Shinkawa, Mitaka-shi
Asian Productivity Organization Library
 (☎ 03-3408-7221) 8-4-14 Akasaka, Minato-ku
Institute of Developing Economics Library
 (☎ 03-3353-4231) 42 Ichigaya Honmurachō, Shinjuku-ku
Japan Information Center of Science and Technology (JICST) Library
 (☎ 03-3976-4141) 2-8-18 Asahichō, Nerima-ku

Japan Textbook Research Center Library
(☎ 03-5606-4311) 1-9-28 Sengoku, Kōtō-ku
Japan-Soviet Library
(☎ 03-3429-8239) 1-11-2 Kyodo, Setagaya-ku
Keidanren (Japan Federation of Economic Organizations) Library
(☎ 03-3279-1411) 1-9-4 Ōtemachi, Chiyoda-ku
Museum of Modern Japanese Literature Library
(☎ 03-3468-4181) 4-3-55 Komaba, Meguro-ku
National Archives
(☎ 03-3214-0621) 3-2 Kitanomaru-kōen, Chiyoda-ku
Tokyo Metropolitan Central Library
(☎ 03-3442-8451) 5-7-13 Minami-Azabu, Minato-ku

CAMPUSES

Tokyo is the educational capital of Japan, and colleges and universities are thick on the ground. Unfortunately, most are uninspiring urban campuses which hardly stand out from their surroundings. It's also difficult to gain access to facilities, especially libraries, at most of these schools. If this doesn't deter you, here are details for a few of Tokyo's major universities:

Meiji University (Map 2)
(☎ 03-3296-4545) 1-1 Kanda Surugadai, Chiyoda-ku
Nihon University (Map 2)
(☎ 03-5275-8000) 4-8-24 Kudan Minami, Chiyoda-ku
University of Tokyo (Map 4)
(☎ 03-3812-2111) 7-3-1 Hongo, Bunkyō-ku
Waseda University (Map 5)
(☎ 03-3203-4141) 1-104 Totsukamachi, Shinjuku-ku

CULTURAL CENTRES

Cultural centres in Tokyo generally act as a focal point of the national group they represent, and usually have good bulletin boards, events, small libraries and language classes.

The British Council (Map 2)
(☎ 03-3235-8031) 1-2 Kagurazaka, Shinjuku-ku
Goethe Institut Tokyo
(☎ 03-3584-3201) 7-5-56 Akasaka, Minato-ku
Institute Franco-Japonais du Tokyo (Map 2)
(☎ 03-5261-3933) 15 Ichigaya Funagawarachō, Shinjuku-ku
Sweden Center Japan KK
(☎ 03-3403-1351) 6-11-9 Roppongi, Minato-ku

DANGERS & ANNOYANCES

Tokyo is generally an extremely safe city, though it does have a few annoyances. Air pollution, for which the city used to be famous (to the point of having oxygen vending machines on street corners), has improved a lot, though it can become somewhat dirty during peak hour traffic. You might also find blaring public and advertising announcements annoying.

Though Tokyo is infinitely better than most other Japanese cities in this respect, you may encounter police who treat foreigners as second-class citizens. This is usually not a problem unless you put yourself in the position of having to deal with them – like visiting a kōban, or actually committing an offence.

If passive smoking worries you, a lot of restaurants and coffee shops are going to be uncomfortable. Nonsmoking areas are a lot more common these days, but Tokyo isn't Singapore. If you are intent on finding clear air, John Kennerdell's *Tokyo Restaurant Guide* lists 23 good restaurants where you can enjoy a smoke-free meal.

Lost & Found

One wonderful thing about Tokyo is that lost property is more often than not returned by the finder. If you've left something on a train, in a taxi or at a restaurant, don't give it up as gone for good. For items lost on JR trains and at stations, ring the JR East Infoline (☎ 03-3423-0111); for TRTA subway trains and stations, ring its Lost & Found Center (☎ 03-3834-5577); Toei subway trains, stations and buses have a Lost & Found Service Corner (☎ 03-5600-2020); and for property left in taxis, ring the Tokyo Taxi Kindaika Center (☎ 03-3648-0300).

Theft

The low incidence of theft and crime in general in Japan is often noted; of course, theft does occur, and its unlikelihood is no reason for carelessness. Airports are reputed to be among the worst places in Japan for pickpockets and other sneak thieves, so take extra care in these places.

FACTS FOR THE VISITOR

Earthquakes

Earthquakes are a risk throughout Japan, but the Tokyo region is particularly prone to them. There is no point in being paranoid, but it is worth checking the emergency exits in your hotel and being aware of earthquake safety procedures. These include turning off anything that might cause a fire, opening a door or window to secure your exit and sheltering in a doorway or under a sturdy table. If an earthquake occurs, NHK will broadcast information and instructions in English on all its TV and radio networks. Tune to Channel 1 on your television, or to NHK (639 AM) or FEN (810 AM) on your radio.

The Big One

Every Tokyo resident's worst fear – the next 'big one' – became a tangible threat on 17 January 1995, when Kōbe was devastated by an earthquake that measured 7.2 on the Richter scale. People began to wonder what would happen if a similar or even stronger quake hit sprawling, densely populated Tokyo.

Though almost imperceptible earthquakes happen nearly every day, the last one to give Tokyo a major shakedown was the 1923 'Great Kantō Earthquake'. Although Tokyo is not the city it was in 1923, the prospect of another major quake remains a grim one. Still, earthquake prediction is hardly an exact science, and no-one is sure if Tokyo is overdue for a major quake or not – tremors of the magnitude of 1923 may be less common than was previously thought. Whatever the case, the recent Kōbe quake was a reminder to the people of Tokyo and elsewhere in Japan that the mighty geological forces that created their islands are still at work. And the devastation in central Kōbe reminded them that no amount of earthquake preparedness is too much. ■

LEGAL MATTERS

The police are granted extraordinary powers in exchange for patrolling one of the safest societies around. This is all fine until you find yourself on the wrong side of the law (or are suspected of being so). If this is the case, it will be an unpleasant experience. Japanese police have the right to detain a suspect without charging them for up to three days, after which a prosecutor can decide to extend this another 20 days. They can also choose whether to allow you to phone your embassy or lawyer, though you should insist that you will not cooperate in any way until you can make such a call. Your embassy is the first place you should call if given the chance.

Police will speak almost no English; insist that an interpreter *(tsuyakusha)* be summoned. Police are legally bound to provide one before proceeding with any questioning. If you speak Japanese, it's best to deny it and stay with your native language.

If you are taken in on a drug offence, get legal representation as soon as possible. Police have been known to use torture in extracting confessions from suspected drug offenders, and having a lawyer will at least make them think twice. Drug laws are very strict – do *not* be tempted in Japan. Other things like public drunkenness, littering and jaywalking are usually ignored.

As a woman dealing with police, sexist treatment is not uncommmon. Try not to see police alone, or be left alone, and let someone know where you are. At the same time, police at *kōban* (police boxes) are usually friendly, helpful sources of information.

For legal counselling in English and some other languages, call the Human Rights Center Information Line (☎ 03-3581-2302) from noon to 5 pm on weekdays. The Gaikokujin Komarigoto Sōdan (Foreigners' Crisis Consultation) centre (☎ 03-3503-8484) can provide telephone interpretation with police if needed.

BUSINESS HOURS

Shops are typically open seven days a week from around 10 am to 8 pm. Department stores close earlier, usually 6.30 or 7 pm, and close one weekday. Department stores close on different days of the week, so that even if, say, Mitsukoshi is closed, Isetan will be open. Large companies usually work a 9 am to 5 pm five day week; some also operate on Saturday morning. Public offices also work a 9 am to 5 pm schedule, and sometimes close for lunch between noon and 1 pm.

Most government-run attractions (such as major museums) usually open from 9.30 am to 4.30 pm. Note that most ticket offices close half an hour before actual closing time. Private galleries, such as those in department stores, tend to open later and close later. Typically, restaurants open for three hours at lunch (about 11.30 am to 2.30 pm) and four or five hours in the evening (6 to 10.30 pm), though there are abundant exceptions. Cheaper, family-run restaurants often stay open from around 11.30 am to 11.30 pm, particularly those around railway stations.

For bank hours, see the Banking Hours entry in the Money section of this chapter.

PUBLIC HOLIDAYS

National holidays are spread across the year, but beware of the three holidays on 29 April, and 3 and 5 May. These make up 'Golden Week', when Japanese are all on international flights or long train and bus journeys, making it very difficult to get around or out of the country. Another difficult time to travel is during O-bon (Festival of the Dead) from 13 to 16 August, when most Japanese try to get back to their home town.

On most public holidays, essential services and stores remain open, and getting around and eating is not a problem. The one major exception is the New Year's holiday period, from 31 December to 2 or 3 January. During this time, about the only places open are convenience stores and fast-food joints; if you don't want to survive on potato chips and fries, make appropriate preparations.

Here is the list of public holidays:

Ganjitsu (New Year's Day)
    1 January
Seijin-no-hi (Adult's Day)
    15 January
Kenkoku Kinen-bi (National Foundation Day)
    11 February
Shunbun-no-hi (Spring Equinox Day)
    21 March (approximately)
Midori-no-hi (Green Day)
    29 April
Kenpo Kinen-bi (Constitution Memorial Day)
    3 May
Kodomo-no-hi (Children's Day)
    5 May

Umi no hi (Marine Day)
    20 July
Keiro-no-hi (Respect-for-the-Aged Day)
    15 September
Shūbun-no-hi (Autumn Equinox Day)
    23 September (approximately)
Taiiku-no-hi (Sports Day)
    10 October
Bunka-no-hi (Culture Day)
    3 November
Kinrō Kansha-no-hi (Labour Thanksgiving Day)
    23 November
Tennō Tanjōbi (Emperor's Birthday)
    23 December

FESTIVALS

The following is a list of the major festivals celebrated in and around Tokyo. There are so many that, no matter when you visit, you're bound to be in time for something. While festivals *(matsuri)* in Japan are usually non-participatory affairs, many other special events call for full participation – this often translates as drinking, which reaches its peak during the New Year's and *hanami* (blossom viewing) seasons.

January-February

Ganjitsu (New Year's Day)
    1 January; it is customary for Japanese to visit Buddhist and Shintō shrines to pray for luck in the coming year. Go to Meiji-jingū Shrine, Sensō-ji Temple or Yasukuni-jinja Shrine. The day after New Year's Day is one of the two occasions each year when the Imperial Palace is open to the public. Enter the inner gardens by Nijū-bashi Bridge between 9 am and 3.30 pm.
Dezome-shiki
    6 January; firemen dressed in Edo-period costumes put on a parade involving acrobatic stunts on top of bamboo ladders. The parade takes place on Chūō-dōri from Harumi from 10 am.
Seijin-no-hi (Adult's Day)
    15 January; a traditional display of archery is held at Meiji-jingū.
Setsubun
    3 or 4 February; held at Zōjō-ji Temple, Kanda-jinja Shrine and Sensō-ji. Sensō-ji offers the added attraction of a classical dance.
Hari-kuyō
    usually early February; a typically quirky Japanese festival held for pins and needles that have been broken in the preceding year. At Sensō-ji, women lay their pins and needles to rest by 'burying' them in tōfu and radishes.

東京東京東京東京東京東京東京東京東

Matsuri

The Japanese year is marked by a colourful abundance of festivals, or *matsuri*, and nowhere more so than in Tokyo. Matsuri are an expression of Shintō, and were originally held in farming communities according to the seasonal planting and harvesting of rice. Spring festivals were held to supplicate the local gods *(kami)* and to secure a plentiful harvest. Autumn festivals were held in thanks and celebration of a rich harvest. Summer and winter matsuri were less common, though summer festivals were sometimes held to ward off the natural disasters that could ravage a crop before harvest. Summer matsuri became a more common event with the rise of large urban settlements like Edo, where they were held in the hope of circumventing pestilence and plague.

There are many elements to matsuri. One that is common to nearly all is a boisterous crowd of scantily clad men puffing and heaving beneath the weight of a portable shrine *(mikoshi)*. In Tokyo's biannual Kanda Festival, 200 mikoshi are paraded through the streets. Apparently the gods also delight in revelry of all kinds, providing an excuse for the swilling of sake, archery contests, horse-riding displays and dancing. The Tōshō-gū Grand Shrine Festival held at Nikkō annually on 17 and 18 May also provides a good opportunity to see these traditional entertainments.

Although purists might complain that the contemporary urban festivals of Japan bear little in common with their traditional origins, having become largely an excuse for a huge ceremonial piss-up, they are still tremendous fun and wonderfully photogenic. The most highly rated city festival? Unfortunately it is not held in Tokyo, but in Kyoto. The Kyoto Gion Matsuri lasts a full month, reaching its climax on 17 July. ■

東京東京東京東京東京東京東京東京東

March-April

Hina Matsuri (Doll Festival)
    3 March (main celebration); from mid-February onwards, a doll fair is held in Asakusabashi – check with the TIC for exact details.

Knickers Giving Day
    14 March; a recent innovation that could only happen in Japan (although people once said that about karaoke). The idea is that boys reciprocate their Valentine chockies with an article of a lady's most intimate apparel.

Kinryū no Mai
    18 March, a golden dragon dance is held at Sensō-ji to celebrate the discovery of the golden image of Kannon that now rests there. Two or three dances are performed during the day.

Gōhan Shiki
    2 April; a rice-harvesting festival held at Rinnō-ji Temple, Nikkō, in which men (in days past, samurai lords) are forced to eat great quantities of rice in a tribute to the bounty supplied by the gods. Sacred dances are also performed by priests as an accompaniment to the ceremonial 'pig-out'.

Hanami (Blossom Viewing)
    early to mid-April; this is one festival you can't help hearing about if you're in Japan when the blossoms come out.

Kamakura Matsuri
    second and third Sunday of April; a whole week of celebrations centred around Hachiman-gū Shrine in Kamakura.

Hana Matsuri (Buddha's Birthday)
    8 April; celebrations are held at Buddhist temples all over Japan. In Tokyo, celebrations take place at Sensō-ji and Zōjō-ji, among others.

Jibeta Matsuri
    15 April; Kawasaki's famous festival celebrates the vanquishing of a sharp-toothed demon residing in a young maiden, by means of an iron phallus (it's true, really!). The festival starts with a procession, followed by a re-enactment of the forging, and is rounded off with a banquet. The action takes place close to Kawasaki-Taishi station.

Yayoi Matsuri
    16-17 April; a procession of portable shrines is held at Futāra-san-jinja Shrine in Nikkō.

Ueno Tōshō-gū Taisai
    17 April; traditional music and dance at Ueno's Tōshō-gū in memory of Tokugawa Ieyasu.

The golden dragon dance, held at the Sensō-ji Temple, is part of the Kinryū no Mai festival.

May-June

Kanda Matsuri

mid-May; this festival is held on odd-numbered years on the Saturday and Sunday closest to 15 May, and is a traditional Edo festival that celebrates a Tokugawa battle victory. A whole range of activities takes place at Kanda-jinja.

Kuro-fune Matsuri (Black Ship Festival)

16-18 May; held in Shimoda on the Izu-hantō Peninsula. It commemorates the first landing of American Commodore Perry with parades and fireworks displays.

Tōshō-gū Shrine Grand Festival

17-18 May; Nikkō's most important annual festival, featuring horseback archery and a 1000-strong costumed re-enactment of the delivery of Tokugawa Ieyasu's remains to Nikkō.

Sanja Matsuri

third Friday, Saturday and Sunday of May; at Sensō-ji up to 100 *mikoshi* (portable shrines) carried by participants dressed in traditional clothes are paraded through the area near the temple.

Sannō-sai

10-16 June; street stalls, traditional music and dancing, and processions of mikoshi are all part of this Edo festival, held at Hie-jinja Shrine, near Akasaka-mitsuke subway station.

July-October

Tarai-nori Kyōsō

first Sunday of July; held in Itō on Izu-hantō; a race that involves paddling down the Matsukawa River in washtubs using rice scoops as oars; what it's in aid of, no-one seems to know.

Tsukudajima Sumiyoshi-jinja Matsuri

Sunday closest to 7 July; a tri-annual festival, with activities centred around the Sumiyoshi-jinja Shrine; it includes dragon dances and mikoshi parades. The last festival was staged in 1995.

O-bon

13-15 July; this major festival takes place at a time when, according to Buddhist belief, the dead briefly revisit the earth. Dances are held and lanterns lighted in their memory. In Tokyo *bon odori* dances are held in different locations around town.

Sumida-gawa Hanabi Taikai

last Saturday of July; the biggest fireworks display of its kind in Tokyo is held on the Sumida-gawa River in Asakusa.

Ashino-ko Kosui Matsuri

31 July; this festival is held at Hakone-jinja Shrine in Moto-Hakone, and features fireworks displays over Ashino-ko Lake.

Fukagawa Hachiman Matsuri

15 August; another tri-annual, three day Edo festival, when foolhardy mikoshi-bearers charge through 8km of frenzied crowds who dash water on them. The action takes place at Tomioka Hachiman-gū Shrine, next to Monzennakachō subway station on the Tōzai line. The last festival was staged in 1995.

Hakone Daimonji-yaki Festival

16 August; in Hakone, torches are lit on Mt Myojoga-take so that they form the shape of the Chinese character for 'great' or 'large'.

Asakusa Samba Carnival

late August (check with the TIC for exact dates); one of Tokyo's most un-Japanese matsuri. Put on by Brazilian-Japanese returnees, it includes a parade down Kaminarimon-dōri by festively (scantily) attired dancers, and attracts a huge crowd.

Hachimangū Matsuri

14-15 September; festivities include a procession of mikoshi, followed by a display of horseback archery on the 16th.

Ningyō-kuyō

25 September; childless couples offer dolls to Kannon in the hope that she will bless them with children. More interesting for spectators is the ceremonial burning by priests of all the dolls that have been held in the temple precinct from the previous year. The ceremony takes place at Kiyomizu-dō Temple in Ueno-kōen Park from 2 to 3.30 pm.

Furusato Tokyo Matsuri (Metropolitan Citizen's Day)

first Saturday and Sunday in October; a wide range of activities is held at different locations around town. In particular, check out Asakusa's Sensō-ji and Ueno-kōen.

Oeshiki

12 October; held in commemoration of Nichiren (1222-82), founder of the Nichiren sect of Buddhism. On that night, people bearing large lanterns and paper flower arrangements make their way to Hommon-ji Temple. The nearest station is Ikegami station on the Tōkyū Ikegami line.

Tōshō-gū Autumn Festival

17 October; in Nikkō, the equestrian archery performance staged during May's Nikkō's grand festival is held again.

Meiji Reidaisai

30 October to 3 November; held at Meiji-jingū in commemoration of the Meiji emperor's birthday. Particularly interesting are displays of horseback archery by riders dressed in traditional clothes. Other events include classical music and dance.

November-December

Hakone Daimyō Gyōretsu

3 November; a re-enactment of a feudal lord's procession by 400 costumed locals; held in Hakone.

Shichi-go-san (Seven-Five-Three Festival)

15 November; as its name suggests, this is for children aged seven, five and three. They make a colourful sight, dressed in traditional clothes and taken to several shrines, notably Meiji-jingū, Yasukuni-jinja and Sannō Hie-jinja.

Gishi-sai

14 December; commemorating the 47 *rōnin* (masterless samurai) who committed *seppuku* (ritual suicide) after avenging the death of their master. The activities involve a parade of warriors to Sengaku-ji – the rōnin's burial place – and a memorial service from 7.30 pm.

WORK

Unless you are highly qualified, Japan is not a good place to look for work. Japanese employers have become more discriminating, and the market is increasingly saturated with young hopefuls looking for a bit-part in the Japanese economic success story. Do your job hunting before you arrive in Japan – foreign professionals are overwhelmingly recruited from overseas. Arriving in Tokyo with a smart suit and an impressive CV is no guarantee against spending a couple of months attending interviews and watching your savings rapidly disappear.

The same is true of English teaching. If you don't have a college or university degree, forget it, since you cannot be issued a working visa to teach without one. Even people with MA degrees in Teaching English as a Foreign Language (TEFL) often spend a month or so answering advertisements before they finally get accepted somewhere. If you want to teach in Japan, try getting a placement from your home country.

Besides English, it may be possible to find work if you have teaching experience and credentials for another major language like French, Spanish, German, Chinese or Korean. But as with English, openings are scarce and go only to those with real ability.

Many foreigners work in the entertainment industry as dancers, singers, hostesses and bartenders. The problem with most of these jobs is that they do not qualify you for a working visa, and you are going to have to live with the constant threat of immigration problems. Some skilled workers also find jobs in the construction industry, both as labourers and carpenters, though the present sluggish economy has severely reduced openings. Skilled proofreaders, translators and editors are also in demand in Tokyo, but you can bet that most of the good jobs are taken by those who have been in the city for a long time.

If you aren't dissuaded by all this, the best place to look for employment is in the Monday edition of the *Japan Times*. You can also check the want ads in the *Tokyo Journal* or the *Tokyo Classified*. Unless you plan on working illegally, which some do, you are going to need to get a work visa.

Getting There & Away

AIR
Airports

Tokyo is serviced by two major airports, Narita and Haneda. All international carriers with the exception of China Airlines fly to/from Narita airport. The bulk of domestic air traffic goes through Haneda. Fortunately, the two airports are connected by a regular bus service. Flights to and from Narita are usually the cheapest way in or out of Japan, but you may find a rare deal to Nagoya, two hours west of Tokyo by *shinkansen* (bullet train) or to Osaka's Kansai international airport (KIX: four hours west of Tokyo by shinkansen) for less. As a rule, Tokyo-bound travellers should fly into Nagoya or Osaka *only* when it means a saving of over ¥30,000, since this is at least what you'd spend on round trip train fare to these airports.

For local transportation details to/from and between Narita and Haneda airports, see the Getting Around chapter.

Narita Narita is 66km and nearly an hour out of Tokyo by the fastest means available, N'EX airport express trains. If you can forget its inconvenient location, Narita is an excellent, modern airport with a host of services.

The airport is divided into Terminal 1 and Terminal 2, which are connected by a free shuttle bus service. From Terminal 1, board this bus at the No 0 bus stop and from Terminal 2, board at the No 8 and 18 stops. Note that some of the airport's services are only available in the newer Terminal 2.

At both terminals there are post offices, currency exchange counters (generally open daily from 7 am to 10 pm, though the one in Terminal 2 on the 1st floor is open to 11 pm), health clinics (in the underground floor of both terminals) as well as lots of restaurants and duty-free shops. Both terminals also offer left-luggage services and baggage shipping/delivery services. ABC is one such company (☎ 03-3545-1131). ABC can also deliver baggage from Tokyo to the airport if you book in advance.

In Terminal 2, you will also find showers and day rooms for napping (main building, 3rd floor; showers ¥600/hour, day rooms ¥2000 for four hours) and a children's play room (free), available to passengers who have completed their emigration procedures (Terminal 2 satellite building, 3rd floor).

There are several information counters in both terminals, and the staff speak some English at all of them; the main counter for foreign visitors is in Terminal 2 on the 1st floor (☎ 0476-34-6251). It's open from 9 am to 8 pm daily.

On the way in or out of Narita airport, you may notice a heavy security/police presence. Narita was built on land rather forcefully appropriated from local farmers, and the airport has a history of demonstrations, even occasional threats of terrorism. This can slow down road access to the airport, but usually doesn't affect rail transport. Customs and passport control procedures are not affected and usually run as smoothly as in airports elsewhere, if not faster.

Haneda Haneda is the airport all Tokyo expats still wish was Tokyo's main air hub. Unfortunately, all international traffic now goes via Narita airport (with the exception of China Airlines), and only domestic fliers can make use of this conveniently located airport. While the range of services at Haneda is not as great as those at Narita, there are post offices, banking services, left-luggage and baggage shipping services. Also, Haneda does not have a dedicated English-language information counter like the one at Narita, but there are several information counters in the airport, and there is usually a staffer on hand who can answer your questions in English. Haneda's information number is ☎ 03-5757-8111, and operators usually speak enough English to answer your questions.

Arriving at Narita Airport
Customs and immigration procedures are usually straightforward, though they're more time-consuming for non-Japanese. A neat appearance will speed your passage through passport control and Customs, while anyone with even a slightly 'hippy' look is asking for a visit to 'the room'.

Everything at Narita is clearly signposted in English, and you can change money in the Customs halls of either terminal or in the arrival halls. The rates will be the same as those offered in town.

The airport Tourist Information Center (TIC; ☎ 0476-34-6251) is an important stop in the arrival lobby of Terminal 2. It has a wealth of information – at the very least, pick up a subway map and the *Tourist Map of Tokyo*. The office is open daily from 9 am to 8 pm. The TIC is to the far right of the A arrival lobby as you exit the Customs hall.

Narita airport also has a Japan Railways (JR) office where you can make bookings and exchange your Japan Rail Pass voucher for a pass, if you're planning to start travelling straight away.

Leaving Tokyo
Check-in procedures are usually very efficient at Narita, but you should arrive at the airport at least two hours before your departure time. Passport control and security procedures are similarly efficient (bring your embarkation card, which you should have received upon arrival; if you don't have one, you can get a blank form before going through passport control).

Departure Tax There is a ¥2040 departure tax at Narita airport, while all those lucky people flying China Airlines from Haneda airport get out of the country for nothing. Until recently, cash was the only way to pay the tax, and this left ill-prepared travellers in a fix. Now, there is a machine which accepts all major credit cards.

Airlines
Following is a list of the major airline offices in Tokyo:

Aeroflot
(☎ 03-3434-9671) No 2 Matsuda Building, 3-4-8 Toranomon, Minato-ku
Air China
(☎ 03-5251-0711) AO1 Building, 3-2-7 Akasaka, Minato-ku
Air India
(☎ 03-3214-1981) Hibiya Park Building, 1-8-1 Yūrakuchō, Chiyoda-ku
Air Lanka
(☎ 03-3573-4261) Dowa Building, 7-2-22 Ginza, Chūō-ku
Air New Zealand
(☎ 03-3287-1641) Shin-Kokusai Building, 3-4-1 Marunouchi, Chiyoda-ku
Alitalia
(☎ 03-3580-2242) Tokyo Club Building, 3-2-6 Kasumigaseki, Chiyoda-ku
All Nippon Airways (ANA)
(☎ 03-3272-1212, 0120-029-333 toll-free, international; ☎ 03-3552-8800, domestic) Kasumigaseki Building, 3-2-5 Kasumigaseki, Chiyoda-ku
American Airlines
(☎ 03-3214-2111) Nichirei Higashi-Ginza Building, 6-19-20 Tsukiji, Chūō-ku
Asiana Airlines
(☎ 03-3582-6600) Ryuen Building, 1-3-1 Shibakōen, Minato-ku
Austrian Airlines
(☎ 03-3597-6100) Kokusai Shin-Akasaka Building, East Tower, 2-14-7 Akasaka, Minato-ku
Biman Bangladesh Airlines
(☎ 03-3593-1252) Kasumigaseki Building, 3-2-5 Kasumigaseki, Chiyoda-ku
British Airways
(☎ 03-3593-8811) Sanshin Building, 1-4-1 Yūrakuchō, Chiyoda-ku
Canadian Airlines International
(☎ 03-3281-7426) Hibiya Park Building, 1-8-1 Yūrakuchō, Chiyoda-ku
Cathay Pacific Airways
(☎ 03-3504-1531) Tōhō Twin Tower Building, 1-5-2 Yūrakuchō, Chiyoda-ku
China Airlines
(☎ 03-3436-1661) Sumitomo Building, 1-12-16 Shiba-Daimon, Minato-ku
China Eastern Airlines
(☎ 03-3506-1166) AO1 Building, 3-2-7 Akasaka, Minato-ku
Continental Micronesia
(☎ 03-3508-6411) Kokusai Building, 3-1-1 Marunouchi, Chiyoda-ku
Delta Air Lines
(☎ 03-5275-7000) Kiochō Building, 3-12 Kiochō, Chiyoda-ku
Egypt Air
(☎ 03-3211-4521) Palace Building, 1-1-1 Marunouchi, Chiyoda-ku

Finnair
(☎ 03-3222-6801) NK Building, 2-14-2 Kōjimachi, Chiyoda-ku
Garuda Indonesia
(☎ 03-3593-1181) Kanzan Kaikan Building, 3-2-4 Kasumigaseki, Chiyoda-ku
Iberia
(☎ 03-3578-3555) Ark Mori Building, 1-12-32 Akasaka, Minato-ku
Japan Airlines (JAL)
(☎ 03-5489-1111, 0120-255-931 toll-free, international; ☎ 03-3456-2111, domestic) Dai-ni Tekko Building, 1-8-2 Marunouchi, Chiyoda-ku
Japan Air Systems (JAS)
(☎ 045-212-2111) 4-47 Ōtemachi, Naka-ku, Yokohama
Japan Asia Airways
(☎ 03-5489-5411) Yūrakuchō Denki Building, 1-7-1 Yūrakuchō, Chiyoda-ku
KLM-Royal Dutch Airlines
(☎ 03-3216-0771) Yūrakuchō Denki Building, 1-7-1 Yūrakuchō, Chiyoda-ku
Korean Air
(☎ 03-5443-3311) Tokyo KAL Building, 3-4-15 Shiba, Minato-ku
Lufthansa Airlines
(☎ 03-3578-6700) 3-2-6 Kasumigaseki, Chiyoda-ku
Malaysia Airlines
(☎ 03-3503-5961) Hankyū International Express Building, 3-3 Shimbashi, Minato-ku
Northwest Airlines
(☎ 03-3533-6000) Forefront Tower, 3-12-1 Kachidoki, Chūō-ku
Olympic Airways
(☎ 03-3201-0611) Yūrakuchō Denki Building, 1-7-1 Yūrakuchō, Chiyoda-ku
Pakistan International Airlines (PIA)
(☎ 03-3216-6511) Hibiya Park Building, 1-8-1 Yūrakuchō, Chiyoda-ku
Philippine Airlines
(☎ 03-3593-2421) Hibiya Mitsui Building, 1-1-2 Yūrakuchō, Chiyoda-ku
Qantas
(☎ 03-3593-7000) Tokyo Chamber of Commerce Building, 3-2-2 Marunouchi, Chiyoda-ku
Sabena
(☎ 03-3585-6151) Address Building, 2-2-19 Akasaka, Minato-ku
Scandinavian Airlines (SAS)
(☎ 03-3503-8101) Tōhō Twin Tower Building, 1-5-2 Yūrakuchō, Chiyoda-ku
Singapore Airlines (SIA)
(☎ 03-3213-3431) Yūrakuchō Building 709, 1-10-1 Yūrakuchō, Chiyoda-ku
Swissair
(☎ 03-3212-1016) Hibiya Park Building, 1-8-1 Yūrakuchō, Chiyoda-ku

Thai Airways International (THAI)
(☎ 03-3503-3311) Asahi Seimei Hibiya Building, 1-5-1 Yūrakuchō, Chiyoda-ku
United Airlines
(☎ 03-3817-4411) Kokusai Building, 3-1-1 Marunouchi, Chiyoda-ku
Virgin Atlantic
(☎ 03-3499-8811) 3-13 Yotsuya, Shinjuku-ku

Buying Tickets

Competition has brought Tokyo ticket prices down in recent years. While it was taken for granted several years ago that prices were much better in Bangkok and Hong Kong, this is no longer a certainty. In Tokyo, start your search in the *Tokyo Journal*, the *Japan Times* or the *Daily Yomiuri*, all of which run ads from the big Tokyo travel agents which specialise in selling tickets to foreigners (see the Travel Agents section in this chapter). The prices offered by these agents are the lowest you will find in Japan, and departures from Tokyo are almost always the cheapest way out of the country.

Be aware that there are three peak travel periods – Christmas/New Year, Golden Week and O-bon – during which ticket prices nearly double (see the Public Holidays section of the Facts for the Visitor chapter for holiday period details). Since Japanese have a hard time getting time off outside of these limited periods, there is little carry-over before and after these times, and if you are willing to advance or delay your travel by only a day or two, you can often enjoy considerable savings. If you must fly during one of the peak seasons, you'll have to reserve well in advance, as Japanese tend to book such tickets many months in advance.

Travel agents in Japan are reliable, and the only way you are likely to get ripped off is if you deal with an obviously fly-by-night operation or buy a ticket from an individual selling a non-refundable ticket which he or she is unable to use (which is inadvisable anyway, as airlines flying in and out of Tokyo usually check tickets against passports). If you buy a ticket in Japan, you will have to pay a deposit, then pay the balance when you pick up the ticket (Japanese travel agents do not usually issue tickets on the spot).

With your ticket, you will receive a copy of the travel agent's ticket refund policy. If you have any questions about the policy, ask to see it before buying your ticket.

Travel agents may want to see your passport when you make a reservation or purchase. This is to insure that you can enter your intended destination without any visa problems.

Travel agents in Japan are very conservative and have been known to refuse to sell tickets to people they believe will have visa problems on the other end. Note that this is also true for those buying round trip tickets back to Japan. If you're refused at one place and are still determined such a ticket, you will eventually find an agent who will sell you one.

Travellers with Special Needs

If you have a special need – a broken leg, a wheelchair, a baby, dietary restrictions, fear of flying – let the airline know early so that it can make arrangements. Remind them when you reconfirm your booking (at least 72 hours prior to departure) and again when you check in at the airport.

Airports and airlines can be quite accommodating to passengers in wheelchairs, but they do need advance warning. Most international airports will provide escorts from the check-in desk to the airplane, and there should be ramps, lift-accessible toilets and reachable phones. Aircraft toilets, however, are likely to present a problem; travellers should discuss this with the airline at an early stage and, if necessary, with their doctor.

Hearing-impaired travellers can request airport and in-flight announcements to be written down for them.

Children under the age of two travel for 10% of the standard fare (or free on some airlines), as long as they don't occupy a seat. (They don't get a baggage allowance.) 'Skycots' should be provided by the airline if requested in advance; these take children weighing up to 10kg. Children between the ages of two and 12 usually occupy a seat for half to two-thirds of the full fare, and do get a baggage allowance. Strollers can often be taken on as hand luggage.

Guide dogs for the visually impaired will often have to travel in a specially pressurised baggage compartment with other animals, though smaller guide dogs may be admitted to the cabin.

Japanese regulations on the importation of live animals are very strict, and are not waived for guide dogs. Dogs brought from countries in which rabies has been eradicated need not be quarantined, provided their owners can show an exportation certification (*yūshutsu shomeisho*). Dogs arriving from countries in which rabies occurs will be placed into quarantine for up to six months, unless their owners can supply an exportation certification, a veterinary examination certification and written proof of rabies vaccination.

USA & Canada

Recent years have seen huge drops in prices for tickets between North America and Japan. The best advice is to shop around a bit before you buy.

From New York, return fares as low as US$700 can be found. Carriers to check include United Airlines, Northwest Airlines, Korean Air, Japan Airlines (JAL) and All Nippon Airways (ANA). From the US west coast, return fares can start from as low as US$550. Check the Sunday travel sections of papers like the *Los Angeles Times* or the *New York Times* for travel bargains.

Council Travel and STA Travel are good discount operations specialising in student fares and other cheap deals. Both are found across the USA and Canada. Overseas Tours (☎ 800-323-8777), 199 California Drive, Millbrae, CA 94030, is reliable, digs up good fares and can arrange mail-order purchases by cheque or money order.

United Airlines is one of the better price bets from the USA to Japan; its schedule and routes are hard to beat for convenience, and its frequent flier program is among the best around.

United also has great Japan-USA (four stops)-Japan tickets for as low as ¥78,000, and Japan-USA (four stops)-Europe (one stop)-Japan tickets for as low as ¥110,000.

Fares from Canada are similar to those from the USA. Travel Cuts, the Canadian student travel organisation, offers cheap one-way and return Vancouver to Tokyo flights (as low as C$800/C$1000), depending on the season. Canadian Airlines International, which operates out of Vancouver, often matches or beats the best fares available from the USA.

Continental Europe

Consider the route offered between Europe and Japan as well as the price: flight times vary widely depending on the route. The most direct way is across Scandinavia and Russia (about 12 hours from London to Tokyo); some flights still go via Anchorage, Alaska (add about five hours); and trans-Asian routes can take from 18 to 30 hours.

Return London-Tokyo economy air fares are around UK£1000, and are valid for 14 days to three months. A ticket valid for a year costs about £1300 on British Airways and JAL. Although a wide variety of cheaper deals are available, generally, the lower the price, the less convenient the route. Expect to pay UK£900 to UK£1000 for a one year return ticket with a good airline via a fast route. For adventurous trans-Asian routes, count on UK£700 for returns and about half that for one-way tickets.

London remains one of the best places in Europe for keenly priced airline tickets, although Amsterdam is also very good. STA Travel (☎ 0171-937-9962) at 74 Old Brompton Rd, London SW7 or 117 Euston Rd, London NW1; Trailfinders (☎ 0171-938-3366) at 46 Earls Court Rd and at 194 Kensington High St, London W8 7RG (☎ 0171-938-3444); and Travel Bug (☎ 0171-835-2000, 0161-721-4000) all offer rock-bottom return flights to Tokyo, and can put together good Round-the-World routes.

The weekly *Time Out* or various give-away papers are good places to look for travel bargains, but take care with shonky bucket shops and prices too low to believe. The really cheap fares will probably involve cash-strapped Eastern European or Middle Eastern airlines, complicated transfers and long waits along the way.

The Far East Travel Centre (☎ 0171-734-9318), at 3 Lower John St, London W1A 4XE, specialises in Korean Airline ticketing, and can fly you from London via Seoul to Tokyo. The Japan Centre (☎ 0171-437-6445), 66-68 Brewer St, London W1R 3PJ, handles all sorts of ticket permutations.

You can also fly to Hong Kong and buy an onward ticket from one of Hong Kong's very competitive travel agencies. London-Hong Kong flights are much more competitively priced than London-Tokyo ones.

Australia & New Zealand

JAL, ANA and Qantas all have direct flights between Australia and Tokyo, flying from most Australian state capitals. The cheapest fares between Australia and Japan are generally with Garuda Indonesia and Philippine Airlines. One-way/return fares with Garuda start at around A$850/1250. Tickets are valid for six months, or for one year (for an additional A$100). Both fares allow a stopover in Bali. Philippine Airlines is somewhat cheaper: one-way/return fares start around A$760/1130, valid for six months (add another A$150 for the full year).

A normal published excursion fare out of Sydney is around A$1559, but will often be discounted to A$1400. Qantas and JAL also offer cheap fares to travellers with working holiday or student visas, but these are normally only available through selected distributors. STA Travel or Flight Centre International are good places to look for discount ticket deals.

Both Air New Zealand and JAL fly Auckland to Tokyo direct; return fares start around NZ$1350. Air New Zealand and Air Pacific offer a stopover in Fiji; Air Pacific flies daily from Auckland to Fiji, and twice a week to Tokyo via Nadi.

Fares to Australia from Tokyo usually start at around ¥65,000 for flights with stops and ¥91,000 for nonstop flights. Flights to New Zealand from Tokyo usually start at around ¥64,000 with stops and ¥100,000 nonstop.

STA Travel has an Australia-wide number (☎ 1-300-360-960) for fast fares; in New Zealand, ring ☎ 0800-100-677. Flight Centre

International's similar Australia service is on ☎ 131-600; for New Zealand, it's ☎ 0800-354-4487. These are all toll-free numbers.

Asia

Most Asian nations have air links with Japan. South Korea is particularly popular, because it's often used as a place to take a short holiday from Japan when one's visa is close to expiring. Immigration authorities treat travellers returning to Japan after a short break in South Korea with great suspicion.

South Korea Numerous flights link Seoul and Pusan with Tokyo. A one-way/return Seoul-Tokyo flight purchased in Seoul costs around US$180/340. From Tokyo, flights to Seoul are the cheapest way out of Japan. Low-season return fares start as low as ¥18,000; there are several departures daily. Getting seats is usually not a problem, even during peak flying season.

China Air China has several flights a week from Beijing to Tokyo, via Shanghai. JAL flies from Beijing and Shanghai to Tokyo, Osaka and Nagasaki. There are also flights between Dailin and Tokyo on ANA. Current Tokyo prices for flights between Tokyo and Beijing start at ¥36,000 return.

Visas for China obtained in Japan are outrageously expensive – US$80 to US$120, depending on which agent you use. Try to purchase the visa elsewhere.

There are lots of direct flights between Hong Kong and Tokyo, though the cheapest flights will involve a stopover. Hong Kong Student Travel Bureau (☎ 2730-3269) or Phoenix Travel (☎ 2722-7378) can offer good one-way deals from around HK$2300, and cheap return tickets from HK$3500 to HK$5000, depending on the route and the period of validity. Leaving Tokyo, you can usually get flights from the bigger travel agents for as low as ¥28,000 return.

Taiwan Agents handling discounted tickets advertise in the English-language *China News* and *China Post*. The average price for a Taipei to Tokyo return flight is NT$11,000,

though cheaper deals are available. Leaving Tokyo, you can find return tickets to Taipei for as low as ¥37,000. If you are stopping off in Taiwan between Hong Kong and Japan, check out China Airlines tickets, which allow a stopover in Taipei before continuing to Tokyo's handy Haneda airport.

Other Asian Centres There are regular flights between Tokyo and other cities like Manila, Bangkok, Kuala Lumpur, Singapore and Jakarta. Bangkok and Penang offer the cheapest South-East Asian prices for flights to Tokyo. Tokyo prices for low-season return tickets include Manila ¥36,000, Bangkok ¥39,000, Kuala Lumpur ¥55,000, Singapore ¥44,000 and Jakarta ¥57,000.

Other Regions

There are also scheduled flights between Japan and South America, Africa and the Middle East.

Domestic Air Services

For travel on Honshū, it is often cheaper and quicker to travel by shinkansen than by air. This will depend on your destination. If you're heading quickly off Honshū (eg to

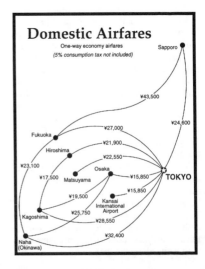

Domestic Airfares

One-way economy airfares
(5% consumption tax not included)

Sapporo

¥43,500

¥24,600

Fukuoka   ¥27,000

Hiroshima   ¥21,900

¥22,550

¥23,100

Osaka

¥17,500   Matsuyama   ¥15,850   **TOKYO**

¥15,850

¥19,500

Kansai International Airport

Kagoshima   ¥25,750

¥28,550

¥32,400

Naha (Okinawa)

Sapporo, Fukuoka/Hakata or Naha), it is well worth considering flying. Most Tokyo domestic flights use Haneda airport.

The main domestic carriers are ANA, JAS and JAL. Japan's major international carrier is JAL, which only offers limited domestic services. Tickets can be purchased at any travel agency or directly through the airlines. There is little discounting of tickets, so it makes no difference how you buy them.

TRAIN

Arriving in Tokyo by train is a simple affair. Most of the major train lines terminate at Tokyo station on the Japan Railways (JR) Yamanote line. For day trips to areas such as Kamakura, Nikkō, Hakone and Yokohama, the most convenient means of transport is usually one of the private lines. With the exception of the Tōbu Nikkō line, which starts in Asakusa, all of them start from somewhere on the Yamanote line.

Japan Railways is actually several separate private railway systems which provide one linked service, but this arrangement makes little difference to the visitor, as JR gives every impression of being a single operation, which indeed it was for more than a century. To most Japanese, JR is known as *kokutetsu* – *koku* means 'national' and *tetsu* means 'line' (literally, iron, short for 'iron road').

There are basically three types of train transport in or out of Tokyo: shinkansen, JR and private trains. See the Getting Around chapter for the subway, which services central Tokyo.

For JR schedules, fares, routes, lost baggage, and discounts on services, hotels and rent-a-cars, call the JR East-Infoline in Tokyo on ☎ 03-3423-0111. The service is available from 10 am to 6 pm Monday to Friday, but not on holidays. The Japan National Tourist Organization (JNTO) also puts out a handy *Railway Timetable* booklet in English. The 'Green Window' *(Midori-no-Madoguchi)* offices in the larger JR stations are also useful places to make train inquiries and bookings.

Osaka/Kyoto/Kansai International Airport

Train travel between Tokyo and these major destinations takes three forms: shinkansen, regular Tōkaidō trains and night trains. Shinkansen (see the Shinkansen section below) is by far the fastest and most convenient way to go. A one way, non-reserved shinkansen seat between Tokyo and Kyoto costs ¥12,970 and takes about 2¾ hours; between Osaka and Tokyo, it's about three hours and ¥13,480.

You can also take regular JR Tōkaidō express trains to Kyoto (about eight hours, ¥7830) to avoid the hefty shinkansen surcharge, but this is going to eat up most of a day and require several changes en route. The Kyoto to Osaka leg will add ¥530 and 30 minutes to this journey.

There are also JR night trains between Tokyo and Kyoto (about seven hours, ¥7980), usually departing around 11.45 pm. While some are reserved-only sleeper trains, most are standard trains with upright seats. Also, some night departures run straight through, while others stop en route, requiring bleary-eyed train changes. Since this is can be a complicated option, we suggest buying your tickets at Tokyo station, where the staff at the information counter at the main ticket office can explain everything in English.

Travel between Kansai international airport (KIX) and Tokyo is best done via Osaka (there are no direct trains between Tokyo and KIX). The fastest route uses the *Haruka* airport express train between the airport and Shin-Osaka station (45 minutes, ¥2930), and the shinkansen between Shin-Osaka and Tokyo (three hours, ¥13,480). You can go via Osaka station or Kyoto, but this will involve more travel time and, in the case of Osaka, at least one more train change.

Shinkansen

There are three main shinkansen lines that connect Tokyo with the rest of Japan: the Tōkaidō line passes through central Honshū, changing names along the way to the San-yō line before terminating at Fukuoka/Hakata in northern Kyūshū; the Tōhoku line runs

GETTING THERE & AWAY

north-east via Utsunomiya and Sendai as far as Morioka (with another sub-route which branches off at Fukushima and travels to Yamagata); and the Jōetsu line runs north to Niigata. The line you'd most likely use is the Tōkaidō line, as it passes through Kyoto and Osaka. All three lines start at Tokyo station, though the Tōhoku and Jōetsu lines also stop at Ueno station.

A new service to Nagano is the Asama shinkansen, with frequent departures daily from around 6 am to 10 pm.

Note that there are different types of shinkansen – the difference being the combination of speed and the number of stops. On the Tōkaidō shinkansen line (for Kyoto, Osaka and KIX), the three types are: *nozomi*, *hikari* and *kodama*. Of these, the nozomi is the fastest and all seats are reserved, the hikari is the next fastest and probably the most useful for the traveller, and the kodama is the slowest (though still infinitely faster than regular Tōkaidō line express trains).

While these trains are clearly labelled in English, both on the trains themselves and on departure boards, you can also tell them apart by appearance: the nozomi is the newest and most streamlined, while the humble kodama looks rather old-fashioned, with a bulbous nose and a patina born of many years of service.

Other JR Lines
As well as the Tōkaidō shinkansen line, there is a Tōkaidō line to the same areas, but stopping at all the stations that the shinkansen zips through. Trains start at Tokyo station and pass through Shimbashi and Shinagawa stations on their way out of town. There are also express services to Yokohama and Izu-hantō Peninsula, via Atami, and from there trains continue to Nagoya, Kyoto and Osaka.

If you are keeping expenses down and travelling long distance on the Tōkaidō line, there are some late-night services that do the Tokyo to Osaka run, arriving early the next morning. One of them will have sleepers available.

Travelling in the same direction as the beginning of the Tōkaidō line, the Yokosuka line offers a much cheaper service to Yokohama and Kamakura. Like the Tōkaidō line, the Yokosuka line starts at Tokyo station and passes through Shimbashi and Shinagawa stations on its way out of Tokyo.

Branching off to the west from Tokyo, running through the centre of the Yamanote line loop and on through Shinjuku and Tachikawa, is the Chūo line. It eventually takes you into Nagano prefecture, containing the Japan Alps and the historical town of Matsumoto.

東京 東京 東京 東京 東京 東京 東京 東

Trans-Siberian Railway
A little-used but fascinating way to enter or leave Japan is via the Trans-Siberian Railway. It won't be useful if you're leaving Japan in a hurry – visas and bookings take time – but despite some bad press, the train can still be a great means of connecting Europe and Asia.

There are actually three trans-Russia railway routes, one of which is to travel directly across Siberia from Moscow, followed by a flight from either Vladivostok or Khabarovsk – an expensive option. Air connections between Japan and Vladivostok and Khabarovsk are via Niigata in northern Honshū. Since these are not discounted, they tend to be expensive: ¥65,000 one way and ¥128,000 return. There are also ferry connections between Niigata and Nakhodka (near Vladivostok).

Cheaper are the Chinese Trans-Mongolian and Russian Trans-Manchurian routes, both of which start in Moscow and end in Beijing. Once you're in China, there are ferry connections with Japan via Tianjin (Tanggu) and Shanghai (see the Boat section of this chapter).

For more information outside Japan, you can contact an overseas JNTO office, China International Travel Service (CITS) or check out deals offered by travel outfits detailed in Lonely Planet's *China* or *Russia, Ukraine & Belarus* guides. In Tokyo, call the TIC (☎ 03-3201-3331) or Eurastours (☎ 03-3432-6161). ■

A retired 'iron rooster'

東京 東京 東京 東京 東京 東京 東京 東

Northbound trains start in Ueno. The Takasaki line goes out to Kumagaya and Takasaki, with connections from Takasaki to Niigata. The Keihin-Tōhoku line follows the Takasaki line as far north as Ōmiya, from where it heads to the far north of Honshū via Sendai and Aomori. Overnight trains also operate, for those intent on saving the expense of a night's accommodation.

Note that the faster express services to any of these destinations require an express surcharge, which is paid on top of the basic local train fare.

Private Lines

Private lines are much shorter than JR lines and generally service Tokyo's sprawling suburbs. Though very few go to places of interest to visitors, private lines are usually cheaper than JR lines. Particularly good bargains are the Tōkyū Tōyoko line, running between Shibuya station and Yokohama; the Odakyū line, from Shinjuku to Odawara and the Hakone region; the Tōbu Nikkō line, running from Asakusa to Nikkō; and the Seibu Shinjuku line from Shinjuku to Kawagoe.

BUS

Generally intercity buses are little or no cheaper than trains, but are sometimes a good alternative for long-distance trips to areas serviced by expressways. The buses will often run direct, so you can relax instead of watching for your stop, as happens on an ordinary train service.

A number of express buses run between Tokyo, Kyoto and Osaka. Overnight buses leave at 10 pm and 11 pm from Tokyo station, and arrive at Kyoto and Osaka between 6 and 7 am the following morning. They cost from ¥8000 to ¥8500. If you plan on coming back the same way, a return ticket saves money, eg Kyoto to Tokyo is ¥8180 one way and ¥14,800 return. A return ticket must be used within six days of purchase. The buses are a JR service and can be booked at a Green Window office in the larger JR stations. The main JR highway bus office (☎ 03-3215-0498) is on the south end of the Yaesu side of Tokyo station. Buses depart from in front of the office. Direct buses also run from Tokyo station to Nagoya, Nara and Kōbe.

From Shinjuku station, buses run to the Fuji and Hakone regions, including, for Mt Fuji climbers, direct services to the fifth stations. See the Mt Fuji section in the Excursions chapter for more details.

BOAT

Japan has ferry services to South Korea, China and Taiwan, but the South Korea and China services run from the Kansai region, not from Tokyo, while Taiwan services operate from faraway Okinawa.

South Korea

This is the closest country to Japan, and a popular visa-renewal point. The main ferry departure/arrival points are Shimonoseki, at Honshū's far western end, and Fukuoka/Hakata, on the southern island of Kyūshū. Both services operate from Pusan in South Korea.

Ferries depart daily from Shimonoseki on the Kampur Ferry service's (☎ 0832-24-3000) vessels *Kampu* or *Pukwan*, both of which leave at 6 pm daily and arrive in Pusan at 8.30 the following morning. One-way fares start at ¥6800 for students, rise to ¥8500 for space on the floor of a large, shared room and peak at ¥12,000 for a cabin. There's a 10% discount for return tickets.

Known as the 'JK Line Hydrofoil', or 'Beetle' (☎ 03-3240-5692 in Tokyo; 092-281-2315 in Fukuoka/Hakata), the hydrofoil costs around ¥13,000 one way and ¥24,000 return from Fukuoka/Hakata to Pusan. It makes the trip in just three hours and runs daily (twice a day on Monday and Wednesday). The Camellia Line (☎ 092-262-2323) ferry departs in the early evening three times a week, and takes 15 hours. Prices start from ¥9000 one way and ¥17,000 return.

China

The Japan-China International Ferry service connects Shanghai and Osaka/Kōbe. The ship departs once a week, one week from Osaka and the next from Kōbe. A 2nd class ticket costs around ¥20,000.

GETTING THERE & AWAY

Ships from Kōbe to Tanggu (near Tianjin) leave from Kōbe every Thursday at noon and arrive in Tanggu the next day. Economy/1st class tickets cost ¥22,500/35,000. Tickets can be bought in Tianjin from the shipping office (☎ 31-2243) at 89 Munan Dao, Heping District. In Kōbe, the office (☎ 078-321-5791) is in the port.

Taiwan

A weekly ferry operates between Taiwan and Okinawa, sometimes via Ishigaki and Miyako in Okinawa prefecture. The Taiwan port alternates between Keelung and Kaohsiung. Departure from Okinawa is on Thursday or Friday; departure from Taiwan is usually on Monday. The trip takes from 16 to 19 hours. Fares from Okinawa range from ¥15,600 (economy) to ¥24,300 (1st class). Fares from Taiwan are slightly cheaper.

You can buy tickets from travel agents in your port of departure or directly from the ferry company, Arimura Sangyo, which has an office in Naha (☎ 0988-64-0087) and Osaka (☎ 02-424-8151). In Taiwan, contact Yeong An Marine Company in Taipei (☎ 02-771-5911), Kaohsiung (☎ 07-551-0281) or Keelung (☎ 02-424-8151).

Domestic Ferries

From Tokyo, there are also long-distance ferries to other islands of Japan: Kushiro on Hokkaidō (¥14,700); Kōchi (¥10,600) and Tokushima (¥8610) on Shikoku; Kokura in northern Kyūshū (¥12,600); and Naha on Okinawa (¥20,050). For information on these services, ring the Ferry Service Center (☎ 03-3501-0889) in Tokyo.

TRAVEL AGENTS

Four well established agents where English is spoken are: No 1 Travel in Shinjuku (☎ 03-3200-8871), Shibuya (☎ 03-3770-1381), Ikebukuro (☎ 03-3986-4291) and Yokohama (☎ 045-322-1701); STA Travel, which is represented in Yotsuya (☎ 03-5269-0751), Shibuya (☎ 03-5485-8380) and Ikebukuro (☎ 03-5391-2922); Across Traveller's Bureau in Shinjuku (☎ 03-3340-6741) and Ikebukuro (☎ 03-5391-2871); and Just Travel in Takadanobaba (☎ 03-3362-3441).

Perhaps the cheapest of the four is No 1 Travel, whose Shinjuku branch (Map 6) is conveniently located on Yasukuni-dōri, about five minutes from Shinjuku station.

Some theatre ticket outlets are also able to provide discounted tickets for domestic air flights and shinkansen journeys. A good place to try is Ikari (☎ 03-3407-3554), opposite Shibuya post office (Map 7) on the 3rd floor of the Gloria Shibuya building.

WARNING

This chapter is particularly vulnerable to change – prices for international travel are volatile, routes are introduced and cancelled, schedules change, special deals come and go, and rules and visa requirements are amended. Airlines and governments seem to take a perverse pleasure in making price structures and regulations as complicated as possible. You should check directly with the airline or travel agent to make sure you understand how a fare (and ticket you may buy) works. In addition, the travel industry is highly competitive, and there are many lurks and perks. The upshot is that you should get opinions, quotes and advice from as many airlines and travel agents as possible before you part with your hard-earned cash. The details provided in this chapter should be treated as pointers, and are not a substitute for careful up-to-date research.

Getting Around

Tokyo has an excellent public transport system. There are very few worthwhile spots around town that aren't conveniently close to a subway or Japan Railways (JR) station. When the rail network lets you down, there are generally bus services, though these are harder to use if you can't read *kanji*.

Most residents of and visitors to Tokyo use the railway system far more than any other means of transport. It is reasonably priced, frequent (generally at most five minutes between trains on major lines in central Tokyo) and stations feature conveniences like pay lockers for baggage storage. In fact, the only real drawback is that the system shuts down at midnight or 1 am and doesn't start up again until 5 or 6 am.

Subway trains do have a habit of stopping halfway along their route when closing time arrives. People who get stranded face an expensive taxi ride home or of waiting for the first morning train. Check time schedules posted on platforms for the last train on the line if you plan to be out late.

Avoiding Tokyo's rush hour is a good idea, but may be impossible if you're on a tight schedule. Commuter congestion tends to ease between 10 am and 4 pm, when travelling around Tokyo can actually be quite pleasant. Before 9.30 am and from about 4.30 pm onward, there'll be cheek-to-jowl crowds on all major train and bus lines.

TO/FROM NARITA AIRPORT

Narita airport (Map 1) is used by almost all the international airlines, but only by a small number of domestic operators. The airport is 66km from central Tokyo, and getting into town is going to take from 50 minutes to two hours, depending on your mode of transport.

Bear in mind that there are now two terminals at Narita. Get off at the terminal used by your airline – all airport transport has prominently displayed lists of airlines and the terminal they use. For flight information at Narita airport, ring ☎ 0476-34-5000. For general information at Narita airport, phone ☎ 0476-32-2802 or ☎ 0476-32-2105. The Tourist Information Center (TIC) counter at Narita can be reached on ☎ 0476-34-6251.

Train

Trains conveniently depart from stations directly under the airport terminals. There are three rail services between both terminals

---

東京 東京 東京 東京 東京 東京 東京 東京 東

Useful Kanji
Transport

limited express train	特急列車
express train	急行列車
local train	普通列車
east exit	東口
west exit	西口
south exit	南口
north exit	北口
ticket office	きっぷ売り場
fare adjustment machine	乗り越し精算機
reserved seats	指定席
this train	この電車
next train	つぎの電車
train after next	次々発
shinkansen	新幹線
nozomi	のぞみ
hikari	ひかり
kodama	こだま

Other Terms

smoking section	喫煙所
nonsmoking	禁煙所
vacant taxi	空車
occupied taxi	満車

禁 煙 車
NON-SMOKING CAR

南出口
SOUTH EXIT

指定席
RESERVED

お手洗
Toilets

ALL PHOTOGRAPHS BY CHRIS ROWTHORN

東京 東京 東京 東京 東京 東京 東京 東京 東

at Narita airport and Tokyo: the private Keisei line, the JR Narita Express (N'EX) and the regular JR 'Airport Narita' rapid train service. The Keisei service runs into Nippori and Ueno; from either you can change to the Yamanote line, which runs to Ikebukuro, Shinjuku, Tokyo station and other destinations. N'EX and the Airport Narita service run into Tokyo station (Map 2) (from where you can change to almost anywhere). N'EX also runs less frequently into Shinjuku, Ikebukuro and Yokohama.

On the private Keisei line, two trains run between Narita airport and Ueno station: the Skyliner, which runs nonstop (one hour, ¥1880); and the limited express *(tokkyū)* service (one hour 11 minutes, ¥980). Both the Keisei stations in Terminals 1 and 2 are clearly signposted in English. The final destination, Ueno, is on the Yamanote line and the Hibiya and Ginza subway lines. Those travelling to Ikebukuro or Shinjuku are advised to get off one stop before Ueno at Nippori station, also on the Yamanote line.

Going to the airport from Ueno, the Keisei station is right next to the JR Ueno station. You can buy advance tickets for the Skyliner service at the ticket counter, while express and limited express tickets are available from the ticket dispensing machines. JR Nippori station has a clearly signposted walkway to the Keisei Nippori station.

The JR N'EX is fast, smooth and comfortable, but does not run as frequently as the private Keisei line. N'EX service is as follows: to/from Tokyo station (53 minutes, ¥2890); Shinjuku station (1¼ hours, ¥3050); Ikebukuro station (1½ hours, ¥3050); and Yokohama station (1½ hours, ¥4100). N'EX runs approximately every half hour between 7 am and 10 pm to Tokyo, less frequently to other destinations. All seats are reserved but can usually be bought just before departure if the train is not full (if it's full, you can buy a standing ticket for the same price). The Airport Narita *(kaisoku)* service takes 1½ hours and costs ¥1260 to Tokyo central. All seats on these trains are unreserved, and are a good option if you cannot get a seat on the N'EX.

Limousine Bus
Ticket offices, marked with the sign 'Limousine', can be found in both wings of the arrival building. Don't be mislead by the name – they're ordinary buses. They take 1½ to two hours (depending on traffic) to travel between Narita airport and a number of major hotels around Tokyo. Check departure times before buying your ticket, as services aren't frequent. The fare to hotels in eastern Tokyo is ¥2700, while to Ikebukuro, Akasaka, Ginza, Shinagawa or Shinjuku, it is ¥3000. You can also go straight to Tokyo station in one hour 20 minutes, or to Shinjuku station (one hour 25 minutes), for ¥3000. Those transferring to domestic flights departing from Haneda airport can take a limousine bus direct for ¥3000. The trip takes about 1¼ hours in light traffic, but leave lots of extra time, as traffic conditions in Tokyo are seldom ideal.

For general airport limousine information, ring ☎ 03-3665-7220.

The Tokyo City Air Terminal (TCAT) in Nihombashi (Map 1) and the Yokohama City Air Terminal (YCAT) at Yokohama station both offer frequent limousine-bus connections to/from Narita airport, as well as check-in services for departing passengers. TCAT buses leave about every 15 minutes and take about one hour, depending on traffic. The fare is ¥2700. The trip from YCAT takes around 1½ hours and costs ¥3500.

If your airline allows you to check your baggage in at TCAT or YCAT, you can take a taxi from your hotel, check it in at either terminal and relax. Allow some extra time if you plan to do this.

There is a subway directly under TCAT – it's the Suitengū-mae subway station on the Hanzōmon line. There is also a frequent shuttle bus service between TCAT and Tokyo station (look for the signs on the station's Yaesu side) for ¥200. There are also plenty of taxis waiting at TCAT. For further information on TCAT and its services, phone ☎ 03-3665-7111. For YCAT information, ring ☎ 045-459-4800.

By the way, a taxi to Narita airport from Tokyo will cost about ¥22,000.

TO/FROM HANEDA AIRPORT

Most domestic flights and China Airlines (Taiwan) flights use the convenient Haneda airport (Map 1) (officially known as Tokyo international airport).

Getting from Haneda to Tokyo is simple: take the monorail to Hamamatsuchō station on the JR Yamanote line. The trip takes 20 minutes; trains leave every 10 minutes and cost ¥270. Taxis to places around central Tokyo will cost around ¥7000.

There's also a regular bus service between Haneda and TCAT (around 30 minutes, ¥900). Buses also run between Haneda and Ikebukuro (¥1100) and Shinjuku (¥1100).

Those with connections at Narita can take a direct bus service between Haneda and Narita (up to two hours, ¥2900). Or you can take the monorail to Tokyo and connect with a Narita-bound train running from a station on the Yamanote line.

For information at Haneda, ring ☎ 03-5757-8111. For China Airlines flights, phone ☎ 03-3747-4942.

TRAIN

The Tokyo train system can be a bit daunting at first, but you soon get the hang of it. Much initial confusion arises from the fact that Tokyo is serviced by a combination of JR, private inner-city subway lines and private suburban lines. This sometimes means switching between both trains and train systems. It's not as bad as it sounds, however, as the lines are well integrated and can often be traversed with just one purchase of a special combination ticket.

Once you get off the JR Yamanote line and the subway lines, watch for express services. Generally, the longer the route, the more likely you are to find faster train services. The fastest regular (non-shinkansen) trains are *tokkyū*, or limited express services, followed by *kyūkō*, or ordinary express, which stops at only a limited number of stations. A variation on kyūkō trains is the *kaisoku*, or rapid service. The slowest trains, which stop at all stations, are called *futsū*.

Train designations are usually written in both Japanese and English on the side of the train and on the platform departure board. When no English translation is provided, you're going to have to ask someone or decipher the kanji yourself.

Since the faster trains do not stop at all stations, you must determine if your destination is serviced by express trains before boarding. There is usually a board on the platform indicating exactly which trains stop where. Trains are colour-coded and you can usually tell what's what even if you don't read Japanese (though smaller destinations are frequently not written in English, so it's a good idea to have your destination written down in Japanese before setting out).

Railway Stations

Modern Japanese spend a good part of their lives in railway stations, and this fact is reflected in the wide range of services at most stations. Most importantly, there is the ticket office. In the case of JR stations, there will be signs (sometimes but not always in both English and Japanese), indicating the *Midori-no-Madoguchi* (Green Window, meaning ticket window or counter). This is usually posted with a green sign. Here, you can buy your tickets and make reservations. In smaller stations, this is where you ask for information as well. Stations also have one or more banks of automatic ticket machines (see the following Buying a Ticket entry).

Most stations also have coin lockers which hold medium-size bags (backpacks won't usually fit). These often come in several sizes, and cost from ¥150 to ¥600. Storage is

CHRIS ROWTHORN

The JR Green Window

GETTING AROUND

good for 24 hours, after which your bags will be removed and taken to the station office.

All railway stations have toilets, almost all of which are free of charge (Shinjuku has a few which charge ¥100). Bring toilet paper, as it is not usually provided (this is why advertising in the form of tissue packets handed out on street corners is big business in Japan).

At many stations, you can also find several options for food. The smallest of these are kiosks, which sell snacks, drinks, magazines, newspapers (many have copies of Japan's four English dailies), film etc. Next up are stores selling *ekiben* (railway station boxed lunches; see the Ekiben – Lunch in Locomotion boxed text in the Places to Eat chapter). Larger stations also have *tachi-kui* restaurants (stand-and-eat restaurants). Most of these places require that you purchase a food ticket from a vending machine, which you hand to an attendant upon entry (most machines have pictures on the buttons to help you order). Large stations may also have a choice of several sit-down places, most of which will have plastic food models displayed out front.

Navigating your way around railway stations in Japan can be confusing, particularly at some of the larger, more complex stations like Tokyo's Shinjuku station. The key is to know where you're going before you get to the station. Most stations have adequate English signposting, and exits are clearly posted with numbers. If possible, find out which exit to use when you get directions to a destination. Many stations simply have four main exits: north, south, east and west. Since one station may have several different *kaisatsu-guchi* (automated turnstiles), each near a different exit, you should take your bearings and decide where to exit while still on the platforms. As a last resort, you can always just exit the station and get your bearings on the ground.

Buying a Ticket For all local journeys, tickets are sold by vending machines called *kippu jidō hanbaiki*. Above the vending machines is a rail map with fares indicated next to the station names. Unfortunately for visitors, the names are often in kanji only. The best way around this problem is to put your money in the machine and push the lowest fare button (usually ¥130). This will get you on the railway; when you get to your destination, you can correct the fare at an attended ticket gate, or with an automatic fare adjustment machine (see the following Fare Adjustment entry). On many JR ticket machines, only the stops closest to the station are written on the price chart, not fare amounts. Thus, you may not find a figure saying ¥130. In this case, push the button all the way to the left (with kanji written on it) and this will be the cheapest fare.

If you want to use a combination of JR and private lines, there are automatic ticket vending machines that enable you to this; the problem is that there is generally insufficient English labelling to make sense of them. Don't stress yourself trying to figure it out. Buy the cheapest ticket and let the station attendants at the other end of your trip figure out how much you owe – as long as you are polite, no-one will mind. If you find yourself without change, there are vending machines for all lines that accept ¥1000 notes and some that accept ¥10,000 (there are pictures of the bills accepted on the machines).

There are two buttons on the machine which may come in handy if you completely bungle the operation. First is the *tori-keshi* (cancel) button, which is usually marked in English. The second is the *yobidashi* (call)

CHRIS ROWTHORN

Most Tokyo stations are well signposted.

GETTING AROUND

button, which will alert a staff member that you need assistance (they usually pop out from a hidden door between the machines – it can be surprising).

Fare Adjustment Many travellers and even long-term residents never bother to figure out the appropriate fare when buying tickets (particularly for short inner-city hops). This is quite a time-saver – while everyone is standing around straining to see the fare chart, you can slide in, grab the cheapest ticket and be on your way. If you choose to do this, you have two choices upon arrival at your destination: the automated fare adjustment machine or an attended ticket gate.

At an attended gate, simply hand over your ticket and the attendant will inform you of the additional fare. An automated fare adjustment machine is almost as simple and saves time if the gate is congested. There's a slot near the top of the machine into which

you insert your ticket. The screen will tell you how much to pay, then spit out your change (if any) and a new ticket. You can use this ticket in the ordinary automated turnstiles. Automated fare adjustment machines usually have some English instructions.

Japan Railways (JR)
Yamanote Line The most useful line in Tokyo is the JR Yamanote line, which does a loop around the city, taking in most of the important areas. The trains are silver with a green stripe. You can do the whole circuit in an hour for the ¥130 minimum fare – a great introduction to the city.

When riding the Yamanote, it can be hard to determine where to get off. The signs indicating the name of the station are sometimes hard to see from inside the train (the stop announcements, if they're audible at all, are usually in a language neither English nor Japanese). Before boarding, look at the board on the platform which shows the stops of the Yamanote and the time to each stop. Count the number of stops: this way you won't have to frantically crane your neck to see where you are each time the train stops.

CHRIS ROWTHORN

A train traveller's best friend.

CHRIS ROWTHORN

This is how you stay in the loop.

GETTING AROUND

Chūō Line The JR Chūō line cuts through the centre of the Yamanote line between Shinjuku and Tokyo stations. Trains on this line are orange. This line is continuous with the Sōbu line until Ochanomizu station. At Ochanomizu the lines split – the Chūō heading down to Tokyo station and the Sōbu heading out to the eastern suburbs. Trains on the Sōbu line are yellow, so telling them apart is easy. The Chūō line is about the fastest route between Shinjuku and Tokyo stations (rivalled by the Marunouchi subway line).

Other Lines The Yokosuka line runs down to Kamakura from Tokyo, Shimbashi and Shinagawa stations. The Tōkaidō line travels in the same direction from Tokyo station, providing access to Izu-hantō Peninsula.

Some other main lines are the north-bound lines (Takasaki, Keihin-Tōhoku, Saikyō) to Saitama Prefecture and beyond, the Jōban and Narita lines to the north-eastern satellite towns in Saitama and Chiba prefectures, and the Sōbu and Keiyō lines heading east towards Chiba city (and Tokyo Disneyland) and the convention city at Makuhari Messe.

Orange Cards If you get tired of fumbling for change, the JR system offers the option of 'orange cards'. These are available in denominations of ¥1000, ¥3000, ¥5000 and ¥10,000. With a ¥5000 card you get an extra credit of ¥300; a ¥10,000 card gives you a bonus of ¥700. Fares are automatically deducted from the cards when you use them in the orange-card vending machines. For longer-term visitors, passes called *teiki-ken* are available between two stops over a fixed period of time, but you really have to use the ticket at least once a day for it to pay off.

Tokyo Rinkai Shin-Kōtsū Line (Yurikamome)

Also known as the Tokyo Waterfront New Transit Line, this new line services the Tokyo Bay area's Odaiba/Daiba/Ariake developments. It's a monorail that leaves from Shimbashi, just south of Ginza, crosses the Rainbow Bridge and terminates in Ariake, on an artificial island in Tokyo Bay. The Shimbashi station is above ground on the east side of JR Shimbashi station (look for the stairs and the English signs saying 'Yurikamome'). Ticket buying procedures are basically the same as on other train lines, and ticket machines provide ample English explanation. The fare from Shimbashi to Ariake is ¥230. En route entertainment is provided by the unconventional English of the stop announcements.

Private Lines

Most of the private lines service suburban areas outside Tokyo, but some of them also connect with popular sightseeing areas. The private lines almost always represent better value for money than the JR lines. The ones you are most likely to use are Shibuya's Tōkyū Tōyoko line, which runs to Yokohama; Shinjuku's Odakyū line, which runs out to Hakone; and Asakusa's Tōbu Nikkō line, which goes out to Nikkō.

SUBWAY

There are 12 subway lines, of which eight are TRTA lines and four are TOEI lines. This is not particularly important to remember, as the services are essentially the same and have good connections from one to the other, although they do operate under separate ticketing systems. The colour-coding and regular

CHRIS ROWTHORN

Hint: the middle *kanji* means down or below.

GETTING AROUND

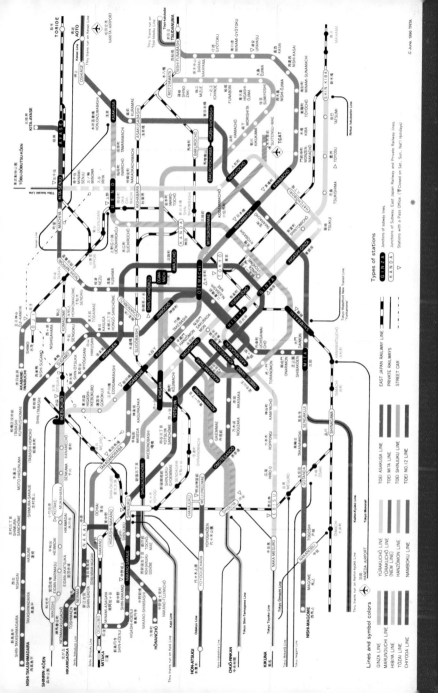

Tokyo's Homeless

Visitors to Tokyo are often surprised by the numbers of homeless they see living in box dwellings in train stations, under bridges and in city parks – a population left behind by the economic 'miracle'. Groups who work with the homeless in Tokyo estimate their numbers in the tens of thousands.

Nowhere is their presence more visible than in the underground passages on the west side of JR Shinjuku station. Here, for the last decade, homeless individuals have been living in a veritable city of cardboard dwellings. Some are remarkable in their construction, with separate rooms, small libraries and sizeable arrays of furniture.

The authorities are hardly pleased about a homeless encampment in a passageway that leads straight to their showcase city hall. For years there have been sporadic efforts to eject the homeless – these have been met with fierce resistance from the homeless and various supporters. For now, it looks like a fragile detente has been achieved. However, authorities have been placing low pillars in certain walkways to prevent further habitation. These look like monotonous art installations until one realises their real purpose.

Japanese homeless do not support themselves by panhandling, and you're not going to be accosted. Indeed, many actually work, doing various forms of menial day labour. Japanese TV even documents the lives of suit-wearing businessmen who return each night from their offices to cardboard box homes in the station. The truth is, many are simply too ashamed by economic failure to return home to their families.

There's a bright spot in this story: if you pass through the cardboard city, you might think that these otherwise drab boxes were painted by a homeless Heronymous Bosch. Actually, two young Tokyo art students, Junichiro Take and Takeo Yoshizaki, have taken it upon themselves to brighten up the lives of the Shinjuku homeless. Without a doubt, the result is one of Tokyo's most compelling free public art galleries.

Performance art meets grim reality in Shinjuku's tunnels. A virtual army of homeless came to stay in the late 80s; in some parts of the city, the yakuza provides support for the homeless where the official authorities don't. All photographs by Chris Rowthorn.

English signposting make the system easy to use – you soon learn that the Ginza line is orange and that the Marunouchi line is red. Perhaps the most confusing part is figuring out where to surface when you have reached your destination – there is almost always a large number of subway exits. Fortunately, the exits are numbered and maps are posted, usually close to the ticket turnstiles.

Generally, the subway system is indispensable for getting to areas that lie inside the loop traced by the Yamanote line. The central Tokyo area is served by a large number of lines that intersect at Nihombashi, Ōtemachi and Ginza, making it possible to get to this part of town from almost anywhere. Most fares within the Yamanote loop are either ¥160 or ¥190.

All TRTA information counters (found near the automatic turnstiles) have a very useful English map and brochure called *Subways in Tokyo* explaining the system in detail.

Buying a Subway Ticket This is essentially the same as buying a regular train ticket. You need different tickets for the two subway systems, but many of the automated ticket machines sell 'combination tickets' which allow you to transfer from one system to another without buying a new ticket. The bad news is that the button is usually marked only in Japanese (it can be found in the top row of buttons on the newer machines). The best advice is to buy an SF Metro Card, which can be used on all subway lines.

SF Metro Card This card is almost indispensable. SF Metro Cards are prepaid magnetic cards good for all the subway lines in Tokyo. You purchase them from ordinary automatic ticket machines marked with the 'SF Metro Card' symbol, in denominations of ¥1000, ¥2000 and ¥3000. Insert the amount, push the 'Metro Card' button, then the cash amount button and the card will appear.

Insert the card into the automatic turnstiles as you would a normal ticket – don't forget to grab it as you exit the turnstile! The turnstiles will automatically deduct ¥160 from the card as you enter the subway system, and

then any amount above that figure, if necessary, when you leave. If you have less than ¥160 left on the card, you will not be able to enter the system. Take the card to a ticket machine, insert it and whatever change is necessary to bring the figure to ¥160. The machine will spit out a new ticket and the now worthless Metro Card.

Tokyo Combination Ticket A Tokyo Combination Ticket is a day pass that can be used on all JR, subway and bus lines within the Tokyo metropolitan area. It costs ¥1580. It is available at Pass offices, which can be found in major subway stations. Stations with Pass offices are marked with a triangle on local subway maps.

Other Ticket Deals The TRTA subway system (the more extensive of the two) has some money-saving ticket offers. An 11 ride ticket can be bought at vending machines and offers 11 rides for the price of 10. The One Day Open ticket can also be bought at vending machines for ¥710, and offers unlimited use of the TRTA system for the day of purchase.

BUS
Many Tokyo residents and visitors spend a considerable amount of time in the city without ever using the bus network. Train services are great, buses are much more difficult to use and they are at the mercy of Tokyo's sluggish traffic. Services also tend to finish fairly early in the evening, making buses a pretty poor alternative all round.

At some bus stops there are signs indicating in English the destinations of the buses that stop there. But most of the time, if you do not read Japanese, you'll have to ask someone at the stop, or use a bus map.

Bus fares are a flat ¥200 for adults and ¥100 for children (primary school age and younger) and are paid into the fare box next to the driver as you enter the bus. Change for ¥1000 notes and coins will be given. A tape recording announces the name of each stop as it is reached, so listen carefully and press the button next to your seat when yours is

GETTING AROUND

東京 東京 東京 東京 東京 東京 東京 東京 東

Tram
Tokyo has a solitary tram service still in operation. It doesn't really go anywhere special, but it runs from the heart of Shitamachi, passing through a couple of areas that haven't (yet) been claimed by redevelopment. You can get on the Toden Arakawa line from opposite Ōtsuka station on the Yamanote line. The line passes the Sunshine City building before passing through Zōshigaya. The latter is an interesting area dotted with small temples and shrines. It is perhaps best known for Zōshigaya Cemetery, the resting place of Lafcadio Hearn, the remarkable cosmopolitan chronicler of everyday Meiji Japan, and of his contemporary, the immensely popular Edo-born writer Natsume Sōseki. From here the tram travels to its terminus in Waseda, not far from Waseda University (where Hearn once taught). ∎

東京 東京 東京 東京 東京 東京 東京 東京 東

announced. If you are planning to make use of the bus system, pick up a copy of the city government's excellent *Toei Bus Route Guide* at the Tokyo Metropolitan Government Offices (Map 6) in west Shinjuku (ask at the information counter). The TIC also has a good English bus route map.

CAR & MOTORCYCLE
Driving yourself around Tokyo is by no means impossible, but is likely to bring unnecessary frustrations. Parking space is limited and expensive, the traffic moves very slowly, traffic lights are posted on virtually every street corner (every 50m or so) and unless you are very familiar with the city, getting lost will be a common occurrence. Overall, you are much better off using public transport. If you do intend to drive in Japan, note that driving is on the left side. If you're going long distance, and intend to use Japan's expressways, the tolls are very expensive, averaging ¥27 a kilometre.

Still interested? Get a copy of *Rules of the Road*, available from the Japan Automobile Federation (JAF; ☎ 03-3436-2454), for ¥1860. The JAF office is close to Kamiyachō subway station on the Hibiya line.

Car Rental
For those who enjoy a challenge, there are car rental agencies in Tokyo that will hire you one of their vehicles upon presentation of an international licence. Nippon Rent-a-Car (☎ 03-3485-7196) is the largest agency in Tokyo, with some 150 branches, but it makes no provisions for English-speaking customers. Three car rental agencies which usually have English speakers on hand are Dollar Rent-a-Car (☎ 03-3567-2818), Hertz (☎ 0120-489-882) and Toyota Rent-a-Lease (☎ 03-3264-0100). Typical rates for small cars are ¥8000 or ¥9000 for the first day, and ¥5500 to ¥7000 a day thereafter. On top of this there is a ¥1000 per day insurance fee. Mileage is usually unlimited.

Motorcycle
Many foreigners living in Tokyo end up getting themselves a motorbike. It can be a good way to get around town, especially after the trains have stopped running. The best place to take a look at what's available and get some information in English is the area of motorbike shops on Korinchō Rd, near Ueno station. Some of the shops there have foreign staff. If you have a motorbike licence, you could also try hiri ng a motorbike. SCS (☎ 03-3827-5432) hires out scooters for around ¥6000 per day, and 250cc bikes from around ¥12,000 and up.

If you buy a motorbike, you will need a motorbike licence (for up to 400cc, your

TONY WHEELER

Still life with motorbikes, Ueno

foreign licence is transferable) and your bike will need to be registered. Bikes up to 125cc are registered at your ward office; bikes over 125cc are registered with the Bureau of Traffic.

TAXI

Taxis are so expensive that you should only use them when there is no alternative. Rates start at ¥630, which buys you 2km (after 11 pm it's 1.5km), then the meter rises by ¥80 every 299m (every 273m after 11 pm). You also click up about ¥80 every two minutes while you relax in a typical Tokyo traffic jam. Taxi vacancy is indicated by a red light; a green light means there's a night-time surcharge and a yellow light means that the cab is on call.

If you have to get a taxi late on a Friday or Saturday night, be prepared for delays and higher prices. The same applies any day of the week for the first hour or so after the last trains run. At these times, *gaijin* (foreigners) may find themselves shunned like lepers because their ride is likely to be a short one, whereas the drunken worker holding up two fingers (to indicate his willingness to pay twice the meter fare) is probably bound for a distant suburb. There is no point getting annoyed. With only around 50,000 taxis operating in Tokyo, complaints of a taxi shortage are rife – even the locals have problems flagging one down once the trains have shut down for the night.

Tokyo taxi drivers can rarely speak any English, so it's a good idea to have your destination written down in Japanese. Even if your destination has an English name, it is unlikely the driver will understand your pronunciation of it. And, lastly, watch out for the automatic doors on taxis. Don't slam the door shut when you get in or leave – the door will shut itself.

BICYCLE

One look at Tokyo will convince even the most ardent cyclist that this is not the place for pedal-powered transport – the roads are crowded, exhaust fumes can get pretty thick, the shoulders of roads are full of parked cars and there are no bike paths. That said, a surprising number of Tokyo residents brave the perils and do get around by bicycle. Don't try picking up a used bike from the piles of discarded bikes found around railway stations – the police are in the habit of pulling over riders and checking the bike's serial numbers. If the one you're riding turns out to have been stolen, you'll have a bit of explaining to do.

WALKING

The only way to explore areas like Shinjuku, Shibuya and Ueno is on foot. Walking between areas, however, is another story. It is possible, for example, to walk from Shibuya to Roppongi in around an hour, but it is not an appealing stroll. Once you leave the commercial areas clustered around railway stations, you can quickly find yourself in a wasteland of grey buildings and noisy overhead expressways.

For keen walkers, there are extensive walks in the Imperial Palace area, around Ueno and in Asakusa. For some ideas, pick up a copy of the TIC's *Walking Tour Courses in Tokyo* and *One Day Hiking Courses from Central Tokyo* pamphlets. Alternatively take off to Nikkō, Kamakura or Hakone, where there are splendid countryside walks with interesting cultural attractions. Also see the walking tours in the Things to See & Do chapter.

BOAT

Vingt-et-un (☎ 03-3436-2121) offers daytime cruises out of Tokyo Bay as either a straight cruise (¥2040) or including a meal (from ¥5100). Evening cruises cost ¥2550 to board and from ¥10,200 with a meal. See the Asakusa section of the Things to See & Do chapter for information on cruises down the Sumida-gawa River.

ORGANISED TOURS

There are tours available for both the Tokyo metropolitan area and for areas further afield. Tours are also given by factories and

GETTING AROUND

commercial institutions (see the Japan Inc Tours boxed text in the Things to See & Do chapter).

For tours of Tokyo, one of the most reliable operators is Hato Bus Tours (☎ 03-3435-6081). Its Panoramic Tour takes in most of Tokyo's major sights and costs ¥9450, including lunch. Probably the widest range of Tokyo tours is available from the Japan Travel Bureau's (JTB) Sunrise Tours office (☎ 03-5260-9500). Sunrise offers general sightseeing tours, such as morning tours (¥4500) and afternoon tours (¥4950). Both Hato and Sunrise offer English-speaking guides and/or taped explanations and headsets.

Night tours of the city are also offered by Sunrise Tours and by Gray Line (☎ 03-3433-5745). Sunrise offers a Kabuki Night tour that includes a sukiyaki dinner, kabuki at Ginza's Kabuki-za Theatre and a geisha show for ¥10,800.

All of these tours pick up their guests at various major hotels around town. Both Sunrise and Gray Line also offer tours to sightseeing spots around Tokyo.

GETTING AROUND

Things to See & Do

It is perhaps best not to think of Tokyo as one city at all, but a ring of cities connected by the JR Yamanote loop line. Those areas not on the Yamanote line, like Roppongi, Tsukiji and Asakusa, are nonetheless within easy reach, as the whole area is crisscrossed by Tokyo's excellent subway system.

This chapter and the remaining Tokyo chapters roughly follow a counterclockwise circuit of the Yamanote line, beginning with the areas around Tokyo station and ending in Akasaka. You'll soon see that each of these subcities has a distinctive character. Here is an introduction to the main hubs on the Yamanote loop.

Imperial Palace, Ginza, Marunouchi & Nihombashi

These areas around Tokyo station are usually considered the true centre of Tokyo, as they contain the main railway station, the imperial residence, the financial district and some of the main shopping areas. With relatively wide streets, lots of open space and mostly dignified architecture, this is one of the more pleasant parts of the city.

Kanda

A few stops north-east of Tokyo station, Kanda is the academic centre of Tokyo, with several major universities and a whole neighbourhood devoted to bookshops. Nearby Akihabara holds perhaps the world's thickest concentration of electronics shops.

Ueno & Asakusa

A few stops to the north of Kanda is Ueno, the cultural centre of Tokyo, with an abundance of museums and performance halls. Ueno and its neighbour Asakusa, two stops away on the Ginza subway line, retain some Shitamachi flavour, and those in search of traditional Japan will find a bit of it here.

Ikebukuro

The next main stop on the Yamanote line after Ueno is Ikebukuro, in limbo between high-tech Tokyo and the tumbledown suburbs of old Edo. One of Tokyo's main shopping and nightlife areas, Ikebukuro is awash with gaudy advertising, strolling shoppers and an army of touts beckoning passers-by into a variety of nightspots.

Shinjuku

Four stops south of Ikebukuro, Shinjuku is the heart of modern Tokyo, with the city government offices on one side of the station and a bustling nightlife district on the other. The east side features the futuristic *Blade Runner* atmosphere of flashing neon associated with Tokyo. If you have the energy, it's great; if you don't, well, keep moving.

Shibuya

A few stops further is Shibuya, the main stomping ground of Tokyo's youth, where it sometimes seems as if everyone over 30 has been banished. What draws youth here are trendy shops, game halls, karaoke boxes and cheap international food.

東京東京東京東京東京東京東京東京東

Words & Sights

Finding sights is easier if you familiarise yourself with these common nouns:

kōen	park	公園
teien/en	garden	庭園／園
ji/dera	temple	寺／寺
jinja/jingū	shrine	神社／神宮
hakubutsukan	museum	博物館
bijutsukan	art museum	美術館
biru/kan/	building/hall	ビル／館／
kaikan		会館
sen	railway line	線
eki	railway station	駅
depāto	department store	デパート
dōri	avenue	通り
bashi	bridge	橋
mon	gate	門

東京東京東京東京東京東京東京東京東

THINGS TO SEE & DO

Other Hubs

In Akasaka, Roppongi, Ebisu, Harajuku, Aoyama and Nishi-Azabu, things are a little less crowded and intense, and some of the better restaurants and nightspots are to be found in these areas.

With all these areas to choose from, you're bound to find at least one which suits you. The best part is, if you get tired of one place, you can hop on the train and find an entirely new 'city' waiting just a stop or two away.

HIGHLIGHTS

Tokyo offers a glimpse into both the future – as the modern metropolis *par excellence* – and Japan's fascinating past. A well-rounded visit should discover both.

For high tech, visit some of the showrooms in Ginza, or some of the towering multifunction buildings that have sprung up in west Shinjuku. Japanese consumer culture is at its best (or worst) in the fashionable areas of Ginza, Shibuya, Harajuku, Aoyama and Akasaka, not to mention Akihabara, the garish discount 'Electric Town'.

Tokyo often looks its best by night, and an evening stroll through the east side of Shinjuku is not to be missed. Ginza and Shibuya are also worth a twilight excursion. For real late-night action, head for the bright lights of Roppongi, an area that parties till the first morning train on weekends.

A taste of traditional Japan can be had by a visit to Meiji-jingū Shrine in Harajuku, Sensō-ji Temple in Asakusa, or any of the many other temples and gardens tucked away throughout the city. If there's time, visit one of the museum re-creations of old Edo. The Edo-Tokyo Museum is the best; the Fukugawa Edo Museum is also very good.

Tokyo has some splendid gardens, such as the Hama Rikyū Detached Palace Garden in Tsukiji (near Ginza), Koishikawa Kōraku-en Garden near Kanda and Rikugi-en Garden between Ikebukuro and Ueno. The Imperial East Palace Garden is a popular stroll garden.

Tokyo is the best place in Japan to visit museums and galleries. Many are concentrated in Ueno-kōen Park, making the park well worth a day's outing. If nothing else, see

the Tokyo National Museum, which holds the world's largest collection of Japanese art.

IMPERIAL PALACE AREA 皇居近辺

The area around the Imperial Palace (Map 2) is one of the best places in Tokyo for leisurely exploration, with lots of open areas and parks. You can catch glimpses of the normally closed palace from the surrounding areas, and the moats are picturesque, especially when the cherry blossoms are out. Just north of the Imperial Palace East Garden and close to Kudanshita subway station are Kitanomaru-kōen Park, with its museums, and Yasukuni-jinja Shrine.

Imperial Palace

This is the home of Japan's emperor and the imperial family. Unfortunately, the palace itself is closed to the public for all but two days a year – 2 January (New Year's Day) and 23 December (the emperor's birthday). But it is possible to wander around its outskirts and visit the gardens, from which you can at least get a partial view of the palace with **Nijū-bashi Bridge** in the foreground.

On the Imperial Palace grounds once stood **Edo-jō Castle**, in its time the largest castle in the world. The palace we see today is a reconstruction, completed in 1968, of the Meiji Imperial Palace, destroyed during the aerial bombing of WWII. Edo-jō was first home to a feudal lord who was assassinated in 1486. The castle fell into disuse until 1590, when Tokugawa Ieyasu chose it as the site for an impregnable castle from which the shōgunate was to rule all Japan until the Meiji Restoration.

Edo-jō was fortified by a complex system of moats, and the grounds included numerous watch towers and armouries. By the time the Meiji emperor moved to Edo in 1868, large sections of the old castle had been destroyed in the upheavals leading to the transfer of power. Much that remained was torn down to make way for the new Imperial Palace.

It is an easy walk from Tokyo station, or from Hibiya and Nijū-bashi-mae subway stations, to Nijū-bashi. The walk involves

THINGS TO SEE & DO

crossing **Babasaki Moat** and the expansive **Imperial Palace Plaza**. This vantage point gives you a picture-postcard view of the palace peeking over its fortifications, with Nijū-bashi in the foreground.

Imperial Palace East Garden

The Imperial Palace East Garden is the only corner of the Imperial Palace proper that is open to the public. It makes for a pleasant retreat after wandering the outskirts of the Imperial Palace or sightseeing in Ginza. Entry is through one of three gates, Ōte-mon, Hirakawa-mon and Kitahanebashi-mon, which were entrances to Edo-jō. Most people enter through Ōte-mon, a 10 minute walk north of Nijū-bashi. This was once the principal gate of Edo-jō, while the garden is at the centre of the old castle site. The garden includes a tea pavilion, a Japanese garden and expansive lawns. It is worth buying a map at the rest house which is on your right shortly after you enter through Ōte-mon. Check out the list of prohibited behaviour on the back of the map, including the stricture against making 'hideous noises'.

There is no entry fee for the garden, which is open from 9 am to 4 pm (last entry is at 3 pm), closed Monday and Friday, and from 15 December to 3 January. When you enter, you'll be given a numbered plastic chip which you must carry with you and return upon exiting the garden. Presumably, this security measure reflects jitters about the garden's proximity to the imperial quarters.

Kitanomaru-kōen Park

The park itself is quite pleasant, and is home to a few museums and **Nihon Budōkan Hall** (☎ 3216-5100), if you want to pay homage to the Budōkan, where so many live recordings have been made. The park is best reached from Kudanshita or Takebashi subway stations. If you're walking from the Imperial Palace East Garden, take Kitahanebashi-mon, turn left and look for Kitanomaru-kōen on the other side of the road.

If you continue past the Budōkan, look for the **Science Museum** (☎ 3212-2440) on your left. With good exhibits, there's little in

the way of English explanations, but the museum provides a useful booklet in English when you buy your ticket (¥600). The museum is open daily from 9.30 am to 4.50 pm.

Toward the back of the park, facing the Imperial Palace East Garden, are the **Tokyo National Museum of Modern Art** (☎ 3211-7781) and the **Craft Museum**. The Museum of Modern Art has a collection of Japanese art from the Meiji period onwards. With over 3000 exhibits, it claims to be the best collection in the country. Admission is ¥420, and it is open Tuesday to Sunday from 10 am to 5 pm. The Craft Museum – an annex of the Museum of Modern Art – houses ceramics, lacquerware and dolls. It is open the same hours as the Museum of Modern Art.

Yasukuni-jinja Shrine

If you take the Tayasu-mon Gate exit (just past the Budōkan) of Kitanomaru-kōen and cross the road, to your left is Yasukuni-jinja, literally 'Peaceful Country Shrine'. Given that it is actually a memorial to Japan's war dead, enshrining some 2.5 million souls who died in combat, by its very name the shrine invites controversy.

Leading up to and during WWII, Yasukuni-jinja became Tokyo's chief shrine of state Shintō. Despite a constitutional commitment to the separation of religion and politics, and a renunciation of militarism, in 1979 a group of class-A war criminals was enshrined here. The shrine has also been visited by leading Liberal Democratic Party (LDP) politicians on the anniversary of Japan's defeat in WWII (15 August).

Whatever your feelings about honouring Japanese war dead, Yasukuni-jinja is interesting to visit. The enormous *torii* (gates) at the entrance are, unusually, made of steel; the second set, of bronze. The inner shrine area is quite beautiful and is laid out in the style of ancient Ise shrines.

In stark contrast to the black *uyoku* (right-wing) vans patrolling the area, the shrine grounds are home to a flock of doves whose presence seems calculated, as these birds are rarely seen in other parts of Tokyo.

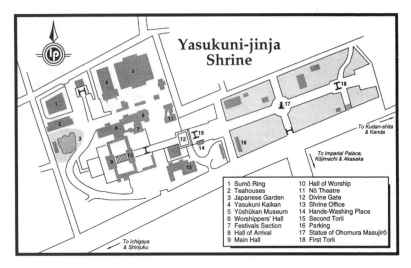

Yasukuni-jinja
Shrine

1 Sumō Ring	10 Hall of Worship
2 Teahouses	11 Nō Theatre
3 Japanese Garden	12 Divine Gate
4 Yasukuni Kaikan	13 Shrine Office
5 Yūshūkan Museum	14 Hands-Washing Place
6 Worshippers' Hall	15 Second Torii
7 Festivals Section	16 Parking
8 Hall of Arrival	17 Statue of Ohomura Masujirō
9 Main Hall	18 First Torii

To Kudan-shita & Kanda

To Imperial Palace, Kōjimachi & Akasaka

To Ichigaya & Shinjuku

Next to the shrine is **Yasukuni Yūshūkan Museum**, with treasures from Yasukuni-jinja and other items commemorating Japanese war dead. An English pamphlet is available. Exhibits include the long torpedo in the large exhibition hall which is in fact a *kaiten*, or human torpedo, a submarine version of the kamikaze airplane. There are displays of military uniforms, samurai armour and a panorama of 'the Divine Thunderbolt Corps in final attack mode at Okinawa'.

There are two exhibits you should see. The first deals with Japan's attack on Pearl Harbor. Lengthy excerpts from books, many written in English by foreign scholars, are on display. Crucial sections are highlighted which argue that Japan was actually forced into launching the attack by American and British foreign policy of the time.

The second is the 'miracle coconut' set afloat by an employee of the Japanese army in the Philippines shortly before his death in 1944. It floated round the Pacific for 31 years before washing up in Japan's Taishi-machi harbour, very near his widow's home town. You can still make out the Japanese characters which the doomed man wrote on the coconut before tossing it into the ocean.

Admission to the museum is ¥300, and it's open daily from 9 am to 5 pm.

You can also walk down the path which leads behind the main hall to a pleasant little pond with some gargantuan ornamental carp. You can feed them with food from a nearby dispenser at ¥100 a handful.

TOKYO STATION AREA　　東京駅近辺
This includes **Tokyo station** (its west side is a replica of Amsterdam's central station), Nihombashi to the east and Marunouchi, Tokyo's most prestigious office district, to the west. Though it is not rich in sights, the station area (Map 2) is home to **Nihombashi Bridge** (the iron pole on its north end indicates the old geographical centre of Tokyo); the prestigious **Mitsukoshi department store**; **Yaesu underground arcade**, with its hundreds of small shops and restaurants; and a couple of art museums.

The **Tokyo Stock Exchange** (☎ 3666-0141) is a 10 minute walk from Nihombashi subway station. You can also take the No 10 or 11 exit of Kayabachō subway station and walk north for around five minutes on the side street to the left of the Yamatane Museum of Art. The exchange has a gallery

Tokyo's Top Ten

Tsukiji Fish Market
The action is early and fast at the biggest fish market in the world.
(photograph by Chris Rowthorn)

Koishikawa Kōraku-en Garden
A stunning 17th century blend of Chinese and Japanese landscaping.
(photograph by Chris Rowthorn)

Imperial Palace
Tokyo's hidden centre is a photographer's dream.
(photograph by Chris Rowthorn)

Ueno-kōen Park
Cherry-blossom parties are the loudest and longest here.
(photograph by Chris Rowthorn)

Meiji-jingū Shrine
The restored elegance of another age; one of Japan's most beautiful shrines.
(photograph by Martin Moos)

Tokyo Metropolitan Government Offices
Amazing architecture, the views from the top and a Roman-style plaza; a vision of every citizen's future?
(photograph by Chris Rowthorn)

Hama Rikyū Detached Palace Garden
One of Tokyo's finest; sublime shrubbery girds a lovely pond with pavilion.
(photograph by Chris Rowthorn)

Sensō-ji Shrine
The heart of old Tokyo beats here in the midst of bawdy Asakusa.
(photograph by Chris Rowthorn)

Edo-Tokyo Museum
A futuristic structure provides hands-on views of Tokyo's past.
(photograph by JNTO)

Yasukuni-jinja Shrine
A stately ode to Shintō, perfect for a peaceful stroll.
(photograph by Chris Rowthorn)

CHRIS ROWTHORN

CHRIS ROWTHORN

CHRIS ROWTHORN

CHRIS ROWTHORN

Top: A simple stone lantern rests amid gorgeous foliage at Koishikawa Kōraku-en, Tokyo's finest garden
Bottom Left: Doves at Yasukuni-jinja Shrine mount a raid on the birdfeed machine.
Bottom Upper: Lotus leaves stand tall in Ueno's Shinobazu Pond, with Benten-dō Temple in the background.
Bottom Lower: Ueno-kōen Park is a green oasis in an ocean of neon, glass and concrete.

on the 2nd floor to observe all the frenzied activity. There are explanatory videos and stock trading simulation games that add to the excitement. The exchange is open from 9 to 11 am and 1 to 4 pm, Monday to Friday. Entry is free. For information on English tours, see the Japan Inc Tours boxed text in this chapter.

Just behind Tōkyū department store is the **Kite Museum** (☎ 3275-2704), which boasts some 4000 kites from all over the world, exhibited on a rotating basis. Although there are some stunning kites, particularly the Jap-anese ones, the museum is very cramped and lacks explanatory material. Take the lift to the 5th floor from Taimeiken restaurant. Entry is ¥200; it's open from 11 am to 5 pm, closed Sunday.

A little east, on the corner of Eitai-dōri, is the **Yamatane Museum of Art** (☎ 3669-7643) on the 8th and 9th floors of the Yamatane Securities building. The museum includes an interior garden and a collection of Japanese paintings. Admission is ¥700 (¥1000 for special exhibits); it is open from 10 am to 5 pm, closed Monday.

東京 東京 東京 東京 東京 東京 東京 東京 東京 東京 東京 東京 東京 東京 東京 東京

Tokyo for Free

There's no getting around it: Tokyo is an expensive city. But those on a tight budget need not despair; if you're willing to use your imagination and do a little walking, Tokyo offers a host of things to do for free. These suggestions will cost no more than the train ticket to get there.

Parks Unlike Tokyo's gardens, Tokyo's parks are free, and provide a welcome escape from the urban sprawl. Just grab a bentō or some baked bread and you've got a picnic. Good spots are Kitanomaru-kōen (see the Other Attractions section in this chapter), Yoyogi-kōen near Harajuku, Ueno-kōen in Ueno and Hibiya-kōen near Ginza.

Galleries Most private galleries don't charge admission. Indeed, these galleries are often rented by individual artists who are delighted by a foreigner's interest in their work. Ginza is the best place to hunt for them. Department store galleries (on upper floors) are another good bet; if these are not free, admission is often cheaper than a museum entry fee.

Temples & Shrines Shrines are almost always free in Tokyo and most temples only charge to enter their *honden* (main hall). Sensō-ji in Asakusa and Meiji-jingū in Harajuku are two good places to start. See also the Nippori to Nishi-Nippori Walk boxed text in this chapter for some lesser known temples and shrines.

Company Showrooms OK, they're really just another form of advertising, but some showrooms in Tokyo are like small museums and they're all free. The Toyota Amlux showroom in Ikebukuro is great for auto enthusiasts and Sony Plaza in Ginza is great for just about anyone. Kids especially love the free video games. Other showrooms can be found in Ginza, Shinjuku and Harajuku/Aoyama. See the Other Attractions section in this chapter for details.

Tsukiji Central Fish Market You can wander the world's biggest fish market and its great External Market for hours at no cost.

Skyscrapers Several skyscrapers have free observation floors, eg Tokyo Metropolitan Government Offices building No 1 in west Shinjuku, Shinjuku Sumitomo building and Tokyo Big Sight (see the Other Attractions section in this chapter). Avoid the pricey observation decks like the one in Ikebukuro's Sunshine Tower.

Free Food Samples It may be a little embarrassing, but you can put together a free and often delicious lunch from the food samples laid out in the larger department stores' food sections. Takashimaya in Ginza and Seibu and Tōbu in Ikebukuro usually have good selections. If you're going to make a daily practice of this, we suggest varying your appearance a little.

Bookshops Unlike some other countries, in Japan no-one will object to you spending hours reading books and magazines on display in bookshops. There's even a word for the practice: *tachiyomi* (a standing read). ■

東京 東京 東京 東京 東京 東京 東京 東京 東京 東京 東京 東京 東京 東京 東京 東京

THINGS TO SEE & DO

If you walk back west to Chūō-dōri and make a left turn, on the far left side of the intersection with Yaesu-dōri is the **Bridge-stone Museum of Art** (☎ 3563-0241). There is a glut of French impressionist art in Tokyo, but this private collection of the Bridgestone Tire Company's founder rates highly. Impressionist paintings by Japanese artists are also featured. Entry is ¥500; it's open from 10 am to 5.30 pm, closed Monday.

Tokyo International Forum

In Yūrakuchō (Map 3), midway between Tokyo station and Ginza, this is a wonderful building. The prominent glass wing looks like a fantastic ship plying the urban waters of central Tokyo – perhaps the maritime touch is intentional, as the building represents a traditionally isolated island nation's efforts toward internationalisation.

The west wing is a phantasma of canti-levered, overhanging spaces and cavernous atriums. Together, the two wings hold a variety of meeting halls and convention centres. On the basement floor on the north side of the building is the main Tokyo **Tourist Information Center** (TIC), the foyer of which is home to an excellent photographic gallery.

There is a variety of restaurants and cafes scattered throughout the building, a small library with mostly Japanese material on the B1 floor, an ATM corner (for Japanese cards) and a self-service fax/photocopy centre on the 4th floor of the glass wing.

It's worth a side trip to see the Forum, truly one of Tokyo's architectural marvels. At night, when the upper floors are illuminated, the glass hall takes on the appearance of a giant space colony. The building is open daily from 8 am to 11 pm. For information call ☎ 5221-9000.

GINZA 銀座

This is the Tokyo shopping district that everyone has heard of. In the 1870s, Ginza (Map 3) was one of the first areas to modern-ise, featuring novel (for Tokyoites of the time) western-style brick buildings. Ginza saw Tokyo's first department stores, side-walks and other western emblems of moder-nity like the gas lamp. Today, other shopping districts rival Ginza in opulence, vitality and popularity, but Ginza retains a distinct snob value. Make a point of checking out some of the topnotch department stores like **Wakō**, **Mitsukoshi** and **Matsuya**. The window displays are always a creative treat. Watch for speciality stores tucked away in the most unlikely places.

Ginza overflows with small galleries, craft shops and showrooms – and you should at least be able to afford a cup of coffee at one of the discount coffee shops huddled among the exclusive boutiques.

The best starting point for a wander is **Sukiyabashi crossing**, a 10 minute walk from the Imperial Palace, or out the Sukiya-bashi crossing exit at Ginza subway station. The streets of Ginza are closed to traffic on weekends and holidays, making these times especially pleasant for a stroll.

Sony Building

Right on Sukiyabashi crossing is the Sony building (☎ 3573-2371), which has fascinat-ing hands-on displays of Sony's many products, including some which have yet to be released. Although there's often a wait, kids love the free video and virtual reality games on the 6th floor. If nothing else, you can put your feet up and relax for a while in one of the building's two Hi-Vision theatres. The building also has a Toyota showroom, an Internet cafe and two of Tokyo's finest restaurants: Sabatini di Firenze and Maxim's de Paris. The showroom is open daily from 11 am to 7 pm; admission is free.

Galleries

Galleries, many so tiny they only take a couple of minutes to see, are scattered throughout Ginza, but are concentrated in the area south of Harumi-dōri, between Ginza-dōri and Chūō-dōri.

Idemitsu Art Museum (☎ 3213-9402) holds an eclectic selection of Japanese, Chinese and western art collected by a petro-leum magnate. The museum also provides an excellent view over the Imperial Palace. It is a five minute walk from Hibiya or Yūrakuchō stations, on the 9th floor of the Kokusai building, next to Teikoku Gekijō Theatre (Imperial Theatre). Entry is ¥500; it is open from 10 am to 5 pm, Tuesday to Sunday.

A quirky, little known option, the **Japan Sake Center** (☎ 3575-0656) on Harumi-dōri offers a history of sake-making. There are no English captions on the indifferent displays, but you can purchase some sake for ¥500. It is open from 10.30 am to 6.30 pm, closed Monday, every fourth Sunday and public holidays. Entry is free.

The best photographic galleries around here are probably **Nikon Salon** (☎ 3562-5756) and the **Contax Gallery** (☎ 3572-1921). Both have free, changing exhibits. Nikon Salon is in the Matsushima Gankyōten building (3rd floor), opposite Matsuya department store on Chūō-dōri, and is open Tuesday to Sunday from 10 am to 6 pm. The Contax Gallery is on the 5th floor of the building next door to the San-ai building on Chūō-dōri; there is no English sign at ground level. It is open Tuesday to Sunday from 10.30 am to 7 pm.

A friendly private art gallery worth a look is **Art Museum Ginza** (☎ 3571-2285), just down the street from the Sony building on Sotobori-dōri. This gallery shows some very experimental art, including video and sculptural installations. Hours vary according to the exhibition, and admission is free.

World Magazine Gallery

Just around the corner from Kabuki-za is the World Magazine Gallery (☎ 3545-7227), open weekdays. It stocks about 1200 magazines from around the world, and although loans cannot be made, you are free to sit down and read anything you please. Twice a year the gallery sells off its magazines for the previous six months – look for announcements in the *Japan Times* or the tourist literature. It also has a coffee shop where you can enjoy a drink while you read.

Kabuki-za Theatre

To the east, along Harumi-dōri, is Kabuki-za Theatre (☎ 3541-3131). Even if you don't plan to attend a kabuki performance, take a look at the building, an interesting fusion of western and Japanese architecture.

Hachikan-jinja Shrine

Hachikan-jinja is so small that you might stroll past and not notice it was there – which is what makes it worth pausing for. Real-estate values in Ginza have generally forced places of worship elsewhere (or relocated them on the rooftops of Ginza's temples of commerce). Located near Shimbashi station, this is one shrine that remains at street level, a feat that was achieved by building over the top of it.

Hibiya-kōen Park

If Ginza has left you yearning for greenery, retrace your steps along Harumi-dōri, back through Sukiyabashi crossing to Hibiya-kōen. The park is actually just west of Ginza in Hibiya, an area notable for the Imperial Theater and its cinema complexes, but it's only a brief walk west of Sukiyabashi crossing. It was Tokyo's first western-style park, and it makes for a pleasant break, especially if you head for the benches overlooking the pond on the park's east side. Also on the park's east side, about midway down, is a small restaurant where you can pause for coffee or ice cream.

TSUKIJI　築地

Tsukiji (Map 3) is famous for its fish market, the world's largest, but there are several other sights here, including **Tsukiji Hongan-ji Temple**, next to Tsukiji subway station, which looks as if it has been magically transported from New Delhi. The Indian touch is a tribute to the birthplace of Buddhism. It can be entered free, from 6 am to 4 pm daily.

Just before the entrance to the market, have a look at the shrine, **Namiyoke-jinja**, where wholesalers and middlemen come to pray before entering the market. Its highlights are the giant gold parade mask in the main hall and the dragon-shaped water spigots over the purification basins.

Quite a walk from the station east along Harumi-dōri is the **Tokyo International Fair**

Ground, with 56,000 sq metres of well-used exhibition space. Next to the fish market on the Shimbashi side is one of Tokyo's most beautiful gardens, the Hama Rikyū Detached Palace Garden.

While most people get to Tsukiji by taking the Hibiya subway line to Tsukiji station, you can also walk from central Ginza in about 15 minutes. If you make the early-morning trip to the fish market, you could return to Ginza on foot, taking in Kabuki-za Theatre and some department stores on the way.

Tsukiji Central Fish Market

This is one of Tokyo's top attractions and definitely worth a visit. If it lives in the sea, it's probably for sale here – acres and acres of fish and fish products passing hands in a lively, almost chaotic atmosphere. Everything is allotted its own area: mountains of octopus, rows of giant tuna, endless varieties of shellfish, tanks of live fish, bundles of wriggling crabs; you name it, it's here in abundance.

To get an idea of the size of Tsukiji Market (called Tsukiji Ichiba), consider this: 2500 *tonnes* of fish are sold here daily, worth over US$23 million; that's 670,000 tonnes of fish worth over US$6 billion a year. To keep all this fish cold, the market goes through 240 tonnes of ice and a mountain of styrofoam boxes every day.

The day begins very early, with the arrival of fish and its wholesale auctioning. The wholesale market is not open to the general public, which is probably a blessing, given that you'd have to be there well before 5 am to see the action. You are free to visit the middlemen's market, though, and wander around the stalls set up to sell directly to restaurants, retail stores and other buyers. It's fun, and you don't have to arrive *that* early; as long as you're there before 8 am, there will be something going on. Wear old shoes – there's a lot of muck and water on the floor – and don't get run down by the electric carts that prowl the narrow aisles.

Also, take a stroll through Tsukiji External Market (Tsukijijō-gaishijō) which you pass through on the way to the main market. This is a good option if you've arrived too late for the action in the main market. Here, you'll find all kinds of seafood, cooking supplies and produce for sale, in addition to durables like baskets and pottery – good, low-cost souvenir alternatives. The produce market is also worth a look. It's north-west of the main fish market.

The done thing is to top off your visit with a sushi breakfast in one of the nearby sushi shops. There are plenty of small, cheap places in the narrow alleys of Tsukiji External Market and larger, more upscale ones off Harumi-dōri and Shin-Ōhashi-dōri. The market is closed on Sunday and public holidays.

Hama Rikyū Detached Palace Garden

Called Hama Rikyū Onshi-teien (☎ 3541-0200), this is one of Tokyo's finest gardens, featuring a large pond with an island and a pavilion. It was a shōgunal palace, and extended into the area now occupied by the fish market. Besides visiting the park as a side trip from Ginza or Tsukiji Market, consider setting out from Asakusa via the Sumida-gawa River cruise (see the Asakusa section later in this chapter). Entry is ¥300, and it is open daily from 9 am to 4.30 pm.

KANDA   神田

Kanda (Map 2) was a bustling commercial and residential district back in the days of old Edo, and it is another area where something of Edo's spirit lingers. It can be found in the specialised commercial districts and in the old-style restaurants that lurk in the side streets. Kanda is not one of Tokyo's main attractions, but for the visitor with time to spare, it is worth a look.

Akihabara

Akihabara is Tokyo's discount electrical and electronics centre, with countless shops ranging from tiny specialist stores to electrical department stores. You could go there with no intention of buying and quickly find half a dozen things that you couldn't possibly live without. See the Shopping chapter for details.

THINGS TO SEE & DO

Yushima Seidō A Confucian school during the Tokugawa regime, Yushima Seidō is one of Tokyo's few Confucian shrines. There is a bronze statue of Confucius in the main hall. The original building was destroyed by WWII bombing. It's near Ochanomizu station.

Transportation Museum Just south of Akihabara station (Electric Town is to the north), on the far side of Kanda-gawa River, is the Transportation Museum (☎ 3251-8481), a great place for kids and adults alike. It has exhibits of modes of transport from bicycles to airplanes, with the emphasis on trains. Many exhibits are hands-on, and kids will especially love the train simulator, which lets them 'drive' a JR Yamanote train around Tokyo. They'll also love the giant model train layout, which comes alive once an hour in a great show with a 'conductor' who operates all the trains and gives a running explanation of the layout. The museum is open from 9.30 am to 5 pm, closed Monday. Entry is ¥310 for adults, ¥150 for children – a bargain in Tokyo.

Russian Orthodox Nikolai Cathedral More of interest to building junkies, Nikolai Cathedral was completed in 1892 after eight years of work. It can be visited easily with Akihabara's Electric Town and the Transportation Museum. From the museum, walk straight ahead, turn right and follow the road along the river to the second bridge. Turn left here onto Hongo-dōri; the cathedral is on the right.

Jimbōchō
This is a neighbourhood of booksellers, close to some of Tokyo's more prestigious private universities and schools (see the Tokyo's Bookshops boxed text in the Facts for the Visitor chapter).

Jimbōchō can be reached in a 15 minute walk from Akihabara by heading south down Chūō-dōri and turning right into Yasukuni-dōri. You can also walk down Yasukuni-dōri from Yasukuni-jinja or catch the subway to Jimbōchō subway station.

東京 東京 東京 東京 東京 東京 東京 東京 東

Fireworks

The Japanese call them *hanabi* (fire-flowers), and when the heat of summer is at its worst, the skies over Tokyo suddenly burst into bloom with these incandescent flowers. If you're in Tokyo in late July or early August, when the biggest displays take place, make every effort to see one.

Huge sums of money are spent on hanabi by corporations keen on public exposure, and Japanese fireworks displays are among the best in the world. They usually start at sunset and continue for up to two hours. The crowds really turn out for hanabi, and public transport is packed both coming and going – arrive early, bring a picnic and linger for a long time after the show. The following are some of Tokyo's best shows; inquire at the TIC for exact dates.

Sumida-gawa River Fireworks Festival
    Taitō-ku, late July; fireworks are launched from two locations, best viewed from between Sakura-bashi and Komagata-bashi bridges; walk from Asakusa station
Edogawa-ku Fireworks Festival
    Edogawa-ku, early August; fireworks are set off from the banks of the Edo-gawa River, best viewed from Shinozaki-kōen Park; walk 15 minutes from Koiwa station, on the JR Sōbu line
Tokyo Bay Big Fireworks Festival
    Chūō-ku, mid-August; fireworks are launched from Harumi Wharf; take the bus from Tokyo station or walk 20 minutes from Tsukiji
Setagaya-ku Tamagawa Fireworks Festival
    Setagaya-ku, late July; fireworks take off from Futako-tamagawa-kōen Park, a short walk from Futako-tamagawa station on the Tōkyū Shin-tamagawa line ■

東京 東京 東京 東京 東京 東京 東京 東京 東

UENO 上野
Ueno Hill was the site of a last-ditch defence of the Tokugawa shōgunate by about 2000 Tokugawa loyalists in 1868. They were duly dispatched by the imperial army, and the new Meiji government decreed that Ueno Hill would become one of Tokyo's first parks.

Today, Ueno-kōen is Ueno's foremost attraction. The park has a number of museums, galleries and a zoo that, by Asian standards at least, is pretty good.

Ueno (Map 4) is interesting for a stroll. Opposite Ueno station is Ameyoko arcade, a market area selling everything from dried fish to fake Rolexes. Two stops from Ueno on the Ginza subway line is Kappabashi-dōri, a great place for real versions of all those plastic food displays.

Shitamachi History Museum

Just around the corner from McDonald's, close to Ueno station, is the Shitamachi History Museum (☎ 3823-7451), which recreates life in the plebeian quarters of old Tokyo through an exhibition of typical Shitamachi buildings. These include a merchant's shop, a sweet shop, the home and business of a copper-boiler maker, and a tenement house (take off your shoes and look around inside). Upstairs, the museum has many utensils and items from the daily life of the average Shitamachi resident. You are free to pick many up and have a closer look. Admission is ¥200, and it is open from 9.30 am to 4.30 pm, closed Monday.

Ueno-kōen Park

There are two entrances to Ueno-kōen. The main one takes you straight into the museum and art gallery area, a course that might leave you worn out before you get to Ueno's temples. It's better to start at the southern entrance between Ueno's JR station and Keisei station, and do a little temple viewing on the way to the museums. From the JR station, take the Keisei station exit and turn right. Just around the corner is a flight of stairs leading up into the park.

Ahead of you and slightly to your right at the top of the stairs is the **Saigō Takamori statue**. This image of a samurai walking his dog proves that between hacking each other to pieces, samurai had the time for more domestic pleasures. The statue is a favourite meeting place.

Bear to the far left and follow a wide tree-lined path until you reach **Kiyōmizu Kannon-dō Temple**. The temple's model is Kiyōmizu-dera in Kyoto, not that there is any real comparison – the Tokyo version might have seen better days. Nevertheless, it's definitely worth a browse. Women who wish to conceive a child leave a doll here for the

senjū Kannon (the 1000-armed goddess of mercy), and the accumulated dolls are burnt ceremoniously on 25 September.

From the temple, continue down to the narrow road that follows Shinobazu Pond. Through a red torii is **Benten-dō Temple**, on an island in the pond. Benten-dō is a memorial to Benten, a patron goddess of the arts. Behind the temple you can hire a peddle boat for 30 minutes (¥500) or a row boat for an hour (same price).

Make your way back to the road that follows Shinobazu Pond and turn left. Where the road begins to curve and leaves the pond behind, there is a stair pathway to the right. Follow the path and take the second turn to the left. This takes you into the grounds of **Tōshō-gū Shrine**. Established in 1627 (the present building dates from 1651), this is a shrine which, like its counterpart in Nikkō, was founded in memory of Tokugawa Ieyasu, declared a divinity after his death. Miraculously, it has survived Tokyo's many disasters, making it one of the few early Edo structures extant. There is a good view of Kanei-ji Temple Pagoda to your right as you take the pathway into the shrine. The pathway itself is fronted by a stone torii and lined with 200 stone lanterns rendered as gifts by *daimyō* (feudal lords) in the Edo period. Entry is ¥200, and it is open from 9 am to 5.30 pm, to 4.30 pm in winter.

Tokyo Metropolitan Museum of Art Not far from Tōshō-gū, the Tokyo Metropolitan Museum of Art (☎ 3823-6921) has a number of galleries running various shows of contemporary Japanese art. It is worth entering just to see what is on display. Galleries feature both western art and Japanese arts such as ink brush and ikebana. Entry to the museum itself is free, but most special exhibits cost ¥900 to ¥1100 to enter. The museum also has an excellent, free art library. It is open from 9 am to 5 pm, closed the third Monday of each month.

Ueno Zoo While it is definitely not worth slotting Ueno Zoo (☎ 3828-5171) into a tight itinerary, in good weather it can make for a pleasant walk. Among the Japanese, the zoo is very popular for its pandas. The best time to see the pandas is during feeding time at 3.30 pm (they're not on view on Friday). There are also two snow leopards born in 1995, nine lowland gorillas and four Bengal tigers. The zoo is divided into two areas, linked by a monorail. The southern half of the zoo contains the children's petting zoo. Note that the outdoor exhibits here are much nicer than the indoor ones, which tend to be a little dark and depressing. Admission is ¥500 for adults, ¥200 for children junior high school age and up, and free for younger kids. The zoo is open from 9.30 am to 4.30 pm, closed Monday.

Tokyo National Museum This is the one museum worth going out of your way to visit. The Tokyo National Museum (☎ 3822-1111) is Japan's largest museum, holding the world's largest collection of Japanese art. Only a portion of the museum's vast collection is displayed at any one time.

The museum has four galleries, the most important of which is the Main Gallery. It is straight ahead as you enter, and houses a very impressive collection of Japanese art, from sculpture and swords to lacquerware and calligraphy. The Gallery of Eastern Antiquities, to the right of the ticket booth, has a collection of art and archaeological finds from all of Asia east of Egypt. Hyōkeikan Hall, to the left of the ticket booth, houses Japanese archaeological finds. There is also a room devoted to Ainu artefacts.

Finally, there is the Gallery of Hōryū-ji Treasures, which is only open on Thursday, and then only 'weather permitting'. The exhibits (masks, scrolls etc) are from Hōryū-ji Temple in Nara. Because these are more than 1000 years old, the building often remains closed if it is raining or humid. Museum entry is ¥420, and it is open from 9 am to 5 pm, closed Monday.

National Science Museum This museum (☎ 3822-0111) is generally nothing special: displays are limited in scope and quality, and can be covered in less than an hour. Excellent special exhibitions are often held, but these cost extra (usually around ¥500). Signs out the front of the museum announce special exhibits, or ask at the park information centre. Most regular exhibits aren't labelled in English, though you can buy a pamphlet (¥300). Admission is ¥420, and it is open from 9 am to 4.30 pm, closed Monday. At least stop by to see the life-sized model of the blue whale outside.

National Museum of Western Art This museum (☎ 3828-5131) holds an impressive collection of western art (probably the most extensive in Asia). The main building was designed by Le Corbusier, and the garden contains originals by Rodin, including the famous statue of *The Thinker*. Inside, there is an emphasis on French impressionists, with paintings and sketches by, among others, Renoir and Monet. Loan exhibitions are also often on display from art museums around the world, although these cost extra. Admission is ¥420; it is open from 9.30 am to 5 pm, closed Monday.

Other Attractions Back toward the south entrance of Ueno-kōen is **Tokyo Metropolitan Festival Hall**, a venue for classical music, and **Ueno-no-Mori Art Museum**, which has a variety of exhibition spaces for changing exhibits, particularly calligraphy. Entry to the museum is free; it's open from 10 am to 5 pm.

Ameyoko Arcade
Directly opposite the southern exit to JR Ueno station is Ameyoko arcade. Cross the road and enter beneath the big romaji sign. This fascinating jumble of market-style shops, game parlours and restaurants huddled together in the shadow of the overhead Yamanote line is worth a wander.

The Ameyoko area was famous as a black-market district in the early years following WWII, and is still a lively bargain shopping area. Many of the same tourist items on sale at inflated prices in Ginza sell here at more reasonable rates. Shopkeepers are also much less restrained than those in other shopping areas in Tokyo, brazenly hawking their goods with guttural cries to the passing crowds. It is one of the few areas in which some of the rough and readiness of old Shitamachi lingers.

Check out the basement of the Ameyoko Center building, where Chinese and Korean merchants have set up their own shopping arcade. If you're looking for Chinese cooking ingredients, this is the place.

Korinchō Rd

Just north of Ueno station is the Korinchō Rd motorcycle centre, and the interesting motorcycle museum on the 3rd and 4th floors of the Corin Motors clothing shop. This is a good area to pick up new and second-hand motorbikes. Several shops have native-English speakers on staff.

ASAKUSA 浅草

The most famous sight in Asakusa (Map 4) is Sensō-ji, also known as Asakusa Kannon-dō. The temple was founded in the 7th century, according to tradition. Asakusa itself emerged as an important commercial and entertainment area during the Edo period. Asakusa and the nearby red-light area of Yoshiwara (now divested of its former glory, lingering in a few bath houses and shabby love hotels) lay at the very heart of Edo's Shitamachi.

Like Ueno, Asakusa is well worth a directionless stroll – the spirit of old Edo hasn't been banished by the razzle-dazzle of modern Tokyo. In early Edo times, Asakusa may have been a halfway stop between the city and Yoshiwara, but in time it emerged as a pleasure quarter in its own right, eventually becoming the hub of that most beloved of Edo entertainments, kabuki. In the very shadow of Sensō-ji, a fairground atmosphere harboured a wealth of decidedly secular entertainment – from kabuki to brothels.

When Japan ended its isolation with the Meiji Restoration, it was in Asakusa that the first cinemas and music halls appeared; western opera first graced the Japanese stage at Asakusa's Teikoku Gekijō Theatre (Imperial Theatre). It was also in Asakusa that

another western export – the striptease – first found a Japanese audience. It almost failed to catch on, such was the popularity of a rival form of risqué entertainment – female sword fighting. The inspired introduction of a bubble-bath show saved the day. A few clubs still operate in the area.

Asakusa never quite recovered from aerial bombing in the closing months of WWII. Although Sensō-ji was rebuilt, the bright lights have shifted elsewhere.

The tourist information office, across the street from Kaminari-mon Gate, has English speakers on hand who can give you handy maps and tips on events and activities.

If you're around at the end of August – call the TIC for exact dates – don't miss the Asakusa Samba Carnival. This, the most un-Japanese of all Tokyo festivals, is put on by Brazilian-born Japanese, and it comes as close as anything to restoring Asakusa to its prewar bawdy glory.

Sensō-ji Temple

Sensō-ji enshrines a golden image of Kannon, which according to legend was miraculously fished out of nearby Sumida-gawa River by two fishermen in 628 AD. In time, a temple was built to house the image, which has remained on the spot through successive rebuildings of the temple.

If you approach Sensō-ji from Asakusa subway station, you will enter through **Kaminari-mon** (Thunder Gate). The gate houses a pair of scowling gods: Fūjin, the god of wind, on the right; and Raijin, the god of thunder, on the left.

Straight on through the gate is **Nakamise-dōri**, a shopping street set within the actual temple precinct. Everything from tourist trinkets to genuine Edo-style crafts is sold here. There's even a shop selling wigs to be worn with a kimono. Be sure to try the *sembei* (savoury rice crackers) that a few shops specialise in – you'll have to queue, though, as they are very popular with Japanese tourists as well.

Nakamise-dōri leads to the main temple compound, but it is hard to say if the Kannon image really is inside, as you cannot see it – not that this stops a steady stream of worshippers making their way up the stairs to the temple, where they cast coins, clap ceremoniously and bow in a gesture of respect. In front of the temple is a large incense cauldron where people go to rub smoke against their bodies to ensure good health. If any part of your body (as far as modesty permits) is giving you trouble, you should give it particular attention when applying the smoke.

The temple itself is a post-1945 concrete reproduction of the original, but the building is not the sole reason to visit. The atmospheric energy is the real attraction.

On your left, just before you reach the temple, is **Dempō-in Garden**. Unfortunately, it is not possible to gain admission to Dempō-in, as the garden is not open to the public – but this does not stop you from peering over the fence and taking a look at one of Tokyo's most beautiful gardens. The garden contains a pond and a replica of a famous Kyoto teahouse.

Behind Sensō-ji, to the right, is **Asakusa-jinja Shrine**. Unlike its Buddhist neighbour, Asakusa-jinja is a Shintō shrine, a tribute to the comfortable coexistence of Japan's religions. It was built in honour of the brothers who discovered the Kannon statue. The shrine dates back to 1649, and is the site of one of Tokyo's most important festivals, the Sanja Festival, a three day extravaganza of costumed parades and lurching *mikoshi* (portable shrines).

Kappabashi-dōri

One stop west of Asakusa on the Ginza line (get off at Tawaramachi) or a 10 minute walk from Sensō-ji is Kappabashi-dōri, a restaurateur's heaven. Gourmet accessories include colourful, patterned *noren* (split doorway curtains), crockery and oodles of wax food models. Whether you want a plate of bolognaise complete with an upright fork, steak and chips, a lurid pizza or a bowl of rāmen, it is all on this street. Most items aren't particularly cheap, but most of them are very convincing and certainly make unusual souvenirs.

Sumida-gawa River Cruise

'Cruise' is a slight overstatement, but in its time Sumida-gawa was a picturesque river punctuated by delicate arched bridges. It's no longer so, but a cruise is a good way to get to or from Asakusa and look at some of Tokyo's new bay area developments. It's also a good option when the summer heat takes the fun out of walking.

The cruise departs from a pier below Asakusa's Azuma-bashi Bridge and goes to Hama Rikyū Onshi-teien, Hinode Pier and Odaiba Seaside Park. The best option is to buy a ticket to Hama Rikyū-teien (you'll still have to pay the ¥300 entry fee for the garden). From the garden it's a 15 minute walk into Ginza. Boats leave daily between 9.50 am and 7.35 pm (¥520 to Hama Rikyū Onshi-teien, ¥560 to Hinode Pier). From Hinode Pier you can catch boats to Odaiba Seaside Park for ¥400 or the Museum of Maritime Science for ¥520. Take an English leaflet when you buy your ticket; it describes the 11 bridges you'll pass under between Asakusa and Hama Rikyū Onshi-teien.

MARTIN MOOS
The floating world of the Sumida-gawa River

東京 東京 東京 東京 東京 東京 東京 東京 東京 東京 東京 東京 東京 東京 東京 東京 東京

Shitamachi Walking Tour (Asakusa)
Time: About two hours
Distance: About 3km
Highlights: Kappabashi-dōri, old stores, Chingo-dō Temple

If you've spent a few days in Tokyo, you'll notice the difference between Asakusa and other parts of the city as soon as you pass into Nakamise-dōri. For the most part, the Japanese vision of the future has swallowed up Tokyo, and for this reason it is worth taking a stroll outside the precincts of Sensō-ji. What you get is not so much an abundance of sights as an alternative to Japan Inc.

To start, exit Sensō-ji the way you entered it – through Hōzō-mon at the temple end of Nakamise-dōri. Turn right here and follow the road around the perimeter of the temple grounds. Look for **Chingo-dō Temple** on your right, next door to the back entrance to Dempō-in. More than anything else, it is an interesting oddity: founded in 1883, the temple was constructed for the 'raccoon dogs' living in the Sensō-ji precincts. It doesn't seem to have done much good, as the animals aren't much in evidence nowadays. This stretch of road also has a flea market feel about it, as there are often stalls set up along the outside of the temple precincts. You can pick up some interesting festival accessories here.

If you follow the road round to the right, you pass an arcade with shops selling traditional items at reasonable prices. Look for shops selling *yukata* (cotton robes) and kimono. Further along is the **Hanayashiki Amusement Park**. It hasn't got a lot to recommend it, unless you are overcome by a hankering to test your resilience on one of the fairly rickety-looking rides. The amusement park dates back to 1853, when it was a botanical garden, and the park pays homage to Asakusa's past with a Panorama Hall that displays photographs of old Asakusa. It is open daily from 10 am to 6 pm; entry is ¥900 for adults and ¥400 for children, after which most rides average ¥200 to ¥300. A pass allowing entry and access to most rides is ¥1600 for adults and ¥1400 for children – ask for a 'furawā bando'.

From Hanayashiki take a left and another left and you will enter what is left of **Rokku**, Asakusa's old cinema district. It is all a little down-at-heel nowadays, and the few remaining cinemas seem to restrict their screenings to Japanese pornography – at least they all carry the familiar lurid posters depicting naked women trussed up like hams, their meek eyes casting plaintive looks at the tattooed torturers standing over them. As you wander through, consider that this was once the most lively of Tokyo's entertainment districts – how times change. Presiding over the area today, just next door to the Big Boy restaurant, is the **Rox building**, a shopping centre that is notable above all else for its failure to endow Asakusa with an air of cosmopolitan modernity. Near the Rox building is Asakusa Engei Hall, where performances of rakugo are held.

Ahead is another arcade. Mostly it is taken up by Japanese restaurants specialising in tempura and so on. However, worth a look are the traditional sembei-making shops. These savoury crackers are very popular, and in the open-fronted shops in the arcade you can watch them being produced.

The arcade takes you back onto Kamanarimon-dōri, which is lined with excellent Japanese restaurants. Turn right here and cross over Kokusai-dōri. Following the small road that runs to Kappabashi-dōri, to your left is a block that is riddled with temples, most of them quite small. The largest is **Tokyo Hongan-ji Temple**, which is on your left just before you get to Kappabashi-dōri.

Kappabashi-dōri is Tokyo's wholesale restaurant supplies area. It's chock-a-block with shops selling wax food models, bamboo cooking utensils, customised cushions and even the red lanterns *(aka-chōchin)* that light the back alleys of Tokyo by night. Turn right into Kappabashi-dōri and walk up the road a few blocks, before crossing over the road and walking back in the other direction.

The landmark that tells you you've reached the end of your Shitamachi tour and done the rounds of the plastic food shops is the **Niimi building**, crowned with an enormous chef's head – you can't miss it. It's on the corner of Asakusa-dōri, and a few minutes down the road to your left is Tawaramachi subway station on the Ginza line. ■

東京 東京 東京 東京 東京 東京 東京 東京 東京 東京 東京 東京 東京 東京 東京 東京 東京

IKEBUKURO 池袋

Ikebukuro (Map 5) has been creeping up-market, giving the area a cosmopolitan sheen. Today, provincial old Ikebukuro is home to some of the world's biggest department stores, one of the tallest buildings in Asia, the world's largest automobile showroom, the escalator from hell and the second busiest station in Tokyo. The obligatory fashionable shopping plazas have started to spring up, and the CD superstore invasion has bestowed branches of HMV and Virgin Records.

For the time being, Ikebukuro lags behind other areas of Tokyo in terms of vibrancy and attractions, but it can be worth spending an afternoon or morning in the area. Most sights are on the eastern side of Ikebukuro station; the west side is mainly notable for the Tokyo Metropolitan Art Space.

Tokyo Metropolitan Art Space
Part of the 'Tokyo Renaissance' plan, the Art Space (☎ 5391-2111) is an attempt to endow Ikebukuro's west side with a touch of high culture. The plaza-like area in front of the building is a popular place to hang out, munch on Big Macs and practise the latest dance moves. The building is designed mainly for performance art, featuring a large, medium and two small halls. If you're not there for a show, it's memorable mainly for its soaring escalator ride. The building is open daily from 9 am to 10 pm.

Metropolitan Plaza
Just across the road from the Metropolitan Art Space, the Metropolitan Plaza is a multi-floor collection of designer boutiques and restaurants. On the ground floor is **Tōbu Art Museum** (☎ 5391-3220), which houses exhibits of contemporary Japanese art. Entry is around ¥1000; it's open from 10 am to 7 pm, closed Wednesday. The 6th floor has a huge HMV store.

Tōbu Department Store
With 29 floors, it's possible to spend all day in this place (try not to). On floors 10 to 17 of the main building, you'll find most of the store's restaurants, while the two basement floors house the 'groceteria' (food section). Tōbu is open daily from 10 am to 8 pm.

Seibu Department Store
On the western side of the station, this is Seibu's biggest branch. The 12th floor has an art museum. Seibu is open from 10 am to 7 pm, closed Thursday.

In the Seibu annex next door, **Sezon Museum of Art** (☎ 5992-0155) holds high-quality art exhibitions. Admission is usually hefty (about ¥1200); it's closed Tuesday.

Sunshine City
Billed as a city in a building, this is basically another opportunity to partake of that quintessential Japanese pastime – shopping.

With 60 floors (mostly office space), there are some diversions. For ¥620, you can take the world's second fastest lift to the 60th floor observatory and gaze out on Tokyo's murky skyline. **Sunshine International Aquarium** (☎ 3989-3466) is one of the best in Tokyo, though entry is expensive (¥1600 for adults; ¥800 for children); it's open from 10 am to 6 pm daily. **Sunshine Planetarium** (☎ 3989-3466) is an option, though shows are in Japanese. Entry is ¥800 for adults, ¥500 for children; it's open from 11 am to 5.30 pm daily.

Not in the Sunshine City building itself, but in the Bunka Kaikan building (7th floor) of Sunshine City, is the **Ancient Orient Museum** (☎ 3989-3491), which is strictly for those with a special interest in ancient odds and ends such as coins and beads. Admission is ¥500; it's open Tuesday to Sunday from 10 am to 4 pm.

Toyota Amlux
Toyota Amlux is touted as the world's largest automobile showroom. It is basically five floors of Toyota products, but with special exhibitions, ambient sound effects and a majestic escalator ride, it is worth a brief detour. Toyota Amlux is next to Sunshine City, 10 minutes from the eastern exit of Ikebukuro station. It's open Tuesday to Saturday from 11 am to 8 pm, closed Monday, and from 10 am to 7.30 pm on Sunday and public holidays.

SHINJUKU　新宿
Shinjuku (Map 6) is a city in itself and without doubt the most vigorous part of Tokyo. If you had only a day in Tokyo, Shinjuku would be the place to go. Two million people a day pass through Shinjuku station, making it one of the busiest stations in the world. Like Ikebukuro station, its crowded, sprawling underground tunnels and caverns can reduce newcomers to gibbering wrecks – avoid the shakes by knowing where you are

東京 東京 東京 東京 東京 東京 東京 東京 東京 東京 東京 東京 東京 東京 東京 東京 東京 東京

West Shinjuku Walking Tour

Time: About three hours
Distance: About 3km
Highlights: Tokyo Metropolitan Government Offices, Shinjuku NS building, Shinjuku Sumitomo building

The west exit of Shinjuku station leads into an underground mall lined with shops and restaurants. There are some good lunch-time specials to be had here. Follow the mall to the Shinjuku post office exit and take the stairs to the right. Ahead of you is the **Shinjuku Center building,** which offers the Toto Super Space, a bathroom and kitchen display venue complete with a 'Toilet Zone' and a free observation port on the 53rd floor. Next door is the **Yasuda Kaisai-Kaijo building.** On the 42nd floor is **Tōgō Seiji Art Museum.** The museum is notable mainly for its purchase, at more than ¥5 billion, of Van Gogh's *Sunflowers*. The museum is, however, mainly a forum for the work of the Japanese artist Tōgō Seiji. Entry is ¥500; the museum is open from 9.30 am to 5 pm, Monday to Friday.

The **Shinjuku Mitsui building** is only worth a detour if you are a photography buff. On the 1st floor is the **Pentax Forum** (☎ 3348-2941). The exhibition space has changing exhibits by photographers sponsored by Pentax. The best part of the Pentax Forum, however, is the vast array of Pentax cameras, lenses and other optical equipment on display. It is completely hands-on – you can snap away with the cameras and use the huge 1000mm lenses to peer through the windows of neighbouring buildings. Admission is free, and it's open daily from 10.30 am to 6.30 pm.

On the opposite corner of the intersection is the **Shinjuku Sumitomo building,** which bills itself as 'a building that's actually a city', a concept the Japanese seem to find particularly appealing (Sunshine City in Ikebukuro is another such building). The Sumitomo building has a hollow core. The ground floor and basement feature a 'jewel palace' (a jewellery shopping mall) and a general shopping centre. There is a free observation platform on the 51st floor, which is a good deal when you consider the inflated prices being charged by Tokyo Tower and Sunshine City for entry to their observatories.

By now you cannot but have noticed the towering **Tokyo Metropolitan Government Offices.** Some 13,000 government workers sweat over the administrative paperwork of running Tokyo in these buildings. The Citizen's Plaza features shops, restaurants, a passport section and, curiously, a blood donation room.

If you are in the mood for a bit of eccentric high tech, the interior of the **Shinjuku NS building,** just down the road, is hollow, like the Sumitomo building, featuring a 1600 sq metre area from which you can gaze upward at the transparent roof. Overhead, at 110m, is a 'sky bridge'. The square itself features a 29m pendulum clock, listed by the *Guinness Book of Records* as the largest in the world. The 29th and 30th floors have a large number of restaurants, including a branch of the Spaghetti Factory. On the 5th floor, you can browse through the showrooms of Japanese computer companies in the OA Centre.

At this point you have basically exhausted west Shinjuku's walking possibilities, unless you opt for a stroll in the rather drab **Shinjuku Central Park.** The best option is probably to walk back to Shinjuku station via the underground arcade and grab a coffee or a bite to eat along the way. ■

東京 東京 東京 東京 東京 東京 東京 東京 東京 東京 東京 東京 東京 東京 東京 東京 東京 東京

going beforehand and keeping a close lookout for the English signposting.

Shinjuku effectively divides into two areas demarcated by the station. On the west side are the skyscrapers, several of which are worth visiting, including the latest addition to the skyline, the imposing Tokyo Metropolitan Government Offices. The eastern side of the station is far and away the liveliest part of Shinjuku.

West Side

As the city's high-rise centre, this is supposed to be one of the few stable areas in earthquake-prone Tokyo – hopefully, that's true.

Tokyo Metropolitan Government Offices

Known as Tokyo Tochō (☎ 5321-1111), these two adjoining buildings are worth a visit for both their stunning architecture and the great views from the twin observation floors of the 202m-tall No 1 building. Despite the critics, most visitors are won over by the buildings' complex symmetry and computer-chip appearance. Particularly impressive is the spacious Citizen's Plaza in front of the No 1 building – more reminiscent of a Roman amphitheatre than anything Japanese.

The No 2 building is also appealing, with its three tiered asymmetrical design. Con-

necting the two buildings is an open plaza called Fureai-Mall. With several modern sculptures scattered about, this is a good spot for a picnic lunch.

To reach the No 1 building's observation

東京 東京 東京 東京 東京 東京 東京 東京 東京 東京 東京 東京 東京 東京 東京 東京 東京

East Shinjuku Walking Tour
Time: About two hours
Distance: About 2km
Highlights: Kabukichō, Golden Gai, department stores

In Shinjuku station, follow the east exit or Kabukichō exit signs. Once you have passed through the ticket gates, take the 'My City' exit. As you surface, directly ahead of you is the **Studio Alta building**. You can't miss its enormous video screen.

Continue walking east down Shinjuku-dōri. This area is good for men's clothing and shoes – there are often bargains here. A little further on is **Kinokuniya bookshop**, with its superb collection of English books (especially books on Japan and Japanese text books) on the 6th floor. Continue walking and you pass **Mitsukoshi department store** on the right and **Isetan** on the left. Isetan, in particular, is a department store that is worth a browse. It has everything from arts and crafts to fashionable boutiques. The top floor harbours **Isetan Museum**, Tokyo's best-regarded department store art gallery.

Turn left at Isetan and walk down to Yasukuni-dōri. Down a lane on the opposite side of the road is **Hanazono-jinja Shrine**. While it is not one of Tokyo's major shrines, it is nestled so close to Tokyo's most infamous red-light district that its clientele can make for some interesting people-watching. The shrine has a reputation for bringing success to business ventures – both legitimate and otherwise.

Exit Hanazono-jinja onto **Golden Gai**, a tiny warren of alleyways devoted entirely to small, stand-up watering holes. Traditionally the haunt of bohemian Tokyoites (writers and the like), it is a safe area to take a walk through, even by night. You may not, however, be welcome in many of the bars – it's regulars only. By day it is usually deserted. It is also an area that is said to be gradually being bought up by Seibu – in which case it will probably not be long before we see another department store going up here. However, for the time being Golden Gai hangs on.

Continue in the same direction along the alleyways that run parallel to Yasukuni-dōri and you reach **Kabukichō**, Tokyo's most notorious red-light district. Despite its reputation, Kabukichō remains a relatively safe area to stroll around. Most of what goes on in these environs is pretty much off limits to foreigners, though single *gaijin* males are likely to be approached by touts offering to take them to an overpriced strip club.

Kabukichō is probably one of the more imaginative red-light areas in the world, with 'soaplands' (massage parlours), love hotels, 'no-pants' coffee shops (it's the waitresses who doff their briefs, not the customers), peep shows, so-called pink cabarets ('pink' is the Japanese equivalent of 'blue' in English), porno-video booths and strip shows that involve audience participation. As you walk through streets lined with neon signs and crowded with drunken salarymen, high-pitched female voices wail out invitations to their establishments through distorting sound systems, and Japanese punks earn a few extra yen passing out advertisements for telephone clubs. *Tere kure*, as these clubs are known, have become particularly popular. Japanese men pay an hourly fee for a room, a telephone and a list of girls' telephone numbers – if the two like the sound of each other, they can make a date to meet.

Follow the walking tour along the perimeter of Kabukichō and look for the **Tokyo Kaisen Ichiba**, or the fish market, on your right. It is not particularly big as fish markets go, but there is a great restaurant upstairs. Turn left here into the square dominated by the enormous **Koma Theatre**. The Koma started its life as a movie theatre, but quickly switched to stage performances. It still hosts performances of a more mainstream variety than those elsewhere in Kabukichō. The square facing the Koma is ringed by cinemas and is also a popular busking spot at night, though yakuza are usually quick about moving anyone too popular along. Look for the **Virtual Theatre** – a high-tech, full-sensory impact cinema – which is also located in this square. Take any of the lanes radiating off the square to see Kabukichō at its best.

From this point wander back to Yasukuni-dōri and take one of the lanes that connect it with Shinjuku-dōri. Like much of Shinjuku, these lanes are lined with restaurants, shot bars and shops. It's another area popular with buskers and good to linger (look for the revolving sushi bars) if the crowds aren't too overwhelming. ■

東京 東京 東京 東京 東京 東京 東京 東京 東京 東京 東京 東京 東京 東京 東京 東京 東京

floors, take one of the two 1st floor lifts. The observatories are open from 9.30 am to 5 pm on weekdays, to 7 pm on weekends and holidays. Admission is free.

East Side

The east side is an area to wander through and wonder. While the west side is showy, administrative and planned, Shinjuku's east side is spontaneous chaos. The chief east-side attractions include **Hanazono-jinja shrine**, the many department stores, and the colourful, if sleazy, **Kabukichō** and **Golden Gai** areas.

From Shinjuku station's eastern exit, your first sight is the **Studio Alta** building, with its huge video screen showing ads and video clips day and night. The sheltered area beneath the screen is Shinjuku's most popular meeting place, though like the Almond coffee shop in Roppongi, it has become so popular that finding the person you're meeting is something of an ordeal. Opposite Studio Alta, close to the My City exit of Shinjuku station, is a small concrete plaza that has become a popular spot for bands to perform in the evenings.

To the right of Studio Alta, about 100m up Shinjuku-dōri, on your left, is **Kinokuniya bookshop**. The sheltered area here is also a popular meeting place. Around Kinokuniya are shops selling discounted clothes and shoes, and some cheap second-hand camera shops thrive on the backstreets. The area abounds in fast-food joints, cheap noodle shops, reasonably priced western food and some of the best Chinese food in Japan.

Of all the department store art museums in Tokyo, **Isetan Museum** (☎ 3352-1111) in Isetan department store is considered the best. Exhibitions change frequently; they never disappoint. The museum is open daily from 10 am to 7.30 pm. Admission changes with exhibitions but is usually ¥500 to ¥1000.

Among the city's newest and largest indoor malls, **Takashimaya Times Square** (☎ 5631-1111) contains a Takashimaya department store, HMV records, an IMAX theatre, two food courts, a Joypolis virtual reality game centre, a Tōkyū Hands department store and countless smaller stores. The giant branch of Kinokuniya bookshop in the annex of the complex (connected by an aerial walkway) houses perhaps the largest collection of English-language books in the city.

HARAJUKU & AOYAMA　原宿／青山

Harajuku and Aoyama melt into each other, yet they are very different areas. Harajuku teems with teenagers swapping pocket money for Mickey Mouse caps and string vests (Takeshita-dōri is the place to see them in action), while Aoyama is the domain of chic boutiques and ersatz Parisian cafes. A stroll down Harajuku's tree-lined Omote-sandō into Aoyama comes as a welcome relief from the push-and-shove chaos of other consumer villages like Shinjuku.

The chief attractions are Meiji-jingū – one of Japan's finest shrines – the bustling action of Takeshita-dōri and Nezu Art Museum in Aoyama. Try and fit in a cup of coffee on Omote-sandō along the way.

East of Harajuku and Aoyama, Nishi-Azabu (Map 7) is a buffer zone between Tokyo chic and the let-it-all-hang-out approach of Roppongi. There aren't many attractions by day in Nishi-Azabu, but it's home to some of Tokyo's best restaurants and clubs.

Harajuku

One of the best (and trendiest) attractions in Harajuku (Map 7) is Omote-sandō. This tree-lined avenue sports al fresco coffee shops, trendy boutiques and a good cross section of restaurants. Omote-sandō is at its best on a Sunday, when the street is closed to traffic and Tokyo's beautiful people come to strut their stuff. (See the Tokyo Cafe Society boxed text in the Places to Eat chapter.)

Further down Omote-sandō at the intersection of Meiji-dōri is a Harajuku landmark, **Laforet**. A large space on the front of the building is used for cryptic advertising. You'll see a fascinating spectrum of trendy types passing in and out – a very popular spot with talent-spotting Japanese photographers. Inside are fashionable boutiques; downstairs is an HMV, where you can check out the latest CDs on the headphones provided.

Turning right onto Meiji-dōri (look for the Condomania shop on the corner), you could walk into Shibuya in around 15 minutes.

Further down Omote-sandō, look for the **Oriental Bazaar** (see the Shopping chapter) and a host of boutiques with names like 'Gallerie de Pop' and 'Coccoon'. The best known of Harajuku's boutiques is the **Hanae Mori building**, designed by Tange Kenzō and featuring the work of Hanae Mori, perhaps Japan's most famous fashion designer. There is also an antiques bazaar in the basement.

Meiji-jingū Shrine Next door to Yoyogi-kōen Park, this is without a doubt Tokyo's, if not Japan's, most splendid Shintō shrine. Completed in 1920, Meiji-jingū was constructed in honour of Emperor Meiji and Empress Shōken. Unfortunately, the shrine was destroyed by WWII bombing. Rebuilding was completed in 1958.

Meiji-jingū might be a reconstruction, but unlike so many others, it was rebuilt with all the features of a Shintō shrine preserved. The shrine itself was built with Japanese cypress, while the cypress for the huge torii came from Ali Shan in Taiwan.

In the grounds of the shrine (on the left, before the second set of torii) is **Meiji-jingū-gyoen Park**. The park, formerly an imperial garden, has some very peaceful walks and is almost deserted on weekdays. It is particularly beautiful in June, when the irises are in bloom. Admission is ¥500; it's open daily from 9 am to 4.30 pm.

As you approach Meiji-jingū, there are so many signs indicating the way to the **Meiji-jingū Treasure Museum** that you tend to feel obliged to pay it a visit. In fact, the collection of items from the lives of the emperor and empress is not very exciting. It includes official garments, portraits and other imperial odds and ends. Entry is ¥200; it's open from 9 am to 4.30 pm, closed on the third Friday of each month.

If you visit the shrine on a Sunday, you'll have to wade through a peculiar gathering which forms on the bridge over the JR tracks leading into the shrine grounds. This is the weekly meeting of Tokyo's 'Goths', a subculture of young women with pale white faces who dress in elaborate, black costumes and listen to the Japanese equivalent of the Smiths and Morrissey. They come here to have their pictures taken, so don't be shy about snapping a few – some of the outfits are truly startling.

Yoyogi-kōen Park Sunday in Yoyogi-kōen used to be one of Tokyo's prime attractions, when local bands gathered to give free concerts on the pathways into the park. Sadly, the police have put a stop to this, and now Yoyogi is just another park. That said, with lots of wide open spaces and some flowering trees, it's not a bad place for a picnic or some sports on the grass.

You can still catch glimpses of the former spectacle if you go on a Sunday, as a few die-hard performers haven't heard that the show is over. In particular, the city's rockabilly fans can still be seen doing highly stylised 50s dance routines to taped music. One wonders how long this cult will survive.

If you cross the pedestrian overpass from the park that leads down toward Shibuya, you may find a flea market in the open space on the other side. There is a bandstand here as well, and on some weekends, Tokyo's hip-hop community gets together and revives another ancient dance style, in this case, break dancing.

Ota Memorial Art Museum This museum (☎ 3403-0880) has an excellent collection of *ukiyo-e* prints and offers a good opportunity to see works by Japanese masters of the art, including Hiroshige. The museum is open from 10.30 am to 5.30 pm, closed Monday and from the 26th to the end of each month. Entry is ¥500; extra for special exhibitions.

Do! Family Art Museum Very close to Ota Memorial Art Museum, Do! Family Art Museum (☎ 3470-4540) has another collection of wood-block prints, with some 2000 exhibits by 84 artists. Most are Japanese, but

American and French works (featuring Paul Jacoulet, who was based in Japan during the 1930s) are also present. It's an interesting contrast to the Ota museum. Entry is ¥300; it's open from 10 am to 6 pm, closed Saturday and Sunday.

Takeshita-dōri This teeming alley veers somewhere between teenage kitsch and subcultural fetish. One of the biggest shops in this vein is about halfway along Takeshita-dōri: Octopus Army. It's more mainstream than some of its competitors, but it offers an interesting browse. Other diversions include punk accessories, trendy hair boutiques, fast-food joints and cuddly toys.

Aoyama

Aoyama (Map 7) is not rich in sights, but it's only a 15 minute walk from Harajuku. The area is worthwhile mainly for the fashionable Killer-dōri, and for several museums and galleries.

If you arrive in Aoyama from Harajuku along Aoyama-dōri, keep walking until you reach Gaien-nishi-dōri. This is better known as **Killer-dōri**, so named for its fashionable boutiques. On the right-hand corner of the intersection is the **Japan Traditional Craft Center** (see the Arts, Crafts & Antiques entry in the Shopping chapter for details). On the corner diagonally opposite the craft center is another boutique building, regarded highly by Tokyoites, **Bell Commons**.

Up Killer-dōri, on the left-hand side, is the **Watari Museum of Contemporary Art** (☎ 3402-3001), which hosts many current exhibits. Admission averages about ¥700. Exhibits are advertised in the lobby, and you can browse their enormous collection of obscure postcards (around ¥150 each). There's an excellent art bookshop and a small coffee shop in the basement, and exhibition space for young nonmainstream artists. It's open from 11 am to 7 pm, closed Monday.

Look for **On Sundays**, a funky little shop nearby with another good supply of postcards and art books.

Back down the other end of Aoyama-dōri,

south of Omote-sandō, are some minor attractions. The **Spiral building** will interest architecture fans. There is a coffee shop in the front of the building, and modern art exhibitions are sometimes held in the atrium. Further down, on the opposite side of the road, is the **Aoyama Oval Plaza**, which has an antiques market. More antiques shops are on Kottō-dōri, which runs south-west off Aoyama-dōri, close to the Spiral building.

Nezu Fine Art Museum This museum (☎ 3400-2536) in Minami-Aoyama is a highly rated exhibition space with a well-established collection of Japanese art – paintings, calligraphy and sculpture – as well as Chinese and Korean art exhibits and a teahouse where tea ceremonies are performed. There are around 7000 exhibits here, including some 'Important Cultural Properties'. As well as some notable Japanese art, Sinophiles will find the collection of Shang dynasty bronzes particularly interesting.

The museum is nestled amid delightful gardens (21,000 sq m) with seven traditional teahouses. From Omote-sandō subway station, walk down Omote-sandō away from Harajuku. Turn right at the end of the road and look for the museum on the left. Entry is ¥1000; it's open from 9.30 am to 4.30 pm, closed Monday.

Honda Welcome Plaza On Aoyama-dōri, beside the Aoyama-itchōme subway station, is the Honda Welcome Plaza (☎ 3423-4118), a showroom in which classic Honda Grand Prix motorcycles and Formula One cars are displayed. Displays also include the latest Honda products and a projection room with a 'sonic floor', where you can watch races with the sensation that you are actually in the thick of it all.

Aoyama Cemetery Known as Aoyama Rei-en, this cemetery dates back to 1872. Occupying some very expensive real estate, it is a prestigious spot from which to retire into the great unknown. It is also a pleasant, leafy retreat from Aoyama chic.

SHIBUYA 渋谷

While it may look like Shinjuku, Shibuya (Map 7) goes about its business with an air of diligently acquired elegance. The area is studded with department stores that vie for the patronage of cash-loaded young Japanese. Shibuya is not rich in sights, but it is a good place for department store browsing, shopping and dining out.

If you leave JR Shibuya station by the north-west (Hachiko) exit, you'll see one of Shibuya's main sights and the exit's namesake: a statue of the dog Hachiko. The story of this dog is rather touching: in the 1920s, a professor who lived near Shibuya station kept a small Akita dog, who would come to the station every day to await his master's return. The master died in 1925, but the dog continued to show up and wait at the station until his own death 11 years later. The poor dog's faithfulness was not lost on the Japanese, and they built a statue to honour his memory. The statue itself is nothing special and is usually surrounded by a pack of sullen youths.

Tepco Electric Energy Museum

Called Denryoku-kan, the Tepco Electric Energy Museum is the building on Jingū-dōri with the R2D2-shaped silver-domed building (visible from the Hachiko statue). It is one of Tokyo's better science museums, offering seven floors of dynamic exhibitions on every conceivable aspect of electricity. There are innumerable hands-on exhibits, and admission is free. Get the excellent, free English handout at the reception desk. The museum is open from 10.30 am to 6.30 pm, closed Wednesday.

NHK Studio Plaza

This is a broadcasting museum (☎ 3485-8034), with sets from Japanese drama serials and exhibitions demonstrating the behind-the-scenes activity on a broadcasting set. It's a reasonably entertaining rainy day activity. The plaza is closer to Harajuku station than it is to Shibuya station. It is open from 10 am to 6 pm, closed one Monday a month. Entry is ¥200.

Tobacco & Salt Museum

Not to be confused with the National Car Wax and Yogurt Museum, this small museum has some fairly interesting exhibits detailing the history of tobacco and the methods of salt production practised in pre-modern Japan (Japan has no salt mines and until recently harvested salt from the sea). As usual, there's little in the way of English explanations, but a lot of the material is self-explanatory. There are no warnings about the risks of smoking and areas are set aside for those who crave a good smoke after touring the museum. It's open from 10 am to 6 pm, closed Monday. Entry is ¥100.

Love Hotel Hill

Take the road up Dogen-zaka to the left of the 109 building, and at the top of the hill, on the side streets that run off the main road, is a concentration of love hotels catering to all tastes. The buildings alone are interesting, representing a range of architectural pastiche, from miniature Gothic castles to kitsch *Arabian Nights*. It's okay to wander in and take a look.

Beam Building

The Beam building is usually cited as one of Tokyo's more startling examples of vulgar architecture. Maybe, but in Shibuya it hardly stands out. The building houses several karaoke parlours and hundreds of the latest electronic games. It's open from 10 am to 8 pm. Admission is free, but the games eat through those ¥100 coins at an alarming rate.

ROPPONGI 六本木

There's no reason to come here by day, but by night it's the capital of Tokyo. See the Entertainment chapter for more.

EBISU 恵比寿

Ebisu (Map 8) cannot compete with big hubs on the Yamanote line, but its small size and comfortable atmosphere make for enjoyable strolling. Ebisu is probably best considered a nightspot, as it houses some good restaurants and bars. If you come during the day, most sights worth seeing are in the new Ebisu

Garden Place, easily reached from JR Ebisu station by an aerial walkway.

Ebisu Garden Place

This is a complex of shops, restaurants and a 39 floor tower surrounded by an open mall area, perfect for hanging out on warmer days. The Garden Place also features the headquarters of **Sapporo Breweries**, which contains the **Beer Museum Yebisu** (☎ 5423-7255). There are lots of good exhibits, the best of which is the 'Tasting Lounge', where you can sample Sapporo's various brews in a pleasant space decorated with rare European beer steins. Entry is free, and the museum is open from 10 am to 6 pm, closed Monday.

Also in the Garden Place complex is **Sapporo Beer Station**, which has reasonably priced draught beer and food like German sausages, steak and seafood. It's open daily from 10.30 am to 10 pm.

There are lots of outdoor cafes scattered around the complex. If you're hungry, most serve light meals as well. The restaurants on the 38th and 39th floors of **Ebisu Garden Place Tower** offer excellent views.

Ebisu Garden Place is also home to the **Tokyo Metropolitan Museum of Photography** (☎ 3280-0031), the city's largest photography exhibition space. Most exhibits are very current, and there is even a wing devoted to computer-generated graphics. Entry is ¥500 for the regular exhibits, ¥600 for special exhibits and ¥1000 for a ticket into all exhibits. It's open from 10 am to 6 pm, closed the second and fourth Wednesday of the month.

AKASAKA 赤坂

Akasaka (Map 3) is the area with the greatest concentration of topnotch hotels, including the ANA, New Ōtani and Akasaka Prince. These effectively form a ring around the centre of Akasaka, a huddle of narrow streets lined largely with restaurants. There may not be much in the way of sights besides Hie-jinja Shrine and the occasional museum, but Akasaka is the place to indulge in some of Tokyo's best food.

Hie-jinja Shrine

The shrine itself is by no means one of Tokyo's major attractions; it's modern, drab and largely cement. The highlight is the walk up to the shrine through a 'tunnel' of orange torii. On a sunny day, the play of the light on the torii is pretty, but Hie-jinja is only worth going out of your way for when the cherry blossoms are out. If you're wondering about the carved monkey clutching one of her young, she is emblematic of the shrine's ability to offer protection against the threat of a miscarriage.

Akasaka Detached Palace

This is known officially as Geihinkan, or State Guesthouse. It was built in 1909 with an eye to Versailles and the Louvre as the residence of the crown prince (Emperor Hirohito), and aimed to bestow the imperial family with a residence matching their royal counterparts in Europe. Today the palace is used as a guesthouse for visiting dignitaries.

The palace can be viewed from the outside at its west entry gate (around 15 minutes walk from Akasaka). It is not possible to enter. It is arguably not worth the effort of trudging up here unless you have an abiding interest in neo-baroque architecture.

National Diet Building

Gaining admission to this austere building is more trouble than it is worth. You will need to organise it with your embassy or via an introduction from a Diet member – fat chance of the latter for the average visitor. Rest assured, however, that you are not missing much. Proceedings within are notoriously dull.

Just north of this is the **National Diet Library**, which houses over five million books, open to anyone over 20 years of age. Behind the National Diet building is the **Parliamentary Museum** and gardens. The exhibition here traces the history of constitutional government in Japan (with some English labelling). It's open weekdays from 9.30 am to 4.30 pm; entry is free.

Suntory Museum of Art

The Suntory Museum of Art (☎ 3470-1073) is on the 11th floor of the Suntory building, and offers a pleasant area in which to view its collection of over 2000 traditional artefacts, including lacquerware and pottery. The premises also have a library and a tea room where you can indulge in that most celebrated of Japanese leisured pursuits, the tea ceremony (an extra charge of ¥500). Entry is ¥700 to ¥1000, depending on the exhibit; it's open from 10 am to 5 pm, closed Monday.

Hotel Sights

Even the luxury hotels in Akasaka deserve a mention. Notable is the **New Ōtani**, which has managed to preserve part of a 400-year-old garden that once belonged to a Tokugawa regent. On the 6th floor of the New Ōtani Garden Court building (the north building), the **New Ōtani Art Museum** (☎ 3221-4111) has a decent collection of modern Japanese and French paintings. Free for guests of the hotel, entry is ¥500 for nonguests and may be higher for special exhibitions. It's open from 10 am to 6 pm, closed Monday. If you're still in Akasaka at night, try a hotel sky-bar and check out the night view of Tokyo.

Ark Hills

Ark stands for 'Akasaka-Roppongi knot' – pinioned between Akasaka and Roppongi is a much-touted 'subcity' featuring display rooms, banks, restaurants, entertainment and even housing. It's worth a browse, as much for an insight into how the Japanese see the future as anything else.

Aoyama-dōri

Down Aoyama-dōri, in the direction of Aoyama-itchōme subway station, are a couple of sights. About halfway to the station, on the left side, is **Sogetsu Kaikan**, a centre for the Sogetsu school of avant-garde ikebana. On the 6th floor is **Sogetsu Art Museum**, with its bewilderingly eclectic collection of art from across the centuries and the four corners of the world – from Indian Buddhas to works by Matisse. Entry

is ¥500; it's open from 10 am to 5 pm, closed Sunday.

OTHER ATTRACTIONS

Many of the attractions listed here are off the main colour maps. Where no map reference is given, see Map 1 for the general location; individual listings give details on transportation and directions.

Tokyo Tower

As a tourist attraction, Tokyo Tower (Map 3) is an anachronism. Built in 1958 for broadcasting through the Kantō region, it was modelled on the Eiffel Tower – it is just over 30m higher than its Parisian counterpart.

As a tourist trap, the tower is probably not worth seeing. The Grand Observation Platform, at only 150m, costs ¥800, while a trip to the Special Observation Platform, a further 100m up, is another ¥600. The Tokyo Tower also features an overpriced aquarium (¥1000), a wax museum (¥750), the uninspired Holographic Mystery Zone (¥300) and showrooms.

The tower is a fair trudge from Roppongi. If you must go, take the Hibiya subway line one stop to Kamiyachō station. Observation platforms are open daily from 9 am to 6 pm (to 8 pm from 16 March to 15 November, but to 9 pm in August).

Parks & Gardens

Many of Tokyo's parks and gardens are described earlier in this chapter. Those listed here are all inside the loop of the Yamanote line and can be easily reached.

Koishikawa Kōraku-en Garden Right next to the Kōraku-en Amusement Park (see the Amusement Parks section) is one of the most beautiful and least-visited (by foreigners at least) gardens in Tokyo. Established in the mid-17th century, it incorporates elements of Chinese and Japanese landscaping. Any visitor to Tokyo with even the slightest interest in gardens should make a point of visiting this one. Admission is ¥300; it's open daily from 9 am to 5 pm.

THINGS TO SEE & DO

Rikugi-en Garden Near JR Komagome station on the Yamanote line, Rikugi-en is a fine stroll garden with landscaped views unfolding at every turn of the pathways that crisscross the grounds. The garden is rich in literary associations: its name is taken from the six principles of *waka* poetry, while the garden invokes famous scenes from Chinese and Japanese literature. Entry is ¥300; it's open daily from 9 am to 4.30 pm.

Nature Study Garden Unique in Tokyo, the garden (Map 8) tries to preserve the original flora of Tokyo in undisciplined profusion. There are some wonderful stress-relieving walks through wild woods and swamps, making this one of Tokyo's least known and most appealing getaways. The garden is open from 9 am to 4 pm (5 pm in summer), closed Monday. Entry is ¥210.

To get there, take the east exit of Meguro station on the Yamanote line and walk straight ahead for around 15 minutes; look for the garden on the left. You can also take any of the buses that leave from in front of the east exit of Meguro station and get off at the first stop (Shirogane-dai).

Shinjuku-gyoen Garden On Shinjuku-dōri, right in front of Shinjuku-gyoen-mae subway station, Shinjuku-gyoen (Map 6) has a Japanese garden, a French garden, a hothouse containing exotic tropical plants and, near the hothouse, a pond with giant carp. Entry is ¥200; it's open from 9 am to 4.30 pm, closed Monday.

Museums & Galleries

As well as the museums and galleries described earlier in this chapter, Tokyo has the following mainstream places. Those with more arcane interests should turn to the TIC's *Museums & Art Galleries* pamphlet or to *Tokyo Museums – A Complete Guide* by Thomas & Ellen Flannigan, which has everything from the Parasitological Museum to the Fisherman's Culture Museum.

Edo-Tokyo Museum Undoubtedly the best recent addition to Tokyo's profusion of museums is Edo-Tokyo Museum (☎ 3626-8000). This massive, futuristic building houses a re-creation of old Edo and post-Meiji Tokyo. The six floors of exhibits and display areas are presented with praiseworthy attention to detail, and you're free to wander and have a hands-on experience of Tokyo's past. The main exhibit is life-size, but there are smaller models, including one of old Edo-jō. It is well worth the ¥600 entry charge. It's open from 10 am to 6 pm (8 pm on Friday), closed Monday. Edo-Tokyo Museum is close to Ryōgoku station on the JR Sōbu line.

Sumō Museum Also close to Ryōgoku station is Kokugikan Sumō Hall and the adjoining Sumō Museum (☎ 3622-0366). Entry is free; it's open Monday to Friday from 9.30 am to 4.30 pm. Note that when sumō tournaments are on at the stadium, only those holding tickets to the matches can enter the museum.

Kantō Earthquake Memorial Museum Another 10 minutes walk on from the Sumō Stadium is the Kantō Earthquake Memorial Museum (☎ 3623-1200), with sobering exhibits of artefacts that survived the 1923 earthquake. Entry is free; it's open from 9 am to 5 pm, closed Monday.

Tokyo Metropolitan Teien Art Museum This museum (☎ 3443-0201) hosts art exhibitions, but its appeal lies principally in the building itself, an Art Deco structure built in 1933 and designed by French architect Henri Rapin. It was originally the home of Prince Asaka (1887-1981), who was associated with the 'Rape of Nanjing' in 1936. It became a museum in 1983, and is open from 10 am to 6 pm, closed the second and fourth Wednesday of the month. Admission fees vary with exhibits; entry to the attached garden is ¥100. To get there, take the east exit of Meguro station on the Yamanote line and walk straight ahead for around 15 minutes; the museum is on the left. Or, take any of the buses that leave from in front of the east exit of Meguro station and get off at the first stop (Shirogane-dai).

Meguro Museum of Art This museum (☎ 3714-1201) is usually worth a visit, but you can check the *Tokyo Journal* to see what's currently on display. The building is a delight – it's airy and well-lit compared with many other Tokyo art museums, and there is a coffee shop with pleasant views of the grounds on the 1st floor. The museum is open from 10 am to 6 pm, closed Monday; entry is ¥900. Take the west exit of Meguro station, walk straight ahead down Meguro-dōri and turn right onto Yamanote-dōri. The museum is on the right.

Fukagawa Edo Museum A rather long way from anywhere else, near Monzen-nakachō subway station on the Tōzai line, is the Fukagawa Edo Museum (☎ 3630-8625). This museum is a real treat, and well worth the effort of getting out to see it. In a cavernous room, the museum re-creates a 17th century Edo neighbourhood. You can slip off your shoes, explore the homes, and handle the daily utensils and children's toys. It's open from 9.30 am to 5 pm, closed the second and fourth Monday of the month. Entry is ¥300.

Japanese Sword Museum Fans of Japanese swords highly recommend this collection of more than 6000 swords. Entry is ¥515; it's open from 9 am to 4 pm, closed Monday. The nearest station is Sangubashi station on the Odakyū line.

Hatakeyama Memorial Hall For anyone with an interest in tea ceremony, check out Hatakeyama Memorial Hall (☎ 3447-5787), east of Shinagawa station. The extensive collection includes many 'Important Cultural Properties' and is complemented by a tea-ceremony garden. Admission is ¥500, and the hall is normally open from 10 am to 4.30 pm, Tuesday to Sunday; best to ring beforehand.

Hara Museum of Contemporary Art In Shinagawa, the Hara Museum of Contemporary Art (☎ 3445-0651) is one of Tokyo's more adventurous art spaces. Given that exhibitions change frequently, it is a good idea to check what's on before making your way out here. The Bauhaus design and the cafe, which overflows into a delightful garden, are attractions in themselves. Entry is ¥700; open from 11 am to 5 pm, closed Monday. The museum is around 15 minutes walk from Shinagawa station on the JR Yamanote line.

Asakura Chōso Museum In Nippori, this is worth a visit for the building and grounds. The museum commemorates sculptor Asakura Fumio (1883-1964), whose primary work consisted of realistic sculptures of people and cats, but the real attraction is the traditional Japanese house and garden at the back of the museum, designed by the artist. You're free to wander the lovely house and sit on the tatami, enjoying the peaceful view over the garden. Upstairs in the Morning Sun Room and the Poised Mind Room are some excellent ink scrolls and beautiful old *tansu* (wooden chests). The museum is open from 9.30 am to 4.30 pm, closed Monday and Friday. Admission is ¥300. For directions, see the Nippori to Nishi-Nippori Walk boxed text further in this section.

Museum of Maritime Science Down in the Daiba/Tokyo Bay area, this large, ship-shaped museum (Map 9) (☎ 5500-1111) looks like a classic tourist trap, but is actually one of Tokyo's better museums. There are four floors of excellent displays dealing with every aspect of ships and shipping, with loads of highly detailed models, including a 4m-long version of the largest battleship ever built, the *Yamato*, stunning in detail and craftsmanship. There are lots of hands-on exhibits which kids will love and a pool on the museum's roof where, for ¥100, they can pilot radio-controlled boats and submarines.

Alongside the main building, two boats are moored: a floating tourist trap (the *Floating Pavilion* and a retired Antarctic survey vessel (the *Soya*). The museum and boats are open from 10 am to 5 pm (6 pm on weekends and holidays). Admission to the main hall is ¥700 for adults, ¥400 for children junior high

THINGS TO SEE & DO

東京 東京 東京 東京 東京 東京 東京 東京 東京 東京 東京 東京 東京 東京 東京 東京 東京 東京

Nippori to Nishi-Nippori Walk
Time: About three hours with stops
Distance: About 2km
Highlights: Yanaka Cemetery, Asakura Chōso Museum, temples
Best Season: Cherry blossom/autumn foliage seasons

Spared aerial bombing during WWII, the area around Nippori and Nishi-Nippori stations retains some of the flavour of Edo. It is an area of small temples, atmospheric old cemeteries and pleasant little shops. With a bit of determined searching, you can even find some old wooden houses of the sort that used to predominate in Edo. More than anything else, the area invites aimless wandering, poking about tiny streets and turning up small reminders of the way things used to be.

The following walk is a suggested route from Nippori to Nishi-Nippori stations on the Yamanote line, but you should take the time to deviate from the path as your whim suggests. Note that there are no admission fees to enter the grounds of the temples listed here, but some charge fees to enter their inner precincts.

To start, take the south exit from Nippori station. Taking a left out of the exit will lead you across the railway tracks to a stairway leading up to **Yanaka Cemetery** (Yanaka Rei-en). You can pause here to orient yourself, using a large area map at the base of the stairs. At the top of the stairs, walk on about 60m until you see a temple on your left. This is **Tenno-ji**, which belongs to the Tendai Buddhist sect. In the main courtyard there is a large Buddha image cast in 1690 which is reminiscent of the Great Buddha in Kamakura.

Leaving Tenno-ji, you enter Yanaka Cemetery proper. You can either stick to the route on the accompanying map and continue straight down the main road which leads past a police box, or take small detours to explore the cemetery. Either way, make your way to the public toilet about 100m past the police box and turn right (west) through the

CHRIS ROWTHORN
Buddhist graves and markers at Yanaka Cemetery

東京 東京 東京 東京 東京 東京 東京 東京 東京 東京 東京 東京 東京 東京 東京 東京 東京 東京

school age and younger. Tickets for the main hall plus boats are ¥1000 for adults and ¥600 for children. To get there, take the Yurikamome New Transit line from Shimbashi station and get off at the Fune-no-kagakukan stop (the museum's name in Japanese).

Temples
Sengaku-ji Temple This temple is included in Tokyo's sights for the story that surrounds it, that of the '47 Rōnin'. A *rōnin* is a masterless samurai, and these ones plotted for two years to have vengeance on the man who caused the death of their master, Lord Asano.

Vengeance was undertaken knowing that they too would have to forfeit their lives. After having brought the head of his enemy to their master's grave, 46 of them were condemned to commit *seppuku* (ritual disembowelment) in the samurai fashion (the 47th apparently got off on a technicality). The story, with its themes of the supreme sacrifice in the name of loyalty, has captured the Japanese imagination as no story has, having been adapted into countless films and plays. The temple is open daily from 9 am to 4.30 pm, and is close to Sengaku-ji subway station on the Toei Asakusa line.

東京 東京 東京 東京 東京 東京 東京 東京 東京 東京 東京 東京 東京 東京 東京 東京 東京 東京

graves toward a residential/mercantile area. After a brief dogleg, this will bring you out in front of a quaint shop selling Buddhist religious goods. Turn right here.

Right after the shop, you will pass **Jōzai-ji**, a temple which is worth a quick look. The next temple on the left is **Chōan-ji**. This Rinzai sect temple was established in 1669. The grounds contain a densely packed graveyard, in the middle of which is the grave of Kano Hogai (1828-88), a famous Japanese painter who established the Tokyo Fine Art School.

About 30m past Chōan-ji, on the left you will see **Matsujuan** soba restaurant, a simple little place with a few food models in the window. This makes a good lunch stop. Try the *tanuki soba* (soba with fried tofu) for ¥500 or, in summer, the *zaru* (cold) soba for ¥550.

Next on the left is **Kannon-ji**, a Shingon sect temple consecrated to Kannon. The grounds contain another small cemetery, which is pleasant for poking around in. Continuing on, you will pass **Kaizō-in**, which is more of an administrative centre than a temple and can safely be missed.

Diagonally across from Kaizō-in, the **Sandara Kōgei** basket store has a good collection of typically Japanese crafts which make good souvenirs. The quality is fairly high and prices are reasonable. Past this, on the left you will see **Ryūsen-ji**, another small Nichiren temple with a cemetery on its grounds. This is worth a quick look.

Soon after Ryūsen-ji, on the right, you will see the **Asakura Chōso Museum**. The perfectly preserved Japanese house in back of the main building is accessed via a door on the 1st floor. See the Other Attractions section in this chapter for details. Before leaving, climb up to the roof of the main building, from which there are good views south to Ueno. The strange Lego-land building visible over Ueno-kōen Park is the Hotel Sofitel Tokyo.

After leaving the museum continue another 100m or so to the next main intersection. Here, in front of you on the right is the entrance to **Keiō-ji**. This is a pleasant little Nichiren temple with an old wooden *honden* (main hall), the sort of which is rarely seen in Tokyo today. Behind the main hall, there is yet another atmospheric old cemetery.

After leaving Keiō-ji, if you're hungry you can walk to nearby **Darjeeling** restaurant for a curry lunch (¥850) or a tea set (¥750); otherwise, take the narrow Suwadai-dōri, which runs along the left side of the temple, heading north toward Nishi-Nippori station.

Eventually, the land drops away on the east side of this road, allowing views over Arakawa-ku. With little but buildings in sight, it can't be said that this vista is particularly prepossessing, but it's easy to image how it must have been in the Edo period when this neighbourhood, known as Dokanyama Hills, was popular for its scenic woodland views.

As you continue north, you will pass several small temples. The most notable of these is **Yōfuku-ji**, the gate of which houses two fierce-looking *nio* guardian figures. Not far beyond this the road leads you straight into **Suwa-jinja**, a shrine established in 1205. Its grounds offer good views over the JR tracks and Nishi-Nippori.

After the shrine, the road leads straight on to **Nishi-Nippori-kōen Park**. Here, turn right and then left, and you will find yourself at Nishi-Nippori station, where you can catch a Yamanote line train or the Chiyoda subway. ■

東京 東京 東京 東京 東京 東京 東京 東京 東京 東京 東京 東京 東京 東京 東京 東京 東京 東京

Zōjō-ji Temple Behind Tokyo Tower is this former funerary temple (Map 3) of the Tokugawas. Like many sights in Tokyo, it has been rebuilt several times in recent history; the last time was in 1974.

Nevertheless, Zōjō-ji remains an interesting temple to visit if you're in the vicinity of the Tokyo Tower. The main gates date from 1605, and are among the nation's 'Important Cultural Properties'. On the temple grounds there is a large collection of statues of Jizō.

Zōjō-ji is about a 10 minute walk north of the Shiba Kōen stop on the Toei Mita subway line (walk in the direction of Tokyo Tower).

Gokoku-ji Temple This is easily reached from Ikebukuro, but gets surprisingly few visitors. One of the few surviving Edo temples, it dates from 1680. The beautiful main hall is labelled an 'Important Cultural Property'. Get there from Gokokuji subway station (look for the English signposting inside the station), two stops from Ikebukuro on the Yūrakuchō line. The temple is approached via a steep flight of stairs.

Cemeteries

Strolling through a cemetery may seem like a grim form of entertainment, but cemeteries

THINGS TO SEE & DO

in Tokyo are usually quite pleasant and make a nice change from the concrete monotony of streets and skyscrapers.

Yanaka Cemetery North of Ueno-kōen and close to Nippori station is Yanaka Cemetery (Map 4), one of Tokyo's oldest. It is worth taking a stroll through the cemetery and continuing to Ueno on foot. The quiet Yanaka area has many old Buddhist temples and speciality shops. (See the Nippori to Nishi-Nippori Walk boxed text earlier in this chapter.)

Zōshigaya Not far south of Sunshine City and Ikebukuro's commercial activity is the old residential district of Zōshigaya (Map 5). Its **cemetery**, around 10 minutes walk south of Sunshine City, is the final resting place of Lafcadio Hearn. It can also be reached from Higashi-Ikebukuro station on the Yūrakuchō line. Take exit No 5, turn right and right again to reach the cemetery.

Just south of the cemetery is the **Zōshigaya Missionary Museum**, a fine wooden structure that was the home of one John Moody McCaleb, who devoted 50 years of his life to good works in Japan. It is well worth a visit. Entry is free; it's open from 9 am to 4.30 pm, closed Monday.

Convention & Exhibition Centres
In the Rinkai-town section of Tokyo Bay, the **Tokyo International Exhibition Center** (Map 9) (☎ 5530-1234) is perhaps the most spacious venue of its kind in the Tokyo region. Better known as 'Tokyo Big Sight', this is one building that's worth a trip just to see it. It's reached by the Yurikamome line which leaves from Shimbashi station.

Makuhari Messe (☎ 043-296-0001), in the Tokyo Bay area of Chiba, attracts more than 10 million people annually to the events held in its exhibition halls.

Hotels and department stores are another often-used forum for major conferences and displays. English-language newspapers and the *Tokyo Journal* regularly list conventions and exhibitions. The Japan External Trade Organization (JETRO; ☎ 3582-5522) pub-

lishes a comprehensive listing of Japan's annual trade fairs. Other large sites include:

Harumi Tokyo International Fair Ground
    (☎ 3533-5311) 5-3-53 Harumi, Chūō-ku, Tokyo
Pacifico Yokohama
    (☎ 045-221-2121) 1-1-1 Minato Mirai, Nishi-ku, Yokohama
Sunshine Convention Center (Map 5)
    (☎ 3989-3486) 3-1 Higashi-Ikebukuro, Toshima-ku, Tokyo
Tokyo Ryūtsū Center (TRC)
    (☎ 3767-2190) 6-1-1 Heiwajima, Ōta-ku, Tokyo
Tokyo Trade Center
    (☎ 3434-4241) Tokyo Trade Center Building, 1-7-8 Kaigan, Minato-ku, Tokyo

Concert Halls & Event Venues
Tokyo plays host to an impressive line-up of events, from concerts to lectures to sporting events. The best way to learn what's going on is the *Tokyo Journal*. You can also pick up the *Tokyo Weekender* from the TIC or ask the staff directly about things of particular interest to you. These are some of Tokyo's larger concert halls and event venues:

Ariake Colosseum (Map 9)
    (☎ 3529-3301) in the Tokyo Bay area, near Kokusai Tenjijō station; tennis, volleyball, pro-wrestling, sumō; 10,000 seats
Kokugikan Sumō Hall
    (☎ 3623-5111) in Sumida-ku, near Ryōgoku station; sumō, boxing, pro-wrestling, concerts; 11,000 seats
Kōrakuen Hall
    (☎ 5800-9999) in Bunkyō-ku, near Kōrakuen station; boxing, pro-wrestling, concerts; 2500 seats
Nihon Budōkan Hall (Map 2)
    (☎ 3216-5100) in Chiyoda, near Kudanshita station; martial arts tournaments, concerts etc; 14,000 seats
Orchard Hall
    (☎ 3477-3244) in Shibuya, near Shibuya station's Hachiko exit; opera, classical music, some sports; 2150 seats
Shibuya Kōkaidō
    (☎ 3463-1211) in Shibuya, near Shibuya station's Hachiko exit; rock/pop concerts, traditional Japanese music concerts; 2318 seats
Tokyo Dome (Big Egg)
    (☎ 5800-9999) in Bunkyō-ku, near Kōrakuen station, three minutes from Suidōbashi station; Yomiuri Giants and Nippon Ham Fighters baseball games, concerts, other sports; 15,000 seats

THINGS TO SEE & DO

東京 東京 東京 東京 東京 東京 東京 東京 東京 東京 東京 東京 東京 東京 東京 東京 東京 東京

Daiba/Tokyo Bay Walking Tour
Time: About four hours with stops
Distance: About 2.5km
Highlights: Harbour views, Museum of Maritime Science, Tokyo Big Sight

Tokyo is rediscovering that it's a waterfront city, and recent years have seen a spate of development in and around the Tokyo Bay area. Perhaps the most popular Tokyo Bay spot is the Daiba/Ariake area (Map 9). Daiba and Ariake are serviced by the difficult-to-pronounce 'Tokyo Rinkai Shinkōtsū Sen', which is usually translated as the 'Tokyo Waterfront New Transit Line'. Luckily, this line also goes by the much shorter name, the 'Yurikamome line'.

While Tokyo Bay isn't as beautiful as some city bays around the world, it does make a nice change from the congestion of central Tokyo. The following day walk takes in a few of the parks, and some of the museums and attractions which have sprung up over recent years. More than a scenic walk, it should be considered a good chance to breathe the sea air and escape the city for a while.

To start, take the Yurikamome line from Shimbashi station near Ginza to Daiba station. The ride itself is interesting, as it crosses **Rainbow Bridge** and affords good views of bay area developments. Upon arrival at Daiba, you have several choices: head to the futuristic **Fuji Television Japan Broadcast Center**, which offers a studio tour and observation platform; head to Shiokaze-kōen Park to relax by the sea; or walk over to the **Decks Tokyo Beach complex** for a bite to eat.

The Fuji Television Center observatory is inside the ball-shaped structure on its upper floors. On clear days, it affords good views of the bay and Rainbow Bridge. A ticket to the observatory also gets you into the Fuji Studio Tour, although this is probably of little interest to foreign visitors as it is all in Japanese. The observatory is open from 10 am to 9 pm, closed Monday. Admission is ¥500.

The Decks Tokyo Beach complex house dozens of trendy restaurants and shops. Since most of the restaurants offer good views to go with the food, the prices tend to be a bit steep. Shiokaze-kōen is a good spot for a waterside picnic on warmer days. Once you've exhausted these possibilities, head to the next stop, the maritime museum. This can be reached by following the shoreline south or by following the map walkways.

The ship-shaped **Museum of Maritime Science** (Fune-no-kagakukan), is one of the better museums in Tokyo. Here, there are scores of excellent ship models and displays. For details on admission and hours, see the museum entry in the Other Attractions section of this chapter.

From the Museum of Maritime Science you have the option of taking the train or walking to the next stop: **Tokyo International Exhibition Center**, better known as 'Tokyo Big Sight' ('Kokusai Tenjijō Big Sight' in Japanese). If you choose to walk (about 20 minutes), follow the 'Center Promenade' walkway. This leads across the flat middle of the island, with the monolithic towers of the bay area rising on all sides (the most distinctive of these is Telecom Center, another building with an observatory from which to view the bay).

The Center Promenade is surrounded on both sides by rather unsuccessful wildflower gardens. After crossing **Dream Bridge**, you will pass the large shopping complex known as **Tokyo Fashion Town**. If you're in the mood for browsing trendy fashion boutiques and the like, stop here; otherwise, continue until Tokyo Big Sight comes into view.

The Big Sight's main hall looks like an Egyptian pyramid which fell to earth upside-down – certainly one of Tokyo's architectural wonders. On the 8th floor of the main hall there is a restaurant and bar, JW's California Grill (☎ 5530-1221), which serves American-style food at mid-budget prices. For a good view of the bay, you can take the lifts or escalators to the roof of the hall, which is open to visitors any time a conference is not in session.

From Tokyo Big Sight, there are two ways to return to central Tokyo: you can either get back on the Yurikamome line and retrace your steps to Shimbashi, or you can walk over to the Rinkai Fukutoshin line and take it two stops to Shin-Kiba station. At Shin-Kiba you can transfer to the JR Keiyō line, which will take you to Tokyo station in less than 10 minutes. ■

東京 東京 東京 東京 東京 東京 東京 東京 東京 東京 東京 東京 東京 東京 東京 東京 東京 東京

Showrooms

The headquarters of most of Japan's big companies are located in Tokyo, and there are ample opportunities to check out their latest products displayed in company showrooms. Since these are all forms of advertising, it goes without saying that they are free. See the relevant area entries for details.

Honda Welcome Plaza (Map 7)
    Aoyama; classic Honda Grand Prix motorcycles and Formula One cars

東京 東京 東京 東京 東京 東京 東京 東京 東京 東京 東京 東京 東京 東京 東京 東京 東京 東京

Japan Inc Tours

Japan is one of the world's mightiest industrial powers, but few people have ever seen how this economic giant operates up close. Guided tours will give you some insight into the day-to-day workings of 'Japan Inc'. The tours listed here are free, regularly scheduled and conducted in English, provided you give advance warning. At most of the contact numbers, someone will be present who speaks English. If this is not the case, or you would like more information, call the TIC (☎ 3201-3331). For additional tours, pick up the TIC's *Industrial Japan* handout. For any of these tours, reserve as early as possible.

Nissan Motors Nissan offers tours of two of its automobile plants in the Tokyo region: the Oppama plant (one hour by train from Tokyo) on the 2nd and 4th Tuesday of each month, two tours starting at 10 am and 2 pm, lasting two hours; and the Murayama plant (45 minutes by train from Tokyo) on the same days as at Oppama, one tour from 10.30 am to noon. For both tours, contact the Nissan Communications Department (☎ 5565-2149; fax 3456-2669).

Honda Motors Honda has tours of three of its automobile plants, Sayama, Suzuka and Hamamatsu, but only the Hamamatsu tour is offered in English. To join the Hamamatsu English tour, you must apply in writing two months in advance to Honda Motor Company, Hamamatsu Factory, 1-13-1, Aoi-Higashiyama, Hamamatsu-shi, Shizuoka Prefecture. Hamamatsu can be reached from Tokyo by train in one or two hours.

Asahi Beer Asahi offers tours (one hour, 20 minutes) of its Sumida Ward brewery three times a day, Monday to Friday. English-speaking guides are available; reservations are necessary for groups of more than five people (☎ 3762-9384).

Suntory Suntory will guide you through its Minato Ward brewery on Monday and Friday, eights times a day. Reserve a few days in advance for the English tour (☎ 3470-1131).

Asahi Newspapers The *Asahi Shimbun* newspaper offers tours of its Chūō Ward office and printing plant three times a day. Reserve at least two days in advance for an English guide (☎ 3545-0366).

Stock Exchange The Tokyo Stock Exchange offers tours in English, by appointment (☎ 3666-0141), Monday to Friday from 9 am to 4 pm.

Bank of Japan The bank offers tours of its operations and international department. Ring for reservations on ☎ 3279-1111, ext 4659. ■

東京 東京 東京 東京 東京 東京 東京 東京 東京 東京 東京 東京 東京 東京 東京 東京 東京 東京

Pentax Forum (Map 6)
West Shinjuku; Japan's best photographers and Pentax' best gear; see the West Shinjuku Walking Tour boxed text in this chapter
Sony Building (Map 3)
Ginza; Tokyo's first and best showroom
Toyota Amlux (Map 5)
Ikebukuro; Toyota's product line on display

Amusement Parks

No 1 on any list of Tokyo amusement parks has to be **Tokyo Disneyland**. Only the Japanese signs reveal that you're a long way from Orange County – Tokyo Disneyland is a near-perfect replica of the famous California original. A few rides may be in slightly different locations, but basically you turn left from the entrance to the African Jungle, head straight on to Fantasyland or turn right to Tomorrowland.

It is open daily (usually from 9 am to 7 pm at least, but ring ☎ 3366-5600 or inquire at the Disneyland information counter at the Yaesu exit of Tokyo station), except for about a dozen days a year (most of them in January).

A variety of tickets is available, including an all-inclusive 'passport' which gives you unlimited access to all the rides for ¥5200 (children aged 12 to 17, ¥4590; those aged four to 11, ¥3570). There are often long queues at popular rides (30 minutes to an hour). Donald Duck-hunting crowds are usually lighter in the morning and heavier on weekends and holidays.

THINGS TO SEE & DO

To get to Tokyo Disneyland, take the Tōzai subway line to Urayasu station. Follow the 'direct bus to Disneyland 340m' sign out of the station. A shop-lined lane leads to the Disneyland bus station, where a ticket will cost ¥200. Or, take the Yūrakuchō subway line to Shin-Kiba station and the JR Keiyō line to Maihama station, right in front of Disneyland's main gate. The Keiyō line runs all the way from Tokyo station. Shuttle buses also run from Tokyo (¥600), Ueno (¥600) and Yokohama (¥1000) stations, from Narita (¥2000) and Haneda (¥700) airports and from the nearby Disneyland hotels.

Next to Kōrakuen subway station on the Marunouchi subway line is **Kōraku-en Amusement Park** (☎ 3817-6098). Some rides here are not for the faint-hearted. 'Ultra-Twister', with its 85° slope, is the most popular ride. Entry (rides not included) is adults/children ¥1500/800; it's open daily from 10 am to 6 pm in winter, to 8 pm in autumn and spring, and to 10 pm in summer.

Similar is **Toshimaen Amusement Park** (☎ 3990-3131). It has thrill rides with names like Cyclone, Hydropolis and Cork-Screw. Most rides average around ¥400, and entry is ¥1600 for adults, ¥800 for children. Its basic opening hours are 9 am to 5 pm daily, though it stays open later in the height of summer. To get to the park, take the Seibu-Ikebukuro line to Toshimaen station.

Game Rooms

Tokyo is chock-a-block with game rooms, ranging from tiny local joints to huge complexes. The big places are concentrated in Shibuya and Shinjuku. If you don't read Japanese, some of the games may be utterly incomprehensible, although kids seem to find Nintendo an international language.

In Shibuya, the **Beam building** is a huge complex which offers something electronic for everybody.

Joypolis is a chain of game rooms which specialises in virtual reality and sports simulation games. The two main locations are in Shinjuku's Times Square complex and down

CHRIS ROWTHORN

At Tokyo's game rooms, virtual universes are only a pocketful of coins away.

東京 東京 東京 東京 東京 東京 東京 東京 東京 東京 東京 東京 東京 東京 東京 東京

Tokyo with Children

Tokyo is a very child-friendly city, with lots of attractions designed especially for kids – and a good excuse for adults to visit, too. The following should get you started:

The National Children's Castle (Kodomo no Shiro) With playrooms, puppet theatres, a swimming pool and lots of events just for children, the castle (Map 7) even has a hotel next door built especially for those with young children. Entrance is ¥400 for adults, ¥300 for children; it's open from 12.30 to 5.30 pm weekdays, from 10 am on weekends. Located off Aoyama-dōri, take the Ginza subway line to Omote-sandō station, go out the B2 exit and walk towards Shibuya.

Tokyo Metropolitan Children's Museum (Tokyo-to Jido Kaikan) There are several play areas, a hands-on art studio where children can make pottery and origami, a library of *manga* comics, and a monthly schedule of events. It's near Shibuya station.

Transportation Museum This is a museum both children and adults can enjoy, with great displays on all modes of transport, especially trains. See the Akihabara section of this chapter for details.

Museum of Maritime Science This ship-shaped museum is filled with detailed model ships, hands-on displays and even a pool for piloting remote-control submarines. The museum is in the Daiba/Tokyo Bay area. See the Other Attractions section in this chapter for details.

Ueno Zoo Although the zoo is pretty much like other zoos round the world, it does have a petting zoo, and its proximity to the other attractions of Ueno-kōen Park is a bonus. See the Ueno section of this chapter for more information.

Game Rooms Your kids will be delighted to try the latest games in some of the world's largest video game halls (see the Other Attractions section in this chapter). You can also find smaller video game centres in almost every neighbourhood.

Feed the Carp Colourful ornamental carp are fascinating, and your kids can feed them at some gardens and shrines, where a bag of carp food is ¥100. The pond behind Yasukuni-jinja Shrine is a good spot; Rikugi-en Garden has perhaps the largest and most beautiful carp in Tokyo.

Tokyo Disneyland If you've exhausted the options above and want a sure-fire hit with the kids, be prepared to spend a little time and money at Tokyo Disneyland (see the Amusement Parks section for details). ■

東京 東京 東京 東京 東京 東京 東京 東京 東京 東京 東京 東京 東京 東京 東京 東京

in the Tokyo Bay area in the Deck's Tokyo Beach building (see the Daiba/Tokyo Bay Walking Tour boxed text in this chapter). At both places, entry is ¥300; a book of five tickets to the bigger rides/games is ¥2600.

If you're tired of shelling out wads of cash for games which end in a matter of minutes, head to the **Sony building** (Map 3) in Ginza, which has several Play Stations with the latest game software which you can play for free. The downside is that you have to queue with a lot of young Tokyoites for the privilege.

ACTIVITIES
Cultural
The TIC has a wealth of information on cultural activities and courses, from Zen meditation to ikebana. The following are contact numbers for some of the many schools and associations around Tokyo. It is also worth checking the regular listings in the *Tokyo Journal* and the English-language newspapers.

Acupuncture Known as *hari*, acupuncture is far more commonly practised in Japan than most people realise. Two places which perform acupuncture and are somewhat used to foreigners are:

Baba Kaiseidō Acupuncture Office
(☎ 3432-0260) 2-4-5-305 Shiba Daimon, Minato-ku

Chinese Acupuncture Studio
(☎ 3464-5819) 2-15-1 Dogenzaka, Shibuya-ku

Bonsai Large hotels and department stores often have bonsai displays. Devotees should make the 30 minute trip outside Tokyo to visit Bonsai Village at Bonsai-machi, Omiya, Saitama.

Calligraphy Known in Japanese as *shodō*, calligraphy lessons are available at the Koyo Calligraphy Art School (☎ 3941-3809) in Ōtsuka.

Cuisine Japanese cooking classes are served up at Egami Cooking School (☎ 3269-0281), very near Ichigaya station. There's also Akasaka B Cooking School (☎ 3582-9074), as well as Cooking House Kuroda (☎ 045-261-5181) in Yokohama.

Ikebana There are lots of ikebana schools around Tokyo. To find out about flower arranging courses, call Ikebana International (☎ 3293-8188), Ochanomizu Square Building, 1-6 Surugadai, Kanda, Chiyoda-ku. Some schools provide instruction in English; prices start at around ¥3000 an hour.

Language The TIC's *Japanese & Japanese Studies* leaflet lists government-accredited schools that belong to the Association of International Education (☎ 3485-6827). The association can also be contacted directly, as can the Association for the Promotion of Japanese Language Education (☎ 5386-0080).

Costs at private Japanese-language schools vary enormously, depending on the school's status and facilities. For part-time or seasonal intensive study, tuition fees average about ¥50,000 per term. For full-time study, there is usually an application fee of ¥5000 to ¥30,000, an administration charge of ¥50,000 to ¥100,000 and annual tuition fees of ¥400,000 to ¥750,000. The benefit of studying full-time is that it entitles you to a student visa, with which you can work up to 20 hours a week, thereby offsetting some of the tuition costs.

Shiatsu Lessons in English are available for shiatsu, or finger-pressure massage. Contact Dr Kimura at the Iokai Shiatsu Center (☎ 3832-2983). These places offer shiatsu massage (call first for an appointment):

Kōjimachi Rebirth
(☎ 3261-3493) 1-5-7 Hirakawachō, Chiyoda-ku
Namikoshi Shiatsu Center
(☎ 3583-9326) 5-5-9 Akasaka, Minato-ku
Shiatsu Nanaka
(☎ 045-743-2134) 3-44 Miyamotochō, Yokohama

Tea Ceremony The Kenkyusha Eigo Center (☎ 5261-8940) in Iidabashi has one-off lessons (¥5000) and three-month courses (¥34,000) in English.

Zen Some organisations and temples around Tokyo hold talks and Zen meditation sessions in English, including Dogen Sanga (☎ 3235-0701) in Hongo-sanchōme. These

---

東京 東京 東京 東京 東京 東京 東京 東京 東

Tea Ceremony

Combining the arts of cooking, ceramics, haiku, calligraphy and flower arrangement with a dash of Zen, tea ceremony *(chanoyu)* is perhaps the most concentrated of all Japanese experiences.

With the right attitude, chanoyu is a wonderful diversion. Just remember: no-one is going to hold it against you if you don't know the exact procedure. The trick is simply to follow the lead of the Japanese in attendance. If there aren't any present, your host will explain what to do. And relax: the point of the ritual is to forget the cares of the world and concentrate on the tea at hand.

The following hotels offer chanoyu to foreign visitors:

Imperial Hotel
(☎ 3504-1111); from 10 am to 4 pm, Monday to Saturday; ¥1500; call for an appointment
Hotel Ōkura
(☎ 3582-0111); daily from 11 am to 5 pm; ¥1030; call for an appointment
Hotel New Ōtani
(☎ 3265-1111); at 11 am and 1 pm, Thursday to Saturday; ¥1030; appointments required for more than five people

東京 東京 東京 東京 東京 東京 東京 東京 東

THINGS TO SEE & DO

Tokyo temples offer regular Zen sessions to beginners and have someone on hand who can speak English:

Eihei-ji Temple (Soto sect)
(☎ 3400-5232) 2-21-34 Nishi-Azabu, Minato-ku
Soun-in Temple (Rinzai sect)
(☎ 3844-3711) 4-1-12 Higashi-Ueno, Taito-ku
Taiso-ji Temple (Soto sect)
(☎ 3917-6290) 7-1-1 Komagome, Toshima-ku
Tokyo Hannya Dojo (Rinzai sect)
(☎ 5245-7678) 1-6-1 Hirano, Kōtō-ku

Friends of the Western Buddhist Order also has regular courses on Buddhism and meditation, and can be contacted through Mr Kevin Duffey (☎ 044-754-6189). Similarly, Tibet House (☎ 3353-4094) in Shinjuku offers courses on Tibetan Buddhism.

Some Buddhist temples in Kamakura offer *zazen* meditation sessions on weekends. Hokoku-ji Temple's sessions are aimed at the beginner, while those run by Kenchō-ji and Engaku-ji temples are more suited to experienced practitioners (see the Kamakura section in the Excursions chapter).

Public Baths & Hot Springs
For details on the *sentō* (public bath) and *onsen* (hot spring) experience, see the Public Baths & Hot Springs entry in the Entertainment chapter.

Traditional Sports
Martial arts traditionally associated with Japan such as *aikidō, jūdō, karate* and *kendō* can be studied in Tokyo, as well as the less popular sports such as *kyūdō* (Japanese archery) and sumō. Addresses in Tokyo include:

All-Japan Jūdō Federation
(☎ 3812-9580) c/o Kodokan, 1-16-30 Kasuga, Bunkyō-ku
Amateur Archery Federation of Japan
(☎ 3481-2387) Kishi Memorial Hall, 1-1-1 Jinan, Shibuya-ku
International Aikidō Federation
(☎ 3203-9236) 17-18 Wakamatsuchō, Shinjuku-ku

Japan Karate Association
(☎ 3462-1415) For information on how to get there, ring Mr Yamamoto, Mr Hashimoto or Mr Yagyu at Wise International (☎ 3436-4567); all three speak English.
Japan Kendō Federation
(☎ 3211-58045) c/o Nihon Budōkan, 2-3 Kitanomaru-kōen, Chiyoda-ku
Nihon Sumō Kyokai
(☎ 3623-5111) Kokugikan Sumō Hall, 1-3-28 Yokoami, Sumida-ku

Participatory Sports
Unless you are based in a five star hotel with its own facilities, most short-term visitors to Tokyo will probably have to do without their favourite sporting activities. High population density and shortage of land mean a high demand for recreational space. This pushes up prices and creates long waiting lists.

Cycling Long-distance cycling in Tokyo isn't much fun. Keen cyclists who want information on bicycle rental, purchase or cycling courses can contact the following organisations, all in the same building in Akasaka (Map 3): Japan Cycling Association (☎ 3583-5628), the Japan Bicycle Promotion Institute (☎ 3583-5444) or the Bicycle Culture Center (☎ 3586-5930).

Golf Tokyo is undoubtedly the most expensive place in the world to play a game of golf. The cheaper option would be a visit to one of the many multistorey golf ranges that dot the landscape.

Skiing & Snowboarding Skiing has been popular for a long time in Japan, and snowboarding is currently all the rage among Japanese youth. There is no lack of places to do either in the Kantō region. The problem is the expense and the difficulty of getting to the ski areas. One place popular with Tokyoites is Akakura. For more information, contact the TIC office, which can give details about prices and transportation.

Surfing Surfing is more popular in Japan than most people realise. Around Tokyo, the most popular surf beaches are those on

Muira-hantō Peninsula and around Kamakura, especially between Kamakura and Enoshima. Unless a typhoon hits, don't expect much in the way of waves; the breaks are mostly beach breaks averaging a metre at best.

Swimming Like everything else, taking a swim in a pool in Tokyo can be costly and bound by unaccustomed rules. In the summer months, it's probably better to head to the beaches of Muira-hantō and around Kamakura. Otherwise, the following places have pools which accept visitors:

Big Box Seibu Sports Plaza (Map 5)
    (☎ 3208-7171) next to Takadanobaba station; open Sunday from noon to 10 pm; ¥1545 for the whole day
Yoyogi National Stadium (Map 7)
    (☎ 3468-1171) close to Harajuku station; open daily from noon to 4 pm; ¥460 for the day

Tennis Court reservations are sometimes needed up to a month in advance. If you are just in Tokyo on a short stay, it's probably better not to bother. You might try the following places if you're really set on a game.

Hibiya-kōen (Map 3)
    (☎ 3501-6428) open daily from 9 am to 9 pm; ¥1300 per hour
National Stadium Tennis Court
    (☎ 3408-4495) close to Gaien-mae subway station; open daily from 9 am to 4.30 pm; ¥700 per person per hour in the morning, ¥900 in the afternoon

Windsurfing Windsurfing is growing in popularity, but as with other equipment-intensive sports in Japan, it is not cheap. The most popular spots in the Tokyo area for windsurfing are the beaches of Kanagawa and Chiba. For details on places that rent boards, call the Tokyo TIC.

Places to Stay

Tokyo offers a diversity of accommodation options. At the upper end of the market are luxury hotels with facilities to rival the best hotels anywhere. At the other end of the scale are youth hostels, capsule hotels and *minshuku* (the Japanese version of B&B). Between these extremes are mid-range business hotels, so-called love hotels (cheap hotels used for trysts by Japanese, but fine for a regular stay) and *ryokan* (traditional Japanese inns).

Youth Hostels

Tokyo's youth hostels are much like youth hostels elsewhere: not much atmosphere, a mixture of dorms and private rooms, and strict rules concerning curfew and check-out time. They can also be very noisy when you're sharing the quarters with a group of students on a school excursion. On the plus side, Japanese youth hostels are used to foreigners and are cleaner than many of their overseas counterparts. A room in a typical youth hostel is about ¥3200, and payment is in cash only. Membership is not usually necessary, but some places will ask you to pay a one-time 'joining fee'.

Capsule Hotels

A slightly more private, if claustrophobic, option is the capsule hotel. Measuring about the size of a coffin, the tiny area packs in a bed, reading light, TV, alarm clock and one insensate human body. Despite their size, capsule hotels are not the bargain you might suppose. Prices for an overnight stay range from ¥3500 to ¥4800, depending on the area and the facilities. Like youth hostels, payment is by cash only.

One drawback to capsule hotels is their relative lack of familiarity with foreign guests; most of their business comes from drunken office workers who have missed the last train home. Sadly, they are also usually male-only. On the plus side, most capsule hotels have a well-appointed bath area similar to a good local *sentō* (public bath).

Love Hotels

Similarly quirky is the love hotel. Rooms here are generally rented out for one or two hours at a time, but late in the evening there will usually be fairly reasonable all-night rates (around ¥7500, no credit cards accepted). Of course, prices can soar if you request the all-leather S&M deluxe suite with the African-safari-meets-Elvis decor ...

Love hotels are distinguished by their discreet entrances – high bushes, large stones out front, underground parking and so on – installed so that patrons can duck in and out in complete anonymity. Once inside, the anonymity continues: you choose a room from a bank of illuminated pictures on the wall. If the picture is not illuminated, the room's already taken. Once you've decided, either push a button or say the number to a hidden clerk. Payment is through a slot in the wall. Once you've paid, you'll be handed a key and must make your own way to the room.

Posted outside love hotels are signs indicating the rates for a one or two hour stay, discreetly referred to as a *kyūkei* (rest), or for an overnight stay, *tomari*. Note that most places will not allow you to check in for an overnight stay until 10 or 11 pm. Furthermore, some of these places are not used to dealing with foreigners. However, if you act like you know what you're doing and can muster a little Japanese (saying 'kyūkei' or 'tomari' will suffice), there should be no

東京 東京 東京 東京 東京 東京 東京 東京 東	
Useful Japanese	
hotel	ホテル
ryokan	旅館
minshuku	民宿
youth hostel	ユースホステル
capsule hotel	カプセルホテル
東京 東京 東京 東京 東京 東京 東京 東京 東	

problems. Be warned that same-sex guests may be refused at some love hotels. If this happens, insist that you are travelling as friends *(tomodachi)* and you may get in.

Ryokan

For those who crave a really traditional Japanese experience with tatami rooms and futons instead of beds, nothing beats a night in a ryokan. Although the more exclusive establishments can charge ¥25,000 (and often much more), there are a number of relatively inexpensive ryokan in Tokyo. These places are generally more accustomed to foreigners than their counterparts in more remote parts of Japan, and the rules tend to be a bit more relaxed as a result.

While some ryokan will allow you to pay by credit card, you should always ask at check-in if you hope to do so. The ryokan listed in this chapter are generally budget; those wishing to stay in mid-range and top-end ryokan should inquire at the Tourist Information Center (TIC), which has listings and will handle reservations.

Minshuku

Similar to ryokan, but generally simpler in

東京東京東京東京東京東京東京東京東京東京東京東京東京東京東京東京東京東京東京

Staying at a Ryokan

The Japanese tendency is to make the procedure at a ryokan seem rather rarefied for foreign comprehension, and some ryokan are wary of accepting foreign guests. However, many are used to catering for foreigners, and once you've grasped the basics, it really isn't that hard to fit in.

On arrival at the ryokan, you leave your shoes at the entrance steps, don a pair of slippers, and are shown by a maid to your room, which has a *tatami* floor. Slippers are taken off before entering tatami rooms. Instead of using numbers, rooms are often named after auspicious flowers, plants or trees.

The room usually contains an alcove *(tokonoma)*, probably decorated with a flower display or a calligraphy scroll. One side of the room will contain a cupboard with sliding doors for the bedding; the other side will have sliding screens covered with rice paper and may open onto a veranda with a garden view.

The room maid usually serves tea with a sweet on the low table surrounded by cushions *(zabuton)* in the centre of the room. At this time you'll be asked to sign the register. A tray is provided with a towel, cotton robe *(yukata)* and belt *(obi)* which you put on before taking your bath *(o-furo)*. Remember to close the left side of the yukata over the right – the reverse order is used for dressing the dead. In colder weather, there will also be an outer jacket *(tanzen)*. Your clothes can be put away in a closet or left on a hanger.

At some ryokan, there are rooms with private baths, but the communal ones are often designed with 'natural' pools or a window looking onto a garden. Bathing is communal, but sexes are segregated. Make sure you can differentiate between the bathroom signs for men and women (see the Toilets & Public Baths section in the Facts for the Visitor chapter) – although ryokan will often have signs in English. Many inns will have family bathrooms for couples or families.

Dressed in your yukata after your bath, you return to your room where the maid will have laid out dinner – in some ryokan, dinner is provided in a separate room but you can still wear your yukata for dining. Dinner usually includes standard dishes such as miso soup, pickles *(tsukemono)*, vegetables in vinegar *(sunomono)*, hors d'oeuvres *(zensai)*, fish either grilled or raw *(sashimi)*, and perhaps *tempura* and a stew. There will also be plenty of bowls for rice, dips and sauces. Depending on the standard of the accommodation, meals at a ryokan can become flamboyant displays of local cuisine or refined arrangements of *kaiseki* (a cuisine which obeys strict rules of form and etiquette for every detail of the meal and setting).

After dinner, while you are pottering around or strolling in the garden – or in the o-furo again – the maid will clear the dishes and prepare your bedding. A mattress *(futon)* is placed on the tatami floor and a quilt put on top.

In the morning, the maid will knock to make sure you are awake, then come in to put away the bedding before serving breakfast – sometimes this is served in a separate room. Breakfast usually consists of pickles, dried seaweed *(nori)*, raw egg, dried fish, miso soup and rice. (Foreign stomachs may need some time to digest this new experience.) After breakfast, the day is yours, fresh in the afterglow of Japanese hospitality. ∎

東京東京東京東京東京東京東京東京東京東京東京東京東京東京東京東京東京東京東京

decor and cheaper, are minshuku. These are private homes which accept visitors and offer food, usually both breakfast and dinner. They are friendly places, and you can often get to know other travellers, both Japanese and foreign, especially in places where meals are taken communally in a dining room.

Minshuku in Tokyo generally cost about ¥6000 to ¥8000 per person (cash only), including two meals, making minshuku one of your better travel bargains. You will find that few minshuku owners speak English. The best way to secure lodging is through the Japan Minshuku Center (☎ 3216-6556, English spoken) in the basement of the Kōtsū Kaikan building (Map 3) in Ginza. It will handle all reservations and payments, and will give you a map to your minshuku. It's closed on Sunday and national holidays.

Business Hotels

A very common form of mid-range accommodation is the so-called 'business hotel'. Generally these are economical and functional places – a step up from the capsule hotel – geared to the lone traveller on business, though many in Tokyo also take couples. In Tokyo, a room in a business hotel will have a pay TV and a tiny bathroom, and cost between ¥6000 and ¥12,000. Like ryokan, some business hotels accept credit cards, but you should always ask upon check-in. There is no room service, and you will usually be required to check out at 10 or 11 am and check in after 3 or 4 pm. At some of the nicer business hotels, there are large shared baths and saunas in addition to the private ones in the guest rooms.

Business hotels are fairly easy to identify by their small size (usually three to five floors), their simple, often concrete, exteriors and a sign, usually in both English and Japanese, out the front. While you can't expect much English from the front desk clerk, if you smile and speak slowly you should be okay.

Hotels

Once you leave the budget and mid-range category and enter the top-end bracket, you can expect to find all the amenities of top hotels anywhere in the world. The staff speak English, the rooms are spotless and the service impeccable. In addition, most hotels in Tokyo have several good restaurants and bars on their premises, many of which offer outstanding views over the city.

Gaijin Houses

Those on a low budget who plan on setting up shop in Tokyo may want to consider a 'gaijin house'. Many of these are private houses or apartments that have been partitioned into rooms and rented out to *gaijin* (foreigners). In general, gaijin houses are not an option for the short-term visitor, but for those planning an extended stay, they may initially be the only affordable option.

Other Options

The TIC can give you information about several other lodging options in and around Tokyo, including *shukubō* (staying on the grounds of a temple), *onsen* (hot-spring resorts) and converted farmhouses. It also has information for travellers with special needs, eg seniors, those with children and disabled visitors.

Tax

Keep in mind that a 5% consumption tax applies to room rates across all accommodation categories, with the exception of gaijin houses and some of the other budget options. For the more expensive styles of accommodation (generally rooms which cost over ¥15,000), a 3% local tax is also added to the 10% to 15% service charge.

Reservations & Information

If you need more information before you leave home, contact your nearest Japan National Tourist Organization (JNTO) office. Or, if you are in Japan, visit the Tokyo or Narita offices of the TIC. These offices can supply useful publications listing ryokan, hotels and business hotels such as *Hotels in Japan*, *Japan Ryokan Guide*, *Japanese Inn Group* and the *Directory of Welcome Inns*. Also at the main JNTO office in Tokyo (Map 3) is a free booking service, provided that you stay at a member of the Japan Welcome Inn hotel group. For those who'd like an authentic hot-spring resort experience, get JNTO's *Japanese Hot Springs*, which details some of the more popular onsen areas within easy reach of Tokyo.

Where to Stay

If you are not on a budget, areas such as Akasaka and Ginza are ideal places to be based. There are even some mid-range hotels in this part of town, though you won't find anything under ¥7500 for a single room. From this point prices spiral ever upward – anything from ¥20,000 for a single to ¥30,000 for a double – as you move into the giddy heights of opulent indulgence offered by hotels of international renown, such as the Hotel Ōkura and the Imperial Hotel. If your budget doesn't reach five star levels, you can find cheaper accommodation with easy access of central Tokyo by staying somewhere on the Yamanote line.

Around the Yamanote line, business and entertainment districts like Shinjuku or Ikebukuro will have capsule hotels from around ¥4000 per night or business-hotel singles from ¥7000 to ¥9000. For the same price, a couple could even find a room in a love hotel from 10 or 11 pm. Shinjuku, a very convenient area in which to be based, has some international-class hotels, mainly concentrated on the west side of the station. Ikebukuro, Kanda and Ueno have some particularly good deals in the business-hotel category.

Most of the more reasonably priced accommodation, such as ryokan, are less conveniently situated. Nevertheless, areas like Ueno and Ikebukuro have a number of budget accommodation options. Asakusa is another area with a number of ryokan popular with foreigners.

PLACES TO STAY – BUDGET

Tokyo is an expensive city. Budget travellers arriving from other parts of Asia are likely to be shocked at the cost of accommodation. Even travellers who come well supplied with funds often find that too large a chunk of their daily expenses go into a place to sleep, and some end up cutting their trip short as a result.

There is really no way around this problem, as there are no true accommodation bargains in the city. Even dormitory lodging (care of Tokyo's two youth hostels) is up around ¥3200. Once you leave the youth hostel bracket, the next option to consider is Kimi Ryokan in Ikebukuro – probably the best entry in the budget category.

A step up in price are the economy hotels banded together as the Welcome Inn Group. The majority of these fall into the budget ryokan category, but some business hotels are also included. Prices average ¥6000 for a single and ¥8000 for a double/twin. The advantage of hotels in this group is that they are accustomed to dealing with foreigners (an important consideration, even in Tokyo), and they can be booked before you leave home.

If you wish to book from overseas, you will have to get a Welcome Inn Group reservation form from your nearest JNTO office. Bookings need to be made at least two weeks before departure, and you will need a confirmed air ticket. If you book for your day of arrival, you will need to be scheduled to land before 3 pm. Bookings can also be made in Tokyo at the Narita and Tokyo TIC offices.

Youth Hostels

The cheapest short-term options in Tokyo are the youth hostels in Iidabashi and Yoyogi.

JNTO

A basic Japanese inn, Tokyo

The drawbacks are the usual youth hostel restrictions – you have to be out of the building between 10 am and 3 pm (10 am and 5 pm at Yoyogi) and you have to be home by 10 pm in the evening – a real drag in a city like Tokyo. Finally, there's a three night limit to your stay, and the hostels can often be booked out during peak holiday periods. The consensus is that the Yoyogi Youth Hostel is the better option of the two.

The *Tokyo International Youth Hostel* (Map 2) (☎ 3235-1107), just south of the station in Iidabashi, might be a showcase for Japan's youth hostels (it's on the 18th floor of a towering office block, providing great views), but a business-like atmosphere prevails. You aren't required to be a member, but you are asked to book ahead and provide some identification (a passport will do) when you arrive. There is a basic charge of ¥3250 per person per night, or ¥4300 with two meals, and a sleeping sheet costs ¥150 for three nights. To get there, exit from Iidabashi station (either JR or subway) and look for the tallest building in sight (it's long, slender and glass fronted). The Narita TIC has an instruction sheet on the cheapest means to get to the hostel from the airport.

Yoyogi Youth Hostel (Map 7) (☎ 3467-9163) requires that you be a youth hostel member to stay, but will accept nonmembers upon payment of a ¥600 'one welcome stamp'. No meals are available, but there are cooking facilities. It's ¥3000 per person per night to stay. Take the Odakyū line to Sangūbashi station and walk toward the Meiji-jingū Shrine gardens. The hostel is in a fenced compound – not a former prison camp, but the National Olympics Memorial Youth Center – in building No 14. Staff may let you exceed the three night limit if it is not crowded.

Ryokan & Other Accommodation

An easy ryokan to reach from Narita airport is *Suzuki Ryokan* (Map 4) (☎ 3821-4944) in Nippori. Some rooms have private bathroom and all have TV. Take the Keisei line from Narita airport and get off at Nippori, the last stop before Ueno. Turn right at the Ueno end of the platform and look for the ryokan to the right as you exit the station. There is an English sign. Singles without a bathroom cost ¥4000 per person; doubles with a bath cost ¥8000. A bonus at this ryokan is the location; it's near one of Tokyo's most pleasant neighbourhoods for a stroll.

Kimi Ryokan (Map 5) (☎ 3971-3766) deserves a special mention. The Kimi is in Ikebukuro, which isn't a bad location from which to see Tokyo; it's 10 minutes from Shinjuku and 20 minutes from Ginza. The rooms are relatively inexpensive by Tokyo standards, nicely designed in Japanese style, and the place is friendly, clean and relaxed about the hours you keep – just remember to inform the staff if you're going to be out late. One nice touch is the constantly changing ikebana in the common areas. The Kimi lounge is a good meeting place, with a useful notice board which has recently expanded into the nearby Kimi Information Center.

Kimi Ryokan is often fully booked, so it's a good idea to phone and book a room as early as possible. The staff speak English. Prices range from ¥4500 for singles to ¥6500 for medium doubles and ¥7500 for large doubles/twins. To get there, go out the west exit of Ikebukuro station, or go to the police box on the west side, just past Marui department store, and say 'Kimi Ryokan' to the policeman on duty. He'll give you a map.

In Ueno (Map 4) are several budget ryokan, all members of the Welcome Inn Group. *Sawanoya Ryokan* (☎ 3822-2251) is close to Nezu subway station on the Chiyoda line. Take the Nezu crossing exit and turn right onto Kototoi-dōri. Turn left at the fourth street on your left – Sawanoya Ryokan is a couple of minutes down the road on your right. If you're coming from Narita, it would probably be easier and just as cheap to share a taxi from Ueno station. Singles/doubles cost from ¥4700/8800; triples cost ¥12,000. It is closed from 29 December to 4 January.

A bit closer to Ueno station, a popular choice with travellers is *Ryokan Katsutaron* (☎ 3821-9808). If you follow the road that runs alongside Shinobazu Pond for about 10 minutes, you'll see the ryokan on the right, just past the police box (don't turn right at the police box; go straight across the intersection). You can also get to the ryokan from Nezu subway station. Singles/doubles/triples cost ¥4500/8400/12,300 without a bath. With bath, rooms are slightly more.

The popular *Asia Center of Japan* ryokan (Map 7) (☎ 3402-6111) is near Aoyama-itchōme subway station on the Ginza line. Like Kimi Ryokan, it attracts many long-term guests, and even though it's a lot bigger than the Kimi, it's still often fully booked. The station is under the easily recognisable Aoyama Twin Tower building on Aoyama-dōri. Walk past the Tower building toward Akasaka-mitsuke and turn right (toward Roppongi); the Asia Center is a short walk up the third street on the left. Rooms have pay TVs, and singles without a bath cost ¥5100, twins/doubles from ¥9500.

Just one stop from Ueno on the Yamanote line (Uguisudani station) is *Sakura Ryokan* (☎ 3876-8118). Take the southern exit and turn left. Pass the Iriya subway station exits on the left – Sakura Ryokan is on the right-hand side of the second street on your left. If you're exiting from Iriya subway station on the Hibiya line, take the No 1 exit and turn left. Singles/doubles cost ¥5250/9000.

Close to Gotanda station on the Yamanote line is *Ryokan Sansuisō* (☎ 3441-7475). This is not the greatest of locations, but it's only a few stops from Shibuya, the nearest main railway station. Take the exit furthest away from Shibuya and go out on the left-hand side. Turn right, take the first right after the big Tōkyū department store and then the first left. Turn left and then right, continue past the bowling centre and look for the sign on the right directing you down the side road to the ryokan. Prices for singles/doubles are ¥5500/8600; triples cost ¥12,000.

Asakusa also has a few reasonably priced ryokan. *Ryokan Mikawaya* (Map 4) (☎ 3843-2345) is in an interesting area, just around the corner from Sensō-ji Temple. It is on a side street off the shop-lined street leading into the temple. From Kaminari-mon Gate, the street is a few streets up on the left – there is a toy shop and a shoe shop on the corner.

The ryokan is on the left-hand side of the road. Singles/doubles without bath cost ¥6000/11,000.

The *YMCA Asia Youth Center* (Map 2) (☎ 3233-0611) takes both men and women. The center is halfway between Suidōbashi and Jimbōchō subway stations. Don't be fooled by the name: it's actually quite close to a business hotel in cost and no different in service. Singles/doubles cost ¥7000/13,000 with bathroom; triples cost ¥16,800.

Just around the corner from Ryokan Mikawaya is the new, clean and friendly *Ryokan Shigetsu* (Map 4) (☎ 3843-2345). Japanese-style singles/doubles are ¥9000/15,000 and larger Japanese-style suites are available for ¥25,000. Western-style singles/doubles are ¥7000/14,000. Try the Japanese bath, which has a view of Sensō-ji's five storey pagoda.

Capsule Hotels

Capsule hotels are generally a male domain, and you find them in large hubs and nightlife districts. Most are open from 5 pm to 10 am.

In Shinjuku, toward Shinjuku-gyoen Park, is the *Winning Inn Shinjuku* (Map 6) (☎ 3350-0601), for ¥3500 per night. Just down the road from the Prince Hotel on Shinjuku's east side is *Green Plaza Shinjuku* (Map 6) (☎ 3207-5411). Your own personal capsule is ¥4200. The front desk of this hotel is on the 3rd floor; take the lift from the basement.

Right in Shinjuku's sleazy Kabukichō is the *Shinjuku-ku Capsule Hotel* (Map 6) (☎ 3232-1110), at ¥4300 per night.

In Akasaka, not far from Akasaka station, is *Capsule Inn Akasaka* (☎ 3588-1811). Follow Akasaka-dōri south-west from the TBS broadcasting station; the hotel's on the left. It costs ¥4500 per night. Closer to Akasaka-mitsuke station is an upmarket capsule hotel, *Capsule Hotel Fontaine Akasaka* (Map 3) (☎ 3583-6554). An overnight stay here is ¥4800. This is one of the few capsule hotels in Tokyo that accepts women, but it does so only on Friday, Saturday and Sunday.

Gaijin Houses

Although a few gaijin houses quote daily or weekly rates, they are generally not an option for short-term visitors. If you are planning a long stay, however, a gaijin house may be the only affordable option. The slowdown in the Japanese economy has led to less foreigners heading to Tokyo in search of work; consequently, it is easier than it used to be to find a room in a gaijin house. Typically prices range from ¥40,000 per month for a bed in a shared room to ¥70,000 for a private room, with no deposits or key money required.

Conditions in gaijin houses vary enormously, and you should definitely check out several places before deciding. The best ways to find a gaijin house are by word of mouth from other foreigners, looking in the *Tokyo Journal* or the *Tokyo Classifieds*, or going through an agency. Agencies are generally the fastest and easiest way to go, as they have extensive listings and will handle all the arrangements with the landlord. The Tokyo agency with the largest listings and best rates is Fontana (☎ 3382-0151).

PLACES TO STAY – MIDDLE

The mid-range bracket mainly comprises business hotels. There's very little to distinguish one from another, and their main attraction is usually convenience. Nearly every area has numerous business hotels with singles/doubles from about ¥7500/ 12,000. Generally, each room will have a built-in bathroom with shower, bath and toilet, a telephone, pay TV and other features like disposable toothbrushes and shaving equipment.

One difficulty for non-Japanese speakers is that very few mid-range hotels have English-speaking staff. As a general rule, the lower the price in a business hotel, the less likely it is that the staff are accustomed to dealing with foreigners. It is highly unusual to be turned away, however. In some cases room prices are listed with consumption tax included – where a round figure is given for a room price, you can expect a 3% consumption tax to be added.

There are plenty of love hotels in any of Tokyo's entertainment districts, but particularly in Shinjuku, Shibuya, Roppongi and Ikebukuro. All-night rooms range in price from about ¥6000 to ¥9000, but 'all night' doesn't start until 10 or 11 pm, when the regular hour-by-hour customers have run out of energy.

Tokyo Station Area

Basically, hotels in this area (Map 2) offer mid-range standards at top-end prices, simply because real estate values are so high. If you opt to stay in this area, you are paying for location.

Between Tokyo station and Takashimaya department store is the fairly economical *Yaesu Terminal Hotel* (☎ 3281-3771). It has a business hotel feel and the rooms are quite small, but the prices are a bargain for this area. Singles/doubles are ¥10,800/15,800, twins ¥15,800.

A little south of the station, very convenient for business at the Tokyo International Forum, is the *Yaesu Fujiya Hotel* (Map 3) (☎ 3273-2111). The rooms here are a bit more spacious than some of the other mid-range hotels in the area. Given its location, it's good value, with singles/doubles/twins starting at ¥12,500/17,000/22,000.

If you can't face any more travel upon arriving at Tokyo station, you can try the *Tokyo Station Hotel* (☎ 3231-2511), on the Marunouchi (west) side of the station. The rooms are pretty basic, but you can't beat the location. Light sleepers should request rooms on the west side of the building, so as not to get woken up by trains. Singles/ doubles start at ¥13,000/19,000, twins at ¥19,000.

Another hotel which is almost directly on top of Tokyo station, on the Yaesu (east) side, is the *Hotel Kokusai Kankō* (☎ 3215-3281). Rooms are fairly basic, but quieter than those at the Tokyo Station Hotel. Singles/doubles/ twins start at ¥14,000/23,000/23,500.

North of the station, above the Tōzai subway line's Ōtemachi station, is the *Marunouchi Hotel* (☎ 3215-2151). This is a fairly basic hotel within walking distance of Tokyo station and on the doorstep of Tokyo's financial district. Singles/doubles/twins start at ¥13,000/23,000/21,000.

Ginza

Ginza (Map 3) is not the best place to look for mid-range accommodation, as prices reflect the posh surroundings, but it's certainly a good area in which to be based.

A bargain for this part of town, the *Hotel Ginza Dai-ei* (☎ 3545-1111), just north of Kabuki-za Theatre, is a standard business hotel. Singles/doubles/twins start at ¥11,400/15,600/17,500. The less than pristine condition of the hotel reflects the prices.

A step up in terms of quality and price is the *Ginza Nikkō Hotel* (☎ 3571-4911). Right on Sotobori-dōri between Ginza and Shimbashi, Ginza Nikkō is a quality hotel in a prime location. Singles/doubles/twins start at ¥10,000/20,000/24,000.

In a similar class to the Ginza Nikko and located nearby, the *Ginza International Hotel* (☎ 3574-1121) offers singles/doubles starting at ¥13,000/18,000 and twins from ¥20,000.

Kanda

The Kanda area (Map 2), comprising Jimbōchō and Akihabara, is neglected by many travellers looking for business hotel accommodation. Kanda is actually a fine place to be based: it's close to central Tokyo and quieter than many other parts of town. You might also appreciate Kanda's college-town atmosphere, with lots of good bookshops and cheap restaurants. Best of all, the hotels in Kanda are a few thousand yen cheaper than comparable hotels in more fashionable parts of town.

About the cheapest business hotel in Kanda is the *Central Hotel* (☎ 3256-6251). Rooms are small and simple, and there are a sauna and large bath, although these are a little seedy. Singles/doubles/twins start at ¥6500/9800/9300.

Part of the same chain as the Central Hotel, the *New Central Hotel* (☎ 3256-2171) is surprisingly cheap considering the new facilities.

There are a large bath and sauna to wash away travel fatigue. Singles/doubles/twins start at ¥7000/7500/9600.

A throwback to a different era, the older and slightly funky *Tokyo Family Hotel* (☎ 3293-3001) is a good option if you want something a little different from a standard business hotel. Singles/twins start at ¥7500/12,000. It's best to have a look first to see if this is your sort of place.

Perhaps the nicest business hotel in Kanda is the clean, new *Tokyo Green Hotel* (☎ 3255-4161). The common areas here have a nice woody/bamboo theme, and the staff are friendly. Simple meals are available in the attached restaurant for reasonable prices. Singles/twins start at ¥8400/14,200.

The *Grand Central Hotel* (☎ 3256-3211), the third link in the 'Central' hotel chain, is a standard-issue business hotel with rooms slightly larger than the other two Centrals. Singles/doubles start at ¥8600/12,200, twins at ¥13,200.

Not far from Ochanomizu station, *Hotel Juraku* (☎ 3251-7222) is somewhere between a regular hotel and a business hotel. The rooms are quite simple and on the small side. On the whole, it's probably better to save the money and go to one of the above business hotels. Singles/doubles/twins start at ¥9500/12,500/14,500.

Hotel New Kanda (☎ 3258-3911), right around the corner from Akihabara, is one of Kanda's only real hotels (as opposed to business hotels). It's your basic hotel, with clean rooms and a few restaurants thrown in. Singles/doubles start at ¥10,700/16,000, twins at ¥17,000.

Ueno

With the Keisei Airport Express only minutes away and with some of Tokyo's most famous cultural attractions, Ueno (Map 4) is not a bad place in which to be based. Mid-range accommodation consists primarily of standard business hotels and a few simple hotels. Also, there are a few ryokan nearby.

The *Kinuya Hotel* (☎ 3833-1911) has a good location, but the staff are rather cool and unused to foreign guests. You may not care about the reception, but prices are competitive at ¥7400/11,200 for singles/doubles, ¥11,200 for twins.

The *Hotel Green Capital* (☎ 3842-2411) is a typical business hotel quite close to Ueno station. The rooms are clean and new, and the staff are polite. Prices are also competitive at ¥7500/10,000/9000 for singles/doubles/twins. It's a little tricky to find; look for a black marble front and a metal sign with green lettering at street level.

Directly across from Ueno station, the *Hotel New Ueno* (☎ 3841-3221) is a good choice in terms of location. The rooms are standard business hotel style, but prices are a little higher than at other Ueno business hotels. Singles/doubles/twins start at ¥8500/14,000/16,000.

In a similar class, the *Ueno Terminal Hotel* (☎ 3831-1110) offers singles/doubles/twins starting at ¥8700/14,000/16,500. The place is clean, and the staff are used to foreign guests. Look for a white building with a white on brown sign in English.

On the south side of Ueno-kōen Park are some good hotels. The *Hotel Pine Hill Ueno* (☎ 3836-5111) is a large, clean hotel with a pleasant, English-speaking staff. Considering its location and quality, the rooms here are a bargain, starting at ¥7800/14,500 for singles/doubles, ¥14,500 for twins.

Overlooking the park itself, the *Hotel Parkside* (☎ 3836-5711) is another good choice, particularly if you can get a room on the front side. The place is pleasant, clean and new. Singles/doubles/twins start at ¥9200/16,100/16,100. Japanese-style rooms are also available for ¥16,600 for two people. Dieters may be interested in what the hotel's brochure describes as a 'semi-sweet room'.

Those who want a change from the typical western-style hotel may want to try the *Suigetsu Hotel* (☎ 3822-4611), on the west side of the park. This hotel has mostly Japanese-style tatami rooms, and there are several large Japanese-style baths. Though the hotel is built round a Japanese garden, its structure is largely western. Japanese-style rooms, including Japanese breakfast, start at ¥16,000 for two people (breakfast and dinner

service is also available). Western-style rooms start at ¥9300 for a single, with breakfast. There is no English sign; look for a white on blue Japanese sign and a grey granite building.

Asakusa

Asakusa (Map 3) is an interesting place to stay, if you don't mind sacrificing central location for a funky Shitamachi atmosphere. Options here are similar to those in Ueno: mostly business hotels and a few simple hotels. If you're going to stay in old Asakusa, you may want to try a ryokan.

As for the business hotels, most are down on Kaminarimon-dōri. The *Asakusa Plaza Hotel* (☎ 3845-2621) is a standard-issue business hotel convenient to the sights. Singles/doubles/twins start at ¥7000/10,500/11,000. The front desk is upstairs, above Dunkin' Donuts.

Slightly nicer is the nearby *Hotel Top Asakusa* (☎ 3847-2222), where singles/doubles start at ¥8200/13,500, twins at ¥15,000. The front desk is on the 3rd floor.

In a different class altogether, the *Asakusa View Hotel* (☎ 3842-2117) is just about Asakusa's only luxury hotel. The 28 storey building boasts an assortment of restaurants, a swimming pool, a Japanese-style floor and a shopping area. A drink in the 28th floor St Cristina bar is a good way to enjoy the night lights of Asakusa. Singles/doubles/twins start at ¥13,000/21,000/25,000.

Ikebukuro

Ikebukuro (Map 5) has lots of mid-range accommodation, most of it business hotels. This being one of Tokyo's nightlife areas, there are also lots of love hotels and a few capsule hotels scattered about. Be warned that the capsule hotels in this neighbourhood are not nearly as accustomed to foreign guests as their cousins in Akasaka or Shinjuku.

Perhaps the cheapest mid-range option is the love hotel *Hotel Castle* (☎ 3988-6711), near the Kimi Ryokan (see the Budget section). Here, an overnight stay will cost ¥6300 for one or two people. This is a real love hotel, and the owners aren't that used to foreign guests.

Business Hotel Ikebukuro Park (☎ 3982-8989) has about the cheapest rooms in its class, but the management appears unaccustomed to foreigners. Singles/doubles/twins start at ¥7000/10,000/10,000.

A friendlier place in the same price range is the *Hotel Star Plaza Ikebukuro* (☎ 3590-0005). Here, singles/doubles start at ¥7000/10,000. It also has Japanese-style rooms for ¥10,000 for two.

On the east side of Ikebukuro station, the *Hotel Grand City* (☎ 3984-5121) is a standard business hotel with relatively inexpensive rates. Singles/twins start at ¥7300/11,800.

The *Ikebukuro Royal Hotel* (☎ 5396-0333) is another basic business hotel not too far from the station, with lots of good restaurants nearby. The rooms are nothing special; singles start at ¥7500, doubles at ¥11,500.

The *Hotel Sun City Ikebukuro* (☎ 3986-1101) has basic rooms with a few on-premises drinking and dining options. Its singles/doubles start at ¥7800/12,600, twins at ¥12,600.

Near the Hotel Grand City, the *Ark Hotel* (☎ 3590-0111) has clean, newish rooms and polite staff. Singles/doubles/twins start at ¥8800/16,000/17,000. Japanese-style rooms are also available for ¥17,000 for two people.

Just up the street from Bic Camera, the *Hotel Sunroute Ikebukuro* (☎ 3980-1911) has pleasant, clean rooms and a friendly staff, some of whom speak English. This hotel is recommended for those who want a break from spartan business hotels. Singles/doubles start at ¥9000/15,600, twins at ¥15,600.

Shinjuku

Shinjuku (Map 6) is a good hunting ground for business hotels accustomed to foreign guests. Moreover, the intense competition in the area helps keep prices down. Along with Kanda, this is one of the best places for mid-range accommodation.

Starting in east Shinjuku, in Nichōme, the oddly named *City Hotel Lornstar* (☎ 3842-2411) is about as cheap a business hotel as

you'll find in these parts. It's small, clean and new, but little English is spoken and staff are not particularly used to foreign guests – smile and speak slowly and you should be fine. Singles/twins/doubles start at ¥7000/10,000/13,000.

Also in east Shinjuku, the *Hotel Sun Light Shinjuku* (☎ 3356-0391) is a good choice. The place is clean and new, and the staff are quite polite. Rooms are small, as are the windows, but well maintained. Singles/doubles are ¥8300/14,000, twins ¥13,500. If the main building is full, ask about the annex.

Just south of the Takashimaya Times Square complex, next to the Kinokuniya annex, is the *Park Hotel* (☎ 3355-3768). While it gets no raves for warm, friendly service, the rooms are a little larger than at most business hotels and the prices competitive. Singles/twins start at ¥7700/13,400.

The decidedly tatty *Central Hotel* (☎ 3354-6611) is worth considering only if the options above are full (which is unlikely). Once you negotiate the smoke-filled lounge, you'll find singles/doubles/twins starting at ¥10,000/16,000/16,000.

In west Shinjuku, the very conveniently located *Star Hotel Tokyo* (☎ 3361-1111) offers singles/doubles/twins from ¥9000/17,000/18,000. The rooms and service are average.

On the far side of Shinjuku's Central Park, the *Shinjuku New City Hotel* (☎ 3375-6511) is very convenient for anyone with business in the Tokyo Metropolitan Government Offices. The rooms are slightly larger than usual for a business hotel, while the prices are average. Singles/doubles/twins start at ¥8800/16,200/17,600.

The *Shinjuku Washington Hotel* (☎ 3343-3111) offers business hotel accommodation with regular hotel-style restaurants and amenities. Rooms are average, but the views from the upper floors are excellent. Singles/doubles/twins start at ¥11,300/17,000/17,500.

The *Hotel Sunroute Tokyo* (☎ 3375-3211), south-west of Shinjuku station, offers rather plain rooms and a convenient location for business in west Shinjuku. Singles/doubles/twins start at ¥12,500/17,000/18,000.

Shibuya

Shibuya (Map 7) is not as rich in accommodation as some of Tokyo's other built-up neighbourhoods. There are very few business hotels, and the regular hotels have little to recommend them over similar options in more interesting parts of Tokyo.

The *Shibuya Business Hotel* (☎ 3409-9300), on a backstreet behind Shibuya post office, is the cheapest choice in the area. The reception appears rather unfamiliar with dealing with foreigners, but will cope. Rooms are small but sufficient. Singles/doubles/twins start at ¥8400/11,200/11,900. There is no English sign; it's in a white building, and the entrance is down a small alley.

The *Shanpia Hotel Aoyama* (☎ 3407-2111) is a better choice, with decent rooms and a few restaurants in the building. It's also quite close to Shibuya sights and shopping. Singles/doubles/twins start at ¥8700/16,600/17,000.

The *Hotel Sun Route Shibuya* (☎ 3464-6411) has singles for ¥6700, if you're willing to make do with a shared bath. Otherwise, singles/doubles start at ¥10,000/13,000, twins at ¥17,500.

The *Shibuya Tōbu Hotel* (☎ 3476-0111) is probably the nicest place to stay in Shibuya. The rooms are clean, the common areas are pleasant, there are loads of in-house restaurants and the staff speak English. Singles/doubles/twins start at ¥11,800/14,400/17,000.

The *Shibuya Tōkyū Inn* (☎ 3462-0109) has singles/doubles from ¥14,600/21,200, twins from ¥22,600. Although it's closer to Shibuya station, it's probably not worth paying this much for rooms similar to those at the Shibuya Tōbu Hotel.

Those travelling with young children may want to consider Shibuya's *Children's Castle Hotel* (☎ 3797-5677). Twins/triples go for ¥13,000/17,400. Very young children, of course, stay for free. The big advantage of staying here is that guests can use the facilities of the adjoining Children's Castle at discounted rates. These include a pool, a gym, and theatres and playrooms designed to keep children entertained. That said, neither the hotel nor the Children's Castle are designed for foreign travellers, and those who don't speak Japanese may find it all a little baffling, though your kids probably won't mind. This place is easy to spot; look for the unusual many-headed statue out front.

Roppongi

Roppongi (Map 7) is not the place to look for accommodation. There are few hotels of any class in this primarily entertainment district. You do have one decent mid-range choice, right near the famous Roppongi crossing: *Hotel Ibis* (☎ 3403-4411). This is a clean, modern hotel with a few restaurants and bars in the building (if you just can't face the insanity on the streets below). This being Roppongi, you can count on the staff being used to foreign guests. Singles/doubles start at ¥11,500/14,100, twins at ¥19,000.

Other than Hotel Ibis, if you're intent on staying near Roppongi's bright lights, look a little to the north in Akasaka.

Akasaka

Akasaka (Map 3) is a good base, if you want access to central Tokyo and a lively nightlife. In addition to all the top-end hotels, there are a few mid-range options, many of which are located on Akasaka-dōri, past the TBS broadcasting station on the way to Roppongi. You can also try one of Akasaka's capsule hotels.

The *Akasaka Yōkō Hotel* (☎ 3586-4050) is a reasonably priced business hotel about midway between Akasaka and Roppongi. Although it's quite simple, the rooms are clean and the staff are friendly. Singles/twins start at ¥8900/14,000.

On the same street, 100m closer to Roppongi, *Marroad Inn Akasaka* (☎ 3585-7611) is another standard business hotel with features similar to the Yōkō Hotel. Singles/doubles/twins start at ¥9400/15,000/13,500.

PLACES TO STAY – TOP END

Although Tokyo is one of the world's most expensive cities, its many top-end hotels are usually no more expensive than similar hotels elsewhere in the world, *and* you get Japan's legendary high standard of service.

Ginza, Akasaka and Shinjuku (mainly the west side) have the highest concentration of top-end hotels. Any of these areas would make a convenient base.

Tokyo Station Area

Directly alongside the Imperial Palace, the *Palace Hotel* (Map 2) (☎ 3211-5211) is in the running for the best location in Tokyo. Many rooms here command impressive views over the palace. If you aren't lucky enough to get a good view from your room, you can always have dinner in the 10th floor Crown Restaurant – a great place to admire the lights of central Tokyo.

The service here is wonderful and the hotel's restaurants are among the best in Tokyo. Singles/doubles start at ¥24,000/29,000, twins at ¥28,000. For those in need of larger space, a business suite is ¥56,000; larger, regular suites start at ¥100,000.

Ginza

Along with Akasaka, Ginza (Map 3) is home to the thickest concentration of elite hotels anywhere in Tokyo. Prices here reflect the glamorous surroundings and proximity to Tokyo station, great shopping, good restaurants and the political/financial districts of the city. Plus, there's no denying that Ginza is a lot more pleasant for strolling than some of the louder and gaudier areas of Shinjuku and Ikebukuro.

The *Mitsui Urban Hotel* (☎ 3527-4131) is a stylish hotel near Shimbashi station. The rooms here have a retro 70s touch. Singles/doubles start at ¥14,000/21,000, twins at ¥21,000.

The *Ginza Tōkyū Hotel* (☎ 3541-2411) is a spacious hotel not far from Tsukiji market. Singles/doubles start at ¥16,000/26,000, twins at ¥24,000.

The *Ginza Dai-Ichi Hotel* (☎ 3542-5311) is similar to the Tōkyū Hotel, but the advantage here is the array of good restaurants and bars which grace its upper and lower floors. Singles/doubles start at ¥16,000/26,000, twins at ¥25,000.

A clean, new hotel just south of Kabuki-za Theatre is the *Ginza Tōbu Hotel* (☎ 3546-0111). The rooms are spacious, and the restaurants and bars are excellent. Singles/doubles start at ¥17,000/23,000, twins at ¥23,000.

Up a level in elegance and price is the *Dai-Ichi Hotel* (☎ 3501-5161). Not far from Hibiya-kōen Park, this fine hotel combines a modern skyscraper with classical interior design. The upper floors afford excellent views over the city. Singles/doubles/twins start at ¥27,000/34,000/30,000. Suites are available from ¥80,000.

Those who want the luxury of the Dai-Ichi Hotel in a somewhat pared-down and more economical package can stay at the nearby *Dai-Ichi Hotel Annex* (☎ 3501-5161). The annex's singles/doubles start at ¥22,000/26,000, twins at ¥42,000.

One of Tokyo's grand old hotels, the *Imperial Hotel* (☎ 3504-1111), is within walking distance of the sights of Ginza and Hibiya-kōen. It has all the standard amenities in a very elegant setting, and rooms are large and tastefully appointed. This hotel is your chance to try Japanese hospitality at its best. In the main building, singles/doubles start at ¥30,000/35,000. Tower rooms are somewhat more expensive. Suites start at ¥110,000.

For an experience of over-the-top service in impossibly dignified surroundings, try the *Hotel Seiyō Ginza* (☎ 3535-1111). This is like no other hotel in Tokyo; indeed, it doesn't even feel like a hotel – it's more like a very wealthy friend's chateau. There's no front desk as such, just a very discreet room with a very discreet staffer who takes care of the details of your stay. Most rooms come with a personal secretary, and this is only the start. Guest rooms range from ¥48,000 to ¥72,000. Suites start at ¥85,000.

Kanda

The only worthy top-end hotel in Kanda is the *Hilltop Hotel* (Map 2) (☎ 3293-2311). On a hill next to Meiji University, one gets the impression that this is where the parents of some of the wealthier students stay when they're in town. The place is an anachronism, like something out of 1930s Hollywood.

It also bills itself as a 'hotel to maintain health' (as opposed to the all-too-common 'inn to destroy health'). What this means is clearly and calmly explained by the brochure: 'Oxygen and negative ions are circulated into the rooms and its refreshing atmosphere is accepted by many, including prominent individuals, as most adequate for work and rest'. Never mind, it is a nice, dignified hotel. Singles/doubles/twins start at ¥17,000/24,000/26,000.

Ueno

The exotic *Hotel Sofitel Tokyo* (Map 4) (☎ 5685-7111) is about the only top-end hotel in Ueno. You can't miss this weird Lego-land structure looming over Ueno-kōen's boating pond. It's described as a 'boutique hotel' – the rooms and common areas are hung with fine art, and the whole hotel has a fashionable air to it. Its unique construction affords good views from every room, particularly those facing Ueno-kōen. Singles/doubles start at ¥17,000/22,000, twins at ¥22,000.

Ikebukuro

Unless you have a good reason to be based here, there seems little point in paying top-end prices to stay in bawdy Ikebukuro. For the same money, you can get good accommodation *and* pleasant surroundings in places like Akasaka, west Shinjuku and even Ginza. However, if you want to be based in Ikebukuro (Map 5), there are two choices in this class.

On the east side of Ikebukuro station, the *Sun City Prince Hotel* (☎ 3988-1111), in the Sunshine City complex, has rather chaotic common areas and the whole place feels slightly tatty. Singles/doubles start at ¥15,000/24,000, twins at ¥22,000.

The better option is the *Hotel Metropolitan* (☎ 3980-1111) on Ikebukuro's west side. This hotel has all the amenities you'd expect, including ample dining and entertainment options, some of which are located on the 27th floor, affording good views over Tokyo

and beyond. Singles/doubles/twins here start at ¥16,500/22,000/22,000.

Shinjuku

In east Shinjuku (Map 6), next to Seibu Shinjuku station, the *Shinjuku Prince Hotel* (☎ 3205-1111) is a rather drab choice in this price bracket. The rooms are plain, and the lobby area is rather chaotic and dimly lit. Singles/doubles start at ¥15,000/17,000, twins at ¥26,000.

In west Shinjuku, the 47 storey *Keiō Plaza Inter-Continental Hotel* (☎ 3344-0111) provides excellent views of the area and quick access to the station. Singles/doubles/twins start at ¥16/000/24,000/24,000.

The *Tokyo Hilton International* (☎ 3344-5111) offers great service, sports facilities, convenient location and a variety of good restaurants. Singles/doubles start at ¥22,000/26,000. Suites are available from ¥60,000. The hotel also has a 'hotel within a hotel' on its upper five floors catering specially to the business traveller, with a fully staffed business centre and a 'guest relations officer' to help organise your affairs.

Nearby, the *Hotel Century Hyatt* (☎ 3348-1234) offers a similar level of service and very spacious rooms, both western and Japanese-style, and a 26th floor penthouse pool. Singles/doubles start at ¥31,000/34,000, twins at ¥34,000. If you happen to be in the neighbourhood, pop into the lobby and see the mother of all chandeliers.

For a hotel experience unlike any other, check out the breathtaking *Park Hyatt Tokyo* (☎ 5322-1234) on the upper floors of the new 53 storey Shinjuku Park Tower – it's an island of luxury in the sky. The rooms are new, clean, very stylish and complemented by some of the most impressive bars and restaurants in Tokyo. Add to this the rooftop pool, the exercise studio overlooking the city and a great spa bath/sauna room, and you've got one of the city's best top-end hotels. Singles/doubles are ¥41,000/46,000. Suites start at ¥100,000. Even if you don't stay here, at least stop by for a drink in the Sky Bar; you'll understand why when you get there.

Roppongi

Sadly, Roppongi is not rich in hotel accommodation of any class; it's better to look just a little to the north in hotel-rich Akasaka. If you're intent on staying in Roppongi, there is one fine choice: the *Roppongi Prince Hotel* (Map 3) (☎ 3587-1111), a fashionable, high-tech hotel where high standards prevail. It's built around a huge atrium with an outdoor heated swimming pool at its centre. After a swim, you can head to one of the hotel's excellent restaurants or bars. If you run out of things to do inside the hotel, the nightlife of Roppongi is only 10 minutes walk away. Singles/doubles/twins start at ¥19,500/24,500/23,000.

Ebisu

Ebisu (Map 8) is a pleasant place to stay if you want a break from larger areas like Shinjuku or Ginza. In this class, there is only one real option: the *Westin Hotel Tokyo* (☎ 5423-7000). This is modelled on a grand European hotel, with elegant common areas and classically designed rooms. There are also six good restaurants and three bars, plus Yebisu Garden Place right on the doorstep. Singles/doubles here start at ¥30,000/36,000 and there are a variety of suites from ¥80,000.

Akasaka

Akasaka (Map 3) probably has such a high concentration of luxury hotels because it is a great area in which to be based: there are loads of good restaurants nearby, the political and business centres are within walking distance and Roppongi's nightlife is just down the road.

The *Akasaka Tōkyū Hotel* (☎ 3580-2311) is right in the heart of Akasaka, just above Akasaka-mitsuke subway station. There are lots of good bars and restaurants scattered throughout the building, several of which are on the 14th floor, giving good views over central Tokyo. The hotel also boasts a large shopping floor with luxury goods from around the world. Prices are on the low side for this area. Singles/doubles/twins start at ¥16,000/28,000/23,000.

The *ANA Hotel Tokyo* (☎ 3505-1111), midway between Akasaka and Roppongi in the fashionable Ark Hills area, is an excellent choice. This modern 37 storey hotel has all the amenities – fitness clubs, an outdoor pool, saunas, salons, shopping, and lots of good bars and restaurants. The Astral Sky Bar affords a view over Tokyo as far as Mt Fuji on clear days. Singles/doubles/twins start at ¥24,000/31,000/28,000.

The *Capitol Tōkyū Hotel* (☎ 3581-4511) is an elegant place up on the same hill as Hie-jinja Shrine. The hotel is built around a fine Japanese garden, with good restaurants and bars to take in the view. In warmer months, you can make use of the outdoor swimming pool. Singles/doubles/twins start at ¥23,000/35,500/35,500.

Another skyscraper hotel, the *Akasaka Prince Hotel* (☎ 3234-1111) is something of a landmark. The rooms provide excellent views and spaciousness, a commodity in short supply in Tokyo. Western-style singles/doubles start at ¥24,000/36,000, twins at ¥32,000. Japanese-style suites start at ¥95,000.

The *Hotel New Ōtani* (Map 7) (☎ 3265-1111), not far from the Akasaka Prince, is renowned for the Japanese garden around which it is constructed. The hotel itself is massive, with all the amenities you'd expect from a hotel of this class, including extensive shopping areas, restaurants and private meeting rooms. The downside to such a large hotel is that it has something of an impersonal feeling. Singles/doubles/twins start at ¥27,500/32,500/40,000. The hotel also has a large variety of suites.

At the top of a very exclusive bunch, the *Hotel Ōkura* (☎ 3582-0111), near the US embassy, is the home of visiting dignitaries and businesspeople. With a fine Japanese garden, elegant common areas and some of Tokyo's best restaurants, there's little reason to leave the hotel. Business travellers will also appreciate the executive salon service, offering all the staff and equipment necessary to run your business on the road. Singles/doubles/twins start at ¥28,500/37,000/40,000.

Other Areas

The following is a brief list of recommended hotels on the periphery of the Tokyo area:

Hotel Pacific Meridian (Map 1)
(☎ 3445-6711; fax 3445-5733) singles/doubles from ¥22,000/25,000; near Shinagawa station
New Takanawa Prince Hotel (Map 1)
(☎ 3442-1111; fax 3444-1234) singles/doubles/twins from ¥21,000/28,000/28,500; close to Shinagawa station
Takanawa Prince Hotel
(☎ 3447-1111; fax 3446-0849) singles/twins from ¥17,500/24,000, doubles from ¥30,000; near Shinagawa station
Tokyo Prince Hotel (Map 3)
(☎ 3432-1111; fax 3434-5551) singles/twins from ¥24,000/25,000, doubles from ¥25,000; near Onarimon subway station

If you need easy access to Narita airport, the following hotels are recommended:

Holiday Inn Tōbu Narita
(☎ 0476-32-1234; fax 32-0617) singles/doubles from ¥12,000/19,000; five minutes by taxi to airport
Hotel Narita Tōkyū
(☎ 0476-33-0109; fax 33-0148) singles/twins/doubles from ¥11,800/19,000/19,200; 10 minutes by taxi to airport
Narita ANA Hotel
(☎ 0476-33-1311; fax 33-0244) singles/doubles from ¥14,000/21,000; 10 minutes by taxi to airport

LONG-TERM
Rental Options

Anyone renting an apartment in Tokyo will have to fork out a lot of money up front. You will often have to go through a real estate agency, whose fee is a month's rent. Then there's the landlord's 'key money' *(reikin)* – two to three months rent, usually required again after two years. You never see it again. After this, there is the deposit (one or two months rent) and an up-front payment of one or two months rent. Imagine getting an apartment for a very reasonable ¥85,000 per month, then add up all these costs and you'll see why people stay so long in gaijin houses.

Luckily, nowadays there are lots of real estate agents in Tokyo who speak English and are familiar with helping foreigners find a place to rent. The Kimi Information Center (Map 5) (☎ 3986-1604) in Ikebukuro has comprehensive listings of apartments at very reasonable prices. In Roppongi, there is Ogura Real Estate (☎ 3586-8017). It's open from 9.30 am to 6 pm, closed Sunday. Also check the *The Japan Times*, the *Tokyo Classifieds* and the *Tokyo Journal* for current listings.

Finally, almost every apartment for rent in Tokyo requires a Japanese guarantor. If you have a full-time job, your boss will generally do this for you. Understandably, however, Japanese are generally not eager to sign on as guarantors, especially to foreigners they have only known briefly. It's best not to embarrass newly acquired friends by asking.

Serviced Apartments

If you are based in Tokyo for a couple of months or longer, serviced apartments are an option. Look in *The Japan Times* or *Tokyo Journal*. Prices vary dramatically depending on size, location and services provided. No key money is required, but you generally pay a one month deposit. For anything halfway decent, be prepared to spend between ¥100,000 and ¥180,000 per month.

Helpful agencies that deal in serviced apartments include Nihon MKD (☎ 3780-2611), Fontana (☎ 3382-0151) and House Builder (☎ 3405-0130) in Tokyo, and Arai Housing in Yokohama (☎ 0473-98-3370). English is spoken on all these numbers.

Places to Eat

No city in Asia can match Tokyo for the sheer variety and quality of its restaurants. As well as refined Japanese cuisine, Tokyo is filled with great international restaurants – everything from Cambodian to African. Really serious gourmands can seek out John Kennerdell's *Tokyo Restaurant Guide*, the best guide available.

But Tokyo is not all culinary elegance and trendy ethnic cuisines at fancy prices. Workers face long hours and distant commutes, and often eat out by necessity. All commercial and residential areas harbour multitudes of cheap eateries where you can grab a quick, economical meal. At lunch time, when workers pour out of offices, most restaurants also provide cheap teishoku.

During the day, the best eating areas are the big shopping districts: Akasaka, Shibuya, Shinjuku, Harajuku and Ginza. Shinjuku may be the best daytime option, with department store *resutoran-gai* (restaurant floors), an endless selection of reasonably priced restaurants and the best affordable Chinese food in town. There are a vast number of restaurants around and under Shinjuku station and in the busy entertainment area.

Good Japanese and international cuisine is more expensive, but if you're happy to spend ¥3000 for a meal and a drink, there is no shortage of excellent choices. And if you want the gourmet best, Tokyo delivers – there's something here for everyone.

Vegetarian

Vegetarian food is less common than you might expect in Tokyo (two of the city's more popular Japanese vegetarian restaurants are in Shibuya). Luckily, many places which aren't strictly vegetarian serve a good variety of non-meat/non-fish dishes, eg Japanese noodle and tofu shops. For more information, pick up the Tourist Information Center's (TIC's) *Vegetarian & Macrobiotic Restaurants in Tokyo* handout. This lists strictly vegetarian restaurants, whole food shops, *shōjin-ryōri* (Buddhist temple fare) restaurants, and Indian restaurants which offer a good selection of vegetarian dishes.

continued on page 149

東京 東京 東京 東京 東京 東京 東京 東京 東

Tokyo Cafe Society

Lately, there's been a boom in open-air restaurants and cafes in Tokyo. Granted, it will never be Paris, but Tokyo now has its own cafe society, and people-watching over a cup of cappuccino has become an economical alternative to shopping as a leisure-time activity.

If the sun is shining and the leaves are on the trees, Harajuku's Omote-sandō is the place to be. The street is dotted with slavish reproductions of French cafes and the constant parade of Tokyo characters makes for superb people-watching.

These are recommended cafes in the area where you can get coffee drinks for around ¥500 a cup, light meals for about ¥1000 and a variety of alcoholic drinks:

Cafe des pres
    The current favourite of Aoyama's hip young things. With its prime position near the Omote-sandō intersection, you're bound to see some of Tokyo's most beautiful people.

Cafe de Rope
    Another central spot; the prices are a little high, but the people-watching is great.

Bamboo
    A little off the main drag, but the great patio more than compensates for its less-than-central location; the sandwiches are cheap as well.

Studio V
    This place can't make up its mind: is it a flower shop or a coffee shop? Actually it's both – a pleasant, mellow place, but not a top spot for people-watching.

Stage Y2
    Another popular cafe right near Harajuku station, perfectly situated for the Sunday afternoon fashion parade.

Spiral Cafe
    All right, it's not outdoors at all, but for a slice of chic Aoyama life and a cool artistic interior, check out this cafe inside the famous Spiral building.

東京 東京 東京 東京 東京 東京 東京 東京 東

FOOD

Japanese food is one of the world's most diverse cuisines. While you may have tried only sushi, tempura and sukiyaki in your home country, there are actually over 20 main types of Japanese cooking, each as different as pizza is from hamburger.

The influence of foreign cuisines and availability of imported ingredients have considerably enriched the Japanese diet, but most meals are still based on the mainstays of rice, *miso* (soy-bean paste) soup and *tsukemono* (Japanese pickles). Of these, rice is very much the central element, so much so that the Japanese words for 'rice' and 'meal' are the same: *gohan*. Everything else is just *okazu* (food to be eaten with rice), from humble pickles to the finest cut of Kōbe beef.

Those in search of a truly Japanese experience will probably want to avoid the ubiquitous fast-food emporiums. However, some may baulk at charging into an unfamiliar restaurant where both the language and the menu are likely to be incomprehensible. The best way to get over this fear is to familiarise yourself with the main types of Japanese restaurants so that you have some idea of what's on offer and how to order it. Those timid of heart should take solace in the fact that the Japanese will go to extraordinary lengths to understand what you want and will help you to order.

With the exception of *shokudō* (all around eateries) and *izakaya* (drinking restaurants), most Japanese restaurants are speciality restaurants serving only one type of cuisine. This naturally makes for delicious eating, but does limit your choice. The following sections introduce the main types of Japanese restaurants, along with the most common dishes served. With a little courage and effort you will soon discover that Japan is a gourmet paradise where good food is taken very seriously.

Shokudō 食堂

A shokudō, or eating place, is the most common restaurant in Japan, found near railway stations, tourist spots and just about any other place where people congregate. Easily distinguished by plastic displays in the window, these inexpensive places usually serve a variety of Japanese *(washoku)* and western *(yōshoku)* foods. At lunch, and sometimes dinner, the easiest way to order at a shokudō is to order a *teishoku*, or set course meal (sometimes also called *ranchi setto*, lunch set, or *kōsu*). This usually includes a main dish of meat or fish, a bowl of rice, miso soup, shredded cabbage and a few tsukemono. Most shokudō also serve a fairly standard selection of *donburi-mono* (rice dishes) and *menrui* (noodle dishes). When you order noodles, you can choose between *soba* and *udon* noodles, both of which are served with a variety of toppings. If you're at a loss as to what to order, simply tell the waiter '*kyō-no-ranchi*' (today's lunch) and they'll do the rest. Expect to spend about ¥800 to ¥1000 for a meal at a shokudō. Some of the more common dishes are:

Box: Sushi (photograph by Glenn Beanland)

Above: Mountain yam (yama-imo) – when grated, this vegetable becomes an oozing starchy mass. It is often served on top of soba noodles or mixed with wasabi, soy sauce and cubes of fresh red tuna.

Rice Dishes

katsu-don	カツ丼	a bowl of rice topped with a fried pork cutlet
oyako-don	親子丼	a bowl of rice topped with egg and chicken
niku-don	肉丼	a bowl of rice topped with thin slices of cooked beef
tendon	天丼	a bowl of rice topped with tempura shrimp and vegetables

Noodle Dishes
(Add 'soba' or 'udon' to the following when ordering)

kake	かけ	plain noodles in broth
kitsune	きつね	noodles with fried tofu
tempura	天ぷら	noodles with tempura shrimp
tsukimi	月見	noodles with raw egg on top

Eating in a Japanese Restaurant

When you enter a restaurant in Japan, you will be greeted with a hearty 'Irasshaimase!' ('Welcome!'). In all but the most casual places the waiter or waitress will next ask you 'Nan-mei sama?' ('How many people?'). Answer with your fingers, which is what the Japanese do.

Once seated you'll be given an oshibori (hot towel), a cup of tea and a menu. The oshibori is for wiping your hands and face. When you're done with it, just roll it up and leave it next to your place.

If your Japanese isn't up to it, ordering is a matter of pointing – either to the script on the menu, other diners' meals or the plastic food displays outside. You can signal for the bill by crossing one index finger over the other to form an 'x'. You can also say 'O-kanjō kudasai'. Remember that there's no tipping in Japan and tea is free of charge. Normally you will be given a bill to take to the cashier at the front of the restaurant – cash isn't usually left on the table. Only the bigger and more international places take credit cards, so cash is always the surer option.

When leaving, it is polite to say, 'Gochisō-sama deshita' to the restaurant staff. ■

Left: If you're between restaurants while sightseeing or on business, bentō (boxed lunches) will help keep you on the go. Many imaginative varieties of bentō are sold at railway stations. For details, see the Ekiben – Lunch in Locomotion boxed text later in this chapter.

Below: Pickled plums – served with almost every meal, the ubiquitous umeboshi has been appreciated by the Japanese for its health-giving properties for hundreds of years.

Izakaya 居酒屋

An izakaya is the Japanese equivalent of a pub, with a wider selection of food. It's a good place to visit when you want a casual meal, plenty of food choices, a hearty atmosphere and, of course, lots of beer and sake. When you enter an izakaya, you are given the choice of sitting around the counter, at a table or on a tatami floor. You usually order a bit at a time, eg yakitori, sashimi and grilled fish, as well as Japanese versions of foods like French fries and beef stew.

Izakaya can be identified by their rustic facades, red lanterns bearing the Chinese characters for izakaya, and crates of sake and beer bottles outside their doors. Since izakaya food is casual drinking fare, it is usually fairly inexpensive. Depending on how much you drink, you can expect to pay ¥2500 to ¥5000 per person. Some of Tokyo's best izakaya can be found in Ginza and Ikebukuro.

In addition to the following dishes, refer to the Yakitori and Sushi & Sashimi sections later on for additional choices.

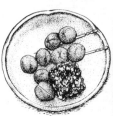

agedashi-dōfu	揚げだし豆腐	deep-fried tofu in a fish stock soup
jaga-batā	ジャガバター	baked potatoes with butter
niku-jaga	肉じゃが	beef and potato stew
shio-yaki-zakana	塩焼魚	a whole fish grilled with salt

yaki-onigiri	焼きおにぎり	a triangle of grilled rice with yakitori sauce
poteto furai	ポテトフライ	French fries
chiizu-age	チーズ揚げ	deep-fried cheese
hiya-yakko	冷奴	a cold block of tofu with soy sauce and scallions
tsuna sarada	ツナサラダ	tuna salad over cabbage
yaki-soba	焼きそば	fried noodles with meat and vegetables
kata yaki-soba	固焼きそば	hard fried noodles with meat and vegetables
sashimi mori-awase	刺身盛りあわせ	a selection of sliced sashimi

Robatayaki 炉端焼

Similar to an izakaya, a *robatayaki* is a rustic drinking restaurant serving a wide variety of foods grilled over charcoal. The name means 'hearthside cooking' and every effort is made to re-create the atmosphere of an old country house – which was always centred around a large hearth, or *irori*. Eating at a robatayaki is a feast for the eyes as well as the taste buds: you sit around a counter with the food spread out in front of you on a layer of ice, behind which is a large charcoal grill. You don't need a word of Japanese to order; just point at whatever looks good. The chef will grill your selection and pass it to you on a long wooden paddle – grab your food quickly before he snatches it back.

Robatayaki fare is largely the same as that at an izakaya. They have menus, but no-one uses them – just point and eat. The drink of choice is beer or sake. Expect to spend about ¥5000 per head. Not as common as izayaka, robatayaki usually have rustic wooden facades modelled on traditional Japanese farmhouses. For a classic, albeit pricey, robatayaki experience, you can't beat Roppongi's Inakaya.

Okonomiyaki お好み焼

The name means 'cook what you like', and an *okonomiyaki* restaurant provides you with an inexpensive opportunity to do just that. At an okonomiyaki, you sit around a *teppan* (iron hotplate) armed with a spatula and chopsticks to cook your choice of meat, seafood and vegetables in a cabbage and vegetable batter.

Some places will do most of the cooking; you season the result with bonito flakes *(katsuo bushi)*, soy sauce *(shōyu)*, parsley, Japanese Worcestershire-style sauce and mayonnaise. Cheaper places will simply hand you a bowl filled with the ingredients. If this happens, don't panic. First, mix the batter and filling thoroughly, then place it on the hot grill, flattening it into a pancake shape. After five minutes or so, use the spatulas to flip it and cook for another five minutes. Then dig in.

Most okonomiyaki places also serve yaki-soba (fried noodles) and *yasai-itame* (stir-fried vegetables), washed down with mugs of draught beer. Don't worry too much about preparation of the food – as a foreigner you'll be expected to be inept and the waiter will keep a sharp eye on you to make sure no real disasters occur. You can expect to pay about ¥1500 per person for a full meal and a beer.

Finding an okonomiyaki restaurant is fairly easy, since most have glass fronts so you can see inside. If not, you'll have to look for the kanji somewhere on the sign.

Soy beans (daizu) – the nutritious base for an endless variety of Japanese foods – soy sauce, miso, tofu and the smelly nattō.

mikkusu okonomiyaki	ミックス お好み焼き	mixed fillings of seafood, meat and vegetables
modan-yaki	モダン焼き	okonomiyaki with fried egg
gyū okonomiyaki	牛お好み焼き	beef okonomiyaki
yasai okonomiyaki	野菜お好み焼き	vegetable okonomiyaki
negi okonomiyaki	ネギお好み焼き	thin okonomiyaki with scallions

Yakitori 焼き鳥

Yakitori means skewers of grilled chicken, a popular after-work accompaniment to beer and sake. At a yakitori restaurant you sit around a counter with the other patrons and watch the chef grill your selections over charcoal. It's best to order a few skewers of several varieties and then order seconds of the ones you really like. Remember that one serving often means two or three skewers (be careful – the price listed on the menu is usually that of a single skewer).

In summer, the beverage of choice at a yakitori restaurant is beer or cold sake (hot in winter). A few drinks and enough skewers to fill you up should cost from ¥3000 to ¥4000 per person. Yakitori joints are usually small places, often near railway stations, and are best identified by a red lantern outside and the smell of grilling chicken.

There are two wonderful places with a yakitori atmosphere, reminiscent of Occupation-era Japan: Yūrakuchō Yakitori Alley and Omoide Yokochō.

yakitori	焼き鳥	plain, grilled white meat
hasami/negima	はさみ／ねぎま	pieces of white meat alternating with leek
sasami	ささみ	skinless chicken breast pieces
kawa	かわ	chicken skin
tsukune	つくね	chicken meat balls
rebā	レバ	chicken livers
tebasaki	手羽先	chicken wings
gyū-niku	牛肉	pieces of beef
shiitake	しいたけ	Japanese mushrooms
piiman	ピーマン	small green peppers
tama-negi	たまねぎ	round, white onions
yaki-onigiri	焼きおにぎり	a triangle of rice grilled with yakitori sauce

GLENN BEANLAND

Yakitori can be bought from pushcarts, used as stomach liner for a night of sake drinking at a Japanese pub or admired for its thoughtful presentation in an elegant restaurant.

Sushi & Sashimi 寿司／刺身

Like yakitori, sushi is considered a side dish for beer and sake. Nonetheless, people often make a meal of it and it's one of the healthiest meals around. Although sushi is now popular in the west, few foreigners are prepared for the delicacy and taste of the real thing. Without a doubt, this is one dish that the visitor to Japan should sample at least once.

There are two main types of sushi: *nigiri-zushi* (served on a small bed of rice – the most common variety) and *maki-zushi* (served in a seaweed roll).

Lesser known varieties include *chirashi-zushi* (a layer of rice covered in egg and fish toppings), *oshi-zushi* (fish pressed in a mould over rice) and *inari-zushi* (rice in a pocket of sweet, fried tofu). Whatever kind of sushi you try, it will be served with lightly vinegared rice. In the case of nigiri-zushi and maki-zushi, it will contain a bit of *wasabi* (hot, green horseradish).

Sushi is not difficult to order. If you sit at the counter of a sushi restaurant you can simply point at what you want. You can also order à la carte from the menu. When ordering, you usually order *ichi-nin mae* (one portion), which usually means two pieces of sushi (though the price on the menu will be that of only one piece). The easiest order is an assorted plate of nigiri-zushi called *mori-awase*. These usually come in three grades: *futsū nigiri* (regular nigiri), *jō nigiri* (special nigiri) and *toku-jō nigiri* (extra-special nigiri). The difference is in the type of fish used. Most mori-awase contain six or seven pieces of sushi. Of course, you can order fish without the rice, in which case it is called sashimi.

Dip the sushi in *shōyu* which you pour from a small decanter into a low dish. If you're not good at using chopsticks, don't worry, sushi is one of the few foods in Japan that is perfectly okay to eat with your hands. Slices of pickled ginger *(gari)* help refresh the palate.

Be warned that a good sushi restaurant can cost upward of ¥10,000, while an average place can cost from ¥3000 to ¥5000 per person. One way to sample the joy of sushi on the cheap is to try an automatic sushi place, usually called *kaiten-zushi*, where the sushi is served on a conveyor belt which runs along a counter. Here you simply reach up and grab whatever looks good. You're charged according to how many plates of sushi you've eaten. Plates are colour-coded according to price, and the cost is written somewhere on the plate itself or on a sign on the wall. You can usually fill yourself up for ¥1000 to ¥2000 per person.

Automatic sushi places often have miniature conveyor belts in the window, while regular sushi restaurants often place fish tanks in the window or a white lantern with the characters for sushi written in black letters.

For the freshest sushi on the planet, head down to Tsukiji, where you can see the raw materials on sale in the giant fish market before sitting down to a fabulous sushi breakfast or brunch.

ama-ebi	甘海老	sweet shrimp
awabi	あわび	abalone
ebi	海老	prawn or shrimp
hamachi	はまち	yellowtail
ika	いか	squid
ikura	イクラ	salmon roe
kai-bashira	貝柱	scallop
kani	かに	crab
katsuo	かつお	bonito
maguro	まぐろ	tuna
tai	鯛	sea bream
tamago	たまご	sweetened egg
toro	とろ	the choicest cut of fatty tuna belly, very expensive
unagi	うなぎ	eel with a sweet sauce
uni	うに	sea urchin roe

Sukiyaki & Shabu-Shabu  すき焼/しゃぶしゃぶ

Restaurants usually specialise in these dishes. Sukiyaki is a favourite of most foreign visitors to Japan. When made with high-quality beef, like Kōbe beef, it is a sublime experience. Sukiyaki consists of thin slices of beef cooked in a broth of soy sauce, sugar and sake, and is accompanied by a variety of vegetables and tofu. After cooking, all the ingredients are dipped in raw egg (the heat of the ingredients tends to lightly cook the egg) before being eaten.

Shabu-shabu consists of thin slices of beef and vegetables cooked by swirling the ingredients in a light broth and then dipping them in a variety of special sesame seed and citrus-based sauces. Both of these dishes are

Okra (lady's fingers) – served raw in salads or lightly cooked in soups, this olive-green, star-shaped vegetable has quite an unusual slippery texture.

Food Etiquette

When it comes to eating in Japan, there are quite a number of implicit rules, but they're fairly easy to remember. If you're worried about putting your foot in it, relax – the Japanese almost expect foreigners to make mistakes in formal situations and are unlikely to be offended as long as you follow the standards of politeness of your own country.

Among the more important eating 'rules' are those regarding chopsticks. Sticking them upright in your rice is considered very bad form: that's how rice is offered to the dead! So is passing food from your chopsticks to someone else's – another Buddhist death rite involves passing the bones of the cremated deceased among members of the family using chopsticks. It's also quite common when taking food from shared plates to avoid using the end of your chopsticks that has touched your mouth – invert them before reaching for that tasty morsel.

Note that it's perfectly acceptable to lift your soup bowl to your mouth and drink from it. It's also fine to lift your rice bowl toward your mouth, and this certainly makes it easier to get the rice to your mouth without dropping it on your lap. When eating noodle dishes like rāmen, soba and udon, it's also acceptable to slurp if you feel like it, but no one will look askance if you don't.

When eating with other people, the general practice is to preface actually digging into the food with the expression '*Itadakimasu*', literally 'I will receive'. Similarly, at the end of the meal you should say '*Gochisō-sama deshita*', a respectful way of saying that the meal was good.

If you're out for a few drinks with Japanese friends or colleagues, remember that you're expected to keep the drinks of your fellow drinkers topped up. Don't fill your own glass: wait for someone to do this for you. It's polite to hold the glass with both hands while it is being filled. The Japanese equivalent of cheers is *kampai*.

In Japan, there is a definite etiquette to bill-paying. If someone invites you to eat or drink with them, they will be paying. Even among groups eating together, it is unusual for bills to be split. Generally, at the end of the meal, something of a struggle will ensue to see who gets the privilege of paying. If this happens, it is polite to at least make an effort to pay the bill. It is extremely unlikely that your Japanese hosts will acquiesce, though exceptions to this rule are likely among younger Japanese. ∎

---

prepared in a pot over a fire at your private table, but you needn't fret about preparation – the waiter will usually help you get started and then keep a close watch as you proceed. The key is to take your time and add the ingredients a little at a time, savouring the flavours as you go.

Sukiyaki and shabu-shabu restaurants usually have a traditional Japanese decor and sometimes a picture of a cow to help you recognise them. Ordering is not difficult. Simply say 'sukiyaki' or 'shabu-shabu' and indicate how many people are eating. Expect to pay between ¥3000 to ¥10,000 a head.

One of the best places to try these dishes made with high-quality beef is Asakusa Imahan.

Tempura 天ぷら

This famous Japanese food is not actually Japanese, but was borrowed from Portuguese traders in the 16th century. Since then, the Japanese have transformed it into something uniquely their own. Good tempura is portions of fish, prawns and vegetables cooked in fluffy, nongreasy batter.

When you sit down at a tempura restaurant, you will be given a small bowl filled with a light brown sauce *(ten-tsuyu)* and a plate of grated *daikon* radish; mix this into the sauce and dip each piece of tempura into it. Tempura is best when it's hot, so don't wait too long – use the sauce to cool each piece and dig in. While you can order à la carte, most diners choose to order a *teishoku* (full set), which includes rice, miso soup and Japanese pickles.

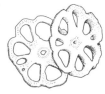

Lotus root (renkon) – appreciated for its firm and crisp texture, slices of this root are often added to pots of steaming nabe or deep-fried as tempura.

Tempura may have been borrowed from 16th century Portugese sea-farers, but it has become a quintessentially Japan-ese food. Popular as 'fast food' in old Edo days, the refined cooking methods used today to subtly unlock the ingredients' essence have made tempura emblematic of Japanese food.

GLENN BEANLAND

Expect to pay between ¥2000 and ¥10,000 for a full tempura meal. Finding these restaurants is tricky, as they have no distinctive facade or decor. If you look through the window, you'll see customers around the counter watching the chefs as they work over large woks filled with oil. Many luxury hotels have tempura restaurants on their premises.

In Tokyo, you need look no further than the famous Ten-Ichi chain for heavenly tempura. For cheaper tempura, head to the area around Sensō-ji Temple in Asakusa.

Rāmen   ラーメン

The Japanese adapted this dish from China and produced one of the world's most delicious fast foods. Rāmen dishes are big bowls of noodles in a meat broth served with a variety of toppings, such as sliced pork, bean sprouts and leeks. In some restaurants you may be asked if you'd prefer kotteri (thick) or assari (thin) soup. Other than this, ordering is simple: just sidle up to the counter and say 'rāmen', or ask for any of the other choices usually on offer. Expect to pay between ¥500 and ¥900 for a bowl. Since rāmen is originally Chinese food, some rāmen restaurants also serve chāhan or yaki-meshi (fried rice), gyōza (dumplings) and kara-age (deep-fried chicken pieces).

Rāmen restaurants are easily distinguished by their long counters lined with customers hunched over steaming bowls. You can also hear a rāmen shop – it is considered polite to slurp the noodles, and aficionados claim that slurping brings out the full flavour of the broth.

Tokyo is home to the world capital of rāmen: the streets surrounding the east exit of JR Shinjuku station. Here, it seems as if there is a rāmen joint for every human in town.

rāmen	ラーメン	standard issue, the cheapest item on the menu – soup and noodles with a sprinkling of meat and vegetables
chāshū-men	チャーシュー麺	rāmen topped with slices of roasted pork
wantan-men	ワンタン麺	rāmen with meat dumplings
miso-rāmen	みそラーメン	rāmen with miso-flavoured broth
chānpon-men	ちゃんぽん麺	Nagasaki-style rāmen with assorted vegetables and meat in the broth

Soba & Udon そば/うどん

Soba noodles are thin, brown, buckwheat noodles, while udon noodles are thick, white, wheat noodles. Most noodle shops serve both soba and udon. Noodles are usually served in a bowl containing a light, bonito-flavoured broth, but you can also order them served cold and piled on a bamboo screen with a cold broth for dipping. By far the most popular type of cold noodles is *zaru soba*, which is served with bits of *nori* (seaweed) on top. This comes with a small plate of wasabi and sliced scallions – put these into the cup of broth and eat the noodles by dipping them in this mixture. The waiter will give you some hot broth to mix with the leftover sauce which you drink like a kind of tea. As with rāmen, feel free to slurp as loudly as you please.

Soba and udon places are usually cheap (about ¥900), but some fancy places can be expensive (the decor is a good indication of the price). Being a traditional food, you can usually spot soba and udon places by their rustic wooden facades, which occasionally have food displays in the window. For great soba and udon in atmospheric surroundings, try Kanda Yabu Soba.

Add 'soba' or 'udon' to the following four dishes when ordering:

kake	かけ	plain noodles in broth
kitsune	きつね	noodles with slices of fried tofu
tempura	天ぷら	noodles with tempura shrimp
tsukimi	月見	noodles with raw egg on top (literally, moon viewing)
zaru soba	ざるそば	cold noodles with seaweed strips served on a bamboo tray

Unagi うなぎ

Unagi is Japanese for eel, an expensive and popular delicacy in Japan – you owe it to yourself to try unagi at least once while in Japan. It's cooked over hot coals and brushed with a rich sauce made from soy sauce and sake. Full unagi dinners can be quite expensive, but many unagi restaurants offer *unagi bentō* (boxed lunches) and lunch sets for around ¥1500. Most unagi restaurants display plastic models of their unagi sets in their front windows and have barrels of live eels to entice passers-by. For good unagi in an elegant setting, try Ueno's Izu-ei restaurant.

unagi teishoku	うなぎ定食	full-set unagi meal with rice, grilled eel, eel-liver soup and pickles
unadon	うな丼	grilled eel over a bowl of rice
unajū	うな重	grilled eel over a flat tray of rice (larger than unadon)
kabayaki	蒲焼き	skewers of grilled eel without rice

GLENN BEANLAND

An order of unajū *is an elegantly presented way to try* unagi *(eel). Ideally, unagi served in this style should be crisp on the outside, with a richly flavoured and tender inside. Unagi is not only exotic and quite tasty – it's also reputed to increase stamina.*

Nabemono 鍋物

Nabemono refers to any of a variety of dishes cooked in large cast-iron pots. Like sukiyaki and shabu-shabu, nabemono are cooked at your table on a small gas burner or a clay *habachi*. Eating nabemono is a participatory experience, with each diner putting in ingredients from trays of prepared, raw food. The most famous nabemono is called *chanko-nabe*, the high-calorie stew eaten by sumō wrestlers during training. Chanko-nabe restaurants are often run by retired wrestlers and the walls are often festooned with sumō arcana.

Since nabemono are filling and hot, they are usually eaten in winter. They are also popular as banquet and party dishes, since the eating of a nabe dish is a very communal experience. It is difficult to pick out a nabe restaurant – the best way is to ask a Japanese friend for a recommendation. We highly recommend Botan in Kanda. This fine old place serves one dish only, chicken nabe, and unless you hate chicken, you'll find it's more than enough.

chanko-nabe	ちゃんこ鍋	sumo wrestler's stew of meat and vegetables
botan-nabe	ぼたん鍋	wild boar stew with vegetables
yose-nabe	寄せ鍋	seafood and chicken stew with vegetables

Fugu ふぐ

The deadly *fugu*, or pufferfish, is eaten more for the thrill than the taste. It's actually rather bland, but acclaimed for its fine texture. Nonetheless, if you have the money to lay out (around ¥10,000), a fugu dinner makes a good 'been there, done that' story back home.

Although the danger of fugu poisoning is negligible, some Japanese joke that you should always let the other person try the first piece. If you need a shot of liquid courage to get started, try a glass of *hirezake* (toasted fugu tail in hot sake) – the traditional accompaniment to a fugu dinner.

Fugu is a seasonal delicacy best eaten in winter. Fugu restaurants usually serve only fugu and can be identified by a picture of a fugu on the sign out the front.

fugu teishoku	ふぐ定食	a set course of fugu served several ways, plus rice and soup
fugu chiri	ふぐちり	a stew made from fugu and vegetables
fugu sashimi	ふぐ刺身	thinly sliced raw fugu
yaki fugu	焼きふぐ	fugu grilled on a habachi at your table

Tonkatsu トンカツ

Tonkatsu is a deep-fried breaded pork cutlet served with a special sauce, usually as part of a set meal *(tonkatsu teishoku)*. Even if you shy away from pork at home, you ought to try this dish – you'll be pleasantly surprised.

Tonkatsu is served both at speciality restaurants and at shokudō. Naturally, the best tonkatsu is at the speciality places, where a full set will run from ¥1500 to ¥2500. When ordering, you can choose between *rōsu*, a fatter cut of pork and *hire*, a leaner cut.

Try Shinjuku's Suzuya for excellent tonkatsu served with all the trimmings.

tonkatsu teishoku	とんかつ定食	a full set meal of tonkatsu, rice, miso soup and shredded cabbage
minchi katsu	ミンチカツ	minced pork cutlet
kushikatsu	串カツ	deep-fried pork and vegetables on skewers

GLENN BEANLAND

JNTO

GLENN BEANLAND

MATTHIAS LEY

GLENN BEANLAND

GLENN BEANLAND

Clockwise from top: Preparation and presentation are two essential concepts in Japanese cuisine: zaru soba, buckwheat noodles served cold on a bamboo screen and sprinkled with nori (seaweed), is a warm-weather favourite; sukiyaki (thinly sliced beef) awaits cooking in a pot over a fire at the table; sashimi is very fresh, skillfully sliced fish served with condiments such as shōyu (soy sauce), shredded daikon (radish) and wasabi (green horseradish); nimono are appetisers made from meat, seafood and vegetables simmered in a seasoned broth and served cold; nigiri sushi, raw fish served with wasabi on a ball of rice sweetened with rice vinegar, elegantly reposes on a rustic tray; bentō boxes range from fast food-style takeaway to delicious haute cuisine served in wooden containers.

CHRIS ROWTHORN

Top: Disturbingly lifelike plastic food models in display cases outside many restaurants make ordering easy; these models, for sale in Kappabashi, also make unusual souvenirs.

CHRIS ROWTHORN

Middle: The common tachi gui (fast-food stand) may be wheeled around to wherever crowds gather, or settled in spots where patrons might like to sit a while.

Bottom Left: Those who consider Japanese food bland probably haven't made use of the many spices available to season the food.

Bottom Right: Somewhere here is a yaki-zakana (grilled whole fish) with your name on it.

MARTIN MOOS

MARTIN MOOS

Kushiage & Kushikatsu　串アゲ／串カツ

Kushiage and *kushikatsu* are deep-fried skewers of meat, seafood and vegetables eaten as an accompaniment to beer. Kushi means skewer, and if it can be fitted onto a skewer, it's probably on the menu. Cabbage is often eaten with the meal to ease the guilt of eating all that grease.

Order kushiage and kushikatsu by the skewer (one skewer is *ippon*, but you can always use your fingers to indicate the number). Like yakitori, this food is popular with office workers and students, and is therefore fairly inexpensive, though upmarket places exist. Expect to pay from ¥2000 to ¥5000 for a full meal and a couple of beers. Not very distinctive in appearance, the best way to find a kushiage and kushikatsu place is to ask a Japanese friend.

ebi	えび	shrimp
ika	いか	squid
renkon	レンコン	lotus root
tama-negi	たまねぎ	white onion
gyū-niku	牛肉	beef pieces
shiitake	しいたけ	Japanese mushrooms
ginnan	銀杏	ginkgo nuts
imo	いも	potato

Kaiseki　懐石

Kaiseki is the pinnacle of Japanese cuisine, where ingredients, preparation, setting and presentation come together to create a dining experience quite unlike any other. Born as an adjunct to the Buddhist-inspired tea ceremony, kaiseki is a largely vegetarian affair. One usually eats kaiseki in the private room of a *ryōtei* (an especially elegant style of traditional restaurant), often overlooking a private, tranquil garden. The meal is served in several small courses, allowing one to admire the plates and bowls which are carefully chosen to complement the food and seasons. Rice is eaten last (usually with an assortment of pickles) and the drink of choice is sake or beer.

This all comes at a steep price – a good kaiseki dinner costs upward of ¥10,000 per person. Kaiseki lunch is much cheaper – most places offer a bentō containing a sampling of their dinner fare for around ¥2500. Kaiseki restaurants can be intimidating places to enter, so you may want to bring a Japanese friend or ask them to call ahead and make arrangements. There is usually only one set course, but some places offer a choice of three courses – graded *ume* (regular), *take* (special) and *matsu* (extra-special).

You can try a fairly casual kaiseki meal at Roppongi's Kisso ryōtei.

Teppanyaki　鉄板焼

Like kaiseki, *teppanyaki* is a luxury food and is usually reserved for special occasions. The main item is steak, though you can also order chicken, seafood and a variety of vegetables. Like robotayaki, part of teppanyaki's appeal is visual, and the preparation of the food, usually right in front of the diner, takes on the air of a performance. Good wine is the perfect accompaniment to teppanyaki and most places have excellent cellars. Teppanyaki does not come cheap, and you can count on spending over ¥10,000 per person, sometimes two or three times that. Most luxury hotels in Tokyo have teppanyaki restaurants on their premises. Otherwise, Roppongi's Seryna is a very accessible place at which to sample top-end teppanyaki.

Mukokuseki　無国籍

Mukokuseki means cuisine without nationality – meaning international spins put on domestic dishes or new creations by whoever is cooking. Usually you order a succession of small dishes and wash them down with beer or sake. Mukokuseki is often served in restaurants which are similar in atmosphere to izakaya, and prices are comparable. Unfortunately, there is no reliable way of distinguishing a mukokuseki restaurant. Reliably good mukokuseki can be had at An An in Ebisu.

Whatever the season, you'll always find a wonderful range of mushrooms (kinoko) in Japan. From the highly acclaimed (and pricey) matsutake that hits upmarket restaurant tables in autumn, to the rich flavour of the shiitake, the pleasant texture of the shimeji or the subtle taste of the long, white enoki, Japan is a virtual paradise for the mushroom-lover.

Yatai 屋台

Yatai are outdoor restaurants, usually tents erected on city sidewalks, but also on temple grounds and at festivals. Like izakaya, yatai are places for both eating and drinking beer and sake. Yatai menus are quite simple and usually include yakitori, a few stewed items, grilled rice balls and in winter, *oden*. A meal at a yatai is a good way to get to know working-class Japanese, who may be a little surprised to find a foreigner in their midst. Ordering is simple, as everything is laid out for you to see. Since yatai owners pay little in the way of rent and upkeep, they are among the cheapest places to eat in Japan – a full meal's worth of food can be had for around ¥1500, and beers cost about ¥600 a mug. Yatai are easy to spot, just look for a tent with a lantern hanging from it.

Oden おでん

Oden is a simple stew of fish cakes, vegetables and tofu cooked for hours in a broth flavoured with kelp. While this may not sound particularly appealing, it's actually good, filling, inexpensive food. Oden is a winter speciality, eaten to fortify oneself against the cold. While there are oden speciality shops scattered about, it's easier to find oden at yakitori and yatai restaurants. You can also buy oden from street vendors. In Tokyo, a good place to look for these is around Ueno-kōen Park. Oden is easy to order; just point at what you'd like. You can easily fill up on oden for less than ¥1000.

DRINKS

Alcoholic Drinks

Alcohol is, in some ways, the glue that holds Japanese society together. Alcohol is drunk by almost every adult, male or female, and a good number of teenagers (alcohol is sold from vending machines and underage drinking is not nearly as frowned upon as it is in some countries). Going out for a few rounds after work with co-workers is both the joy and bane of the Japanese salaryman's life. After a few drinks, workers feel secure enough to vent their frustrations and speak their minds, confident that all will be forgiven by the time they arrive at the office in the morning. Occasionally, drinking crosses the boundary between good-natured fun and ugly inebriation, as anyone who has been in a public park during cherry blossom season can attest. However, drunkenness rarely leads to violence in Japan, so the visitor does not have to be overly concerned.

Box: Sake casks (photograph by Charlotte Hindle).

Above: Tokkuri bottles – coming in all shapes and sizes, many restaurants and sake brewers design their own.

Beer Introduced at the end of the last century, beer *(biiru)* is now the favourite tipple of the Japanese. The quality is generally excellent and the most popular type is light lager, although recently some breweries have been experimenting with darker brews. The major breweries are Kirin, Asahi, Sapporo and Suntory. Beer is dispensed everywhere, from vending machines to beer halls and even in some temple lodgings. A standard can of beer from a vending machine is about ¥250, although some of the monstrous cans cost over ¥1000. At bars, a beer starts at ¥500 and climbs depending on the establishment. Draught beer *(nama biiru)* is widely available, as are imported beers.

Sake Rice wine has been brewed for centuries in Japan. Once restricted to imperial brewers, it was later produced at temples and shrines across the country. In recent years, consumption of beer has overtaken that of sake, but it's still a standard item in homes, restaurants and drinking places. Large casks of sake are often seen piled up as offerings outside temples and shrines, and it plays an important part in most celebrations and festivals.

Most westerners come to Japan with a bad image of sake; the result of having consumed low-grade brands overseas. Although it won't appeal to

TONY WHEELER

You can often see casks of sake left as temple and shrine offerings. Sake is as old as Shintō, and has long been offered to the kami (gods) who watch over the rice harvest. Sake-making was once a communal affair: the entire village chewed a mixture of rice, millet and chestnuts, then spat the results into a vat. Methods have changed with the times, especially after WWII, when rice shortages required glucose and pure alcohol to be mixed with rice mash to increase yields of the drink. Nearly all sake is still produced this way today.

all palates, some of the higher grades are actually very good, and a trip to a restaurant specialising in sake is a great way to sample some of the better brews.

There are several major types of sake, including *nigori* (cloudy), *nama* (unrefined) and regular, clear sake. Of these, the clear sake is by far the most common. Clear sake is usually divided into three grades: *tokkyū* (premium), *ikkyū* (first grade) and *nikkyū* (second grade). Nikkyū is the routine choice. These are further divided into *karakuchi* (dry) and *amakuchi* (sweet). Apart from the national brewing giants, there are thousands of provincial brewers producing local brews called *jizake*.

Sake is served *atsukan* (warm) and *reishū* (cold), the former being more popular in the winter. When you order sake, it will usually be served in a small flask called *tokkuri*. Tokkuri come in two sizes, so you should specify whether you want *ichigo* (small) or *nigo* (large). From these flasks you pour the sake into small ceramic cups called *o-choko* or *sakazuki*. Another way to sample sake is to drink it from a small wooden box called *masu*, with a bit of salt at the rim.

However you drink it, with a 17% alcohol content, sake is likely to go right to your head, particularly the warm stuff. After a few bouts with sake you'll come to understand why the Japanese drink it in such small cups. Particularly memorable is a real sake hangover born of too much cheap sake. The best advice is not to indulge the day before you have to get on a plane.

Shōchū For those looking for a quick and cheap escape route from their sorrows, *shōchū* is the answer. It's a distilled spirit (30% alcohol) which has been resurrected from low esteem (it was used as a disinfectant in the Edo period) to the status of a trendy drink. You can drink it as *oyu-wari* (with hot water) or as *chūhai* (a highball with soda and lemon). A 720ml bottle sells for about ¥600, which makes it a relatively cheap option compared to other spirits.

Wine, Imported Drinks & Whisky Japanese wines are available from areas such as Yamanashi, Nagano, Tōhoku and Hokkaidō. Standard wines are often blended with imports from South America or eastern Europe. The major producers are Suntory, Mann's and Mercian. Prices are high – expect to pay at least ¥1000 for a bottle of something drinkable.

Imported wines are often stocked by large liquor stores or department stores. Bargains are sometimes available at ¥600, but most of the imports are considerably more expensive.

Prices of imported spirits have been coming down in recent years and bargain liquor stores have been popping up. However, it is probably a good idea to pick up a duty-free bottle or two on your way through the airport.

Whisky is available at most drinking establishments and is usually drunk *mizu-wari* (with water and ice) or *onzarokku* (on the rocks). Local brands, such as Suntory and Nikka, are sensibly priced and most measure up to foreign standards. Expensive foreign labels are popular as gifts.

Most other imported spirits are available. Bars with a large foreign clientele, including hotel bars, can usually mix anything at your request. If not, they will certainly tailor a drink to your specifications.

Drinking Places What you pay for your drink depends on where you drink and, in the case of a hostess bar, with whom you drink. As a rule, hostess bars are the most expensive places to drink (up to ¥10,000 per drink), followed by upmarket traditional Japanese bars, hotel bars, beer halls and casual pubs. If you are not sure about a place, ask about prices and cover charges before sitting down. As a rule, if you are served a small snack with your first round, you'll be paying a cover charge (usually a few hundred yen, but sometimes much more).

Japanese-style places to drink include *izakaya* and *yakitori-ya*. These are cheap places which serve beer, sake and food in a casual atmosphere resembling that of a pub. *Aka-chōchin*, also known as *nomiya*, display a red lantern outside. These are pubs for the working class – down-to-earth in price and decor. The cheapest of these places are known as *tachi-nomiya*, where there are no chairs and everyone just stands around and slugs it back.

Nonalcoholic Drinks

Most familiar drinks are available in Japan, with a few colourfully named additions like Pocari Sweat and Calpis Water, and drink machines are on virtually every street corner – for ¥110, refreshment is rarely more than a few steps away.

Coffee & Tea Coffee *(kōhii)* is usually expensive in Japan (¥350 to ¥500 a cup), with some places charging up to ¥1000. Some of the newer chains of coffee restaurants like Doutor or Pronto, or donut shops like Mr Donut (which offers free refills), are cheaper options. Cheaper still is a can of coffee, hot or cold, from a vending machine. Although unpleasantly sweet, at ¥110 the price is hard to beat.

At a coffee shop you'll be asked whether you like your coffee *hotto* (hot) or *aisu* (cold). Black tea also comes hot or cold, with *miruku* (milk) or *remon* (lemon). A good way to start the day is with a *mōningu setto* (morning set) of tea or coffee, toast and eggs, which costs around ¥350. The following are some of the more common drinks available in *kissaten* (Japanese coffee shops).

kōhii	コーヒー	regular coffee
burendo kōhii	ブレンドコーヒー	blended coffee, fairly strong
american kōhii	アメリカンコーヒー	weak coffee
kōcha	紅茶	black, British-style tea
kafe ōre	カフェオーレ	café au lait, hot or cold
orenji jūsu	オレンジジュース	orange juice

Japanese Tea Unlike black tea, Japanese tea is green and contains a lot of vitamin C and caffeine. The powdered form used in tea ceremony is called *matcha* and is drunk after being whipped into a frothy consistency. More common is leafy green tea *(o-cha)*, which is drunk after being steeped in a pot. While *sencha* is one popular variety of green tea, most restaurants will serve a free cup of brownish tea called *bancha*. In summer a cold beverage called *mugicha* (roasted barley tea) is served in private homes.

Japanese tea is very healthy and refreshing, and is said by some to prevent cancer. Most department stores carry a wide selection of Japanese teas.

continued from page135

PLACES TO EAT – BUDGET

It is by no means difficult to eat well on a budget in Tokyo. Apart from self-catering options (sandwiches and so on), economical restaurants for people on the go are everywhere. Probably the most common of these is the rāmen shop. The cheapest dish is always rāmen itself, a hearty bowl of noodles with limited condiments (¥450 to ¥500). Variations can be found in Japanese noodle shops serving udon and soba.

Japanese

The best places to look for inexpensive Japanese food are Shinjuku, Asakusa, Ueno and Ikebukuro. You can always find some cheap places in and around railway stations, on the restaurant floors of department stores and in shopping arcades. The key when hunting is to look for simple, relatively unadorned places. You can also watch where office workers go to eat.

If you're really trying to pinch yen, look for a *tachi-kui* (stand-and-eat) place, where you can get simple dishes for as low as ¥200. These are most commonly found inside the busier railway stations. At a tachi-kui, you usually choose the dish you'd like from a vending machine outside the store, which, if you're lucky, has pictures of the dishes above the buttons. The machine will issue a plastic token which you hand to one of the workers inside.

Tokyo Station Area The area in and around Tokyo station (Map 2) is not the best place to look for good restaurants, but it is possible to find cheap eats. Below the station itself, there is an underground shopping mall with all manner of inexpensive Japanese and western-style restaurants, most of which have plastic food models on display. Japanese dishes include noodles, tonkatsu, teishoku and extensive coffee shop fare.

Out of the station you'll find some bargains on the restaurant floors of nearby department stores. Takashimaya seems to have the best selection – stroll through its wonderful B1 food floor (and try a few free

samples). In the sub-basement (B2), there's a cafeteria-style eatery with standard lunch items, many of them as set meals, ranging from ¥800 to ¥2000. Choose what you'd like from the display case (they're identified by number), buy a ticket from the attendant and give it to your waiter.

If you're willing to spend a little more, there's much tastier food in restaurants on the 6th floor of Takashimaya's annex (the floor is called Konomi Shokudō. Here, for remarkably reasonable prices, you can choose from tempura, unagi, sushi, noodles and Kyoto cuisine, all served by speciality restaurants with plastic food models out the front. Prices range from ¥700 to ¥3000.

Ginza Despite its reputation as Tokyo's ritziest area, Ginza (Map 3) is home to some very reasonably priced restaurants. Indeed, if you're put off by the gaudy lights and in-your-face advertising of Shinjuku or Ikebukuro, Ginza is a great place to look for good restaurants in pleasant surroundings.

For inexpensive lunch and dinner sets, try Ginza's department stores, in particular the 8th floor of Matsuya, the 2nd basement floor of Matsuzakaya and the 1st and 2nd basement floors of Hankyū. On the 2nd basement floor of Hankyū you'll find *Naokyū Rāmen*, one of the cheapest and most popular rāmen places in town – at ¥400 for rāmen and ¥300 for gyōza (Chinese dumplings), it's understandably packed for lunch and dinner – try off-peak. There's no English sign, but it's right next to the Spud coffee shop.

For inexpensive noodles, try *Dondon*, on the other side of the tracks from Ginza in the direction of Hibiya. Lunch sets start at ¥800. Try the tempura udon for ¥900. For an even cheaper meal, *Tendon Tenya*, with a branch in Ginza, offers fast-food tempura for as low as ¥460.

Don-don Tei is a standard-issue lunch place where filling lunch sets start at ¥980. It usually displays its daily special out front.

There's also a tasty beef tongue speciality restaurant, *Shinjuku Negishi*, which advertises its fare as health food – it comes with vegetables, a clear soup and a bowl of tororo rice (rice served with ground sticky potato). Order the negishi teishoku for ¥880, or the double teishoku, if you're really hungry, for ¥1050. There's a picture menu, but no sign. It's easy to spot, though – look for the glass front and polished-wood interior. Don't forget to pour the tororo over your rice!

Kanda This is a student neighbourhood (Map 2) and there are plenty of drab cafeteria-style places serving cheap lunch sets. A step up from these is *Hisago*, a hip place which has been feeding Meiji University students for years. The many lunch and dinner sets start from less than ¥1000. Hisago is in the sporting goods section of town. Look for the rustic wooden facade.

Another Kanda institution is *Kanda Yabu Soba*, a celebrated buckwheat noodle shop. It's possible to eat here for ¥700, and it's equally possible to triple that. The real treat is the authentic surroundings – look for the traditional building with a wooden fence round the outside; it's on a corner.

Ueno The Ueno area (Map 4) is a happy hunting ground for cheap food. You'll find a good variety of cheap Japanese places in and around Ameyoko arcade. Many display food models in the window, and lunch specials and teishoku are likely to cost around ¥800. There's lots of rāmen and automatic sushi on the station end of the arcade. You can also pick up take-away foods like yakitori, rice balls and fruit from vendors in the arcade.

Near the arcade, just south of Marui department store, *Ueno Yabu Soba* is a famous soba shop which sells the basic article for only ¥600. To really fill up, however, get the tenseiro set, which includes tempura, for ¥1800. The black on white sign to look for is in Japanese but the large picture menu will make ordering a snap.

An excellent place across from the station is *Magurokāsan*. 'Maguro' means tuna, and if it can be made from tuna, it's probably on the menu, including exotic and tasty maguro gyōza (tuna-filled dumplings) for ¥400. The lunch sets are great: to go with a large bowl of tuna-topped rice (seafood donburi), there are salads for ¥880 or cold udon for ¥950. The restaurant is nonsmoking during lunch hours and the atmosphere is pleasant any time. Look for the bamboo in the front and a white on green Japanese sign.

Asakusa Not surprisingly, the old Shitamachi area of Asakusa (Map 4) is teeming with Japanese restaurants. The best place to look is Kaminarimon-dōri and the small streets surrounding Nakamise-dōri. If you just want a snack, the authentic sembei (cracker) stores of Nakamise-dōri and the food tents in front of Sensō-ji Temple are a good bet.

Rāmen-tei, opposite Dempō-in Garden, serves about the cheapest rāmen in town (¥290). A nicer option is its spicy Shikoku rāmen (¥460). Look for the pictures of rāmen in the window.

Nearby *Edokko* serves that great Asakusa speciality, tempura, in a very authentic atmosphere. Try its tendon at lunch for ¥1300. The place has a traditional facade and a couple of food models in the window.

On Kaminarimon-dōri, *Tenya* serves roughly the same fare as Edokko, but in a fast-food atmosphere at fast-food prices. This is only recommended if you are in a real hurry or on a very tight budget.

Also on Kaminarimon-dōri, just to the right of Kaminari-mon Gate, is the small family-run restaurant *Tonkyu*, which serves good tonkatsu at reasonable prices. Its rōsu katsu teishoku is recommended (¥1000). It is closed on Thursday. Look for the food models in the window, as there is no English sign.

Ikebukuro If you can't find a budget meal in Ikebukuro (Map 5), you aren't trying very hard. All you have to do is walk a few minutes from the station and look for the plastic food displays, conveniently labelled with prices.

On the station's east side, look for the revolving sushi restaurants. Worth recommending is *Komazushi*, a popular place with a friendly atmosphere, where plates start at ¥120. It's near a giant pachinko parlour.

On the west side, *Tonbo* serves good tonkatsu, fried shrimp and related fare. Tonbo tonkatsu teishoku (pork cutlet set meal) is ¥850, a chicken set meal is ¥950 and ebi furai teishoku (fried-shrimp set meal) is ¥1400.

Seibu, Tōbu and Marui department stores all have restaurant floors in their upper reaches – Seibu alone has around 50 restaurants, many specialising in Japanese regional cuisines. The dishes are all on display in plastic outside. Enjoy.

Takadanobaba In 'Baba (Map 5), *Sumika Rāmen* is down a little side street not far from the station. It serves good rāmen and a range of shūmai meat dumplings for ¥300 an order. Itamiso rāmen is a good main choice for ¥700. There is no English sign, but there are pictures of rāmen in the window.

In the basement of the F1 building, across from the station, you'll find *Ichiban Dori*, a simple restaurant specialising in chicken dishes. Lunch sets are a good deal – try the chicken teriyaki donburi (rice bowl) for ¥680. Again, there is no English sign; you'll see it in front of you as you descend the stairs to the basement.

Shinjuku Speed-loving Shinjuku (Map 6) is a good place to hunt for bargain meals. However, the intense competition has resulted in a lot of *bad* cheap food. Beware of the tabehōdai (all-you-can-eat) specials offered by many places at lunch – the quality is usually as low as the price. The automatic sushi places are pretty grim as well; it may be only ¥120 per plate, but for leathery sushi of unknown origin, it's probably safer to pay more at a good place. But if you look carefully, Shinjuku still has probably Tokyo's best selection of bargain eats. Look on the streets on the east side of Shinjuku station.

There's a lot of rāmen in Shinjuku (goes with the drinking), but most of it is dismal stuff. *Tenkaippin* is a cut above the rest. Most bowls start at ¥600, and sets include fried rice and dumplings. Specify 'kotteri' for thick soup or 'asari' for thin. Look for the red lanterns and red and white decor.

For authentic rāmen, *Keika Kumamoto Rāmen* is out toward Shinjuku Sanchōme. Try the chashūmen for ¥800. There's no English sign, but it's the only rāmen place in the neighbourhood and there are food models in the window.

Up in Kabukichō, not far from the Prince Hotel, *Shinjuku Negishi* serves beef tongue and beef stew sets for around ¥1000. It's tasty stuff, and the set meal it comes with is healthy fare. This cosy little spot is sandwiched between Beijing Rāmen and Tainan Taami Taiwanese restaurant. Look for the wood carvings over the door.

Harajuku, Aoyama & Nishi-Azabu These areas are more cosmopolitan than most others; as a result of the culinary colonisation, there is little in the way of inexpensive Japanese food.

Shibuya Japanese restaurants in Shibuya (Map 7) are slowly succumbing to a tide of foreign invaders, but you can still find some budget places. The *food floors* of large department stores will yield lots of noodle, fried cutlet and set-meal restaurants.

Tenmi, across the street from the Tepco Energy Museum, is a great place for tasty and inexpensive vegetarian fare. Since John Lennon ate here the place has enjoyed considerable esteem among Tokyo diners. A well-prepared lunch bentō meal costs ¥1000. Tenmi is on the 2nd floor above the Pure Food Natural Square.

Shizenkan, on the other side of the station, is a slightly more expensive version of Tenmi. It serves a variety of set meals, all displayed outside with prices and caloric contents. Lunch and dinner here cost about ¥1500. Look for the English sign: 'Healthy Boutique' (and we thought it was a restaurant ...).

Ebisu You can find lots of cheap, standard-issue lunch places in the Ebisu JR station building (Map 8), but for more interesting fare, you'll be looking at mid-range prices.

Roppongi Although it's regarded as Tokyo's foreign playground, you can still grab a cheap bite of Japanese food in Roppongi (Map 7). The popular *Bikkuri Sushi* automatic sushi restaurant is only a few minutes walk from the Roppongi crossing. Many people sit here gobbling sushi while waiting for friends. Plates start at ¥130. Since it's open to 5 am, quite a few people use this as a late-night snack spot as well.

For teishoku, try *Shōjikiya*, very close to the Roppongi crossing. The name means 'honest store', and that's what you'll get: honest Japanese cooking, with unagi sets for ¥1950 or simpler sets for ¥1000. There is no English sign, and the place is set back a little from the street; look for the plants near the door.

Akasaka There is not much bargain Japanese food in upper-crust Akasaka (Map 3). However, a few of the mid-range Japanese places offer lunch specials for around ¥1000.

International Cuisine

Tokyo has some fine international restaurants, but few are cheap. However, the ones listed in this section all serve lunch sets for less than ¥1000. At dinner, some prices rise.

Ginza For good dumplings and other Japanese-style Chinese dishes, try *Gyoza Ichiban*, under the tracks in southern Ginza (Map 3). Order eight gyōza for only ¥450 or go for the yaki-meshi (fried rice) set, which comes with six dumplings and soup (¥750).

Just north of Matsuzaka department store is the multi-ethnic *Potohar*. Billed as a Malaysian and Pakistani restaurant, this place covers a lot of ground. Its business lunch is a great deal: a choice of four curries, tea or lassi, and all the naan and rice you can eat for ¥890. The price goes up at dinner. It's on the 8th floor of the Star building; look for the portable sign on the street.

For steaks and salads from ¥1000 to ¥2000, try *Volks* steakhouse around the corner from Matsuya department store. There is a picture menu to help you order.

Kanda Though Kanda (Map 2) has some cheap international restaurants, the mid-range places are where the action is. If you're

on a budget, you might want to try some of these places for lunch.

Ueno This is not the place to look for bargain international cuisine, unless you consider McDonald's 'cuisine'. But there are two decent Indian restaurants near Ameyoko arcade (Map 4) with lunch specials for around ¥1000. *Maharaja* offers a lunch-time 'viking' (all-you-can-eat special) with four curries, rice and naan for ¥1000 on weekdays and ¥1300 on the weekend. *Samrat* offers its own all-you-can-eat lunch deal for ¥890.

Asakusa In old Shitamachi, you can't really expect much good cosmopolitan food; you're pretty much limited to fast-food chains (Map 4), all of which are represented in the small streets around the Nakamise-dōri arcade. Happily, *Capricciosa* serves enough-for-two portions of Italian food at budget prices. For dessert, you can try the *Real Italian Gelato* down the street.

Ikebukuro There are lots of cheap international places to eat in Ikebukuro (Map 5). Right around the corner from the Kimi Ryokan, the Chinese restaurant *Ryūjō* serves a variety of good lunch and dinner sets for about ¥800. You know this place is authentic – both the customers and the staff speak Chinese. The manager also speaks good English, and will be happy to walk you through the menu. There's no English sign, but look for the bright lights and the long counter within.

Really hungry? The *Oriental Kitchen* serves a vast all-you-can-eat buffet of just about every major Asian food you'd care to name, and it's pretty good considering the price. A one hour lunch binge costs ¥980; a two hour dinner feast runs to ¥1980. There's also an all-you-can-drink special (¥1280) for those who really don't care where they do their drinking. It's on the 2nd floor of its building, look for the large karaoke box sign.

Just down from Marui department store, *Mekong* serves a passable all-you-can-eat Thai lunch buffet for ¥1000 (the soups tend to be the strong point). The atmosphere is better left unmentioned. Dinner prices are firmly mid-range.

For large portions of cheap Italian food, head to *Capricciosa*. At lunch you can eat for around ¥1000. Count on double that for dinner.

You can also head for the excellent restaurant floors of Tōbu, Seibu or Mitsukoshi department stores.

Takadanobaba In addition to all the standard fast-food outlets, those in search of economical international food in 'Baba (Map 5) may want to sample the filling Italian fare at *Capricciosa*.

Shinjuku This is the place to look for good deals on international food. However, as with Japanese cuisine, there's a lot of real junk mixed in with the bargains in Shinjuku (Map 6). Beware of all-you-can-eat specials and other such deals – there's a reason why the food is so cheap.

For good Chinese-style rāmen, head to *Beijing* in Kabukichō. It gets no awards for warm and friendly service, but the noodles are authentic, and so are the Chinese staff. Rāmen starts at ¥800 and six gyōza go for ¥300. Look for the Japanese sign, red awning and pictures of rāmen in the window.

The closest thing you'll get to a South-East Asian night market is the *Yatai Mura* (street stall village) behind the Shinjuku ward office. The quality here varies, but for around ¥1500 you can put together a meal from Thai, Korean, Japanese and Chinese food. This is best enjoyed with a few friends and lots of beer.

Istanbul, out by Sanchōme, offers very good Turkish food at bottom-end prices at lunch – the three filling lunch sets start at ¥780. The atmosphere is pleasant as well. At dinner the prices rise, but the quality does not change.

Court Lodge in west Shinjuku serves a very good Sri Lankan lunch set with two curries for ¥800. Try the godamba roti. At dinner, the prices go up.

For a more adventurous eating experience, walk through downmarket Kabukichō

to the Asian neighbourhoods of Shokuan-dōri or Shin-Ōkubo-dōri. You'll know you've arrived when you stop hearing Japanese; it's a foreign language here.

For authentic Korean food in this area, head to Korea Town (just off the northern end of Map 6), on Shokuan-dōri, east of the JR tracks. Here, all the Korean specialities are available, like yaki-niku (Korean barbecue; 'kalbi' or 'pulgogi' in Korean) and industrial-strength kimchi'i (spicy fermented vegetables).

With an atmosphere as bad as the food is good, *Kankoku-fu*, diagonally across from the AM/PM convenience store, is a winner. Order any dish and they'll serve you a table full of side dishes to accompany it. The 'bibimbap' (a rice dish with vegetables) is a good, filling choice. Don't even try speaking Japanese here – it's Korean or sign language. Look for the red, white and green sign, and the brightly lit interior.

If you walk east from Kankoku-fu and take the first left, you'll find *Shin-sekai* on your left after about 150m. This is an Asian night market under one roof. It's worth going just to check out the patrons. There's a small English sign and a large picture menu. The place stays open all night, every night.

Harajuku, Aoyama & Nishi-Azabu If you want international cuisine, this is the place. Between them, these areas (Map 7) have more bistros, cafes and trattorias than most small European cities. This doesn't necessarily mean great food, since atmosphere usually takes precedence over cuisine, but it does mean a pleasant place to sit and watch the world go by.

The heart of it all is the famous promenade of Tokyo's young and beautiful: Omotesandō. The street is lined with outdoor cafes, most of which are slavish reproductions of the French ones – some are so realistic that courteous Japanese service seems distinctly out of place (see the earlier Tokyo Cafe Society boxed text). Other options exist along Aoyama-dōri and on the pleasant streets of Nishi-Azabu. Be warned that this is one of Tokyo's more glamorous areas, and you're paying for the location as much as anything else. There are some bargains, however, so read on.

Apetito is a popular little shop which sells sandwiches far superior to the limp versions you find in convenience stores. It also sells a variety of coffee shop drinks – and there's a patio. With lunch or dinner in the ¥700 range (including a drink), this is about the best budget option in these parts. Apetito is right next to Royal Host family restaurant.

Another great option for a light lunch or snack is the *Pita Shop Atena*, which sells Turkish-style lamb pita sandwiches, souvlaki, tuna and salad pitas. Unfortunately, seating is limited to one or two benches nearby. Consider taking food away to a local park. Pita sets with salad are around ¥500.

Miss the islands? For a taste of the south seas, head to the Indonesian *Bengawan Solo* out on Roppongi-dōri. This has been around for ages, and the food never disappoints. The ¥700 gado-gado lunch is a bargain, and the ¥1100 beef in coconut cream is delicious. Look for the food models displayed outside.

For good curries in a casual atmosphere a little off the main Harajuku drag, *Ghee* is a great, offbeat choice. It serves daily curry sets for ¥1000; other menu options are worth a try as well. Look for the white plaster facade and a small English sign.

Shibuya There are lots of cheap international restaurants catering to the youthful masses who descend on Shibuya (Map 7) each day. Many are on the food floors of the huge department stores that crowd the area, among which the sandwich shop and cafe *Fungo* is most likely to appeal to foreign tastes. In addition to good sandwiches, Fungo serves expresso, cappuccino and American micro-brewed beers. It's on the 3rd floor of the Parco Part III department store. For other foreign fare, look along the smaller streets surrounding the station.

Charlie House is a Cantonese noodle restaurant on Kōen-dōri where a bowl of authentic Chinese noodles or a noodle set with rice costs less than ¥1000. The good food is complemented by a rustic wood interior.

Turn at the tobacco machines down the small side street and look for the English sign.

Closer to the station, *Samrat* serves the usual Indian curries and curry sets for less than ¥1000. It's just around the corner from the popular foreigner's bar Hub. There's usually a tout outside beckoning people in.

For more imaginative Indian and Sri Lankan food, head south to *Court Lodge*. Lunch here averages around ¥1000, and there is an excellent three curry dinner for ¥2000. Look for the large yellow English sign.

Ebisu The requisite fast-food chains are scattered around JR Ebisu station (Map 8), but that's about it for budget international food.

Roppongi It only makes sense that in Roppongi (Map 7), Tokyo's foreign nightlife playground, there would be a lot of international restaurants. The problem is, this is a pretty ritzy playground. There are a few cheap restaurants in the area, however, where you can bulk up before wading into all those Roppongi bars.

One of the best places to start a Roppongi evening is at the casual *Havana Cafe*. In addition to great happy hour drink specials, it serves reliable stuff like burritos and sandwiches for less than ¥1000. The place opens onto a quiet backstreet, and as you sip that first drink, it's difficult to imagine that Roppongi lurks just round the corner.

Paco's Cafe is another winner for an early dinner or late-night snack and a few drinks; they even serve breakfast (until 2 pm the next day, by which time we hope you've stopped drinking). Burritos, tacos and other Tex-Mex favourites all go for less than ¥1000, and the beer is ¥500 a glass. It's on the B1 floor of the building just north of McDonald's.

The *Hamburger Inn* is a kind of Roppongi institution, but few people rave about the food; most just fall in and are grateful for whatever is put in front of them. Perhaps the main draw is that it's open all night. If you want a hamburger that's a little better than what Ronald offers across the street, ¥1000 should do it.

For much better hamburgers and lots of other American fare, try *Johnny Rockets*, right at the Roppongi intersection. It's at least ¥1500 to fill up, but there's no doubt that the grub is better than what's offered at the competition.

Akasaka Along with nearby Roppongi, Akasaka (Map 3) is one of Tokyo's most cosmopolitan neighbourhoods. While most of the action is in the mid-range bracket, a stroll around the narrow streets just west of Akasaka-mitsuke subway station will turn up a number of good lunch-time deals.

Three Indian restaurants are located in the above-mentioned area: the slightly upmarket *Mughal* and two branches of *Moti*, perhaps Tokyo's best Indian chain. While dinner prices at these places are a lot higher, they all offer lunch specials starting at around ¥800. The pick of the litter is the northern branch of Moti.

Capricciosa dishes out heaping portions of passable spaghetti, one order of which will usually feed two people. The rice balls are a Japanese twist on Italian cuisine, and are actually pretty good. Expect to pay about ¥1000 per head for lunch or ¥2500 for dinner.

Fast Food
You very rarely have to walk far to find a McDonald's or a KFC in Tokyo. A slightly healthier option is a sandwich at Subway or a western-style bakery.

On the whole, fast-food joints are more expensive than eating in rāmen shops, eg two pieces of chicken and fries at KFC costs ¥650. Still, many newcomers end up eating at these places simply because of familiarity with the food and ease of ordering.

Japanese versions of burgers can be found in chains like *Mos Burger*, *Lotteria* and *Love Burger*, featuring teriyaki burgers and so on. Those in the know rate Mos Burger as the best of the bunch.

Bakeries & Ice Cream
Often overlooked, bakeries are the budget traveller's best friend. Tokyoites are waking up to the joys of well-made bread, and even simple local bakeries have a good selection.

Most places also sell sandwiches, and a whole range of sweets and cakes. While bakeries are in just about every neighbourhood, the best bakeries are on the food floors of large department stores.

Those in search of ice cream can choose from local Japanese offerings, which are usually small places selling sofuto-kuriimu (soft ice cream in cones, with green tea a popular flavour) and imports like Häagen Dazs, which have proliferated in the more popular central areas.

Self-Catering
Of course, it is always possible to put your own meal together. While convenience stores are the most frequently raided suppliers of do-it-yourself meals, department store food floors are another favourite option. Apart from all the handout samples, there are often specials available – especially at closing time. Department store bakeries make it fairly easy to put together a decent lunch for around ¥500.

Another favourite of Tokyo travellers on a budget is the local bentō store. These provide take-away meals at very reasonable rates (starting at around ¥400). The meals come in packs and usually include rice, some vegetables and meat or fish.

There are also a couple of western-style supermarkets in Tokyo that, while often exorbitantly expensive, allow the homesick foreigner to indulge in hard-to-find items from home. Two of the more established supermarkets are *Kinokuniya International* (Map 7) (☎ 3400-0022) in Kita-Aoyama, and *Meijiya* (☎ 3271-1111) in Kyōbashi, Ginza (Map 3) and Roppongi (Map 7).

PLACES TO EAT – MIDDLE
Mid-range dining is where Tokyo really comes into its own. Along with all the wonderful Japanese cuisine, it's also well worth checking out some of the international restaurants for which Tokyo is justly famous.

Japanese
Tokyo Station Area If you're looking for delicious food around here, the best advice

is to walk south 15 minutes to Ginza (one stop on the Marunouchi subway line). But if you're intent on eating near the station (Map 2), there are some options.

The nearby izakaya *Banya* serves standard izakaya fare in a rustic farmhouse atmosphere. A dinner here with a few beers will cost about ¥3000 a head. Unlike most izakaya, it also serves lunch on weekdays. There's no English sign, but it's directly next to a Doutor coffee shop. Look for the faux traditional facade.

Around the corner from Banya in the direction of Takashimaya department store, you'll find several cosy yakitori places. *Nanban-tei* is a good place to start. Here, a few beers and enough yakitori to fill you up will cost about ¥3000 per person. There's no English sign, but you can identify the place by the picture of a chicken on the sign.

Ginza We're not sure how it came to pass, but Ginza (Map 3) seems to be the yakitori capital of Tokyo. Under the JR tracks just south of Harumi-dōri is a warren of yakitori restaurants known as Yūrakuchō Yakitori Alley. If you want to sample yakitori in atmospheric surroundings, this is the place. Most of the restaurants here are outside, but if the weather's cold, they put heaters and tents up to keep you warm. While most places serve the same fare for the same price, *Tonton*, in the east-west tunnel beneath the tracks, is the most friendly and has an English menu. Count on spending about ¥3000 here to fill up on food and beer. If Tonton is full, walk out the east side of the tunnel and turn left, where you'll be welcomed by the next-friendliest place.

For good yakitori in slightly more up-market surroundings, walk east into the heart of Ginza. Here, you'll find the authentic, very popular little *New Torigin* hidden away down a very narrow back alley, but signposted in English. There's an English menu, and it does excellent food, including yakitori at ¥120 to ¥200 per stick and the steamed rice dish known as kamameshi (¥700). A complete meal with a few beers is about ¥3500. It is also good for a little sake sampling.

Back near the railway tracks is one of Tokyo's most celebrated izakaya, *Robata*. This is one place where, if you don't speak Japanese, you're going to have to bring a friend who does, point at what your neighbour is eating, or throw yourself at the mercy of the staff and say 'omakase shimasu' ('you decide'). It's hard to spot the sign, even if you can read Japanese; it's better just to look for the rustic weathered facade.

Another atmospheric spot is *Chichibu Nishiki*, a traditional nomiya with good, cheap food in a very authentic setting. It's tucked away behind the Kabuki-za Theatre, north of the Ginza Dai-Ichi Hotel.

If want slightly more prestigious fare, head back toward Yūrakuchō and pop into *Funachū* restaurant, where a mini-kaiseki meal is ¥2400. There is also yakitori, and large beers are only ¥680.

While most sushi restaurants in Ginza are wildly expensive, *Ichi-zushi*, on the 1st floor of the Ginza Dai-Ichi Hotel, is very reasonable – and you don't need an interpreter. A delicious sushi lunch is ¥2300; for dinner, try the elegant sushi kaiseki for ¥7000.

Tsukiji If you make that early-morning trip to Tsukiji's fish market (Map 3), you have to do it properly – and a sushi breakfast or lunch is *de rigueur*. There are quite a few sushi shops close to the market, particularly in the narrow alleys of the Tsukiji External Market, which serve sushi breakfasts of varying quality. For excellent sushi in pleasant surroundings, it's better to visit some of the larger, more established places near Harumi-dōri and Shin-Ōhashi-dōri. These are open for lunch and dinner only, usually from 11 am.

Edogin Sushi is famous for fresh, oversized sushi toppings. It offers the three standard grades of take/ume/matsu sushi sets at lunch for ¥1000/1400/1600. Tempura teishoku is ¥1300 and sashimi teishoku is ¥1000. At dinnertime, sushi sets start at ¥2000, but it's worth paying a little extra to get the tokujō nigiri sushi set for ¥2500. There is no English sign on the restaurant, but it's easily identified by the plastic sushi in the window.

東京 東京 東京 東京 東京 東京 東京 東京 東

Old Tokyo Restaurants

Although tall buildings, flashing neon lights and vast shopping complexes are exciting, there's no doubt that visitors to Tokyo often feel that they are missing out on a 'real Japanese experience'. A great way to make up for this is to sit down for a meal in a traditional Japanese restaurant. The following are a few select old Tokyo restaurants – for details, see their respective sections in this chapter.

Botan	– Kanda
Kanda Yabu Soba	– Kanda
Echikatsu	– Ueno
Chichibu Nishiki	– Ginza
Komagata Dojō	– Asakusa
Inakaya	– Roppongi
Yūrakuchō Yakitori Alley	– Ginza

東京 東京 東京 東京 東京 東京 東京 東京 東

Another Tsukiji institution is *Sushi Iwa* on Harumi-dōri. Here, sushi sets start at ¥1000. Recommended is the ¥2000 ume sushi set. Look for the large Japanese sign written in gold on green.

A smallish place which serves good sushi is *Sushidai* on Harumi-dōri. Here, the 'A ranchi' (lunch) is a good chance to try the catch of the day for ¥1200. There's a small English sign out the front.

Kanda This area (Map 2) has some very famous long-running Japanese restaurants. One of the few Tokyo restaurants to have survived WWII bombing is *Botan* (☎ 3251-0577). It is a speciality restaurant serving just one dish: chicken nabe (torisuki), a traditional Edo pot-stew. This is a good chance to sample Japanese nabe cooking, where everyone sits round one boiling pot, plucking out what looks good with their chopsticks. The cost is ¥6000 per head. It is open from noon to 9 pm, closed Sunday and holidays.

If the idea of spending ¥6000 on chicken stew shocks you, it is possible to dine for less than ¥1000 at what is probably Tokyo's most famous soba restaurant: *Kanda Yabu Soba* (☎ 3251-0287). You may have to queue for your buckwheat noodles, and the faint-hearted may quail at the idea of seiro (cold noodles

with sauce), but Yabu Soba is a Tokyo institution – it's well worth the effort of seeking out.

Another excellent, authentic choice is the izakaya *Ichi-no-chaya* (☎ 3251-8517). This is a sake connoisseur's heaven. The food is also good, with sashimi and nabe heading the list. This is one place where a little Japanese ability, or a Japanese friend, will go a long way. Expect to pay around ¥7000 per head.

Ueno There is plenty of mid-range Japanese food in Ueno (Map 4). Perhaps the most approachable place is *Ganko-zushi*, on the 6th floor of the Nagafuji building opposite McDonald's. There's a large selection of good sushi and other fare, including several economical set meals. It has a picture menu and seems fairly accustomed to foreign customers. On the cheaper side, try the sushi mori-awase (assortment) for ¥1380 or the tempura bentō (¥1080) for lunch or dinner. Ordering à la carte will cost about ¥3000 a head, more with a few drinks.

Just around the corner from McDonald's, the elegant *Kameya* serves high-class food for around ¥3000 per head for lunch, and about double that for dinner. The daily lunch set is displayed outside. You aren't going to get far with English here. Look for noren curtains over the doorway.

Izu-ei is another elegant choice for authentic Japanese food. The speciality here is unagi and it's done well. The Izu-ei unagi bentō is ¥2500 and includes tempura. Other choices cost from ¥2000 to ¥4000. There is a limited picture menu. Look for the black building with a small pine tree and waterfall out the front.

For excellent sukiyaki in exquisite surroundings, walk up the hill south-west of Shinobazu Pond for a few hundred metres to *Echikatsu* (☎ 3811-5293). In a grand old Japanese house, memorable sukiyaki is served in private rooms, many of them overlooking small gardens. Sukiyaki courses range from ¥6000 to ¥11,000, as do shabu-shabu courses. The staff don't speak English, but will make an honest effort to communicate. Since you should make reservations, if you don't speak Japanese the person who calls for you can take care of ordering then. Echikatsu is off Kasuga-dōri, 70m past Hotel Yushima on the left side; look for the wooden gate.

Another memorable experience can be had at the famous *Sasa-no-yuki* (☎ 3873-1145) tofu restaurant near Uguisudani station on the Yamanote line. This is the oldest tofu restaurant in Tokyo, and the food is delicious. Set menus start at ¥2000. Again, little English is spoken, but there's a small English menu. Take the Yamanote line to Uguisudani station, go out the north exit, walk under the elevated highway, and it's about 200m on the left, just past a footbridge.

Asakusa A good selection of Japanese restaurants can be explored here (Map 4). A speciality in Asakusa is tempura, and the place to get it is *Daikokuya*, just outside Nakamise arcade. The place is authentic and the tempura is excellent. Expect to pay about ¥1800 for a meal at lunch (try the tempura donburi) and at least ¥3000 for dinner.

In a similar vein, but not nearly as atmospheric, *Owariya*, on Kaminarimon-dōri, serves tempura and a variety of noodle dishes. Try the tempura donburi for ¥1300.

For good yakitori with a picture menu, check out *Akiyoshi Yakitori*, near the Asakusa View Hotel. In addition to standard yakitori, try a kushi-katsu and rice dish. A full meal and a couple of beers is about ¥3500 per head.

Just down the street, *Asakusa Imahan* is a great place to try sukiyaki or shabu-shabu. The meat is high quality, the preparation is excellent and the atmosphere is dignified. You're going to have to pay for it, however, as sukiyaki sets cost about ¥7000 per person. Look for the white building on the corner.

A few blocks south of Asakusa station near the river, you'll find a very traditional-looking building next to a small park. This is *Komagata Dojō* (☎ 3842-4001), an old Shitamachi restaurant which serves a fish called dojō (something like an eel) in elegant set courses starting at ¥3000 per person. This place is highly recommended.

Ikebukuro The best dining in Ikebukuro (Map 5) is international. If you are on the lookout for good Japanese food, the best advice is to head to Seibu or Tōbu department stores; the 7th and 8th floors of the Metropolitan Plaza are another option.

Ikebukuro has plenty of izakaya, like *Toneria*, a busy place with friendly staff who are used to the occasional gaijin calling in. Prices are reasonable, but they add up quickly – especially if you include a few drinks. Look for all the empty sake bottles piled up outside.

Yōrōnotaki is one of the most famous izakaya chains. Illustrated menus take the hassle out of ordering, and while the food isn't exactly overwhelming, it certainly goes down well with some beer or sake – both are extremely cheap. Try the agedashi dōfu, the yakitori or the sushi – or even fried potatoes. To find the branch here, look for the red and black neon sign (no English) – it's a big place; you can't miss it.

For a much more dignified izakaya experience, try *Sasashu*, a venerable sake specialist where you can try some of Japan's finest sakes and some excellent traditional cuisine. A little Japanese language ability would come in handy, but it's worth braving a bit of awkwardness when ordering for the good quality of the sake and food. Count on about ¥5000 per head. There is no English sign, but the dignified old Japanese facade stands out from its seedy neighbours.

Nearby, *Sushi Kazu* is a good, standard-issue sushi bar which will definitely be a step up from all those revolving sushi bars in the neighbourhood. Whatever you choose, a decent amount of sushi and some beer or sake to wash it down will cost between ¥3000 and ¥5000 per head.

For tasty yakitori in approachable, laid-back surroundings, try *Akiyoshi*. There's a large picture menu to help you order, and the food is pretty cheap. Depending upon how much you drink, you'll be able to fill up here for between ¥2500 and ¥4000. There's no English sign, but you can easily spot the long counters and smoky grills inside from out on the street.

Shinjuku Mid-range Japanese food is abundant in Shinjuku (Map 6). While most of it is in the built-up area on the east side of the station, you can also find some good lunch deals in any of the hotels on the west side.

For good tonkatsu head to *Suzuya* on Yasukuni-dōri. The katsu here are high quality (not greasy) and come with filling sets which include rice and miso soup. Recommended are the hire katsu teishoku for ¥1450 as well as the meibutsu chazuke set (¥1400). It's on the 2nd floor, with signs at street level on the corner.

For an experience of Occupation-era Tokyo – tiny restaurants packed willy-nilly into a wonderfully atmospheric old alley – try *Omoide-yokochō* street beside the JR tracks just north-west of Shinjuku station. Here, local workers stop off for yakitori, oden, noodles and beer before braving the trains back home. It's pointless to make recommendations; most of the places serve the same thing and few have names. What they serve will be piled high on the counters; just point and eat. Expect to pay about ¥2500 per person for a memorable time.

For good tempura at amazingly reasonable prices, try *Tsunahachi Tsunohazuan* (☎ 3358-2788) behind Mitsukoshi department store. Its ¥2500 tempura teishoku is highly recommended. You can choose a table in a tatami room or at the counter, which offers good views of the cooking action. Best of all, there's an English menu and the staff seem accustomed to foreign customers. There's no English sign; look for the brown building and blue noren curtains in the doorway.

When we first recommended *Ibuki* (☎ 3342-4787), an excellent sukiyaki and shabu-shabu restaurant, some five years ago, there was no English sign and it looked dangerously temporary. It's still going strong, has an English menu and sign, and gets a lot of foreign visitors. Pop in and try a sukiyaki course for ¥2500 or shabu-shabu for ¥3200. Sake is ¥500 for a small bottle.

Also in Kabukichō is a unique restaurant known as *Tokyo Kaisen Ichiba* (Tokyo Seafood Market). You can't miss the building, a

girder-and-glass construction with a honkin' great fish on the front. Downstairs is a fish market; upstairs you get to eat the fish. The prices are slightly upmarket, but simply picking the cheapest things on the English menu at random (around ¥1500 per serve) will provide some delicious surprises. A late-night visit makes for some great people-watching.

Daikokuya, with its all-you-can-eat yaki-niku (¥1500), shabu-shabu (¥1950) and sukiyaki (¥3500) courses (add ¥1300 and it's all-you-can-drink too), is popular with students, and can be a good place to meet young Japanese, whose inhibitions start to dissolve with a few beers.

Over on Yasukuni-dōri, on the 6th floor of the Piccadilly movie house just east of Wendy's, is *Irohanihoheto*, a big, lively izakaya with affordable prices. Plan on about ¥3000 per head. If you can still say the name of the place, keep drinking.

Kurumaya serves tasty teppanyaki in elegant surroundings for east Shinjuku. It does seafood and steak sets for around ¥4000. For a splurge, try the ise ebi (Japanese lobster) and steak set for ¥5800. Lunches are a better buy at around ¥2000. There's no English sign, but it's directly across from Kirin City beer hall.

Harajuku, Aoyama & Nishi-Azabu This is a cosmopolitan part of town – for good mid-range Japanese choices, head to nearby Shinjuku, Roppongi, Akasaka or Ginza.

Shibuya There are relatively few good options in Shibuya (Map 7), but there are some.

Akiyoshi is a pleasant, approachable yakitori restaurant with a large picture menu – it's also a good place to knock back a few beers. Dinner here should cost about ¥3000. When you've eaten your fill, you can always move on to the Kirin City beer hall across the street.

Sakana-tei is a casual izakaya where the emphasis is on good-quality sake and simple but tasty food. The concrete decor may not fit everyone's image of an izakaya, but the excellent food and drink more than make up for it. You'll pay around ¥4000 for a good meal and a few flasks of sake. A little Japanese language ability would be useful here.

Ebisu There are two good spots in Ebisu (Map 8). *Fujii*, a five minute walk from the station, is a good place to sample fresh, hand-made udon noodles. The story goes that the master here searched all over Japan for the perfect noodle recipe before finding one that satisfied him in Kansai. We recommend the tempura udon for ¥1500. There is no English sign, but you'll see food models in the window just up the street from KFC.

An An is an offbeat izakaya where the master turns out modern versions of traditional favourites, with a generous sprinkling of international choices thrown in. Seating is communal, and if you don't speak Japanese, just point at whatever looks good from among your neighbours' plates. Look for the very subdued wooden front and the portable sign on the sidewalk.

Roppongi Much of the Japanese fare in Roppongi (Map 7) goes for top-end prices, but there are a few mid-range choices to consider. The oddly named *Panic Cafe*, a fair walk from the Roppongi crossing, is a good place to try teppanyaki with imaginative side dishes and good salads. Expect to pay between ¥3500 and ¥5000 for a meal here. It's a little tricky to find. Once you've passed the Porsche dealer, keep an eye peeled on the left. You'll see it after about 60m; it's in a basement.

Gokoku is close to the top-end category, but if you're conservative with your drink orders, you can eat a fine meal here for around ¥6000, which is mid-budget for Roppongi. The menu changes daily, but it is always hearty Edo-style fare. Unless you speak Japanese, or have a friend who does, you're just going to have to say 'Omakase' ('Please decide for me') to the waiter.

Akasaka In spite of the proliferation of foreign restaurants in the area, Akasaka (Map 3) is still home to some great domestic food. Most of the restaurants are on the narrow streets just west of Akasaka-mitsuke subway station.

Sushi-sei is the real deal: great sushi in a great sushi-bar atmosphere. Everyone sits at long counters, the chefs are in constant motion and the customers often stand in line to partake. If you can't be bothered to choose, try the jō-nigiri set for lunch (¥1300). At dinner, prices go up and the best thing to do, if you don't speak Japanese, is just to point at whatever looks good; all the fish is laid out for you to see. A sushi dinner here, with some beer or sake, will cost around ¥5000 a head. There's no English sign; look for the noren curtains in the doorway. The place is set back a little off the street.

Tōfuya is another reliable spot for real Japanese cuisine, in this case tofu, prepared more ways than you'd think possible. The atmosphere is authentic too. In addition to tofu, there's grilled fish and rice dishes. Lunch is a great deal: there are usually four sets, starting at ¥800. Dinner will run closer to ¥4000. The place is a little tricky to find; it's on a small side street, one street west of Sotobori-dōri. Look for a traditional exterior across from an electronics shop.

If you head down Akasaka-dōri west toward Roppongi, you'll find *Yakitori Louis*. This is a good yakitori restaurant, with skewers from ¥180. It also offers courses from ¥2000. The place is in a basement, but there's a display case on street level with food models and a large plastic beer mug. It's about 10 minutes west of the TBS building.

International Cuisine

If you're willing to pay for it, Tokyo has a fantastic array of good international restaurants – its international cuisine rivals that of any city in the world. As with Japanese food, however, you can expect to pay a lot more at dinner.

Ginza Since Ginza (Map 3) was the first part of Tokyo to 'go international' it's only natural that it's still home to some great international restaurants. One of Tokyo's great ethnic favourites is Indian food. Down

Chūō-dōri, just south of Matsuzakaya department store, is an old Tokyo standby: *Ashoka*. While lunch sets start at ¥850, you'll find that ordering à la carte quickly pushes up the bill. Don't worry: in this case, it's worth it. Vegetarians take note: there are several good meatless dishes here.

On Harumi-dōri, diagonally opposite Mitsukoshi department store, is *Maharajah*. It has a variety of lunch and dinner sets for around ¥1500, among which the tandoori delight is a good choice. Look for the sign at street level; the restaurant is downstairs.

The popular *Nair's* Indian restaurant (in east Ginza toward Tsukiji) always seems to have a queue at lunch, and the reason is that Nair's small scale allows the proper attention to be paid to the food. Expect to pay about ¥1500 for lunch.

The rather obviously named *Brasserie de Paris* serves up so-so versions of the French originals on what must be one of Ginza's most expensive corners. Perhaps a safer bet than the food is the coffee and cake set for ¥950. It's certainly not a bad place to relax after traipsing round the shops all day.

For Italian food, head to the 2nd floor of the Nishi Ginza department store (in front of the Mullion building), where *Buono Buono* (☎ 3566-4031) has great food at upper mid-range prices, and stays open until 11.30 pm.

Kanda Mostly due to the fine efforts of three related restaurants in Jimbōchō, Kanda (Map 2) is one of our favourite destinations for good international food at reasonable prices.

The first, *Muang Thai Nabe* (☎ 3239-6939) is a must for Thai-food lovers. At dinner, it serves a Thai version of shabu-shabu called Thai nabe (about ¥3000 a head). At lunch, however, is when the restaurant really comes into its own; it offers one of the best Thai lunch sets in town for ¥1100, including an authentic Thai curry, soup and a spicy salad. It's on the B1 floor of the Iwanami Hall building.

Muang Thai Nabe has a more formal branch on the 2nd floor of the same building called *Menam no Hotori* (☎ 3238-9597),

which serves upmarket Thai fare of similar quality.

Across the street and downstairs is *Mandala* (☎ 3265-0498), an Indian restaurant which spends a lot more time on the food than it does on faux-Indian decor. The best deal is the curry lunch for ¥1100. Choose from five grades of spiciness and several kinds of curry. Between 2 and 5 pm you can sample its more generous minicourse (there's nothing mini about it) for ¥2200. The full dinner course is for special occasions when you can really stretch out and take your time.

Fans of Brazilian food will want to try *Muito Bom* (☎ 3238-7946). The food here is of the same high standards as at its sister restaurants. This is also the cheapest of the lot, with lunch specials starting at ¥900. It's upstairs from Muang Thai Nabe.

If you're in the mood for an outdoor, Taiwanese feast, try *Taiwan Yatai*, on the other side of Kanda. The food is standard Taiwanese, or at least Japanese versions thereof. Expect to pay about ¥2500 per head.

Asakusa The only decent choices in Asakusa (Map 4) are just across Azuma-bashi Bridge in the *Asahi Beer Flamme d'Or* complex (you can't miss it – it's got the giant 'golden turd' on top). There are three eateries in the main black building and a brew-pub/restaurant in the nearby circular glass annex.

At lunch, the restaurant on the 1st floor of Asahi's main building has an all-you-can-eat buffet for ¥1020, which includes salad, bread, some Chinese and western fare, and a variety of drinks. None of it is very special, but it's worth paying the price to check out the decor – unless you've been living on board a rather chic spaceship, you probably haven't seen the likes of this. Best of all is the bathroom, which resembles nothing so much as the transporter room of the starship *Enterprise* – good luck trying to figure out the sink. Upstairs are a French and a Chinese restaurant which both serve set courses for lunch and dinner starting at ¥3000.

Next door, in the *Sumida River Brewing Company*, you can get average pub grub from ¥600 a plate and knock it back with one of three types of fresh beer, which start at ¥530 for a small glass.

Ikebukuro There's no lack of mid-range choices here (Map 5). Look behind Marui department store – just stroll around and see what the nightly specials are (meals are often prepared and displayed out the front to lure you inside).

Very near Kimi Ryokan, *Taiwan Hsiao Tiao* serves good Taiwanese fare in casual, slightly rustic surroundings. There's an extensive picture menu, and the owners are friendly and used to foreign diners. Try the steamed gyōza, the 'healthy' Chinese sake and the crispy duck dishes. At dinner you'll pay around ¥3000. Lunch sets are a bargain at less than ¥1000. Look for the pictures of food in the window.

Near Ikebukuro station, *Beijing-tei* serves the standard Chinese specialities at somewhat inflated prices. Check what specials are displayed in the window before going in.

On a corner across from Nishi-Ikebukuro-kōen Park is one of Tokyo's few Malaysian restaurants: *Malaychan*. The food here is so-so, but it's easy to order from the big picture menu and the drinks are good. Nasi lemak is a filling introduction to Malaysian food at ¥1070. Lunch sets here start at ¥700.

For a fine meal in relaxing surroundings, *Chez Kibeau* serves continental cuisine in a pleasant basement which feels far removed from the chaos on the streets above. If you can't decide what to drink, English-speaking owner Kibo-san will gladly make a recommendation. In fact, the best thing to do here is simply let Kibo-san make all the decisions, and sit back and enjoy. Expect to pay around ¥5000 per head.

Takadanobaba Here are three suggestions for worthwhile international food in 'Baba (Map 5): *Kao Thai*, *Yeti* and *Cambodia*. Yeti serves good Nepali and Indian cuisine in a casual restaurant that feels almost like someone's living room. Kao Thai is among the cheaper of Tokyo's many Thai restaurants, and serves remarkably authentic food,

spicy enough even for the most seasoned Thai traveller. Cambodia is the most expensive of the three places, but has a mellow atmosphere and tasty, authentic food. These places do lunch for around ¥1000 and dinner for as low as ¥2000, except at Cambodia, where it costs about ¥3000.

Shinjuku Though mid-range Japanese food is the strong point in Shinjuku (Map 6), in addition to some street level offerings, all of the big hotels in west Shinjuku have high-quality international restaurants on their upper and lower floors, some of which offer affordable lunch specials.

For inexpensive Mexican food in a real hole-in-the-wall atmosphere, check out *El Borracho*. As with most Japanese versions of Mexican food, it's not too authentic, but this place isn't bad. El Borracho is next to Mos Burger; look for the Aztec motif.

For authentic thick-skinned Beijing-style gyōza and other Chinese fare, try *Raobian Gyozakan* (☎ 3348-5810), across the street from Keiō department store. The gyōza here are so good that you don't need sauce for dipping. The atmosphere is pure retro Tokyo, especially the back, with waiters and waitresses materialising from secret passageways. Note, however, that portions are small and you'll have to pay at least ¥3000 to get full. It's best to go with a group and order one of the courses. It has an English menu.

For great Taiwanese cuisine in a rowdy izakaya atmosphere, try *Tainan Taami*. There are branches in Roppongi (☎ 3408-2111), Suidōbashi (☎ 3263-4530), Ginza (☎ 3571-3624), Shinjuku (☎ 3232-8839) and Shibuya (☎ 3464-7544), but the best is the Shinjuku branch. The menu is complete with photographs of the dishes. Most of the dishes are small, ranging in price from ¥300 to ¥600.

For yum cha or dim sum, one of the few possibilities is *Tokyo Dai Hanten* (☎ 3202-0121), on the 3rd floor of the unfortunately named Oriental Wave building. Most of the food is overpriced and not particularly special, but the yum cha service is not bad. This is one of the few places in Tokyo where correct yum cha form is observed by bringing the snacks around on trolleys. With a pot or two of good Chinese tea, expect to fill up for about ¥4000 a head. Go on a Sunday, take your time and sit near the main aisles.

African restaurants are not exactly thick on the ground in Tokyo, so *Rose de Sahara* has cornered the market, and tends to charge accordingly. Nevertheless, with its African decor and sounds, this place creates a good atmosphere – try the guinea fowl in orange sauce. Courses start at ¥3500.

Harajuku, Aoyama & Nishi-Azabu This is the least Japanese of all Tokyo areas – you may even feel as though you've been transported to Europe – and the area (Map 7) is chock-a-block with good international cuisine. A lot of the offerings are scattered along the Omote-sandō promenade, but you'll also find some good restaurants in Nishi-Azabu and along Aoyama-dōri. And don't forget the cafes for some great people-watching (see the earlier Tokyo Cafe Society boxed text at the start of this chapter).

A good place to combine drinking and dinner is *Tacos del Amigo*, a Mexican restaurant near Harajuku station with a pleasant indoor/outdoor atmosphere. The food is average and the prices a bit steep, but it's fun all the same. Across the street, *Zest* serves Mexican food of similar quality for similar prices. For tastier Mexican, head to Nishi-Azabu, where *Casa Monnon* serves the good stuff in cosy, casual surroundings.

For more generalised Latin fare (Cuban, Brazilian, Peruvian etc) try *El Mocambo* near Aoyama Cemetery. It's a casual place to hang out and drink after you've filled up on food. Look for the small English sign; the restaurant is in the basement.

Topkapi is a tiny little basement joint where everyone squeezes round the same table for some of Tokyo's best Turkish food. Expect to pay around ¥2000 per head. It's tricky to find – look for the pink stairwell and the odd Turkish posters hanging above the doorway.

Son of the Dragon ('Ryunoko' in Japanese) serves pretty good Sichuan cuisine in a smoky basement off Meiji-dōri. Try the banbanji (cold chicken and sesame sauce) and any of the noodle dishes. You can fill up here for around ¥2500 per head.

Quit your diet? Try *Tony Roma's* on Aoyama-dōri for some American-style ribs and onion rings. There are also passable salads for the nonravenous.

An area imitating Paris would naturally have a plethora of French restaurants. *Brasserie Flo* serves French brasserie fare in a full-on replica of a Parisian brasserie. Specials are displayed on a blackboard outside; lunch runs to about ¥3000 and dinner ¥5000.

Another French restaurant is *Bistro de la Cite* (☎ 3406-5475), out in Nishi-Azabu. Though dinners border on top-end, lunch sets are reasonable at around ¥2500. The cosy, wooden decor provides a nice escape from the madness outside – close your eyes and imagine you're in Provence.

Nishi-Azabu is a prime hunting ground for Thai food, and most of the places are above average in quality. *Rice Terrace* is everyone's favourite here for tasty Thai food in cool surroundings. Lunch sets go from ¥1000, dinner will run closer to ¥3000. It's down a small street off of Gaien-nishi-dōri.

Nearby, *Monsoon Cafe* serves decent Thai fare in a semi-outdoor cafe-style place. This is a good option for tropical drinks and just hanging out. *Maenam* looks like a big miss, with it's tacky decor and garish neon, but the food is actually decent. All the Thai favourites are available, and dinner will cost about ¥2000. This is also a good spot for a few drinks with some spicy snacks.

Surprisingly, Indian food is rather rare in these parts. One place worth tracking down is *Bindi*, off Roppongi-dōri. The friendly couple who run this place turn out reliable Indian food for reasonable prices. It's in the basement of the building next to the Lawson convenience store.

For a look at Tokyo expat life in pleasant, expansive surroundings, check out *Las Chicas*. This is where cool and wannabe-cool expats come to pose and peer. The yuppie-style food is pretty good too – from pizzas to salads to sandwiches – and the wine

PLACES TO EAT

list is solid. There's also a bar to repair to and a computer with free Internet access (you may have to wait in line).

Shibuya There's no shortage of good international cuisine here (Map 7). The best places to look are the small streets around the station and the built-up shopping areas around the giant department stores.

Tainan Taami is a great choice for good Taiwanese fare in raucous, if slightly smoky, surroundings. Plan on around ¥3000 per person. For similar Taiwanese fare and surroundings, check out *Reikyō*, where prices are in the same range and the smoke may be even thicker. It's in a triangular red-brick building. There is no English sign.

Bouganvillea, across from Bunkamura, serves Vietnamese food. It's no great shakes, but if you've got a hankering for South-East Asian, this will probably do the trick. You should be able to fill up on ¥3000.

Kantipur is a Nepali restaurant which seems to borrow a lot from India (perhaps dal bhat is a limited menu for a restaurant). This place is a little bit back from the street and can be tough to spot. Head south from the Kirin City beer hall, and you'll see it on your right after about 10m. Prices are similar to the above-mentioned restaurants.

Ebisu *Mai-Thai* (Map 8) serves plenty of interesting alternatives to those old Thai standards, tom-yam-koon and pad-thai. We recommend any of the yam salads and spicy shrimp dishes. If you've been to Thailand, you'll have no trouble recognising the real Bangkok tuk-tuk parked outside. Lunch sets here go for about ¥1000; dinner will run about ¥3500.

Roppongi Clustered within 10 minutes walk of the Roppongi crossing (Map 7) are dozens of fine foreign restaurants, many of which double as drinking spots for post-dinner relaxation.

Tainam Taami has a branch here: bring a few friends, order lots of dishes and don't be afraid to pick something unusual from the large picture menu. This is a great place to get your Roppongi evening rolling.

Very close by, *Cerveza* sounds like it's a Mexican restaurant – it's not. It's a beer specialist where you can try to work your way through the 100 beer menu while putting away good international food, from Chinese to American. As at other Tokyo beer specialists, you're going to have to pay for it, as good imported beers are in the ¥1000 range.

There are two branches of the hugely popular *Moti* Indian restaurant in Roppongi, one on Roppongi-dōri right above the subway station and the other, called *Moti Darbar*, on Gaien-higashi-dōri. There's no question that both of these serve up some of Tokyo's best Indian food, but the nod goes to Moti Darbar for the whole package of food, ambience and attentive service. Both places do lunch sets for around ¥1000; dinner averages ¥3000.

For good Italian food and excellent streetside people watching, try *Bellini's Pizza Kitchen*. In addition to a wide selection of Italian favourites, there are lots of drink choices, including cappuccino and expresso. Lunch here is around ¥1500 and dinner ¥3000.

Hard Rock Cafe and *Tony Roma's* are in the same building. We figure you know what to expect from the former – loud music, oversized portions of passable American food and plenty of reasonably priced drinks. Tony Roma's has been doing pretty good business in Tokyo as a purveyor of American-style barbecued spare ribs with all the fixings. At either place, a good dinner is in the ¥3000 range, with Tony Roma's the more expensive of the two.

Bernd's Bar (Map 3) is something of a toss-up between a bar and a good German restaurant. German favourites are served with some excellent German beer to wash them down. A filling meal with a few good brews will cost about ¥3500.

Akasaka Akasaka (Map 3) has lots of mid-range international choices. Most of the good places are on the small streets just west of Akasaka-mitsuke subway station, with a few scattered along Akasaka-dōri on the way to Roppongi.

Trattoria Marumo is a pizzeria which does a range of Italian fare for reasonable prices. The atmosphere is pleasant and the food is pretty good. There are loads of food models in the window. Count on about ¥1500 for lunch and ¥3000 for dinner. There's a more formal Marumo out on Akasaka-dōri.

Mugyodon is a popular Korean place which is open for dinner only. This is your chance to sample the real Korean stuff, not the usual Japanese versions. A good feed will run to about ¥3000. It's upstairs from Uskudar Turkish restaurant.

Chez Prisi is a small Swiss place which serves reliable food in pleasant surroundings. The daily lunch specials, which start at around ¥1700, are advertised on a blackboard in the window. Dinner will be closer to ¥5000 with something to drink. It's just past the police box; look for the English sign.

Finally, here are two seafood restaurants: *Tokyo Joe's* and *Fisherman's Wharf*. Fisherman's Wharf is heavy on the nautical theme and the food is just what you'd expect: crab, shrimp, oysters etc prepared American style. Lunch starts at ¥3000, and a good

dinner will double that. Tokyo Joe's doesn't overdo the decor, and its speciality is stone crab, imported daily from Florida. It's tasty stuff, and the ¥3000 lunch set is the best way to try it.

PLACES TO EAT – TOP END

Business travellers beware: Tokyo has been rated the most expensive city in the world for dining out. Luckily, now that the heady days of the bubble economy are behind us, even the most elegant establishments have lowered their prices. It's still possible to drop ¥100,000 on a sumptuous sushi feast in Ginza, but it's now also possible to enjoy food almost as good for a tenth of that price.

Top-end dining in Tokyo is generally going to cost a minimum of ¥10,000 per head. If this doesn't faze you, there is no shortage of elegant establishments in which to indulge a passion for haute cuisine. The following is a very selective list; guests at Tokyo's five-star hotels will also find top-end dining options just an elevator ride away.

Japanese
Ginza If you're looking for budget-busting Tokyo restaurants, dine in Ginza (Map 3). Fortunately, the really outrageous places don't really cater to foreigners and are hardly identifiable as restaurants anyway – you'll need a wealthy Japanese friend to get you through their discreet doors. That said, there are several more down-to-earth places in Ginza where you can sample first-rate food.

One of Tokyo's oldest and best tempura restaurants is *Ten-Ichi* (☎ 3572-1698), about five minutes from Sukibayashi crossing. This is the place to try tempura the way it's meant to be: light and crispy, without any greasiness. Lunch starts at ¥7000 and dinner ¥8500. If this branch is full, there's another one in the basement of the Sony building.

With Tsukiji just down the street, it's not surprising that Ginza boasts some of Tokyo's best sushi restaurants. *Kyubei*, in southern Ginza near Shimbashi, is an elegant place where sushi dinners easily cost ¥10,000. It's not just the sushi you're paying for, it's the wonderful surroundings. You'll have a tough

東京 東京 東京 東京 東京 東京 東京 東

Ekiben – Lunch in Locomotion
Ekiben are one of those delightful Japanese institutions. A contraction of the words *eki* (railway station) and *bentō* (lunch box), every railway station worth its salt has an ekiben stand, and some stations are famous for their ekiben.

Legend has it that the first ekiben were served in 1885 at Utsunomiya station, not far from Tokyo. Back in those days, pickles and rice balls were standard fare. How times change. There are close to 3000 varieties nowadays, and stations contend to produce ever more exotic ones – a station might feature mushroom, marinated boar or trout ekiben. Prices are reasonable, if you consider that you're not buying a hastily flung-together takeout. Famous ekiben tend to go from ¥1000 upward, although cheaper ones are often available on trains. ■

東京 東京 東京 東京 東京 東京 東京 東

time finding the place if you look for the Japanese sign. Instead, look for the very elegant Japanese facade set back a little from the street.

Considered by some to be the best sushi in Tokyo, *Jiro Sushi* (☎ 3535-7053) serves sublime sushi. Expect to pay about ¥30,000 per person, and expect to be put off lesser sushi for the rest of your days. Jiro Sushi is in the basement of the building opposite the Sony building.

If you've been looking for a place to try kaiseki, drop into *Munakata* (☎ 3574-9356). This is a relatively cheap and approachable kaiseki restaurant, in the basement of the Mitsui Urban Hotel. Recommended is the ¥5000 kaiseki set course. Dinner will run closer to ¥10,000.

Roppongi For thoroughly approachable top-end Japanese restaurants, Roppongi (Map 7) is the place. People here are so used to foreigners wandering in off the street that they hardly blink.

Kisso (☎ 3582-4191), on the B1 floor of the Axis building (Map 3), is a good place to sample Japan's gourmet cuisine: kaiseki ryōri. There are other places with more elegant kaiseki, but you'll pay three times as much, and may not get in without a Japanese introduction. Here, you can comfortably walk in and sit down to an unforgettable feast. Dinner costs about ¥10,000 per person; it's best to order a course and leave everything up to the chef.

Fukuzushi (☎ 3402-4116) serves some of the best sushi in town in an atmosphere that is decidedly more relaxed than at some of the more traditional places in Ginza and Tsukiji. You can relax and enjoy the good stuff without fearing that you are breaching some hallowed rule of sushi etiquette. The fish here is fresh, the portions large and there's even a cocktail bar. Expect to pay around ¥10,000 each.

Seryna (☎ 3402-1051) has been a long-time favourite of Tokyo expats for a special splurge. There are actually three restaurants under the Seryna roof: the *Seryna Honten* (main store), which serves shabu-shabu and

sukiyaki; *Mon Cher Ton Ton*, serving Kōbe beef steaks; and *Kani Seryna*, where crab dishes are the speciality. At any one of these, you can sample some of the best luxury food Japan has to offer in elegant, foreigner-friendly surroundings. Meals cost between ¥10,000 and ¥15,000 per person without drinks.

Inakaya (☎ 3405-9866), at the Nogizaka end of Gaien-higashi-dōri in Roppongi, has achieved fame and favour as a top-end robatayaki. It does raucous, bustling, 'don't stand on ceremony' robatayaki with gusto. It's possible to spend lots of money (about ¥10,000 a head) *and* have fun. There is also a branch in Akasaka (☎ 3586-3054). It is open daily from 5 to 11 pm.

Akasaka Luxury hotels are the best place to look for approachable top-end Japanese cuisine in Akasaka (Map 3). Try the *restaurant floors* of the New Ōtani, the Ōkura or the Akasaka Prince. One place worth a walk is the Akasaka branch of Ginza's famous tempura restaurant, *Ten-Ichi* (☎ 3583-0107).

International Cuisine

Ginza For superior French cuisine, head to the basement of Ginza's Sony building (Map 3), where you will find *Maxim's de Paris* (☎ 3572-3621). The interior and the menu are dead ringers for the original in Paris. Lunch sets start at ¥6000 and dinner courses at ¥20,000.

In the same building, *Sabatine di Firenze* (☎ 3573-0013) serves excellent northern Italian fare in a faithful reproduction of its twin in Florence. Everything is over-the-top Italian, but the prices are not excessive considering the location. Expect prices in league with those at Maxim's de Paris.

Shinjuku Among all the fine restaurants in the hotels of west Shinjuku (Map 6), one place worth going out of your way for is the *New York Grill* (☎ 5323-3458) on the 52nd floor of the Park Hyatt Tower. This is power dining at its best – hearty portions of steak and seafood and a drop-dead view. One bargain worth mentioning is the ¥3900 Sunday brunch. On the way in, you can warm up with a few drinks at the adjoining New York Bar.

Harajuku, Aoyama & Nishi-Azabu Trendy Harajuku (Map 7) is the closest thing Tokyo comes to having a 'Little Paris', and the many French restaurants are proof.

L'Amphore (☎ 3402-6486) is often mentioned as one of the best French restaurants in the city. The atmosphere is spot-on and it avoids the overly formal feeling which is the bane of so many top-end French places in Tokyo. An excellent dinner with good wine will run to about ¥25,000 for two, and lunch about half that. It's easy to spot; look for the French sign and the authentic decor.

L'Orangerie de Paris (☎ 3407-7461), in the Hanae Mori building on Omote-sandō, is another elegant choice. The ¥4000 lunch set is good value, and dinners are reliable. Recommended is the ¥4000 Sunday brunch.

How about boutique Chinese cuisine served in the style of a fine French restaurant? It's possible, and *Aux Sept Bonheurs* (☎ 3498-8144) is one of Tokyo's most highly regarded restaurants. The secret is to order one of the courses and let the chef do the rest; what follows is a fabulous succession of small but wonderfully prepared delicacies. Plan on at least ¥10,000 per head.

Ebisu Here is one of Tokyo's most outrageous re-creations of a fine French restaurant, *Taillevent-Robuchon* (Map 8) (☎ 5424-1338). It is inside a full-scale reproduction of a French chateau on the grounds of the Ebisu Garden Place Tower complex. With a tie-in to two of France's most esteemed restaurants, the food is predictably good. Lunch with a good bottle of wine will approach ¥8000 per person, and dinners will be double that.

Roppongi Most of the top-end dining here is Japanese, but those who like Californian cuisine may want to stop in at the Tokyo branch of *Spago* (Map 7) (☎ 3423-4025). Even this bastion of Beverly Hills wealth has had to come to terms with economic realities, and you can now get a fairly reasonable lunch here for around ¥3000. Dinners will comfortably be double that with a few drinks.

Akasaka The best place to look in Akasaka (Map 3) is in the main luxury hotels: the Hotel Ōkura, the New Ōtani, the Akasaka Prince and the Capital Tōkyū.

Tohkalin (☎ 3582-0111), on the 6th floor of the Hotel Ōkura, is reported to have the best Chinese food in Tokyo, and that's saying a lot. It is possible to eat here for mid-range prices if you stick to the simpler dishes, but you'll be under serious pressure to splurge when you see what else is on the menu. An added bonus is access to Ōkura's wine cellar.

For excellent continental cuisine, *Keyaki Grill* (☎ 3581-4511) on the B1 floor of the Capital Tōkyū hotel is a sure bet. Those in the know report that this is the best of its kind in Tokyo.

Entertainment

Tokyo is easily the entertainment capital of Asia – from cinema to sumō, there's more than enough to keep you amused.

The best place to find out what's happening is the *Tokyo Journal*. *Tokyo Classifieds*, *Tokyo Weekender*, the online *Tokyo Q* and *Pia* are also good resources. See the Magazines and Online Services sections of the Facts for the Visitor chapter for details on where to find these.

CINEMA

Foreign movies are screened with original soundtracks and Japanese subtitles. American films predominate, but there's also British, Australian, French, German, Italian and Chinese films. In addition to big-name films, Tokyo is home to smaller cinemas which regularly screen art-house and cult films.

You may also want to check out some Japanese films: *anime* (animated films) are currently booming, and you can find good first-run anime (don't expect any English subtitles or dubbing, though). Revival houses also run Japanese film classics.

The quality of Japanese cinemas has improved drastically in recent years. Most mainstream cinemas in areas like Shinjuku and Shibuya have good sound systems and comfortable seating. Ticket prices, however, are probably the highest in the world, averaging between ¥1700 and ¥2300.

If you can plan ahead, tickets can be bought at certain outlets at discounted prices. Typically, a ¥1700 ticket will cost ¥1300 or less this way. Ticket outlets are in the basement of the Tokyo Kōtsū Kaikan building (Map 3) in Ginza, Shinjuku's Studio Alta building (5th floor) (Map 6), Harajuku's Laforet building (1st floor) (Map 7) and Shibuya's 109 building (2nd floor) (Map 7).

PERFORMING ARTS

Despite the language barrier many will face, Japanese theatre is a unique and rewarding experience. The Tourist Information Center (TIC) or theatres can give you performance and booking details.

Bunraku

Osaka is the bunraku centre, but performances do take place in Tokyo in February, May, September and December at Japan's national theatre, *Kokuritsu Geikijō Theatre* (Map 2) (☎ 3265-7411) in Nagatachō.

Butō

Unfortunately for the visitor, most butō troupes are small, underground affairs. The TIC can help track current ones down.

Kabuki

The best place to see kabuki in Tokyo is the Kabuki-za Theatre (Map 3) (☎ 3541-3131, 5565-6000) in Ginza. Performances and times vary from month to month. For phone

Making a fashion statement on stage.

bookings, ring at least a day ahead, as the theatre won't take bookings for the same day. Earphones providing 'comments and explanations' in English are available at ¥600 (¥1000 deposit) – well worth it. Ticket prices vary from ¥2520 to ¥16,800, depending on how keen you are to see the stage. One distraction you may encounter is a large group of school children – the excitement of the proceedings gives rise to a lot of chatting and giggling.

Performances can be quite a marathon, lasting 4½ to five hours. If you're not up to it, you can get tickets for the gallery on the 4th floor (¥500 to ¥1200) and watch just one act. Unfortunately, earphone guides are not available in these seats. Fourth-floor tickets can be bought on the day of the performance. There are generally two performances daily, starting at around 11 am and 4 pm.

The national theatre (see the earlier Bunraku section) also has kabuki performances, with seat prices from ¥1300 to ¥7800. Again, earphone guides are available.

Nō

Performances are held at various locations around Tokyo. Tickets cost between ¥3000 and ¥10,000, and it's best to get them at the theatre itself.

Kanze Nō-gakudō Theatre (Map 7) (☎ 3469-6241) is a 10 to 15 minute walk from Shibuya station. From the Hachikō exit, turn right at the 109 building and follow the road straight ahead past Tōkyū department store. The theatre is on the right, a couple of minutes down the third street on the left after Tōkyū.

Theatrical fan with a rising sun motif

Ginza Nō-gakudō Theatre (Map 3) (☎ 3571-0197) is a five minute walk from Ginza subway station. Turn right onto Sotobori-dōri in the direction of Shimbashi at the Sukiyabashi crossing; look for the theatre on the left.

Kokuritsu Nō-gakudō Theatre (Map 6) (☎ 3423-1331), or National Nō Theatre, is in Sendagaya on the Chūō/Sōbu line. Exit Sendagaya station in the direction of Shinjuku and follow the road which hugs the railway tracks; the theatre is on the left.

Rakugo

Students of Japanese who want to test their language skills to the hilt can see rakugo at the *Asakusa Engei Hall* (Map 4) (☎ 3841-6545) in Asakusa or at the *Suzumoto Engeijō Hall* (Map 4) (☎ 3834-5905) in Ueno.

Theatre

Tokyo's contemporary theatre scene is effectively off limits to non-Japanese speakers. One much cited instance in which language skills are of limited importance is the *Tokyo Takarazuka Theatre* (Map 3) (☎ 3591-1711). Takarazuka are all-female operatic reviews which partake of a potpourri of styles (from aria through pop music to old folk songs). The Tokyo theatre has a devoted following, largely in teenage girls. Performances are a rich extravaganza of colour and song, and definitely make for an interesting – if somewhat bizarre – evening out. The Tokyo Takarazuka Theatre is just across the road from the Imperial Hotel in Yūrakuchō. Performances usually start at 1 and 5.30 pm, and tickets range from around ¥1000 to ¥5000.

There are also occasional theatre performances in English given by local and international theatre groups.

CLASSICAL MUSIC

Classical music fans will not be disappointed in Tokyo; most nights have orchestral or chamber music performances. In general, performances by Japanese symphonies are cheaper to attend than those by visiting symphonies, eg a recent performance by the Tokyo Symphony at the Suntory Hall cost

ENTERTAINMENT

from ¥5000 to ¥9000, while the Chamber Orchestra of Europe at the same venue was ¥10,000 to ¥14,000.

Four of the main classical performance venues in Tokyo are the *Tokyo Metropolitan Festival Hall* (Map 4) (☎ 3828-2111) in Ueno, the *Tokyo Metropolitan Art Space* (Map 5) (☎ 5391-2111) in Ikebukuro, *Bunkamura* (Map 7) (☎ 3477-9111) in Shibuya and *Suntory Hall* (Map 3) (☎ 3505-1001) in Akasaka.

ROCK

Tokyo doesn't have the thriving live music scene that many western cities do. The local scene suffers from a lack of venues, and shows tend to start and finish early (often around 9 pm). Tokyo does see a lot of international acts, however. Advance ticket prices range from ¥4500 to ¥7000.

Live Houses

The local live music scene, such as it is, can be found in so-called 'live houses'. Most of them are in the outlying student areas like Shimo-Kitazawa, but there are a few scattered around central Tokyo. There is usually an entry charge (¥2000 to ¥3000).

A long-running Tokyo live house is *Loft* (☎ 3365-0698) on the western side of the Yamanote line between Shinjuku and Shin-Ōkubo stations – look for a delightfully ramshackle building with the English sign 'Live House Loft'. Cover charges range from ¥1500 to ¥3000, depending on who is playing, and it is open from 6.30 pm to 1 am, and until 2 am on Friday and Saturday.

In Harajuku, *Crocodile* (☎ 3499-5205) has something happening every night. To get there from Harajuku station, walk down Omote-sandō and turn right at Meiji-dōri. Cross the road and continue straight ahead, passing an overhead walkway. Crocodile is on your left, in the basement of the New Sekiguchi building. Entry is usually ¥2000 with one or two drink tickets.

Shibuya (Map 7) has a few interesting live music venues. Two clubs, *The Cave* (☎ 3780-0715) and *Club Quattro* (☎ 3477-8750), are venues for high quality international and

local acts, and have dance floors as well. Entry for both clubs is around ¥3000 to ¥4000. Also in Shibuya, usually featuring local performers at more reasonable entry rates, are *Eggman* (☎ 3496-1561) and *La Mama* (☎ 3464-0801).

In Ebisu, *Milk* (Map 8) (☎ 5458-2826) is one of Tokyo's best small live clubs, featuring international punk, rock and alternative, along with some of Tokyo's better underground acts. This is a cool space, with three underground levels and a crowd of local characters you just can't imagine meeting on the street. Entry is ¥2000 to ¥3000 and includes one or two drink tickets. The club is in the basement of the building which houses the English-style bar What the Dickens (see the Bars & Small Clubs section later in this chapter).

A good live house is *Rock Mother* (☎ 3460-1479), down in Shimo-Kitazawa. The whole area around there is worth a look: it's a kind of down-market Harajuku or a youth-oriented Shinjuku, with lots of cheap places to eat and drink – very popular with students. To get to Rock Mother, take the Odakyū line to Shimo-Kitazawa station and exit via the south exit ('minami-guchi'). After you leave the station, turn left, then right, and then left again. Follow the road around to the right and look for the club on your left.

Cover Band Venues

One of the best is *Hot Co-Rocket* (Map 7) (☎ 3583-9409) in Roppongi. Reggae bands are featured in a suitably Caribbean setting. For 50s covers, *Kento's* (Map 7) (☎ 3401-5755) has branches all over Japan, and attracts a young, enthusiastic, bobby-soxed crowd of jivers. The cover charge at Kento's is usually around ¥1300. Japanese Beatles cover bands perform faultless renditions of fab-four tunes at Roppongi's *Cavern Club* (Map 7) (☎ 3405-5207). Entry is ¥1300.

JAZZ

There are probably more hardcore jazz fans in Tokyo than anywhere in the world. To keep these folks happy, most major jazz bands include Tokyo on their tour schedules. Thus, Tokyo is a prime spot to catch bands which may be impossible to see elsewhere. The downside is that jazz is expensive in Tokyo, and even small places charge upwards of ¥5000 for a show.

The premier Tokyo jazz spot is the *Blue Note* (Map 7) (☎ 3407-5781) in Aoyama. The top acts all come here and the place is home to some serious cognoscenti, all of whom are willing to pay ¥7000 to ¥15,000 for one show. While this edition was being researched, the Blue Note played host to such acts as Branford Marsalis, Carl Anderson, Tito Puente and the Latin Jazz All Stars, and Maysa Leak.

The *Shinjuku Pit Inn* (☎ 3354-2024) is another spot to look for good jazz shows. Most shows at the Pit Inn cost around ¥3000, but entry can be ¥10,000-plus if the act is well known. To get there, take the C5 exit of Sanchōme subway station; look for the Pit Inn on Gyoen-dōri, below Kobe Ranpu-tei restaurant.

In Roppongi, there's another *Pit Inn* (Map 7) (☎ 3585-1063), where the music is reportedly less traditional than that played at its Shinjuku counterpart. Walking away from Roppongi subway station, turn right at Almond coffee shop, cross over the road and look for the Pit Inn on your left, about 100m down the road.

Dinner & Drinks with a View

How about a little perspective on the rat race? Any of Tokyo's many skyscraper bars and restaurants are sure to give you a feeling of being above it all. While many places charge exorbitant rates to go with their views, some are remarkably reasonable, hardly more than you'd pay down on street level. The following are some recommended spots.

Tokyo Park Hyatt In west Shinjuku, this new Park Hyatt Hotel in the Park Tower (Map 6) is *the* place for power drinking in stunning surroundings. If you've got the extra change, you owe it to yourself to knock back a few here – you'll feel like you own the world. On weekday evenings the *Sky Bar* on the 41st floor has a happy-hour special (5 to 9 pm) with all you can eat/drink for ¥3800 for women and ¥4500 for men. At other times, drinks usually go for about ¥1500 each. The Sky Bar is open from 5 to 11.30 pm, Monday to Saturday, and from noon to 10.30 pm on Sunday and holidays.

On the next floor, the *New York Bar* offers a similarly stunning view in a cool piano bar atmosphere. On weekdays from 5 to 7.30 pm, an hors d'oeuvre plate and two drinks is ¥2500. Otherwise, the hours and prices are the same as the Sky Bar's. The *New York Grill*, on the same floor, offers great food at top-end prices.

Aurora Lounge Also in west Shinjuku, the *Aurora Lounge*, on the 45th floor of the Keiō Plaza Hotel (Map 6), offers great views and drinks (from ¥1000). It also does a good coffee set during the day. It's open daily from 11.30 am to 11.30 pm.

On the same floor, the *Polestar* bar is built for gazing out over the city, with each seat facing the windows. Drinks start at ¥1450. It's open daily from 5 to 11.30 pm.

Top of Akasaka Over in Akasaka, on the 40th floor of the Akasaka Prince Hotel (Map 3), this bar offers a great view over central Tokyo in a lounge atmosphere. Drinks start at ¥1300. It's open from 1 pm to 2 am, Monday to Saturday, until midnight on Sunday and holidays.

Sunset Lounge For good Bay area views, this lounge, on the 6th floor of the Hotel Intercontinental in Kaigan in Minato-ku, is the place to go. While not all that high, the waterfront location allows unobstructed views of Rainbow Bridge and shipping in the harbour. Drinks start at ¥900. It's open daily from 10 am to midnight.

Trianon Up in Ikebukuro, on the 59th floor of the Sunshine 60 building (Map 5), the *Trianon* bar has a good weekend/holiday tart and sandwich buffet for only ¥1600, including drinks, from noon to 4 pm. At night, the bar serves drinks from ¥1000. Bar service runs from 6 pm to midnight, Monday to Saturday, until 11 pm on Sunday and holidays. ∎

ENTERTAINMENT

Another Roppongi jazz club is *Birdland* (☎ 3478-3456), in the basement of the Square building, the hub of disco activity in Roppongi. Entry is around ¥3000. Cross the intersection at the Almond coffee shop, continue walking away from Roppongi subway station, take the second right turn and you'll bump into the Square building. Look for all the beautiful people outside waiting to see where the happening spot is tonight.

DISCOS & BIG CLUBS

The Tokyo club scene is at its hottest during the summer months, though there is action of one kind or another year round. For straight disco action, Roppongi is the place to be. Entry to most discos is steep at around ¥4000 (with some drinks tickets thrown in), which is a risky proposition if you aren't allowed to take a look first. There is so much competition, and discos fluctuate so rapidly in popularity, that there is always a chance that some of the big ones will be near deserted even on a Saturday night.

Entry to clubs is usually cheaper (in the ¥2000 range), and clubs are booming in Tokyo. A quick look at the nightlife listings of the English-language monthlies reveals any number of techno, trance, trip-hop, ambient, drum 'n' bass and jungle happenings at clubs around town. Serious clubbers should take a look at the Clubs and Bars section of the *Tokyo Journal*, the *Tokyo Classifieds*, *Tokyo Q*, or wander in to HMV in Shinjuku or Shibuya.

Shinjuku

Shinjuku (Map 6) is more of a bar/small club scene, but there are a few big dance venues scattered about.

Code (☎ 3209-0702) is a gigantic new club in the Shinjuku Koma theatre building. The place has an open, hip feel and tends to get crowded with younger Tokyoites. The music is mostly house, with some trance and drum 'n' bass mixed in. The huge dance floor invites hours of dancing and there is a good seating area in which to take a break. The cover averages about ¥2000 with one or two drinks.

Also in Shinjuku's Kabukichō, check out the schedule for the *Liquid Room* (☎ 3200-6831). This slick club is usually reserved for live events, but there is a club night at least once a month.

Harajuku, Aoyama & Nishi-Azabu

Aoyama (Map 7) is a hipper, mellower version of Roppongi. This is where a lot of expats go after the initial fascination with Roppongi wears off. The problem is, many of the better clubs here are maddeningly hard to find. Ideally, collar a resident and get a guided tour. Failing that, these should be good starting points.

Apollo (☎ 3478-6007) is a good spot for dancing and mingling. It's fairly mainstream hip-hop and R&B, and the crowd is usually pretty lively. A ¥2500 cover includes two drinks. Entrance is down an alley to the left of the building (look for the florist).

Blue (☎ 3797-1591) is popular with mod Tokyo student types and hots up from time to time. The highlight is its cool interior design and cave-like atmosphere. The music is mostly acid jazz. It's quite a walk from central Aoyama, past the Blue Note (see the earlier Jazz section). Once you get into the area, look for a portable sign on street level. Entrance is down a small walkway, and the club is in the basement. Entry is usually ¥1500 and includes one drink.

Shibuya

Club Asia (Map 7) (☎ 5458-5963) plays host to some of Tokyo's bigger DJ events. Music runs toward techno, trance, drum 'n' bass and house. Entry is ¥2000 including one drink. The place is a little secretive looking; look for the 1st floor, which has the appearance of a cafe.

Roppongi

Roppongi (Map 7) basically has something for everyone, though most of the hipper clubs are on the fringes of the area or down near the Nishi-Azabu crossing.

For mainstream disco, there's *Velfarre* (☎ 3746-0055), a disco extravaganza of little interest to the average punter – for a start, there is a ¥5000 cover for men and ¥4000 for women, and the place shuts down at midnight. Still, if you want a disco with all the trimmings, this is it.

Lexington Queen (☎ 3401-1661) is definitely a Tokyo institution. Local celebrity Bill Hersey manages to make sure that the who's who of the international film and music worlds put in an appearance while in town. The music is a little staid, but the crowd never is. Lexington has the usual cover (around ¥5500), including drinks and a serving from the Lex Sushi Bar.

By the Nishi-Azabu crossing, *Yellow* (☎ 3479-0690) is one of the most progressive places in town. Call in and pick up a monthly calendar – house, acid jazz, techno and foreign DJ nights are all featured.

Gay Clubs

There are not many specifically gay clubs in Tokyo, but plenty which are host to a mixed scene. See the above sections for information on *Yellow*, *Blue* and *Apollo*. Check the *Tokyo Journal*, *Tokyo Q*, and Shinjuku and Shibuya HMV stores for information on gay events, including the Ring party, which is held at various clubs around Tokyo.

BARS & SMALL CLUBS

A lot of heavy drinking goes on in Tokyo, something you will realise very quickly if you hop on any train from around 10 pm onwards. Fortunately, although there is a lot of falling down and the occasional heaving, the Japanese are very rarely violent drunks.

All that drinking makes for a lot of bars. As a general rule, avoid places with closed doors. You probably won't get in even if you try, but if you do, the chances are that it is a hostess bar with extortionate drink prices. The best bet is to duck into one of the many bars with mixed Japanese/foreign crowds; they are as a rule affordable and friendly.

No doubt, Roppongi is the 'gaijin bar' capital of Tokyo. There are more small clubs, bars and pubs here than in most medium-sized cities back home. Shinjuku is probably Tokyo's drinking capital, and many bars and pubs here are receptive to foreigners. You

東京東京東京東京東京東京東京東京東

Beer Gardens

When summer temperatures soar in July and August, the best way to beat the heat is to head to one of Tokyo's many rooftop beer gardens. Most of these places offer some kind of all-you-can-eat/drink special, and you can fill up for around ¥3000. Most places have a time limit, so if you want to get your money's worth, you're going to have to go early and work fast.

Matsuzakaya Lion Beer Garden
  (☎ 3572-1111) Ginza; all-you-can-eat/drink for ¥2980; roof of Matsuzakaya department store; daily, 5 to 9.30 pm.
Ikebukuro Parco Tai Tai
  (☎ 3987-0552) Ikebukuro; all-you-can-eat/drink for ¥3000 for men and ¥2500 for women for two hours; roof of Parco department store; daily, 5 to 10 pm.
My City Beer Garden
  (☎ 5360-7144) Shinjuku; all-you-can-eat/drink for ¥3000 for men and ¥2500 for women for two hours; roof of My City store; Sunday, 4 to 10 pm.
Shibuya Tōkyū Honten
  (☎ 3477-3478) Shibuya; enough yaki-niku (Korean barbecue) for four people for ¥2500, large draught beer for ¥950; Tōkyū department store's main store; daily, 5 to 9.30 pm.
Tokyo ANA Hotel Beer Garden
  (☎ 3505-1111) Akasaka; all-you-can-eat, ¥5000 for two people, beer from ¥600. Akasaka ANA Hotel; daily, 6 to 9.30 pm.

東京東京東京東京東京東京東京東京東

can also find lots of good watering holes in Shibuya, Harajuku, Aoyama, Nishi-Azabu, Ginza and Ikebukuro.

If you don't feel like braving a regular bar down on the streets, you can always try a hotel bar, many of which offer great views to go with your drinks.

Ginza

Despite Ginza's reputation as one of Tokyo's pricier areas, there are lots of places scattered about where you can have a few drinks for no more than you would pay in Roppongi or Shinjuku. Indeed, if you don't want to deal with the madness of those areas, Ginza (Map 3) is a good place for a drink in relaxing surroundings.

ENTERTAINMENT

Over by the JR tracks, *Henry Africa* is the most consciously foreigner-oriented of Ginza's drinking spots. This is part of a chain of British-style pubs and, at least as far as decorations go, it does a pretty good imitation of merry old England. You can start with fish and chips for less than ¥1000 and move on to beers for about ¥800 a pop.

For true beer hall ambience and a great selection of beers, head to *Pilsen* (☎ 3571-3443) in central Ginza. The food is widely hailed as some of Ginza's worst, but if a few greasy snacks before drinking are all you want, it should suffice. Big mugs of beer start at ¥800.

For a bigger, Japanese-style beer hall, head to the nearby *Lion Beer Hall* (☎ 3571-2590). This is a sprawling complex of eating and drinking halls smack in the middle of Ginza. While the food is marginally better than that at Pilsen, the atmosphere leaves plenty to be desired. Beers start at ¥700, food items from ¥500.

For something completely different, head to *Old Imperial Bar* (☎ 3504-1111) in the Imperial Hotel over in Hibiya. This is an impossibly dignified hotel bar. Drinks start at ¥1000.

Asakusa

Asakusa (Map 4) is not the place to look for good night spots in Tokyo. Sure, there are a few izakaya scattered about, but generally the area shuts down early. That said, there is one decent spot for a drink: *Kamiya* (☎ 3841-5400). Opened in 1880, this was the first western-style bar in Japan. The 1st floor is a beer hall, where you pay for drinks as you enter. The 2nd floor is a restaurant. Kamiya is closed Tuesday.

Ikebukuro

A lot of nightlife in Ikebukuro (Map 5) consists of sleazy hostess clubs which won't let you in no matter how politely you ask. There are some good izakaya around, but for western-style places, two decent ones have popped up. *The Dubliners* (☎ 5951-3614), in the Spice 2 building near the Tokyo Metropolitan Art Space, is a faux-Irish pub offering

Kilkenny and Guinness draught for ¥850, and fish and chips for ¥750. The only bummer here is that it shuts down at 11 pm.

If you want to continue drinking, head over to *Persona* (☎ 3980-8875) on the 3rd floor of the Milano building. This is a fairly generic space, but there's table soccer, darts and good music. Catch the happy-hour special between 5 and 9 pm: cocktails and beer for ¥350, a real bargain in Tokyo.

Takadanobaba

'Baba (Map 5), as it is known to locals, is a scaled-down, budget version of Ikebukuro and Shinjuku. There are some good restaurants and a couple of places to have a drink. See the Useful Organisations section of the Facts for the Visitor chapter for information on *Mickey House*, a conversation club cum bar that serves inexpensive drinks and is one of the friendliest places in town for newcomers to drop into.

When things wind down at Mickey House (around 11.30 pm), the action often moves on to *Billy Barew's Beer Bar* (☎ 3209-0952). Billy's claims to stock 150 brands of beer (about ¥800 each) – see if you can come up with an ungrantable request. It also serves a small selection of food (mostly overpriced and in small portions).

Shinjuku

Evenings in Shinjuku (Map 6) are underrated by many of Tokyo's residents. There's actually plenty here, but you have to know where to look. Just promenading under the bright lights of Kabukichō and ducking into a revolving sushi shop or yakitori bar for a bite to eat is a good prelude to a fun night out.

Most of the drinking spots are on the east side of the station. Just a few minute's walk from the My City exit, you'll find *Kirin City* (☎ 3350-8935), a popular beer hall with a few outdoor tables where you can watch the constant parade of Shinjuku characters. There always seems to be a gang of big dudes at the best outside table, so you may have to make do with another (unless you're one of the big dudes). Beers here start at

¥500, making it one of the cheaper options around.

On Yasukuni-dōri, *Top's Bar* (☎ 3354-6808) is a good standard-issue bar for a few rounds in peaceful surroundings. It's dimly lit, patronised by civilised sorts and a cut above most other places in this part of town. Drinks start at ¥800.

If you want to forget that you're even in Japan, try *The Dubliners Irish Pub* (☎ 3352-6606) in the Lion building, just a few minute's walk from the My City exit. This place is pretty popular with Tokyo expats. Guinness is on tap for ¥800 and pub foods are around ¥900 a serving.

Just across Yasukuni-dōri, next to a big pachinko parlour, the Pole Star building is home to two excellent small clubs. *Catalyst* (☎ 3209-4102) is a good, laid-back club where you can dance to salsa, hip-hop and reggae with a nice bunch of Japanese folks and hip expats. Or, just sit at the bar and chill; no-one will hassle you. Entry is ¥2000 and includes two drinks. In the same building, *Garam* (☎ 3205-8668) is a cool little reggae club with a friendly owner. This place makes a nice change from many Shinjuku reggae clubs, which are often packed with rasta-poseurs. Entry is ¥2000 on weekends and includes two drinks; on weekdays entry is free.

Out toward Shinjuku-nichōme, *Rolling Stone* (☎ 3354-7347) is definitely not for the faint-hearted. The music is rock & roll from the 70s onwards (with a heavy emphasis on Stones material), and it's a hang-out for Tokyo's heavy metal kids – lots of leather jackets, outrageous hairdos and cool posing. It's fairly quiet on weekdays, but really hots up on Friday and Saturday night, when things often get a little out of control. There's a ¥500 cover charge and it's ¥800 for a bottle of beer. Look for it in the basement next door to a 'soapland'.

Harajuku, Aoyama & Nishi-Azabu

These adjoining areas (Map 7) hold some of Tokyo's best nightlife options, and provide a pleasant escape when the Roppongi crush is too much to bear.

Oh God (☎ 3406-3206) has been going for years; miraculously, it is still going. The format seems a little tired, but if your needs run to pool tables and movie screenings, it's just the ticket. Walk down Omote-sandō and take the first lane on the right after Meiji-dōri. Oh God is in the basement of the building at the end of the lane. Practically next door is *Zest* (☎ 3499-0976), another popular pub, which also serves food.

In Aoyama you'll find several good small club options. The first, *Kiss* (☎ 3401-8165) has four floors to explore, including an expresso bar, an Internet cafe which serves light snacks, a disco which plays all kinds of funk, soul, disco and electronic sounds, and a bar on the top floor. It's ¥2000 to enter the bar and disco. All in all, this is a cool place to build an evening around.

Back towards the Omote-sandō crossing, there's the tiny, hole-in-the-wall *Mix* (☎ 3797-1313). You can usually count on this club even when others in the neighbourhood are flat. It's small, smoky, crowded and always friendly. Music ranges from reggae to hip-hop. Cover charges vary and drinks start at ¥700. It's rather hard to find; turn at the SG Dupont Paris store and look for the stairs.

Out in Nishi-Azabu, midway between Aoyama and Roppongi, *328* (or *San-nippa*; ☎ 3401-4968) is a funky little club-cum-bar with a ¥2500 cover on Saturday night. It attracts a good crowd of international types and locals, and is a refuge from the trendier clubs up in Roppongi. Music is mostly R&B and soul. Roll in at midnight and you're bound to have a good time. It's right near the corner; look for the stairs leading to the basement.

Las Chicas restaurant (☎ 3407-6865) has a bar and a member's club, both of which are good spots for a drink.

Shibuya

Shibuya (Map 7) is one of the more happening places in Tokyo for a drink. There are lots of bars and clubs scattered about, mostly on the west side of the station hidden between all those big department stores.

The Cave (☎ 3780-0715) is a cramped

ENTERTAINMENT

spot hidden down a narrow street near Tōbu department store. There's electronic music, and the atmosphere is fittingly cool. This was *the* place in the early 90s; now it's just another of Tokyo's many good clubs. Entry averages ¥2000 with one or two drink tickets.

Hub Pub is part of a chain of English-style pubs with branches all over Tokyo. If you like faux-English ambience, pub food and a decent selection of beers, this should satisfy.

For a bar reminiscent of the Occupation era, try *Panama Joe's* (☎ 3461-9047) up on Dōgenzaka-dōri. If you just want to sit alone or with a friend and enjoy an honest drink, you'll like Joe's. There's a ¥200 table charge and a small range of food is available. Look for the red brick building.

Jazz fans take note: *Jazz Swing* (☎ 3463-3889) is a dimly lit coffee shop-cum-bar up on the hill. It's very mellow, and serves the standard lubricants to good jazz: whiskey and beer.

On the other side of the station, *Kirin City* is your run-of-the-mill Japanese beer hall, serving a variety of inexpensive food and beers from just ¥500.

Roppongi

Roppongi (Map 7) has traditionally been the place for foreigners to drink. With Tokyo's highest concentration of gaijin bars tucked into a small area, it's relatively easy to navigate, and is much more approachable than some other neighbourhoods. If you have only one night on the town, Roppongi is undoubtedly the place to go.

Some of the less expensive gaijin bars get very crowded and rowdy on Friday and Saturday night. Second-hand cigarette smoke is thick, and unaccompanied women may get hassled in some bars (by foreigners). All things considered, if you want to have some drinks and do some dancing, it's worth forking out the cover for one of Roppongi's or Aoyama's clubs, where the clientele tends to be hipper and more laid back.

On the north side of Roppongi-dōri are several interesting choices. A great place to start is *Havana Cafe* (see the Places to Eat

chapter). Happy-hour specials are good, and there's lots of tasty, inexpensive food to line your stomach for a night of drinking. Nearby, in a somewhat hard-to-find basement, *People's Bar* (☎ 3479-4898) attracts an interesting crew and entertains them with good reggae, hip-hop and R&B. The fruit drinks are freshly squeezed and start at ¥600. Sometimes this place is hopping, other times it's flat. Poke your head in for a look.

Around the corner, *Paranoia* (☎ 5411-8018) is a shrine to the eponymous horror movie – the walls are covered with rubber ghoul masks, the video plays only horror movie clips and the customers are people only this place would attract. It's worth popping in for a reasonably priced quick one. Look for the giant eye on the front of the building, peering down like an alien cyclops.

In the same area, *Hub* is a decent, plain English-style place, with some bar games, a lot of foreigners hanging about and a few good brews on tap.

On the other side of Gaien-higashi-dōri, *Salsa Sudada* (☎ 5474-8806) is perhaps the most popular salsa club in salsa-mad Tokyo. If you like salsa, climb the steps and get busy. Entry is ¥1500 on weekends, otherwise it's free.

Right near the famous Roppongi crossing, you'll find *Geronimo* (☎ 3478-7449) on the 2nd floor of the Yamamuro building. Described as a shot bar, it gets packed out with all sorts of off-work Tokyo expats and a few of their Japanese associates. At happy hour (6 to 8 pm) all drinks, which usually run around ¥1000, are half price. Beers are ¥800 no matter what time you go. This is a serious drinking bar with a hardcore clientele.

On the south side of Roppongi-dōri, you'll find three good choices clustered next to one another just a little way down Imoarai-zaka-dōri. Here, the street comes to a pointed corner. Right at the corner, the English-style pub *Aston* is a dimly lit spot for a calm drink (Guinness is on tap). Right around the corner from Aston is *Mogambo* (☎ 3403-4833), sister club of Geronimo. The deal here is the same as at Geronimo, and the crowd is pretty similar, too. This bar doesn't bother with

CHRIS ROWTHORN

JNTO

MATTHIAS LEY

RICHARD I'ANSON

om top left to bottom: Figures, gestures and silence take on new meanings in a nō drama; e stately Edo-style facade of Kabuki-za Theatre, Ginza; outdoor performance of modern *gura* dance; limbering up and striking a pose before a sumō bout.

CHRIS TAYLOR

CHRIS TAYLOR

MATTHIAS LEY

わき、おどる。

CHRIS TAYLOR

MARTIN MOOS

It's an aquired taste, but Japanese pop music does have its own style. Japanese all bands were into 'girl power' long before it became a marketing tool in the west. Japan musicians have also been credited with reviving the flagging energy of American punk alternative rock in the 90s.

CHRIS TAYLOR

MARTIN MOOS

MATTHIAS LEY

The visual assault of signs: one of Akihabara's discount electronics outlets (top left), flags advertising the contestants at an upcoming sumō bout at Ryōgoku (top right) and a barrage of messages at a Shinjuku intersection (bottom).

Vending Machines

There are no prizes for guessing that Japan has the most vending machines per capita on the planet. Estimates are in the range of 20 million machines, and you'd swear they were all in Tokyo. A major reason for the numbers is that in Japan they go unmolested – in most countries, plonking a beer vending machine on a suburban street corner would be inviting disaster, or at least a free street party.

You can buy almost anything from vending machines – soft drinks, coffee, cigarettes, beer, sake and whiskey, of course, but also everything from rice and vegetables to cup noodles, burgers, jeans, neckties and computer software. Machines outside some pharmacies dispense condoms (conveniently matched to your blood type, the key to your personality); porno machines (magazines and video) can be found in some areas.

MARTIN MOOS

Vending machines can be socially responsible, too. New vending systems are ecologically correct: 'eco vender' is a system that keeps drinks cold even when switched off; 'eco ice' uses the drinks' own liquid to cool the machine.

Then there's recycling, as with the used panties machine. Ostensibly once owned and worn by female high-school students, undies come in vacuum-sealed packs of three (with a photo of the erstwhile owner) and are targeted at the average fetishistic man about town. The cost? Around ¥3000 to ¥5000, making them an ideal souvenir.

Box: Machines, alone or amassed in arcades, dispense nearly anything that can be spat out of a slot. UCC coffee machines are everywhere, but for a real thirst quencher, there's always Pokari Sweat. (Photograph by Tony Wheeler)

Upper Right: Maybe the phone's there to call mum before you buy anything ...

Bottom Left & Right: Machines dispensing beer, sake and whiskey are common sights in Tokyo.

MARTIN MOOS

MARTIN MOOS

flashing lights and fancy drinks, just good rock 'n' roll.

Just next door, *Castillo* (☎ 3475-1629) is a small club which plays a lot of disco and soul classics. Many people come here to dance, but you can just as easily pull up a chair and sit back for a drink. If you're in the neighbourhood, definitely look in. Drinks start at ¥600.

Across the street is another zone thick with drinking places. On the first street in from the corner, *Motown House* (☎ 5474-4605) used to be the hang-out of Tokyo's expat business types; now it draws a more eclectic group. The music is standard rock 'n' roll, the bar is long, drinks start at ¥800 and it's a good place to meet people. Look for it on the 2nd floor of the building on the corner. In the basement of the same building is *Milwaukee* (☎ 5410-4319), which has been described as an American college bar airlifted to Tokyo. It's your standard jukebox bar, but at ¥500 a beer, it's cheap enough to check out.

Down the same street, in the Marina building on the 3rd floor, *Gas Panic Club* (☎ 3402-7054) is a slightly upmarket version of its rowdy progenitor, Gas Panic bar. If you like the Gas Panic chain (and you know who you are), give the club version a try.

Further down the same road, the MT building houses two large club-type bars where you can really stretch out and enjoy some cheap drinks. On the B2 floor *Cars* (☎ 3470-5944) has a silly automotive theme, but there's good music and frequent live shows. Beers start at ¥600. On the 3rd floor you'll find *Bar, Isn't It?* (☎ 3746-1598), an offshoot of a very successful Osaka bar chain. The formula here is simple: a big space, so-so bar food and all drinks for ¥500. All together, it works pretty well, and it's a good place to meet people.

Charleston (☎ 3402-1096) is just a few streets further south. This used to be an institution of sleaze; now it's just a good small bar where you can put away a pizza while you drink.

One of Roppongi's rowdier cul-de-sacs is formed by what used to be one big gaijin bar,

Gas Panic (☎ 3405-0633), which has split into three bars. Along with the original there's the *Gas Panic Executive Bar* and the *Miller Bar Gas Panic*. The Executive Bar on the 2nd floor tries to reign in the yahoos by enforcing a dress code, while Miller Bar serves up some pretty good pizza to go with the beer. All three have plenty of good happy-hour specials, so if all you want is cheap beer, give one a try. On the downside, they tend to get packed and smoky, and have a reputation for fights.

Déjà Vu (☎ 3403-8777) is right next to Gas Panic. Its popularity seems to have slumped, but Saturday night can still find it packed. Drinks are ¥700. *Bogey's Bar* (☎ 3478-1997) is on the 4th floor of the same building. Modelled on Rick's Cafe in the celluloid Casablanca, it's one of Roppongi's more sophisticated stops, with drinks from ¥800. It is a good place for couples, not so great for meeting people.

Overlooking the Gas Panic cul-de-sac, *Fontana* (☎ 3405-0677) seems miles away. There's an open deck for nonsmokers, and drinks start at ¥800. The place gets packed late on weekends, but at other times it's a mellower spot for a drink than its neighbours.

Paddy Foley's (☎ 3423-2250) is a good Irish-style pub, very popular with the expat business community. It has an outside area to hold the overflow when the weather is warm. If you want a good pint, convivial surroundings and some space to breathe, join the after-work crowd here.

Ebisu

Ebisu (Map 8) is often overlooked as a night-life destination – too bad, considering the good clubs and bars to be found there.

What the Dickens (☎ 3780-2099) is one of Tokyo's better English-style pubs. The place has a pleasant, spacious feel, and there's usually a band in the corner playing good mellow music. There's nice, hearty food and Guinness on tap. What more do you want?

Shanghai (☎ 3715-2207) is a good place to meet for a light meal and drinks (from

ENTERTAINMENT

¥600). By day it's a coffee shop and at night it still has that feel.

Very close by, *Bodeguita* (☎ 3715-7721) is a centre of Tokyo's booming Latin craze. As soon as everyone's finished eating (there's a good selection of Latin dishes from ¥800) they clear away the tables and it's salsa time – either join in or be crushed. Look for the English sign on the facade; the bar is on the 2nd floor.

Just around the corner from Bodeguita is another happening ethnic music enclave, in this case African. *Piga Piga* (☎ 3715-3431) is one of the few venues around which hosts live African music, and is often filled with the sort of Japanese African-wannabes that have to make you wonder. On weekdays there's no cover; on weekends entry is ¥3000 with a few drink tickets. Look for the place in the basement on the corner.

If Bodeguita hasn't quenched your thirst for things Latin, head to *Zona Rosa* (☎ 3440-3878). It has good margaritas, Mexican beers and a wholesome variety of Latin (mostly Mexican) food. Drinks start at ¥800. It's underneath the Red Pepper restaurant.

Akasaka

Nightlife options in Akasaka (Map 3) are mostly limited to hotel bars. Fortunately, Akasaka's hotel bars are among the best in town, and travellers on business may find themselves in after-hours negotiations at one or more of them, courtesy of their hosts.

Hotel Ōkura's *Highlander* (☎ 3505-6077) is a classic, dignified bar with an attentive staff. If you're more interested in a fine drink than in glitzy surroundings, beers here start at ¥850, and mixed drinks and whiskies go from ¥1400.

Gay Bars

Tokyo's gay enclave is Shinjuku-nichōme (Map 6), east of Gyoen-dōri between Shinjuku-dōri and Yasukuni-dōri. There are lots of little bars here, but some can seem rather daunting to enter. *Arty Farty* (☎ 3356-5388) is one place which anyone can comfortably walk into. Drinks start at ¥800; there's also a ¥500 table charge. Meeting people is easy

The Modern Floating World
During the late Tokugawa period, a colourful world was born in which kabuki actors, prostitutes, poets and high-living merchants cavorted in pleasure quarters like Tokyo's Yoshiwara district. This was the so-called 'floating world' *(ukiyo)*, an ephemeral world of night pleasures (called *mizu shōbai*, or 'the water trade') centred around geisha houses and drinking establishments.

Although prostitution was made illegal during the Allied occupation of Japan following WWII, the water trade is alive and well in Japan, and a new form of floating world exists, one in which gaily painted kimonos have been replaced by gaudy mini-skirts and flashing neon lights, particularly in the modern red-light districts of Shinjuku's Kabukichō and the areas around Ikebukuro station.

Although it is easy to romanticise the exploits of those otherworldly figures who live on in ukiyo-e prints, the modern floating world allows for little in the way of sentimentality – today's floating world is primarily a sleazy underworld of illegal South-East Asian sex workers and economically disadvantaged Japanese young women controlled by thoroughly unromantic yakuza bosses. ∎

here, and it's a good place to learn about the area's other possibilities.

Check out the *Tokyo Journal's* Cityscope section, which sometimes has a special insert called 'Tokyo Out'. See also the Gay & Lesbian Travellers section in the Facts for the Visitor chapter for more resources on current entertainment options.

JAPANESE STYLE

You've come all this way to Japan only to find yourself drinking in bars which could be in New York, London or Sydney. What to do? No worries: Tokyo has lots of drinking places where you really *do* feel like you're in a foreign country.

The types of places that welcome gaijin are izakaya, nomiya, yakitori joints and yatai (for details on what these places are and how to find them, see the Japanese Food boxed text in the Places to Eat chapter). When you go drinking at these, it will help to know a few words of Japanese, but you can usually get by with a smile and some hand signals. Some places will be completely at ease with foreign guests, while others may be a little lost or put out. The trick is to get that first order in, then sit back and enjoy. Chances are one of your Japanese neighbours will cautiously approach, and before you know it, you'll be pouring each other sake and laughing at half-understood jokes.

Ginza

Ginza (Map 3) has two good izakaya to try: *Chichibu Nishiki* and *Robata*. The former is a casual, old-style place and the latter is a mid-budget spot famous for its excellent food.

The renowned *Yūrakuchō Yakitori* alley is under the JR tracks. The yakitori places here aren't drinking spots per se, but you'll soon realise that chicken on a stick is not the only reason people come here – this is drinking food! Beer is as cheap here as anywhere in Ginza and the atmosphere is, well, Japanese. For details, see the Places to Eat chapter.

Ikebukuro

Ikebukuro (Map 5) is a good spot for izakaya. Among the choices are *Sasashu*, *Toneria* and *Yoronotaki*. Sasashu is a high-class place which serves some of the best sake in town. The other two are cheaper, and serve good, inexpensive food, cheap beer and drinkable sake. For details on all three, see the Places to Eat chapter.

CHRIS ROWTHORN
Izakaya often display their wares out front.

Shinjuku

A little-known treat in Shinjuku (Map 6) is *Yamagoya*, not far east of Isetan department store. Draught beer and sake, plus yakitori and other snacks, are served in a dungeon-like atmosphere while Japanese crooners mount a cage-like stage and perform a touch of karaoke. Feel free to put in a performance of your own, but don't worry, no-one's going to drag you on stage. Enter Yamagoya by a narrow flight of stairs and you'll end up in what seems like the hull of an old wooden ship. Huge, graffiti-covered wooden beams crisscross overhead. Wooden stairs continue down two more levels. The bottom level is the gloomiest, most dungeon-like and definitely the most fun – try not to think about earthquakes. Look for the kanji sign outside and the rickety stairs descending into the bar.

Omoide Yokochō arcade offers really cheap yakitori, and plenty of beer and sake to wash it down. Like Yūrakuchō Yakitori alley in Ginza, the places here aren't just for drinking, but that's all a lot of the customers do, and it doesn't hurt to have all those good snacks in arm's reach. Note that some places here are a little wary of foreigners. A good trick is to walk slowly down the alley, peering hopefully into places that look good. When one of the masters invites you in with a hearty 'Irasshaimase!' ('Welcome!'), you'll know you've found a good spot.

Golden Gai For a great area that is hard to categorise, try Golden Gai (Map 6). The bars here look western-style, but ten seconds in any of them will quickly dispel any illusions. For the adventurous traveller, this is one of the city's most interesting night zones. Even if you don't feel like a drink, take a night stroll through this warren of tightly packed establishments just to feel the atmosphere – the whole place seems lost in a boozy, rundown time warp.

Most places can hold no more than five or six people at a time, and many keep the dishwashers out on the street to squeeze in one more. Each bar has its own personality, and they run the gamut from gay bars to

ENTERTAINMENT

sports, karaoke and jazz bars, with everything in between.

Being so thoroughly Japanese, it's understandable that some of these places are a little leery of foreigners. You're just going to have to feel them out as you go. One sure-fire spot is *Bon's*. There's a sign reading 'American Bar' on its front, but Bon's is about as American as pachinko. There's usually a ¥900 cover, and drinks start at ¥700. Look for it next to the police box.

Once you leave the security of Bon's, you're on your own, but that's part of the fun. Before long, one of those 'Irasshai!' will be directed at you. Most places charge about ¥900 to enter and ¥1000 per beer – overpriced, but you're paying for an institution.

One last warning: be on the lookout for avaricious grannies who will attempt to lure you in with sweet-sounding promises of free karaoke, then pull the plug halfway through 'Yesterday' and demand fat stacks of yen.

Other Areas

You can find Japanese-style drinking spots wherever you look in Tokyo. Shibuya, Kanda and Asakusa have more than their share, and you can even find a few in pricier areas like around Tokyo station and in Akasaka. Basically, if you keep an eye out for the telltale red lantern and crates of empty sake and beer bottles, you'll find one.

PUBLIC BATHS & HOT SPRINGS

Taking a bath may not sound like your idea of an evening's entertainment, but a good *sentō* (public bath) or *onsen* (hot spring) is more than just a place to wash; it's a place to relax, socialise and forget about the world outside.

Sentō is a vanishing institution in Tokyo, and it's worth visiting one while it's still possible. The following are a few of Tokyo's more accessible sentō and onsen.

東京 東京 東京 東京 東京 東京 東京 東京 東京 東京 東京 東京 東京 東京 東京 東京 東京 東京

Sentō

Until quite recently, most private homes in Japan did not have baths, so every evening, people gathered their toiletries into a bowl and headed off to the local neighbourhood *sentō*, or public bath. More than just a place to wash oneself, the sentō served as kind of a community meeting hall, where news and gossip were traded and social ties strengthened.

Unfortunately, the number of sentō in Japan is rapidly declining, but there are still enough sentō left in Tokyo and Yokohama for you to sample this most traditional aspect of Japanese life. More than just a cultural experience, however, a soak in a sentō is the ideal way to cure the sore muscles born of a day of sightseeing.

Sentō can be identified by their distinctive *noren* (half-length curtains over the doorway). Sentō noren usually bear the hiragana for hot water (occasionally, this will be written in kanji). At the bottom of the noren, look for the kanji for men and for women (for these kanji characters, see the Toilets & Public Baths entry in the Facts for the Visitor chapter).

Once you've located a sentō, determine the men's or women's side, take off your shoes, place them in a locker in the entryway and slide open the door to the changing room. As you enter, you'll see the attendant, who sits midway between the men's and women's changing rooms, collecting the entry fee. Sentō usually cost between ¥300 and ¥400. Most are only open from around 3 pm to midnight.

In the changing room, you'll see a bank of lockers and stacks of wicker or plastic baskets. Grab a basket and drop your clothes into it. Find one of the common washbowls *(senmenki)* and place your toiletries in it, then place your basket in a locker (these have keys on elastic bands). Now you're ready for your bath.

Do not step into the bath until you have thoroughly washed your body. This is done at the banks of low showers and water spigots that line the walls of the place. Grab a low stool and plant yourself at an open spot.

Once you've washed thoroughly and removed all the soap, you are ready for a soak in the tubs. At a good sentō, you'll have a choice of hot tub, scalding tub, cold tub, whirlpool bath, sauna and, believe it or not, electric bath (which is meant to simulate swimming with electric eels!).

After soaking away the strains of the day, if you've done everything correctly, you will have achieved a state called *yude-dako*, or boiled octopus. Now stagger home and collapse onto your futon. ■

東京 東京 東京 東京 東京 東京 東京 東京 東京 東京 東京 東京 東京 東京 東京 東京 東京 東京

Rokuryu (Map 4) (☎ 3821-3826) may feel like a good neighbourhood sentō, but it's actually an onsen, since the water comes from a hot spring. The bubbling amber water contains minerals claimed to cure a number of ailments. It's open from 3.30 to 11 pm, closed Monday. Admission is ¥380. To get there, start from the Ikenohata Keisei exit of Ueno station. Turn right and walk down Dōbutsuen-dōri past Shinobazu Pond. Turn left down the second street after the Suigetsu Hotel. You'll soon see it on the right; look for the traditional Japanese facade and the noren curtains hanging over the entrance.

Azabu-Juban Onsen (Map 7) is one of the few true onsen within Tokyo city limits. While it can't compete with rural onsen, it's a good introduction to the pleasures of a hot-spring bath. There are actually two baths here: downstairs is *Koshino-yu* (☎ 3401-8324) and upstairs is *Azabu-Juban Onsen* (☎ 3403-2610). The former is a simple place popular with locals (entry is ¥385) and the latter is an upmarket bath popular with visitors (¥1260). At both, the rust-coloured water is said to have curative powers.

Koshino-yu is open from 3 to 11 pm, closed Tuesday. Azabu-Juban Onsen is open from 11 am to 9 pm, also closed Tuesday. To get there, start from Roppongi, walk southeast down Gaien-higashi-dōri toward Tokyo Tower, turn left on Tori-zaka-dōri (just after the Roi building), walk about 500m past the Singapore embassy and across a wide street – you'll see the baths on your right in the first block.

Yutopia (☎ 3398-4126) is closer to a 'bathland' than a humble sentō, with five floors of baths and saunas open 24 hours (though the baths themselves are closed from 2 to 5 am). Towels, pyjamas and whatever else you might need are provided, including 40 minute massages on the 5th floor for ¥3000. Yutopia is open every day except national holidays. To get there, take the Marunouchi subway line to Ogikubo station, exit the west side, turn left and walk about 50m; you'll see it on the left. Entry is ¥2200, though some special discounts are available (ask at reception).

SPECTATOR SPORTS
Sumō
Sumō is the only traditional Japanese sport that pulls big crowds and dominates prime time TV. Sumō is a fascinating, highly ritualised activity steeped in Shintō tradition. It's also accessible: unlike say, kabuki, the proceedings are readily comprehensible to the visitor, and sumō is as much spectacle as sport. A visit to a sumō match is a memorable experience of Japanese culture.

Sumō tournaments at *Ryōgoku Kokugikan Stadium* (Map 1) (☎ 3623-5111) in Ryōgoku take place in January, May and September, and last 15 days. The best seats are bought up by those with the right connections, but upstairs seats are usually available from ¥2300 to ¥7000. Non-reserved seats at the back sell for ¥1500. If you don't mind standing, you can get in for around ¥500. Tickets can be bought up to a month prior to the tournament, or you can simply turn up on the day. The ticket office opens at 9 am, and it's advisable to get there early – keen punters start queuing the night before. Note that only one ticket is sold per person, a device used to foil scalpers. The stadium is adjacent to Ryōgoku station on the Sōbu line, on the north side of the railway tracks.

Baseball
Baseball is Japan's most popular sport, and six of Japan's 12 pro baseball teams are based in Tokyo. The best place to catch a ball game is the *Tokyo Dome* (☎ 5800-9999), affectionately known as the Big Egg, close to Kōrakuen and Suidōbashi subway stations (Map 2). The dome is the home ground of Japan's most popular team, the Yomiuri Giants.

A trip to a Japanese ballpark is truly a cultural experience – the crowd behaviour is completely unlike what you're probably used to at home. The home team's fans often turn up in matching *happi* half-length coats and perform intricate cheering rituals in perfect unison led by special cheerleaders, one for each section, who seem to make a job out of whipping fans into a well-ordered frenzy.

J-League Soccer

Soccer is currently booming in Japan. Since the national team gained a berth in the 1998 World Cup, its popularity has soared even higher. There are 12 J-League pro soccer teams and their games, with a 30 minute sudden-death overtime and shootout if needed, are pretty exciting. Plus, Japanese teams have been actively recruiting soccer stars from other countries to beef up the level of play. Two places to catch a game are the *National Stadium* (Map 7) in Sendagaya (☎ 3403-1151) or at the *Tokyo Dome*.

Horse Racing

There are two big racing tracks in the Tokyo area which host some pretty major races, and offer the punter a good chance to wager some money – while prizes in places like pachinko parlours are strictly limited by law, winning big at the races is permitted in Japan. *Tokyo Keibajō* (☎ 0423-63-3141) is near Fuchū-Keibajō-Nishinomae station on the Keiō line and *Ōi Keibajō* (☎ 3763-2151) is near Ōi-Keibajō-mae station on the monorail from Hamamatsuchō. Races are generally held on weekends from 11 am to 4 pm.

ENTERTAINMENT

Shopping

Even more than its Asian neighbours, Hong Kong and Singapore, Tokyo is the shopper's city *par excellence*. There is something about consumer culture in Tokyo that is definitive of the city itself. The near-sacred halls in contemporary Tokyo are the enormous, opulent *depāto*, or department stores. These are usually open six days a week until about 7 pm, and are always crowded. Service standards are very high and products are usually presented quite strikingly. With so much on offer and such excellent service, it is easy to get infected with the shopping syndrome. It's hard to leave Tokyo without having bought *something*.

Shopping in Tokyo is a simple matter of going out and looking around; the area around the next railway station on your sightseeing route will offer hours of potential window shopping. Choosing what to buy may take a little more effort; it's been a while since Japan regularly stunned the consumer world with new products and innovative designs. Lately a lot effort seems to have gone into items that fill a void in Japanese life, like automated pets – 'Daddy's home kids, turn on the dog!' – or key-chain bound virtual companion-animals (the Tamagotchi could have only been hatched in Japan) that become global fads. If you want a toaster that looks like a cute pig, hand deodorant or a device to detect bad breath, Tokyo will supply it.

That said, Japan is still the land of quality manufacturing (though a lot of it is now done 'offshore', where labour costs and legal work standards are much lower), and new products (eg digital cameras) and designs appear constantly. Keep your eyes open, and keep prices in perspective – a beautiful nō mask may be ¥6000, but what are the chances of finding one like it at home?

Although Tokyo is an expensive city, certain things can be considerably cheaper than in other countries, eg many electrical items in Akihabara can be very reasonably priced. The same applies for camera accessories. There are also numerous shops around selling second-hand cameras and lenses (especially in Ginza and Shinjuku).

For souvenir items, almost all the big department stores have good selections of traditional crafts such as Japanese dolls, ceramics, lacquerware, kimono, fans etc – but department stores often sell their goods at inflated prices, unless you are lucky enough to be around during a sale. You're likely to find less glamorous but possibly more interesting souvenirs in Tokyo's flea markets, where you can buy Japanese antiques and curiosities (see the Antique Fairs & Flea Markets boxed text in this chapter).

WHERE TO SHOP

If you don't have a hectic schedule, before doing any shopping, go and watch how the locals do it. Some of Tokyo's major department stores are experiences in themselves, and the energy levels inside run very high. Ikebukuro has a couple of the largest department stores in Japan, if not the world. You could spend a day exploring the Ikebukuro branches of either Seibu or Tōbu.

CHRIS ROWTHORN

If it can be plugged in or it runs on batteries, it's probably for sale in one of Akihabara's many electronic shops, where the joys of bargaining are also to be found.

For a total shopping experience, visit Shibuya. The Parco I, II and III stores are quite remarkable, featuring the latest in fashion, traditional Japanese items, art galleries and restaurant floors. There is also a branch of Seibu in Shibuya, with one building for women's clothing and another for men's. Other Shibuya high points include the Seibu Seed building (boutiques), the 109 building (fashion), Loft (indescribable youth-oriented items – great browsing), Tōkyū Plaza (boutiques), HMV Records and Tower Records, and last but not least, Tōkyū Hands, perhaps the biggest do-it-yourself shop in the world.

Most of Tokyo's major urban hubs have their own distinct mercantile character. While areas like Shinjuku and Ikebukuro tend to be home to the whole range of options, most other areas tend to specialise. Shibuya, for example, has a high-fashion orientation, but is dominated by the large department stores. Harajuku and Aoyama are also fashion centres, but the emphasis is on boutiques or collections of boutiques, as in the Laforet building. Akihabara is an area given over almost entirely to cut-price electrical stores; Jimbōchō (in Kanda) is an area of bookshops; Kappabashi (see the Asakusa section of the Things to See & Do chapter) is where you buy the mouth-watering plastic food that graces restaurant window displays; Ueno is the place for motorbikes; and Asakusabashi is well known for its traditional Japanese dolls.

What about Ginza? It's true Ginza is the most famous Tokyo shopping district, and it's still recommended for a browse, but it's worth remembering that Ginza is about prestige, respectability and having the money to spend there. Check the prices elsewhere before you do any buying, but relax: window-shopping is free.

WHAT TO BUY

If there's any market for it whatsoever, you can buy it in Tokyo. The question comes down to whether the price that's being asked for it is reasonable or not.

Arts, Crafts & Antiques

As much for the convenience of being able to look at a wide range of traditional arts and crafts in one location as anything else, it's worth taking a look in some of the big department stores. You may find a deal or two as well, since there are often sale bins in the department stores, especially for Japanese-style dining ware.

For genuine antiques, there are a few places in Harajuku and Aoyama that you should visit. One of the best spots to look is the basement of the Hanae Mori building (Map 7) (☎ 3406-1021) in Harajuku, where there are more than 30 antique shops, open daily. Not far from the Hanae Mori building, the Oriental Bazaar (☎ 3400-3933) is open every day except Thursday and has a wide-ranging selection of antiques and tourist items, some at very reasonable prices. Items on sale include fans, folding screens, pottery, porcelain and kimono.

On the corner of Aoyama-dōri and Killer-dōri is the Japan Traditional Crafts Center (Map 7) (☎ 3403-2460). The centre has changing displays of Japanese crafts as well as items for sale. Also in Aoyama is the so-called Antique Street, in a side street to the left of Aoyama-dōri as you move in the

Japanese ceramics make beautiful, if fragile, gifts.

direction of Shibuya. Hidden among the trendy boutiques are some 30 antique shops.

Akasaka's Inachu Lacquerware (Map 3) (☎ 3582-4451) is a renowned lacquerware shop, but it's strictly for those who want the genuine item and are prepared to pay for it.

Not far from Ikebukuro station's eastern exit, on the 1st floor of the Satomi building (Map 5) (☎ 3980-8228), are more than 30 antique dealers. They are open Friday to Wednesday from 10 am to 7 pm.

Definitely along more touristy lines, there's the International Arcade in Ginza (Map 3). Also in Ginza are a couple of small shops with high-quality Japanese souvenirs. Takumi (☎ 3571-2017) has been around for some 60 years, and has aquired an elegant selection of traditional crafts from around Japan. Close to the International Arcade is the Taiko Festival Shop, a small retailer with a beautiful selection of Japanese festival souvenirs.

Also worth a look is Nakamise-dōri, in front of Sensō-ji Temple in Asakusa (Map 4). Among the items on sale here are traditional wigs, combs, fans and dolls.

After exploring Nakamise-dōri, another fun possibility for picking up traditional souvenirs is to try out some of the flea markets and antique fairs held around the city.

The large Tokyo Antique Fair takes place three times a year and brings together more than 200 antique dealers. The Antique Fair's schedule changes annually; for information on this year's schedule, ring the Tokyo TIC.

Audio

Japanese recordings are renowned for their high fidelity, and Tokyo has numerous music stores with enormous collections of discs and tapes to sift through. Some of the best places to check out are the Virgin Megastores in Shinjuku and Ikebukuro; HMV Records in Harajuku, Shibuya, Shinjuku and Ikebukuro; Wave in Roppongi, Shibuya and Ikebukuro; Tower Records in Shibuya; and Yamaha in Ginza. Wave, in particular, is notable for its AV displays (including hi-definition TV) and extensive audio selections. Tokyo also has lots of used record stores and you can find old LPs here that are difficult to find

東京東京東京東京東京東京東京東京東

Antique Fairs & Flea Markets

After days of perfectly ordered department stores, one longs for the colourful anarchy of a good flea market. Tokyo has loads of flea markets and antique fairs – many held on temple or shrine grounds – where you can spend hours among the bric-a-brac.

Don't get your hopes up about treasures, though, for gone are the days when astute buyers could turn up at a flea market and cart off antique *tansu* (wooden chests) worth thousands of dollars. More likely, you'll find some quirky gifts at considerable savings over department store prices. Things to look for include old kimono, scrolls, pottery, Chinese snuff bottles, old Japanese postcards, antique toys and costume jewellery.

The joy of these markets and fairs is that bargaining is permitted. Remember: have a good time at it and never drive too hard a bargain. If your Japanese is lacking, bring a pad of paper and a pencil.

The following are some of Tokyo's better flea markets and antique fairs. Check with the TIC before going, as shrine and temple events sometimes interfere with the scheduling of markets.

Arai Yakushi-ji Temple antique market
  five minutes from Arai-yakushi-mae station on the Seibu Shinjuku Line; 8th, 18th and 28th of every month, dawn to dusk
Hanazono-jinja Shrine flea market
  five minutes from Shinjuku Sanchōme station on the Marunouchi subway line; Sunday, dawn to dusk
Kawagoe Narita Fūdo antique fair
  15 minutes from Hon-Kawagoe station on the Seibu Shinjuku Line; 28th of every month, dawn to dusk
Nogi-jija Shrine flea market
  one minute from Nogizaka station on the Chiyoda subway line; 2nd Sunday of every month, dawn to dusk
Salvation Army Bazaar
  10 minutes from Nakano Fujimichō station on the Marunouchi subway line; Saturday, 9 am to 1 pm
Tōgo Shrine flea market
  three minutes walk from Harajuku station; 1st and 4th Sunday of every month, dawn to 2 pm

東京東京東京東京東京東京東京東京東

SHOPPING

back home, usually in excellent condition. The best places to look for used record shops are in the streets of Shibuya, Aoyama, Harajuku and Nishi-Azabu.

Cameras & Film

Apart from wandering around straining your neck at concrete monoliths, Shinjuku's west side (Map 6) is the best place in Tokyo to buy photographic supplies. The city's largest camera stores can be found here. The most famous are Yodobashi Camera (☎ 3346-1010) and Sakuraya Camera (☎ 3354-3636). Yodobashi in particular stocks anything and everything connected with photography – film, darkroom equipment, tripods, cameras, lenses and other accessories. Its prices are very competitive and foreigners, resident or not, are waived Japanese consumption taxes. The store even has a limited selection of second-hand photographic equipment.

Many other places deal in second-hand photographic equipment. Foreign-made large-format equipment is usually ridiculously expensive, but Japanese equipment can often be had at very good prices (note that the big shops in places like Shinjuku sell photographic equipment tax-free to tourists, but may ask you to produce a passport to verify that you are not a resident in Japan).

Surprisingly, one of the best areas in which to look for used cameras is Ginza (Map 3) – maybe it's all the photo galleries in the neighbourhood. On Harumi-dōri there's a good place opposite the Sony building on the Sukiyabashi crossing. On the same side as the Sony building, towards the Kabuki-za Theatre, are a couple more places. They're all on ground level and the windows are full of cameras and lenses.

Photographic film and processing in Japan are very expensive. It's advisable to bring your own and process it after you leave if possible. Otherwise, you might try Bic Camera (Map 5) (☎ 3988-0002) on the east side of Ikebukuro, where there are big bargain bins of film that is approaching its expiry date – the merchandise is usually fine. Bic Camera claims to be the cheapest camera store in Japan, a claim hotly disputed by Yodobashi and Sakuraya camera stores. There's also a branch in Shibuya. The big camera shops on the west side of Shinjuku station also have enormous selections of film, some at cut-rate prices.

Clothes & Shoes

Tokyo is a very fashionable city, and the range of clothes and shoes is enormous. Where you shop, however, depends on your budget. Shinjuku, Ikebukuro and Ueno are good areas for picking up clothes and shoes at discounted prices. Harajuku, Aoyama, Shibuya and Ginza are good for boutique browsing and making quality purchases.

Reasonably priced clothing stores are scattered all over the east side of Shinjuku (Map 6) – there are quite a few around Kinokuniya bookshop. In Harajuku (Map 7), Omote-sandō and Takeshita-dōri make good hunting grounds, although the market here is very youth oriented. Take a look at Octopus Army on Takeshita-dōri and the Chicago Thrift Shop, with its large collection of good quality second-hand clothes, on Omote-sandō. These are also both good areas for buying shoes. In Ikebukuro (Map 5), around the western exit of the station, are many discount fashion shops. Also take a look at Ueno's Ameyoko arcade (Map 4), which has a number of shops selling clothes and shoes at cheaper prices than other parts of Tokyo.

If you want to make a fashion statement and spend some money, head for the boutiques of Harajuku and Aoyama or the department stores of Shibuya. The Laforet building (Map 7) in Harajuku houses a number of designer boutiques in one building. Cushioned between Kiddyland and the Oriental Bazaar in Harajuku is Vivre 21 (Map 7), another fashion forum. One of the more famous of Aoyama's boutique buildings is Bell Commons (Map 7), right on the corner of Killer-dōri. In Shibuya (Map 7), the Parco stores, Seibu, Seibu Seed and the 109 building are all rated highly by shoppers with style.

The high prices asked for new kimono (¥100,000 and up) and other traditional Japanese clothing make second-hand shops the best option. Both the Oriental Bazaar and the basement of the Hanae Mori building in Harajuku are good places to look (see the Arts, Crafts & Antiques section). If you've got money to burn and are set on getting a new kimono or a similar item, check the big department stores like Isetan and Seibu. In March and September, there are big sales of rental kimono at Daimaru. January and July are generally the other big sales months for the retail industry. Also look for the bargain sales listing in the *Tokyo Journal* to learn what off-season sales are on.

Western-Size Clothes If you require large-size shoes and clothes (which by Japanese standards means shoes over 27cm in length and anything long enough to fit a person over 180cm tall), the first rule is: get it before you come. If, by some unlucky turn of events, you wind up needing something new while you're here, the best advice is to avoid the regular stores altogether – they don't have the larger sizes in stock.

This leaves two choices. If you're in town long enough, you can order from an overseas company. Two mail-order companies with Tokyo numbers are REI (☎ 5424-3471) and LL Bean (☎ 5350-8801). Or, you can visit one of Tokyo's big-and-tall stores. Shibuya's Perche (☎ 5467-5586) has a good selection of large shoes and clothes. Don't expect any bargains, however, as large-size items tend to be about double the price of comparable regular-size ones.

Computers

Tokyo is not a good place to buy computers. Prices tend to be higher than they are in Hong Kong, Taiwan or Singapore – and higher even than in the west. If you remain determined, try giving Linc Computer (Map 7) (☎ 3409-6510) in Shibuya a ring. English is spoken here and it has a wide range of computers, both Apple and IBM, and software. In west Shinjuku, you can check T Zone Computers (Map 6) (☎ 3257-2650), which stocks a good selection of software and computer goods (and new computers at prices about average for Tokyo).

Electronics

Ideally, you should have an idea of prices back home or in other places on your travel agenda before you buy any electronic goods in Tokyo. Nevertheless, there are some good

CHRIS ROWTHORN

Try out the latest games before you buy.

bargains to be got, and Akihabara (Map 2) is the place to get them. The range of products is mind boggling, but before you rush into buying, remember that most Japanese companies use the domestic market as a testing ground. Many products end their days in Japan without ever making it onto overseas markets. This may pose difficulties if you take something home and later need to have a fault repaired. Check the voltage, too. Some larger stores (Laox is a reliable option) have tax-free sections with export models for sale. For audio goods, try Laox or Shintoku Echo; for TV and video, Hirose Musen has a good selection that includes export models.

Though it is unusual to find prices that match those of dealers in Hong Kong or Singapore, you should be able to knock 10% off the marked prices by bargaining in Akihabara. To find the shops, take the 'Electric Town' exit at Akihabara station. You will see the sign on the platform if you come in on the Yamanote line.

Food & Alcohol

Japanese food and alcohol are often overlooked as souvenir choices. Check out any of the food floors of the larger department stores for a great selection of things like Japanese tea, sweets, spices and alcohol. While sake tends to be an acquired taste, folks back home will usually be delighted by

SHOPPING

a bottle of good Japanese *ume-shu* (plum wine). As for spices, traditional Japanese ones should please anyone interested in cooking. The best choices are *shichimi* (a mix of seven spices) and *sanshō* (a three spice mix). These can be bought in interesting bamboo dispensers which can be recycled as salt and pepper shakers (full of spice these can be had for less than ¥2000 at department stores). Japanese tea also comes in interesting containers and makes a great gift item.

Japanese Dolls

Edo-dōri, next to Asakusabashi subway station on the Toei Asakusa line, is the place to go if you're interested in Japanese dolls. Both sides of the road have many shops specialising in traditional Japanese dolls as well as their contemporary counterparts. This is actually an area for retailers to buy their goods, so the prices should be substantially lower than buying in the department stores. It's also acceptable to bargain a little.

Akasaka Sakuradō (Map 3) in Akasaka is only a small shop, but its dolls are all beautifully handcrafted in innovative designs. It's possible to buy a smaller piece for around ¥1500. For the larger ones? We saw one with a price tag of ¥300,000.

Japanese dolls range from kitschy to exquisite, with prices to match the quality.

Kids' Stuff

The Japanese are an inventive lot; consequently Tokyo can be a wonderful place to pick up toys and games. Loft (Map 7) in Shibuya has a great selection of wacky kids' stuff, and in Harajuku there's Kiddyland (Map 7) (☎ 3409-3431), with five floors of products that your children would probably be better off not knowing about. Along similar lines is Hakuhinkan Toy Park (Map 3) (☎ 3571-8008) in Ginza. It claims to be the biggest toy shop in Japan, and even has a theatre and restaurants on its upper floors.

Pearls

It was in Japan that cultured pearls were first developed, and pearls are still cheaper here than in many other parts of the world. Ginza's Mikimoto Pearl (Map 3) (☎ 3535-5511), perhaps the most famous of Tokyo's pearl shops, was founded by the man who first developed the cultured pearl, Mikimoto Kokichi, and has been running since 1899. It's next to Wakō department store, opposite Mitsukoshi. Another store worth checking out is Takasaki Shinju (☎ 5561-8880) in Akasaka.

Washi (Japanese Paper)

Japanese hand-made paper is one of the cheaper and more interesting souvenir possibilities. A sheet of colourfully dyed paper about 1m square can often be had for ¥1000 or less. Most people find this paper too beautiful for writing and wind up using is as a decoration or as wrapping paper. One place which stocks a good selection of washi is Haibara (☎ 3272-3801) in Ginza. All the major department stores also have a section devoted to washi.

Itoya (Map 3) (☎ 3561-8311) in Ginza has nine floors of every kind of stationery item you can imagine. What's more, it also stocks washi. You can also get things printed or copied here. It's open from 9.30 am to 7 pm Monday to Saturday, to 6 pm Sunday.

Ideas

If you're at a loss for what to buy, here are a few suggestions.

Odds & Ends One fascinating place which offers the imaginative souvenir hunter a wide range of inexpensive Japanese goods is Tsukiji External Market (Tsukijijō-gaishijō), which is outside the Tsukiji Central Fish Market. The External Market (Map 3) is open all day (closed Sunday and holidays). There are hundreds of little stalls here selling pottery, cooking equipment, food supplies, baskets and cutlery for a fraction of the prices charged by department stores.

Another area to explore for ideas is Asakusa's Kappabashi-dōri (Map 4), where all manner of restaurant and gourmet tools and supplies are sold wholesale.

Comics & Books Fans of *manga* comics might want to pick up some used ones in the bookstores of Jimbōchō (Map 2) in the Kanda area. Several shops here specialise in used manga. You can choose from valuable 1st edition classics and more common editions which can be had for less that ¥100. You can also find a wide range of old Japanese calendars, postcards and picture books. Tuttle editions of translated Japanese novels and poetry can make nice gifts as well.

For information on bookshops which sell a range of English-language texts from art to Zen, see the Tokyo Bookshops boxed text in the Facts for the Visitor chapter.

Traditional Clothes & Crafts For a variety of traditional Japanese clothes and craft items, the shopping arcade known as Hisago-dōri (Map 4), just north of Rokku-Broadway-dōri in Asakusa, is an excellent choice. Takumi Crafts Gallery (☎ 3842-

1990) has displays on the history and production of Shitamachi crafts, and sells some traditional goods. The stores alongside the gallery sell *happi* (half-length coats), *yukata* (summer-weight kimonos), *geta* (wooden shoes), and a whole range of crafts like combs and writing supplies.

Offbeat Items For non-traditional and off-the-wall gift ideas, head to Shibuya (Map 7) and drop in to Tōkyū Hands or Seibu's Loft store (there are also branches of both in Ikebukuro). Both stores offer an enormous range of goodies that most sensible people would never even consider shopping for. Tōkyū Hands, in particular, is the do-it-yourself capital of Tokyo, selling everything from sewing repair kits to chainsaws. The toy department is certainly also worth a browse. Tōkyū Hands is open from 10 am to 8 pm, closed the second and third Wednesday of every month.

The Axis building (Map 3) (☎ 3587-2781) in Roppongi is also an excellent place to catch up on some of Japan's most innovative design ideas and interior design goods. The complex, with its 20 or so retail shops and galleries, is on Gaien-higashi-dōri, and is open 11 am to 7 pm, Monday to Saturday.

Wrapping It Up
So where do you get all these goodies wrapped up to give to the folks back home? In Shibuya the Tsutsumu Factory (Map 7) (☎ 5478-1330) – *tsutsumu* means 'to wrap' in Japanese – is a store devoted entirely to wrapping things up. Choose your materials and the staff will do the wrapping for you.

SHOPPING

Excursions

Tokyo may be a tangled sprawl of expressways, railway lines, office buildings and housing estates, but an hour or so away by train are some of Japan's best travel destinations. The places in this chapter can be visited as day trips, although in several cases it would be worth staying overnight.

Foremost among these is Nikkō, which is a must-see on any trip to Tokyo. Kamakura's peaceful temples are a lovely break from the big city; Hakone and the Mt Fuji region can provide magnificent views of Mt Fuji.

Most other destinations around Tokyo are less interesting to short-term visitors, despite heavy promotion by the Tourist Information Center (TIC). Both Izu-hantō Peninsula and Dogashima are pleasant retreats from Tokyo, but they are geared to Japanese tourists – many of the sights have entry fees, roped walkways and orderly queues.

There are numerous bus tours operating out of Tokyo to nearby sightseeing areas. The two main operators with English guides are Sunrise Tours (☎ 03-5260-9500) and Gray Line Tours (☎ 03-3433-5745). Some Sunrise one-day deals (including lunch) are Mt Fuji and Hakone (¥12,000), Nikkō (¥13,000) and Kamakura (¥12,000).

YOKOHAMA　横浜

Japan's second largest city is in many ways an extension of Tokyo, but city planners are hard at work to make Yokohama a destination in its own right. As an early foreign enclave, the city has always had a relatively large 'gaijin' population, including a sizeable Chinese community. Many foreign residents choose to reside in Yokohama and commute to Tokyo because of its hilly terrain and comparative abundance of greenery. Attractions include Chinatown, a foreigners' cemetery, the harbour area, the Minato Mirai 21 complex and Sankei-en Garden. Also worth a look is the elegant 860m Yokohama Bay Bridge, south of Yamashita-kōen Park.

Despite its fame, Yokohama is best considered a lower priority for visitors to Tokyo – Kamakura, Nikkō and Hakone are far more worthwhile day trips.

Orientation

Arriving in Yokohama can be slightly confusing. Most sights are on the harbour-front, quite a way from Yokohama station. It makes more sense to go to Sakuragi-chō, Kannai or Ishikawa-chō station. From Sakuragi-chō station the Minato Mirai 21 development, with the enormous Landmark Tower, is very close. Kannai station is closer to Yamashita-kōen, the harbour area and a number of sights, like the Silk Museum. Ishikawa-chō station is convenient for the fashionable Motomachi shopping district, Chinatown and the foreigners' cemetery.

Information

The Yokohama International Tourist Association (☎ 045-641-5824) and the Kanagawa Prefectural Tourist Association (☎ 045-681-0007) are both on the ground floor of the building housing the Silk Museum. Both have someone who speaks English. The best of their free brochures is the *Yokohama City Guide – Yokohama Paradise*. The Minato Mirai 21 Complex also has a tourist office, but no English is spoken. It's worth picking up a copy of the TIC's excellent *Yokohama* handout before leaving Tokyo.

Sankei-en Garden

This garden is foremost among Yokohama's attractions. It's beautifully landscaped, featuring a three storey pagoda that is 500 years old. The garden is open daily from 9 am to 4.30 pm. The No 8 bus, from the road running parallel to the harbour behind the Marine Tower, operates with less than commendable frequency, but if one does happen along, ask for the Sankei-en-mae bus stop. Sankei-en is also accessible from JR Negishi

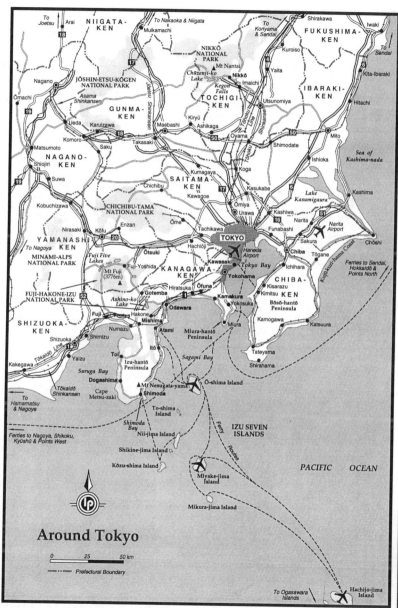

Around Tokyo

```
0        25        50 km
```
━ ━ ━ Prefectural Boundary

Yokohama

0   250   500 m

Port of Yokohama

To Yokohama Bay Bridge
Expressway

To Yokohama Bay Bridge & Yokosuka

To Sankei-en Garden

Harbour View Park

Foreigners' Cemetery

Nakamura River

Motomachi Shopping Centre

Ferry to Natsudote & Oksido Pier

Yamashita Pier

Hikawa Maru

Osanbashi Pier (South Pier)

Yamashita-kōen Park

See Chinatown Map (Page 194)

Chinatown

19 ⬛

18 ●

17 ◆

16 ⬛

15 ⬛ 14 🏛

13 ▼

Nihon Ōdori

21 ⬛ 20 ⬛

22 🏛

To Isogo & Ōfuna

Ishikawa-chō

Kaigan-dōri

Honchō

12 ▼ 11 ▼

10 ▼

9 ● 8 ●

Yokohama-kōen Park
Yokohama Stadium

Shinko Pier (Centre Pier)

Nippon-Maru Memorial Park

Minato Mirai 21 Complex

To Rinko Park & Minato Mirai 21 Pier

Landmark Tower

Sakuragi-chō

Moving Walkway

Kaihin-Tōhoku Line

Bashamichi

7 ▼

Kannai

Kannai

Negishi Line

Ōdori

Isezaki-chōjamachi

Iida

Sakuragi-chō

Takashima-chō

To Yokohama Station
To Tokyo

Tōkyū Toyoko Line

Municipal Subway Line

Ōoka River

Ōdori Shopping Centre

Nishi-waku Shopping Centre

Hinodechō

Keihin-Kyūkō Line

Bandōbashi

5 ⬛ 6 🏛

Expressway

Takashima-chō

PLACES TO STAY

2 Yokohama Royal Park
  Hotel Nikkō
  横浜ロイヤルパーク
  ホテルニッコー
5 Kanagawa Youth Hostel
  神奈川ユース
  ホステル
16 Hotel Yokohama
  ホテルヨコハマ
17 Hotel New Grand
  ホテルニューグランド
20 Aster Hotel
  アスターホテル
21 Yokohama
  International Seaman's
  Hall
  海員会館

PLACES TO EAT

7 Victoria Station
  ビクトリアステーション
10 Pot Luck Bar
  ポットラック
11 Baiko Emmie's
  梅香亭
12 Cape Cod Bar
  ケープコッド
13 Suginoki; Scandia
  杉の木
15 Parkside Gourmet Plaza
  パークサイドグルメ
  プラザ

OTHER

1 Yokohama Museum of Art
  横浜美術館

3 Yokohama Maritime Museum
  横浜マリタイム
  ミュージアム
4 Tourist Information
  観光案内所
6 Iseyama Shrine
  伊勢山神社
8 Yokohama City Hall
  横浜市役所
9 JTB Travel Agent
  ＪＴＢ
14 Silk Museum
  シルク博物館
18 Marine Tower
  マリンタワー
19 Yokohama Doll Museum
  人形の家
22 Empei-mon Gate

station, where you can catch a bus bound for Sakuragi-chō (No 54, 58, 99, 101 or 108). Get off at the Honmoku stop, and it's a five minute walk.

Minato Mirai 21

The '21' stands for '21st century', and this complex represents Yokohama's vision of its future. Its most impressive feature is the Landmark Tower (296m), the tallest building in Japan, complete with the world's fastest lift and a viewing platform on the 70th floor. It's open daily from 10 am to 9 pm (to 10 pm Saturday and every night during July and August); entry is ¥1000.

Chinatown

Close to the harbour is Yokohama's Chinatown, the largest in Japan. 'Chūkagai', as it's known, is an interesting area to stroll and absorb the slightly synthetic ambience. But the best reason to come is to sample the excellent Chinese food.

To get there, go to Ishikawa-chō station, exit and head north along the tracks about 100m before heading east toward the harbour. You'll soon see Empei-mon Gate. Pass through and continue straight; Chinatown is about 200m ahead.

Other Sights

Clustered around the Landmark Tower are a number of so-so attractions. Probably the best is the Yokohama Maritime Museum and *Nippon Maru* sailing ship. Entry to the park containing both is ¥600; it's open from 10 am to 5 pm, closed Monday. The Yokohama Museum of Art is devoted to modern art; entry is ¥500. It's open from 10 am to 5 pm, closed Thursday.

Near Yamashita-kōen, the Marine Tower offers an unimpressive viewing platform for ¥700. The Silk Museum (☎ 045-641-0841) deals with every aspect of silk and silk production with Japanese thoroughness. Entry is ¥300; it's open from 9 am to 4.30 pm, closed Monday. Yamashita-kōen itself is an average park; next to it is the *Hikawa Maru*, a passenger liner that you can board and explore. In summer, the ship is open until 9 pm and has a beer garden. Entry is ¥800.

Harbour cruises operate from the pier next to the *Hikawa Maru* and take from 40 minutes (¥900) to 1½ hours (¥2000). Close to the Marine Tower, the Yokohama Doll Museum (☎ 045-671-9361) has 1200 dolls from around the world (admission is ¥300; open from 10 am to 5 pm, closed Monday). Just beyond the expressway and in the

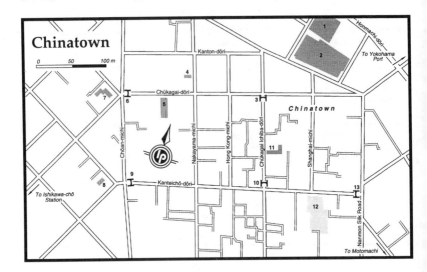

1 Satellite Hotel Yokohama サテライトホテル ヨコハマ	4 Raishanson 苓香尊	9 Jikyū-mon Gate 地久門
2 Hotel Holiday Inn Yokohama; Jūkeihanten ホテルホリデーイン 横浜；重慶飯店	5 Kanton Hanten 広東飯店 6 Zenrin-mon Gate 善隣門	10 Ichibadōri-mon South Gate 市場通り門南口 11 Suuroku Saikan Shinkan 四五六菜館新館
3 Ichibadōri-mon North Gate 市場通り門北口	7 Taishinrō 太新楼 8 Keifukurō 慶福楼	12 Yamashitachō-kōen Park 山下町公園 13 Tenchō-mon Gate 天長門

Yamate hill area is the **Harbour View Park** and, close by, the **Foreigners' Cemetery**, containing the sombre graves of more than 4000 foreigners. This area is best reached by walking through the trendy Motomachi shopping street from Ishikawa-chō station.

The sprawling **Yokohama Hakkeijima Sea Paradise** (☎ 045-788-8888) complex has a great aquarium, amusement park rides, restaurant areas, upmarket shopping – even a yacht harbour and expensive accommodation. The complex is best reached from Minato Mirai 21 pier by the Paradise Line Ferry (¥2000). Or, take the Keihin-Kyūkō line to Kanazawa-hakkei station, change to the Kanazawa Seaside Line and get off at Hakkeijima. Entry is free, though most entertainments cost ¥500 to ¥1000. It is open daily from 8.30 am to 10.30 pm.

The gargantuan **Wild Blue Yokohama** (☎ 045-511-2323) is a water sports park. Unlike many such parks around Tokyo, it is open year-round. Attractions include surfing on artificial waves, water slides and artificial rivers. Entry is ¥3900 for adults, ¥3100 for high school students and ¥2600 for children aged four to 12. It is open daily from 10 am to 9 pm, and can be reached by shuttle bus from Tsurumi station on the Keihin-Tōhoku line.

EXCURSIONS

Places to Stay

It makes most sense to visit Yokohama from Tokyo, as the longest the journey will take is 40 minutes. Those determined to make a night of it will generally find Yokohama accommodation either expensive or inconveniently located.

The *Kanagawa Youth Hostel* (☎ 045-241-6503) is your cheapest option (¥2600). From Sakuragi-chō station, exit on the opposite side to the harbour, turn right and follow the road alongside the railway tracks. Cross the main road and turn left into the steep street with a bridge and cobblestoned section. The youth hostel is up the road on the right.

Most other accommodation is aimed at business travellers. *Yokohama International Seamen's Hall* (☎ 045-681-2358) has singles/doubles for ¥5800/12,200. Very close by is the *Aster Hotel* (☎ 045-651-0141). Singles/doubles are ¥7700/14,500.

Hotel Yokohama (☎ 045-662-1321) is an upmarket option by the waterfront, offering singles from ¥17,000. Doubles/twins start at ¥24,000/28,000 (rooms without a seaside view are slightly less). *Hotel New Grand* (☎ 045-681-1841) has singles/doubles for ¥10,000/28,000. The hotels are located near Yamashita-kōen.

Places to Eat

Chinatown is undoubtedly the place for a meal in Yokohama. Front window displays are common in the many restaurants, and long queues of patient Japanese pinpoint the best places.

Kanton Hanten (☎ 045-681-7676), near Zenrin-mon Gate, is a good spot for dim-sum (yumu-cha or ten-shin in Japanese). You order from a wide selection of small dishes including dumplings, fried yuba rolls and sliced pork, all of which cost around ¥500 per serving. While dim-sum is traditionally a Sunday lunch meal in China, here you can try it all day, every day.

Another good choice is *Taishinrō* (☎ 045-681-7826), across from Zenrin-mon Gate (look for the gaudy Chinese-style facade, and the steamed dumplings and buns for sale outside). Its ¥2500 yumu-cha course takes the pain out of ordering and includes eight small servings of dim-sum, and your choice of Chinese tea. Otherwise, most dim-sum dishes cost around ¥600.

Suuroku Saikan Shinkan (☎ 045-664-4569), offers nine varieties of dumplings alone. Most dim-sum choices cost ¥600. Try the fukahira (shark fin) dumpling or the shūmai dumpling with crab and pork filling.

Raishanson (☎ 045-651-5055) is a good choice for varied sets of Cantonese at reasonable prices. It offers four daily lunch specials for around ¥1000 each. Dinner tends to be closer to ¥4000 without drinks. It's a lot more casual than at some places with over-the-top Chinese decorations.

Keifukurō (☎ 045-681-5256) serves good Beijing-style cooking in fairly casual surroundings. A large picture menu out front lets you choose from dishes like spicy fried beef or sweet-and-sour frog legs (both ¥1800).

The slightly more upmarket *Jūkeihanten* (☎ 045-641-8288) is one of Chinatown's more approachable restaurants, located in the Hotel Holiday Inn Yokohama (3rd floor). Try the delicious unbairū (sliced pork with a spicy Shisen-style sauce) for ¥2000. Dinner here can reach ¥10,000 each if you order freely and include drinks. Lunch can be had for about ¥4000.

Yokohama's reputation doesn't just rest on Chinese food – the area between Kannai station and Yamashita-kōen is packed with bars, coffee shops and restaurants. Wander the side streets of this area in the evening and you'll find plenty of excellent choices. There are two good bars here: *Cape Cod* and *Bar Bar Bar*. The latter has a long saloon-style bar on the 1st floor and live music upstairs.

A wonderful little place is *Baiko Emmie's* (☎ 045-681-4870), with its rather touching sign outside promising 'English spoken'. If Emmie's looks like it's been around for a while, it has. Established in 1924, it was moved to its current spot in the 50s. Try the hayashi or curry rice for ¥750. It's closed Sunday.

For salads, fries and the like, call into *Pot Luck* (☎ 045-662-0525), an American-style kitchen (complete with a Budweiser sign outside); the 'trucker salad' at ¥1800 is enough for three. Another good salad and steak stop is the Yokohama branch of *Victoria Station* (☎ 045-631-0393).

Yamashita-kōen also has some interesting options, though much is western food at marked-up prices. Go at lunch for some good specials. *Scandia* (☎ 045-201-2262), just across the road from the Silk Museum, is probably the only Danish restaurant in Japan. *Suginoki* (☎ 045-212-4143) is just around the corner, and serves what it alleges is Spanish cuisine for reasonable prices.

The Sakuragi-chō station area has a few good spots for a snack or a meal. *Becker's Hamburgers* is an American-style burger joint; *Kirin City* does good cappuccino and cakes – a good breakfast stop.

In the Yokohama station area, try the basement mall that leads out from the station or the 10th floor of Sogō department store. The area around Ishikawa-chō station is also packed with restaurants, many of which display their daily offering out front.

Getting There & Away
There are numerous trains from Tokyo, the cheapest being the Tōkyū Tōyoko line from Shibuya station to Sakuragi-chō station for ¥290. The trip takes 44 minutes by ordinary train and 35 minutes by limited express (same price).

The Keihin-Tōhoku line goes to Yokohama (¥440) and Kannai (¥610) stations from Tokyo and Shinagawa stations. If you only want to go as far as Yokohama station, you can save 10 minutes by taking the Tōkaidō line from Tokyo, Shimbashi or Shinagawa stations (30 minutes, ¥470).

The Yokosuka line can also take you from Tokyo, Shimbashi or Shinagawa station to Yokohama station. This is a convenient line to continue on to Kamakura from Yokohama (¥370). There is also a shinkansen connection to the Kansai region at Shin-Yokohama station, a fair way to the north-east of town.

Getting Around
Shin-Yokohama station connects to Yokohama, Sakuragi-chō and Kannai stations via the Yokohama municipal subway line. Yokohama, Sakuragi-chō and Kannai stations are also linked via the JR Negishi line. Buses around town cost a flat ¥210 each trip; a day pass costs ¥600.

KAMAKURA　鎌倉
Kamakura had a spell of glory as the nation's capital from 1192 to 1333. The Minamoto and later the Hōjo clans ruled Japan from Kamakura for more than a century, until finally in 1333, weakened by the heavy cost of maintaining defences against threats of attack from Kublai Khan in China, the Hōjo clan fell from power at the hands of the forces of Emperor Go-Daigo. Though the restoration of imperial authority was somewhat illusory, the capital nevertheless shifted back to Kyoto and Kamakura disappeared from the history books.

Today, Kamakura may not offer as much as Kyoto or Nara, but a wealth of notable temples and shrines make it one of Tokyo's most rewarding day trips. The town offers relaxing walks and a peacefulness that is hard to come by in Kyoto, where the sights are so often swamped with tourists.

Orientation & Information
The sights are spread over a fairly wide area and, although most of them can be visited by foot, there are times when it may be necessary to catch a bus. There's not much chance of getting lost, however, as the temples are well signposted in English and Japanese. You may want to pick up the Tokyo TIC's *Hakone and Kamakura* pamphlet, which has details on transport and some of the attractions. There is a tourist information office at the east exit of Kamakura station.

Things to See
Kita-Kamakura Station Area The best route is to start at Kita-Kamakura station and visit the temples between there and Kamakura on foot. As you exit the station, there are vendors selling useful bi-lingual maps.

Engaku-ji Temple is on the left as you exit Kita-Kamakura station. It is one of the five main Rinzai Zen temples in Kamakura, and dates from 1282. Entry is ¥200, and it is open daily from 8 am to 4 pm.

Across the railway tracks from Engaku-ji is **Tōkei-ji Temple**, notable for its grounds as much as for the temple itself. On weekdays, when there are few visitors, it can be a veryrelaxing place. Walk up to the cemetery and wander around. Women were once officially recognised as divorced if they spent three years as nuns in the temple precinct. It's open daily from 8.30 am to 5 pm, and entry is ¥50.

A couple of minutes further from Tōkei-ji is **Jōchi-ji Temple**, another temple with tranquil environs. Founded in 1283, this is considered one of Kamakura's five great Zen temples. Jōchi-ji is open daily from 9 am to 4.30 pm, and entry is ¥100.

Kenchō-ji Temple is about a 10 minute walk beyond Jōchi-ji. It is on the left after you pass through a tunnel. This is not only Kamakura's most important Zen temple but something of a showcase generally. The grounds and the buildings are well maintained and still in use. The first of the main buildings, the Buddha Hall, was moved to its present site and reassembled in 1647. The second building, the Hall of Law, is used for *zazen* meditation. Further back is the Dragon King Hall, a Chinese-style building with a garden to its rear. The temple bell, the second largest in Kamakura, has been designated a 'National Treasure'. The temple is open daily from 9 am to 4.30 pm; entry is ¥200.

Across the road from Kenchō-ji is **Ennō-ji Temple**, distinguished primarily by its collection of statues depicting the judges of hell. The temple is open daily from 10 am to 4 pm.

Further down the road is **Hachiman-gū Shrine**. Hachiman, the deity to whom the shrine is dedicated, is both the god of war and the guardian deity of the Minamoto clan. The shrine offers a dramatic contrast to the quiet repose of the Zen temples clustered around Kita-Kamakura station. Notice the gingko tree at the foot of the stairs leading to the square. It is said that an assassination was carried out beneath it in 1219, making the tree very old indeed. Nearby is a dancing platform and a steeply arched bridge, which in times past was reserved for the passage of the shōgun alone.

To the left of the dancing platform is the **National Treasure Museum** (☎ 0467-22-0753). This museum is recommended, as it is a unique opportunity to see Kamakura art, most of which is cloistered away in temples. The museum is open Tuesday to Sunday from 9 am to 4 pm; entry is ¥150.

Kamakura Station Area Apart from Hachiman-gū, there aren't any sites of historic importance in the immediate vicinity; most places require a short bus trip from in front of the station. The most worthwhile trip is to the Great Buddha.

The **Daibutsu** (Great Buddha) was completed in 1252 and is Kamakura's most famous sight. Once housed in a huge hall, the statue today sits in the open, its home having been washed away by a *tsunami* (tidal wave) in 1495. Cast in bronze and weighing close to 850 tonnes, the statue is 11.4m tall. Its construction was inspired by the even bigger Daibutsu in Nara, though it is agreed that Kamakura's is artistically superior.

To get there, take a bus from the No 2, 7 or 10 bus stops in front of Kamakura station and get off at the Daibutsu-mae bus stop. The Daibutsu is open daily from 7 am to 5.30 pm; admission is ¥150.

If you walk back towards Kamakura station and turn right at the intersection where the bus goes left, this small street will take you to **Hase-dera Temple**, also known as Hase Kannon-dō Temple. There is a garden and an interesting collection of statues of Jizō, the protector of travellers and souls of departed children. The main point of interest, however, is the **Kannon statue**.

Kannon is the goddess of mercy, and her compassion is often invoked as a source of succour. The 9m wooden *jūichimen* (11 faced Kannon) is believed to date from the 8th century. The 11 faces actually comprise one major face and 10 minor faces, the latter representing 10 stages of enlightenment. Unfortunately, though the hall containing this statue is open to the public, the statue itself is normally off-limits. From October to

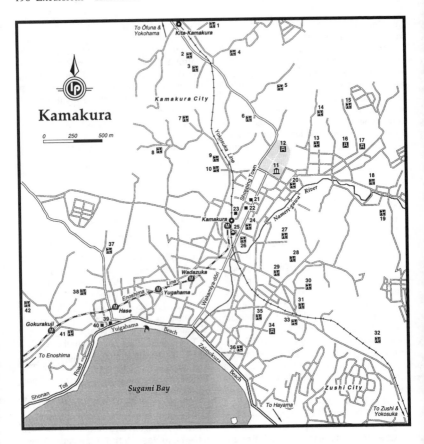

February, Hase-dera is open from 7 am to 4.40 pm. The rest of the year it closes at 5.40 pm. Admission to the temple is ¥200.

Other Shrines & Temples There are plenty of these in and around Kamakura, which has something like 70 temples and shrines (the Kamakura map indicates the main ones). From the Great Buddha, it's best to return to Kamakura station by bus and take another bus out to the temples in the eastern part of town. These have the advantage of being less popular with tourists than the temples of Kita-Kamakura. They may lack the grandeur

of some of the town's more famous temples, but they make up for it with their charm. There is also a delightfully restful, village-like atmosphere in the town's outer fringes.

Egara Ten-jin Shrine is popular with students, who pray here for academic success. Many write their academic aspirations on *ema* (small wooden plaques) which are then hung to the right of the shrine. Buses from stop No 6 in front of Kamakura station run out to Egara Ten-jin Shrine; get off at the Tenjin-mae bus stop.

Zuisen-ji Temple is a pleasant Zen temple which affords relaxing strolling through its

PLACES TO STAY

21 City Pension Shangri La
シティーペンション
シャングリラ

22 Tsurugaoka Kaikan Hotel
鶴ヶ岡会館

23 Ryokan Ushio
旅館うしお

39 BB House
ＢＢハウス

40 Kamakura Kagetsuen
Youth Hostel
鎌倉花月園ユース
ホステル

OTHER

1 Engaku-ji Temple
円覚寺

2 Tōkei-ji Temple
東慶寺

3 Jōchi-ji Temple
浄智寺

4 Meigetsu-in Temple
明月院

5 Kenchō-ji Temple
建長寺

6 Ennō-ji Temple
円応寺

7 Kaizō-ji Temple
海蔵寺

8 Zeniarai-benten
銭洗弁天

9 Eishō-ji Temple
英勝寺

10 Jufuku-ji Temple
寿福寺

11 National Treasure Museum
鎌倉国宝館

12 Hachiman-gū Shrine
鶴岡八幡宮

13 Tomb of Minamoto Yoritomo
源頼朝の墓

14 Raigō-ji Temple
来迎寺

15 Kakuen-ji Temple
覚園寺

16 Egara Ten-jin Shrine
荏柄天神

17 Kamakura-gū Shrine
鎌倉宮

18 Sugimoto-dera Temple
杉本寺

19 Hōkoku-ji Temple
報国寺

20 Hōkai-ji Temple
宝戒寺

24 Daigyō-ji Temple
大巧寺

25 Bus Station
バスステーション

26 Hongaku-ji Temple
本覚寺

27 Myōhon-ji Temple
妙本寺

28 Daihō-ji Temple
大宝寺

29 Anyō-in Temple
安養院

30 Myōhō-ji Temple
妙法寺

31 Ankokuron-ji Temple
安国論寺

32 Hossho-ji Temple
法性寺

33 Chōshō-ji Temple
長勝寺

34 Gosho-jinja Shrine
五所神社

35 Myōchō-ji Temple
妙長寺

36 Kuhonu-ji Temple
九品寺

37 Daibutsu (Great Buddha)
鎌倉大仏

38 Hase-dera Temple
長谷寺

41 Jōjuin Temple
成就院

42 Gokurakuji Temple
極楽寺

gardens (laid out by the temple's founder, Musō Kokushi, during the Kamakura era). It's open daily from 9 am to 5 pm; entry is ¥100. You can walk from Egara Ten-jin in about 15 minutes; turn right where the bus turns left in front of the shrine, take the next left and keep following this road.

Sugimoto-dera Temple is an interesting little temple founded in 734 AD, which makes it the oldest in Kamakura. Ferocious guardian figures are poised at the entrance and the main hall houses three Kannon statues, which are not quite on a par with the one at Hase-dera. Entry is ¥100 and the temple is open daily from 8.30 am to 4.30 pm. To get there, take a bus from the No 5 bus stop in front of Kamakura station and get off at Sugimoto Kannon bus stop.

Hōkoku-ji Temple is down the road (away from Kamakura station) from Sugimoto-dera. This is a Rinzai Zen temple with quiet landscaped gardens where you can relax under a parasol with a cup of green tea. This is one of Kamakura's more active Zen temples, regularly holding zazen meditation classes for beginners. Entry is ¥100. The temple is open daily from 9 am to 4.30 pm.

Places to Stay

Kamakura Kagetsuen Youth Hostel (☎ 0467-25-1238) has beds for ¥3150 and requires membership. Breakfast costs ¥600. You can walk to the hostel from Hase-dera or take an Enoden train to Hase station and walk five minutes south-west of the station (just north of the seafront).

EXCURSIONS

Not far from the youth hostel is *BB House* (☎ 0467-25-5859), which provides accommodation for women only and costs ¥5000 per person, including breakfast.

Just around the corner from Kamakura station is the *Ryokan Ushio* (☎ 0467-22-7016), which has singles from ¥5000. Follow the busy shopping street that runs parallel to the railway tracks next to the station (there's a torii at its entrance) and take the third left. About 20m down this road, you should see a sign on the left pointing into an alley. The ryokan is at the bottom of the alley.

東京東京東京東京東京東京東京東京東

Buddhism in Kamakura

Though Buddhism came to Japan in the 6th century AD, it was 500 years later, during the Kamakura period, that Buddhism spread to all of Japan. Initially the Kamakura period was marked by secular disillusionment with Buddhist institutions and the monastic orders, and a widespread belief that the world had entered Mappō (the Later Age), a period of Buddhist decline when individuals would no longer be able to achieve enlightenment through their own efforts alone. This led to the flourishing of alternatives to established Buddhist doctrine – notably Zen and the 'Pure Land' school of Buddhism.

The Pure Land school preached that in the Later Age salvation could only be achieved through devotion to the transcendent Buddha Amida – all who called on him sincerely would achieve salvation in the Pure Land after death. This populist stroke opened Buddhism in Japan to the masses, who had been largely excluded from the more esoteric branches of Buddhism. This also contrasted with Zen, which sought Buddhahood through meditative practice aimed at the empty centre of the self.

With its rigorous training and self-discipline, Zen found support among an ascendant warrior class and made a considerable contribution to the samurai ethic. Differences on the question of whether *satori* (enlightenment) could be attained suddenly or whether it was a gradual process accounted for Zen breaking into the Rinzai and Sōtō sects.

The contending schools of Pure Land and Zen, along with the views of charismatic leaders such as the influential 13th century priest Nichiren, led to revitalisation of Buddhism within Japan during the Kamakura period. The major Japanese Buddhist sects can trace their antecedents to that era. ■

東京東京東京東京東京東京東京東京東

The *City Pension Shangri La* (☎ 0467-25-6363) is nearby and has twins for ¥6000, plus four-person rooms at economical rates. It's in a modern white building on the left as you walk up the road from the station. A few doors down is the pricey *Tsurugaoka Kaikan Hotel* (☎ 0467-24-1111), where rooms cost ¥16,000 (with two meals).

Places to Eat

Around the square facing Kamakura station are some fast-food places. For more palatable food, head up to Shopping Town street or the main road to Hachiman-gū, both of which run north-east of the station.

On the main road there's *Sakuraya*, just north of Tsurugaoka Kaikan Hotel, a no-frills lunch stop with generic dishes like katsudon and soba – inexpensive and tasty. Just south of here is *Riccione Milano*, an Italian place that does a decent pasta lunch from ¥850.

On Shopping Town street there's a branch of the izakaya chain *Yōrōnotaki* on the right just before you enter the station square; opposite this is *Hirano Rāmen*, a basic shop where a standard bowl of noodles costs ¥500. Further up the road, close to Ryokan Ushio, is *Niraku-sō*, a good Chinese restaurant.

Getting There & Away

Trains on the Yokosuka line run to Kamakura and Kita-Kamakura stations. The trip takes 55 minutes from Tokyo; fares to Kamakura are ¥880 from Tokyo station, ¥760 from Shimbashi and ¥680 from Shinagawa. You can also catch a train from Yokohama on the Yokosuka line (27 minutes; ¥290 to Kita-Kamakura, ¥370 to Kamakura). If you're getting off at Kita-Kamakura station, it's the stop after Ōfuna.

You can go on to Enoshima via the scenic Enoden (Enoshima Dentetsu) line from Kamakura station or by bus from stop No 9 in front of the station. The train (25 minutes, ¥240) is the simpler and cheaper option.

Getting Around

The transportation hub here is Kamakura station. A lack of English signposting makes the bus network hard to use, but the station's tourist information centre should have the latest details on which *noriba* (bus stops/boarding points) serve which destinations. Local bus trips cost either ¥170 or ¥190.

ENOSHIMA 江ノ島

Avoid this popular beach on weekends, when it's packed with day-trippers. At the end of the beach is a bridge to **Enoshima Island**, where the **Enoshima-jinja Shrine** is reached by an 'outdoor escalator' that costs ¥270, but you *can* walk through. It houses a *hadaka-benzaiten* – a nude statue of the Indian goddess of beauty. Other sights around the island include the **Enoshima Shokubutsu-en** (Tropical Garden), open from 9 am to 5 pm daily (¥200).

Enoshima's beaches are good for a bit of meditative wandering after Kamakura's temples and shrines, particularly around the rocky headlands on the southern side of the island. On fair days, Mt Fuji is clearly visible from the south and west sides of the island. In the late afternoon, you might stop for a drink in one of the cliff-side restaurants and watch the sun set over the mountain.

Getting There & Away

Buses and trains run frequently between Kamakura and Enoshima (see the previous Kamakura Getting There & Away section). The Tōkaidō line goes to Ōfuna station from Tokyo station (¥760). At Ōfuna, change to the Shōnan monorail and go to Shōnan-Enoshima station (¥290). Trains also run on the Odakyū line from Shinjuku station to Katase-Enoshima station. The 'Romance Car' runs direct and takes 70 minutes (¥1220); an express takes 10 minutes longer and involves changing trains, but costs only ¥610.

IZU-HANTŌ PENINSULA 伊豆半島

Izu-hantō is noted for its abundant *onsen* (hot springs) and rural landscapes. There's little of historical interest – it's simply a relaxing day trip or overnight stay. You can get around the peninsula in one long and hurried day or stay overnight at a halfway point such as Shimoda. If you stay, make a point of treating yourself to a night in a hot-spring hotel.

A suggested itinerary for Izu-hantō is to start at Atami and travel down the east coast to Shimoda; from there you can cut across to Dogashima and travel up to Mishima or Numazu, where there are railway stations with direct access to Tokyo. There are frequent and reliable buses between the peninsula's main towns, and some towns are also serviced by ferries.

Atami

Atami has more appeal as a naughty hot-spring weekend destination for Japanese couples than it has to westerners for its sightseeing potential. Its easy access from Tokyo by shinkansen and its fame as a hot-spring resort make it an expensive place to spend the night – Itō or Shimoda are better accommodation options. There's an information counter at Atami station (☎ 0557-81-6002).

Atami's prime attraction is **MOA Art Museum**, with a collection of Japanese and Chinese art that includes a few 'National Treasures' and a good number of 'Important Cultural Properties'. It's open Friday to Wednesday from 9.30 am to 4.30 pm. Admission is a hefty ¥1500. Take a bus from the No 4 bus stop outside the station to the 'MOA Bijitsukan' (10 minutes, ¥140).

Getting There & Away An ordinary Tōkaidō line train from Tokyo station to Atami is one hour 50 minutes and ¥1850. The shinkansen takes only 50 minutes, but costs ¥4000. Ordinary trains leave Tokyo every 40 minutes during the day. It is also possible to approach Atami via Shinjuku by taking the Odakyū line to Odawara (one hour 10 minutes, ¥1550), then connecting with the Tōkaidō line to Atami (20 minutes, ¥390).

By far the most comfortable way to travel down to Izu-hantō is by *Odoriko*, a state-of-the-art express service which departs Tokyo station regularly during the day and stops at Atami, Itō, Izu-Inatori and Shimoda. To Atami, the standard Odoriko costs ¥3690; it's ¥3990 for the deluxe *Super Odoriko*.

EXCURSIONS

Itō

Itō, a hot-spring resort, is famous as the place where Anjin-san (William Adams), the hero of James Clavell's book *Shogun*, built a ship for the Tokugawa shōgunate. Among the sights in around Itō are the gourd-shaped **Ippeki-ko Lake**, the **Cycle Sports Centre** and the **Izu Cactus Garden** (ask for Izu Shaboten-kōen), 35 minutes by bus from Izu station and a prickly ¥1550 to enter.

The **Ikeda 20th Century Art Museum** has a collection of paintings and sculptures by Matisse, Picasso, Dali and others. The museum, 25 minutes from Itō station, is open daily from 10 am to 4.30 pm. Entry is ¥720.

Places to Stay There are a couple of youth hostels with accommodation for around ¥2570 in the vicinity of Itō. *Itō Youth Hostel* (☎ 0557-45-0224) is 15 minutes out of town by bus. From Itō station take an Ōshima bus to the Shōgyō Gakkō-mae stop; from there it's a 1km walk.

The *Business Hotel Itō* (☎ 0557-36-1515) is one of the cheapest deals in town: singles/twins are ¥5150/9270. Look for the four storey building around 300m east of the railway station, close to the waterfront.

The Lake Ippeki-ko area is good for pension – small western-style places based on the European pension. *Pension Itōsansō* (☎ 0557-36-4454) has rooms from ¥7500. Most of the other pensions start at ¥9000 per night. There is also a host of accommodation in the Izu-kōgen Plateau area, which is easily accessible from Izu-kōgen station.

Getting There & Away Itō is about 25 minutes from Atami station on the JR Itō line, and the fare is ¥310. There is also a JR limited express *Odoriko* service from Tokyo station to Itō (1¾ hours, ¥4300). Direct ordinary trains from Tokyo station are quite a bit cheaper at ¥2160 and take about two hours 10 minutes.

Shimoda

If you only have time for one town on the peninsula, make it Shimoda, the most pleasant of the hot-spring resorts and former

residence of the American Townsend Harris, the first western diplomat to live in Japan. It's a peaceful place with a few historical sites in addition to the usual touristy stuff.

Things to See Look for the cablecars in front of the station that lurch their way up **Mt Nesugata-yama** every 10 minutes. The park on the top has good views of Shimoda and Shimoda Bay, and a reasonably priced restaurant. A return cablecar trip, including admission to the park, costs ¥1200. The park is open from 9 am to 5.30 pm.

About a 25 minute walk from Shimoda station is **Ryōsen-ji Temple**, famous as the site of a treaty signed by Commodore Perry and representatives of the Tokugawa shōgunate. Next door is **Chōraku-ji Temple**, which has a collection of erotic knick-knacks in its **sex museum**. There also pictures depicting the life of Okichi-san, the courtesan who gave up the man she loved to attend to the needs of the barbarian Harris. Entry is ¥500; it's open daily from 8.30 am to 5 pm.

To get to the temples, turn right from the square with the bus ranks in front of Shimoda station. Bear left after you cross the bridge and follow the road around in the same direction as you were walking before crossing the bridge. The temples are to your left, on the opposite side of the road, at the T junction. On the way you will pass **Hōfuku-ji Temple**, which has a museum that commemorates the life of Okichi-san and includes scenes from the various movie adaptations of her life.

Places to Stay As in the other peninsula resort towns, there is a wealth of accommodation in Shimoda. Staff at the information counter (☎ 0558-22-1351) across the square from the station will book places to stay. If you want a cheap room, ask for a *minshuku* or *kokuminshukusha* (people's lodge); you should be able to get a room for ¥5000 to ¥7000. If you want to find something yourself, the best hunting ground is the area that fronts onto Shimoda Bay. Turn right as you leave the station square, take the second left and cross the bridge. Follow this road around and bear left when it approaches the bay. The left side of the road is crowded with a kilometre of hotels, ryokan and minshuku.

The *Gensu Youth Hostel* (☎ 0558-62-0035) is 25 minutes by bus from the town and has beds for ¥2800. The hostel is opposite a bus stop and a post office. The *Station Hotel Shimoda* (☎ 0558-22-8885), right next to the station, is a reasonably priced business hotel. Singles/twins cost ¥5800/11,500.

Getting There & Away Shimoda is as far as you can go by train on the peninsula; the limited express from Tokyo station takes 2¾ hours (¥6150). An Izu Kyūkō line train from Itō station takes about an hour (¥1440). There are a few express services each day from Atami station, but the surcharges make them expensive. The deluxe *Odoriko* from Tokyo will cost ¥5850, and ¥6150 for the *Super Odoriko* service.

Bus platform No 5 in front of the station is for buses going to Dogashima, while platform No 7 is for those bound for Shuzenji.

West to North Izu-hantō

From Shimoda's No 5 bus stop in front of the station, it's a very scenic bus journey to **Dogashima**, on the other side of the peninsula. Along the way is **Cape Matsu-zaki**, recommended for its traditional-style houses and quiet sandy beach. The bus to Dogashima takes about 30 minutes (¥1290).

The unusual rock formations lining the shore are Dogashima's main attraction. Boat trips allow better views: a 20 minute trip costs ¥900, while two hour tours are ¥1950.

To complete the circuit, there are a number of bus stops in Dogashima on the road opposite the jetty. The fare to **Shuzenji** – another resort town with a rail link via the Tōkaidō line to Tokyo – from stop No 2 is ¥2030. There are many ryokan and minshuku in this area. A more interesting and not much more expensive alternative is to catch a high-speed ferry to **Numazu**, also on the Tōkaidō line (1¼ hours, ¥3090; six departures a day from 10 am to 4.45 pm). Boats also go to **Tōi** (25 minutes, ¥820), where you could stay at the *Takasagoya Youth Hostel*, continue on to

Shuzenji by bus or take another boat to Numazu. Half an hour by rail from Shuzenji is **Mishima**, a town that is short on interesting sights but serviced by the Tōkaidō line. The shinkansen from Mishima to Tokyo station takes 65 minutes and costs ¥4310. Ordinary trains take twice as long and cost ¥2160. Ten minutes by train from Mishima is Numazu, from where you can continue into Izu-hantō by boat or bus.

HAKONE 箱根

If the weather cooperates and Mt Fuji is clearly visible, the Hakone region can make a memorable day trip from Tokyo. You can enjoy cablecar rides, visit an open-air museum, poke around smelly volcanic hot-water springs and cruise Ashino-ko Lake. The weather, however, is crucial, for without Mt Fuji hovering in the background, much of what Hakone has to offer is likely to diminish in interest.

A good loop through the region takes you from Tokyo to Hakone-Yumoto station by train and then 'toy train' (a two car mountain train) to Gōra; by funicular and cable car up Mt Soun-zan and down to Ashino-ko; by boat around the lake to Moto-Hakone, where you can walk a short stretch of the Edo-era Tōkaidō Highway; and from there by bus back to Odawara, where you catch the train to Tokyo. (If you're feeling energetic, you could spend 3½ hours walking the old highway back to Hakone-Yumoto, which is connected to Tokyo by rail.)

Information

The Tokyo TIC has some useful pamphlets, particularly if you're planning on staying. If you want to try some of the area's onsen, definitely get the TIC's *Open-Air Hot Springs in Hakone*. Note that Hakone gets busy on weekends and during the holiday season – reservations are recommended.

Hakone Free Pass The Odakyū line offers a Hakone *furii pasu* (free pass) which costs ¥5400 for adults and ¥2700 for children; it allows you to use any mode of transport within the Hakone region for three days and

Hakone

EXCURSIONS

provides discounts on some sights. The fare between Shinjuku and Hakone-Yumoto station is also included in the pass, although you'll have to pay a ¥850 surcharge if you want to take the Romance Car. If you have a Japan rail pass, you'd be advised to buy a Free Pass in Odawara for ¥4050 and ¥2030 for children, as this doesn't include the fare from Shinjuku. Altogether it's a good deal for a Hakone circuit, as the pass will save at least ¥1000 even on a one day visit to the region.

Things to See

Between Odawara and Gōra on the toy-train Hakone-Tōzan line is the **Hakone Open-Air Art Museum** (☎ 0460-2-1161). The art museum is next to Chōkoku-no-mori station, a little before Gōra station. It features sculptures by western artists such as Rodin and Moore in a 30 sq km park. Admission is a hefty ¥1500, though the Hakone Free Pass will earn you a discount. It's open from 9 am to 5 pm between March and October; during the rest of the year it closes at 4 pm.

The end of the Hakone-Tōzan line and the start of the funicular and cable-car trip to Togendai on Ashino-ko Lake is **Gōra**. This small town also has a couple of attractions, including **Gōra-kōen Park**, just a short walk beside the funicular tracks up Mt Soun-zan. Further up the hill, 10 minutes from Gōra station, is **Hakone Art Museum** (☎ 0460-2-2623), which has a moss garden and a collection of ceramics from Japan and other Asian nations. Admission is ¥900; it's open from 9 am to 4.30 pm, closed on Thursday.

Take the funicular from Gōra up **Mt Sōun-zan**. If you don't have a Hakone Free Pass, you'll need to buy a ticket at the booth to the right of the platform exit for ¥400. The ride takes 10 minutes. Mt Sōun-zan is the starting point for what the Japanese refer to as a 'ropeway', a 30 minute, 4km cablecar ride to **Togendai**, next to Ashino-ko. On the way, the gondolas pass through Ōwakudani. Get out at this point and take a look at the volcanic hot springs. If the weather is fine, there are great views of Mt Fuji, both from the gondolas and from Ōwakudani. The journey

from Gōra to Togendai costs ¥1300 one way, ¥2300 return; keep the ticket if you pause at Ōwakudani. The **Ōwakudani Natural Science Museum** (☎ 0460-4-9149) has displays on the geography and natural history of Hakone. It's open daily from 9 am to 4.30 pm; entry is ¥400.

From Ōwakudani, the cablecar continues to **Ashino-ko Lake**, touted as the primary attraction of the Hakone region. Majestic Mt Fuji rises above the surrounding hills, its snow-clad slopes shimmering on the mirror-like surface of the lake. That is, if the venerable volcano is not hidden behind a dirty grey bank of clouds.

From Togendai there are ferry services to Hakone-en, Moto-Hakone and Hakone-machi. At **Hakone-en**, you can take a cablecar (¥610 one way, ¥1030 return) to the top of **Mt Komaga-take**, where you get good views of the lake and Mt Fuji. You can leave the mountain by the same route or by taking a five minute funicular descent (¥360) to Komaga-take-nobori-kuchi. Buses run from there to Odawara for ¥770.

Most people take the ferry from Togendai to Moto-Hakone (¥105). **Moto-Hakone** has a few places to eat or get an overpriced cup of coffee, and there are a couple of interesting sights within an easy walk of the jetty. These include **Hakone-jinja Shrine**, which is impossible to miss, with its red torii rising from the lake. The shrine is nothing special, but the effect is quite evocative. It's open from 9.30 am to 4 pm, and costs ¥300.

Up the hill from the lakeside Moto-Hakone bus stop runs the **Old Tōkaidō Highway**, the road that once linked the ancient capital Kyoto with Edo (Tokyo). It's a 3½ hour walk on the old road to Hakone-Yumoto station, passing **Amazake-jaya Teahouse**, the **Old Tōkaidō Road Museum** and **Soun-ji Temple** along the way.

A less arduous walk follows **Cryptomeria Ave**, or Sugi-namiki, a 500m path between Moto-Hakone and Hakone-machi, lined with cryptomeria trees planted some 360 years ago. The path runs behind the lakeside road used by the buses and other traffic. **Hakone-machi** itself was once the **Hakone**

Checkpoint, run by the Tokugawa regime from 1619 to 1869 as a means of controlling the movement of everything from people to ideas in and out of Edo. The present-day checkpoint is a recent reproduction. It's open daily from 8.30 am to 4.30 pm.

Buses run from Moto-Hakone back to **Odawara** for ¥1070. Odawara is billed as an 'old castle town', which it is, except that the castle is an uninspiring reconstruction of the original. If you're still interested, Odawara castle is a 10 minute walk from Odawara station. Admission is ¥300; it's open 9 am to 4.30 pm.

Places to Stay

Hakone's popularity with Japanese weekenders is reflected in the high price of most accommodation in the area. The former hostel *Hakone Sōun-zan* (☎ 0465-62-7514) costs ¥2500. It is on the left side of the road that goes off to the right of the cablecar. Look for the wooden sign with Japanese writing and the YHA triangle outside. Alternatively, it's ¥1000 to pitch a tent at the *Kojiri Campground*, and six-person huts are available for ¥10,000.

The *Hakone Sengokuhara Youth Hostel* (☎ 0460-4-8966) has beds for ¥2800. The *Fuji Hakone Guest House* (☎ 0460-4-6577) has singles from ¥5000 to ¥6000 and doubles from ¥10,000 to ¥12,000. To get to both the hostel and guesthouse, take a No 4 bus from Odawara station to the Senkyōrō-mae bus stop (50 minutes, ¥1000). There is an English sign close by. A natural hot spa is available for bathing.

The *Moto Hakone Guest House* (☎ 0460-3-7880), which is conveniently located in Moto-Hakone, costs ¥5000 per person.

For the best, *Fujiya Hotel* (☎ 0460-2-2211) is famous as one of Japan's earliest western-style hotels. Singles/doubles are around ¥20,000/25,000. Prices vary seasonally and rise substantially on weekends and public holidays. The hotel is five minutes walk from Miyanoshita station on the Hakone-Tōzan line; if you ring from the station, someone will give you instructions in English on how to get there.

There are many more options around Hakone's many onsen areas – Yumoto Onsen, Gōra Onsen, Sengokuhara Onsen and Ashino-ko Onsen – which contain many onsen and onsen ryokan, some of which welcome day visitors. Contact the Tokyo TIC for details.

Getting There & Away

There are basically three ways of getting to the Hakone region: by the Odakyū express bus service from the Shinjuku bus terminal on the western side of Shinjuku station; by JR from Tokyo station; and by the private Odakyū line from Shinjuku station.

Train JR trains run on the Tōkaidō line between Tokyo station and Odawara. Ordinary trains (1½ hours, ¥1420) run every 15 minutes or so. Limited express trains take 70 minutes (the express surcharge is ¥1430). Shinkansen (40 minutes, ¥3570) leave Tokyo station every 20 minutes – but make sure you are on a train that stops at Odawara (the *kodama* shinkansen does).

Trains run to Odawara from Shinjuku station on the Odakyū line. Quickest and most comfortable is the Romance Car (one hour 25 minutes, ¥1780), which leaves every half hour. There's also an express service (one hour 35 minutes, ¥990), by far the cheapest way of reaching Odawara.

At Odawara, you can change to the Hakone-Tōzan line, which takes you to Gōra. If you are already on the Odakyū line, you can continue to Hakone-Yumoto and change to the Hakone-Tōzan line simply by walking across the platform.

Bus The Odakyū express bus service has the advantage of running directly into the Hakone region, to Ashino-ko and to Hakone-machi for ¥1830. The disadvantage is that the bus trip is much less interesting than the combination of Romance Car, toy train (Hakone-Tōzan line), funicular, cablecar (ropeway) and ferry. Buses leave from bus stop No 35 in front of Odakyū department store on the west side of Shinjuku station.

continued on page 210

Mt Fuji Area

Mt Fuji, Japan's highest mountain, stands 3776m high, and when it's capped with snow, it's a postcard-perfect volcano cone. Fuji-san, as it's reverently called, last blew its top in 1707, when streets in Edo were covered in volcanic ash. Unfortunately, Mt Fuji is a notoriously reclusive mountain, often hidden by cloud. Views are usually best in winter and early spring, when the snow cap adds to the scene. *Climbing Mt Fuji* and *Mt Fuji & Fuji Five Lakes* brochures are available from the TIC and provide exhaustive detail on transport to the mountain and how to climb it, complete with climbing schedules worked out to the minute. There is an information office in front of Kawaguchi-ko station.

Fuji Views

You can get a classic view of Mt Fuji from the shinkansen as it passes the city of Fuji. There are also good views from the Hakone area and the Nagao Pass on the road from Hakone to Gotemba. The road that encircles the mountain offers good views, particularly near Yamanaka-ko and Sai-ko lakes.

MARTIN MOOS

Box: Passing through a torii on the way up reminds the walker that Fuji is sacred terrain (photograph by Martin Moos).

Left: Fuji the ordinary town and Fuji the extraordinary mountain – the sort of view a modern-day Hiroshige might have made immortal in a wood-block print.

Climbing Mt Fuji

Officially the climbing season on Fuji is July and August, and the Japanese pack in during those busy months. Climbing may be just as good either side of the official season, but transport services to and from Mt Fuji are less frequent then and many of the mountain huts are closed. You can climb Mt Fuji at any time of year, but a mid-winter ascent is strictly for experienced mountaineers.

Bear in mind that although this is a popular climb, Mt Fuji is high enough for altitude sickness, and the weather can be viciously changeable. On the summit it can quickly go from clear but cold to cloudy, wet, windy and freezing cold – not just miserable but downright dangerous. Don't climb without adequate clothing for cold and wet weather – even on a good day in summer, the temperature on top is likely to be close to freezing.

The mountain is divided into 10 'stations' from base to summit, but these days most climbers start from one of the fifth stations, which you can reach by road. Count on a 4½ hour ascent and about 2½ hours to descend. Once you're on the top, it takes about an hour to make a circuit of the crater.

To time your arrival for the sunrise (also when the mountain is least likely to be shrouded in cloud) you can either start up in the afternoon, stay overnight in a mountain hut and continue early in the morning, or climb the whole way at night. You do not want to arrive on the top too long before dawn, as it's likely to be very cold and windy.

When the traffic below is unbearable, head for the cloud-covered paths of Mt Fuji. Bring your bicycle along for the ride.

CHARLOTTE HINDLE

Fifth Stations There are four 'fifth stations' around Fuji, and it's quite feasible to climb from one and descend to another. On the northern side of Fuji is Kawaguchi-ko Fifth Station, at 2305m, which is reached from the town of Kawaguchi-ko. This station is very popular with climbers starting from Tokyo. The Yoshida route, which starts much lower down, close to the town of Fuji-Yoshida, is the same as the Kawaguchi-ko route for much of the way.

Subashiri Fifth Station is at 1980m, and the route from there meets Kawaguchi-ko just after the eighth station. Gotemba Fifth Station is reached from the town of Gotemba and, at 1440m, is much lower than the other fifth stations. From Gotemba station it takes seven or eight hours to reach the top, as opposed to the 4½ to five hours it takes on the other routes. Fujinomiya/Mishima Fifth Station, at 2380m, is more convenient for climbers approaching from the west than for those coming from Tokyo. It meets the Gotemba route right at the top.

Equipment Make sure you have clothing suitable for cold and wet weather, including a hat and gloves. Bring drinking water and some snack food. If you're going to climb at night, bring a torch (flashlight). Even at night it would be difficult to get seriously lost, as the trails are very clear, but it's easy to put a foot wrong in the dark.

Places to Stay There are 'lodges' dotted up the mountainside but they're expensive – ¥4500 for a mattress on the floor squeezed between countless climbers – and you don't get much opportunity to sleep anyway, as you have to be up well before dawn to start the final slog to the top. No matter how miserable the nights, don't plan to shelter or rest in the huts without paying. The huts also prepare simple meals for their guests and for passing climbers. Camping on the mountain is not permitted.

Getting There & Away The three routes that are used by climbers from Tokyo are serviced by the two centres of Kawaguchi-ko and Gotemba. For the Kawaguchi-ko ascent, you're best to take the direct bus from Shinjuku bus terminal to Kawaguchi-ko Fifth Station (2½ hours, ¥2600). If you take two trains and a bus, the same trip can cost ¥6000 – by Chūō line train from Shinjuku to Ōtsuki, Fuji Kyūkō line to Kawaguchi-ko and by bus from there to the Fifth Station.

From Gotemba station there are buses both for the Gotemba route (45 minutes, ¥1080) and the Subashiri route (55 minutes, ¥1500). Trains run to Gotemba via the Gotemba line and then the Odakyū line (1¾ hours, ¥2150). Tōmei buses run from Tokyo station to Tōmei Gotemba, about 1km from Gotemba (about 1¾ hours, ¥1350).

MARTIN MOOS

CHRIS TAYLOR

MARTIN MOOS

ft: Kamakura's Daibutsu (Great Buddha) serenely sits in the lotus meditation position.
ght: Once the shōgun's privileged route to Tōshōgū Shrine, Shinkyō Bridge in Nikkō dates
m 1636; it was rebuilt in 1907 after a flood.
ttom: An early morning fishing competition at Fuji Five Lakes.

CHRIS TAYLOR

CHRIS TAYLOR

CHRIS TAYLOR

MARTIN MOOS

Top Left: Edo-period fashion comes out of the closet on certain festive days.
Top Right: Musicians pipe at the Sanja Matsuri (Sanja Festival) at Sensō-ji Temple, Asaku
Middle: If you ask school children for directions, this is the likely response.
Bottom: Expressions of the Japanese soul – people waiting to pray at Meiji-jingū Shrine

MARTIN MOOS

To climb Mt Fuji is to accrue merit for rebirth and favour with the gods; to hope to get any sleep in a mountain resthouse is probably crazy talk.

Fuji Five Lakes

The five lakes scattered around the northern side of Mt Fuji are major attractions for Tokyo day-trippers, offering water sports and some good views of Mt Fuji. For visitors to Tokyo, the views of the lakes and Mt Fuji are the area's biggest draw. Perhaps the best way to make the most of this is to avail yourself of the area's comprehensive bus network, which includes regular buses from Fuji-Yoshida station. They pass the four smaller lakes and travel around the mountain to Fujinomiya on the south-western side. From Kawaguchi-ko, there are nine to 11 buses daily making the two hour trip to Mishima on the shinkansen line.

Places to Stay There are three youth hostels in the Fuji area: *Fuji Yoshida* (☎ 0555-22-0533), *Kawaguchi-ko* (☎ 0555-72-1431) and *Fuji Sai-ko* (☎ 0555-82-2616). Fuji Yoshida costs ¥2500 a night, Kawaguchi-ko is ¥2800 and Fuji Sai-ko is ¥2300 or ¥2450, depending on the season. Fuji Yoshida is about 1km south of Fuji Yoshida station, just off Route 139 (look out for the Lawson's convenience store on the left-hand corner if you're walking north). Kawaguchi-ko is about 500m south-east of Kawaguchi station. Fuji Sai-ko is on the north-eastern end of the lake with the same name, on the road that circles the lake. It conveniently has its own bus stop (Yūsu hosuteru mae), and buses from Kawaguchi station take around 35 minutes to get there (ask for the bus bound for Saiko Minshuku).

There are numerous hotels, ryokan, minshuku and pensions around the Fuji Five Lakes, particularly at Kawaguchi-ko. The tourist information office at Kawaguchi-ko station can make reservations. The Japanese Inn Group is represented by the *Hotel Ashiwada* (☎ 0555-82-2321), at the western end of Kawaguchi-ko Lake. Singles/doubles are ¥7000/13,000.

Getting There & Away Fuji-Yoshida and Kawaguchi-ko are the two main travel centres in the Fuji Five Lakes area. Frequent buses run directly to Kawaguchi-ko (1¾ hours, ¥1700) from the Shinjuku bus terminal in the Yasuda Seimei second building, beside the main Shinjuku station in Tokyo. Some buses continue to Yamanaka-ko and Motosu-ko lakes.

You can also get to the lakes by train, although it takes longer and costs more. JR Chūō line trains go from Shinjuku to Ōtsuki (one hour; ¥2890 by limited express, ¥1260 by local train). At Ōtsuki you cross the platform to the Fuji Kyūkō line local train which takes about 50 minutes and ¥1110 to Kawaguchi-ko. The train actually goes to Fuji-Yoshida first (¥990), then reverses out for the short leg to Kawaguchi-ko. On Sunday and holidays from March to November, there is a direct local train from Shinjuku (two to 2½ hours, ¥2330).

continued from page 206

NIKKŌ 日光

Nikkō is not only one of the most popular day trips from Tokyo, it's also one of Japan's major tourist attractions, due to the splendour of its shrines and temples. You should pick a weekday to visit, when the crowds are lighter, but whatever you do, don't miss it. Nikkō should be included on even the most whirlwind tour of Japan.

History

Nikkō's history as a sacred site stretches back to the middle of the 8th century, when a Buddhist priest established a hermitage there. In 1617 it was chosen as the site for the mausoleum of Tokugawa Ieyasu. In 1634, Tokugawa Iemitsu, the grandson of the deceased Ieyasu, commenced work on the shrine that can be seen today. Tōshō-gū Shrine was built using a huge army of some 15,000 artisans from all over Japan.

The results continue to receive mixed reviews. In contrast with the minimalism associated with Japanese art, every available space of Ieyasu's shrine and mausoleum is crowded with detail. Animals, mythical and otherwise, jostle among the glimmering gold-leaf and red lacquerwork. The skills involved in creating these is awe-inspiring.

PLACES TO STAY
1   Nikkō Green Hotel
　日光グリーンホテル
3   Annex Turtle Hotori-an
　アネックスタートル ほとり庵
4   Turtle Inn Nikkō
　タートルイン日光

5   Nikkō Daiyagawa Youth Hostel
　日光大谷川ユース ホステル
6   Nikkō Youth Hostel
　日光ユースホステル

PLACES TO EAT
9   Yōrō-no-Taki
　養老乃瀧

OTHER
2   Nikkō Museum
　日光博物館
7   Nikkō Post Office
　日光郵便局
8   Nikkō Kyōdo Center
　日光郷土センター

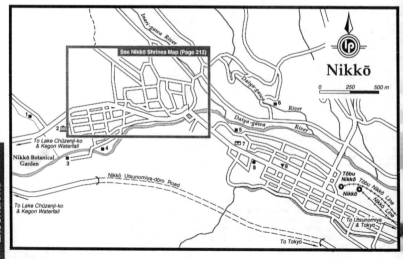

The overall effect is perhaps more Chinese than Japanese, but don't let this put you off – Tōshō-gū remains a grand experience.

Orientation
It's a straight 30 minute walk uphill from the JR and Tōbu stations to the shrine area. You can also take bus No 1, 2, 3 or 4 up to the Shin-kyō bus stop for ¥190.

Information
The Kyōdo Centre (☎ 0288-53-3795), with its useful tourist information office, can be found on the road up to Tōshō-gū Shrine. There is another tourist office in the Tōbu Nikkō station, and one near Rinnō-ji Temple.

Hikers should pick up a copy of the *Nikkō-Yumoto-Chuzenji Area Hiking Guide* (¥150), available from some of the area's pensions and from information counters in Nikkō.

Tickets Ticketing arrangements in Nikkō have improved, but there's still room for confusion. Basically it's like this: Futarasan-jinja Shrine is free, Rinnō-ji Temple costs ¥880 and Tōshō-gū Shrine is ¥1250.

You can save money and effort by buying a 'two-shrines-one-temple' ticket *(nisha-ichiji-kōtsū-baikan-ken)* for ¥900. This ticket covers all three of the above sights, though not the Nemuri-neko (Sleeping Cat) in Tōshō-gū. Entry to the latter is a further ¥430. Even so, this is a considerable saving on buying each of the tickets separately.

Things to See
Close to the Tōshō-gū area is **Shin-kyō Bridge**. The story goes that Shōdō Shōnin, who first established a hermitage in Nikkō in 782, was carried across the river at this point on the backs of two huge serpents. Today's bridge is a 1907 reconstruction of the mid-17th century original. It costs ¥300 to cross the bridge on foot.

The next stop is **Rinnō-ji Temple**, also founded by Shōdō Shōnin (of the Buddhist Tendai sect). **Sambutsu-dō** (Three Buddha Hall) has huge gold-lacquered images – the most impressive is *senjū* (1000-armed Kannon). The central image is Amida Nyorai,

flanked by Batō, a horse-headed Kannon whose domain is the animal kingdom.

Hōmutsu-den (Treasure Hall), also on the temple grounds, has a collection of treasures associated with the temple, but admission (¥300) is not included in the two-shrine-one-temple ticket.

A huge stone torii marks the entrance to **Tōshō-gū Shrine**, while to the left is a five storey pagoda, dating from 1650 but reconstructed in 1818. The pagoda is remarkable for its lack of foundations – the interior contains a long suspended pole that apparently swings like a pendulum in order to maintain equilibrium during an earthquake.

The true entrance to Tōshō-gū is through the torii at Omote-mon Gate, protected on either side by Deva kings. Through the entrance to the right is **Sanjinko** (Three Sacred Storehouses), the upper storey of which is renowned for the imaginative relief carvings of elephants by an artist who had never seen the real thing. To the left of the entrance is the **Sacred Stable**, a suitably plain building housing a carved white horse. The stable's only adornment is an allegorical series of relief carvings depicting the life-cycle of the monkey. They include the famous 'hear no evil, see no evil, speak no evil' trio that is now emblematic of Nikkō.

Pass through another torii, climb another flight of stairs, and on the left and right are a drum tower and a belfry. To the left of the drum tower is **Honji-dō Hall**, with its huge ceiling painting of a dragon in flight known as the 'Roaring Dragon'. The dragon will roar if you clap your hands beneath it.

Next comes **Yōmei-mon Gate**, adorned with a multitude of reliefs of Chinese sages, children, and dragons and other mythical creatures. So much effort and skill went into the gate that its creators worried that its perfection might arouse envy in the gods, so the final supporting pillar on the left side was placed upside down as a deliberate error.

Through Yōmei-mon and to the right is **Nemuri-neko** (Sleeping Cat). Sakashita-mon Gate here opens onto a path that climbs up through towering cedars to **Ieyasu's Tomb**, a relatively simple affair. If you are

PLACES TO STAY
8 Nikkō Pension Green Age
日光ペンション
グリーンエイジ
26 Hotel Seikōen
ホテル清晃苑
27 Nikkō Tōkan-sō Ryokan
日光東観荘旅館
36 Nikkō Kanaya Hotel
日光金谷ホテル

PLACES TO EAT
35 Yakitori-ya
焼き鳥屋

OTHER
1 Taiyūin-byō
大猷院廟
2 Yasha-mon Gate
夜叉門
3 Niō-mon Gate
仁王門
4 Futara-san-jinja
Shrine
二荒山神社
5 Kara-mon Gate
唐門
6 Bronze Torii
銅鳥居

7 Hokke-dō Hall
法華堂
9 Treasury
東照宮宝物館
10 Ticket Office
券売所
11 Sacred Stable
神厩舎
12 Drum Tower
鼓楼
13 Honji-dō Hall
本地堂
14 Tōshō-gū Shrine
東照宮
15 Tomb of Ieyasu
奥社
16 Honden
本殿
17 Honden
本殿
18 Haiden
拝殿
19 Sakashita-mon Gate
坂下門
20 Nemuri-neko
眠猫

21 Yōmei-mon Gate
陽明門
22 Sanjinko
三神庫
23 Omote-mon Gate
表門
24 Pagoda (5 stories)
五重塔
25 Granite Torii
一ノ鳥居
28 Gohoten-dō Hall
護法天堂
29 Sambutsu-dō Hall
三仏堂
30 Rinnō-ji Temple
輪王寺
31 Tourist
Information
観光案内所
32 Nanshō-in
南照院
33 Shihonryū-ji Temple
四本竜寺
34 Hongū Shrine
本宮神社

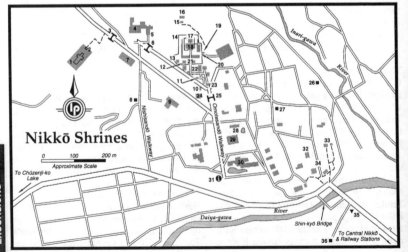

using the ¥900 ticket, it will cost an extra ¥430 to see the cat and the tomb. To the left of Yōmei-mon is **Jinyōsha**, a storage depot for Nikkō's *mikoshi* (portable shrines), which come alive during the May and October festivals. The Honden (Main Hall) and Haiden (Hall of Worship) can also be seen in the enclosure.

Nearby is **Futara-san-jinja Shrine**, dedicated to Mt Nantai, its consort Nyotai and their mountainous progeny Tarō. Also in the vicinity is **Taiyūin-byō**, which enshrines Ieyasu's grandson Iemitsu (1604-51) and is a smaller version of Tōshō-gū. The smaller size gives it a less extravagant air, and some consider it more aesthetically worthy than its larger neighbour.

Chūzenji-ko Lake

On a quiet day it's a 50 minute bus trip from Nikkō up to Chūzenji-ko along a winding road complete with hairpin bends. There's some stunning scenery, including the 97m **Kegon Waterfall** and the lake, but don't cut short a visit to the shrine area just to fit in Chūzenji-ko. There's an elevator (¥520 return) down to a platform where you can observe the full force of the plunging waterfall. Also worth a visit is the third of the **Futara-san-jinja shrines**, which complements the ones near Tōshō-gū and on Mt Nantai.

Buses run frequently from Tōbu Nikkō station to Chūzenji Onsen from 6.20 am to 7.30 pm (50 minutes, ¥1100).

Places to Stay

Because of Nikkō's importance as a tourist attraction, it is one of the few places outside Tokyo and Kyoto where travellers on a budget get some choice in accommodation. If you're willing to spend ¥2000 or so over standard youth hostel rates, there are some very good options close to the central shrine and temple area.

Youth Hostels Of the town's two hostels, *Nikkō Daiyagawa Youth Hostel* (☎ 0288-54-1974) is the more popular. It costs ¥2600 per night (¥3400 with two meals) and is just to

the rear of the post office opposite the Shyakusho-mae bus stop. It's closed from 25 December to 1 January.

A 10 minute walk away, on the other side of the Daiya-gawa River, *Nikkō Youth Hostel* (☎ 0288-54-1013) has beds for ¥2450 or ¥2650, depending on the time of year. It's closed from 28 December to 3 January.

Pensions & Ryokan Nikkō's many pensions offer very reasonable rates and clean, comfortable surroundings. Per-person costs are around ¥5000, but you can often reduce this by sharing rooms with other travellers. Nikkō is very popular, so book well in advance. All the following pensions have someone who can speak a little English.

Far and away the most popular of Nikkō's pensions is the *Turtle Inn Nikkō* (☎ 0288-53-3168), with rooms from ¥3900 per person without bath, ¥5000 with (prices vary seasonally). Meals are ¥1000 for breakfast and ¥2000 for dinner. Turtle Inn Nikkō is by the river, beyond the shrine area. From the station, take a bus to the Sōgō-kaikan-mae bus stop, backtrack around 50m to the fork in the road and follow the river for around five minutes.

To the west, over the river but on the same road, is *Annex Turtle Hotori-An* (☎ 0288-53-3663), where Japanese and western-style rooms range from ¥5200; meals are the same price as at Turtle Inn.

Two great places are the wonderfully named *Nikkō Pension Green Age* (☎ 0288-54-3636), which looks like a Tudor mansion, and *Nikkō Tōkan-sō Ryokan* (☎ 0288-54-0611). Rates at the former start at ¥9800 with two meals, while at the latter the same deal is about ¥15,000.

Hotels The *Nikkō Green Hotel* (☎ 0288-54-1756) has rooms from ¥6500 to ¥18,000; meals are available. *Hotel Seikōen* (☎ 0288-53-5555) starts at ¥13,000 with two meals. Both are rather drab places.

Not far from Shin-kyo Bridge is *Nikkō Kanaya Hotel* (☎ 0288-54-0001), Nikkō's classiest. Twins cost ¥12,000 to ¥50,000; doubles from ¥15,000 to ¥32,000. During

EXCURSIONS

peak holiday periods like Golden Week and the summer holidays, room prices nearly double.

Places to Eat

Many travellers prefer to eat at their ryokan or pension, but there are a number of places to eat on the main road between the stations and shrine area. Across the road from the fire station is a branch of the popular izakaya chain *Yōrō-no-taki* which has cheap beer and a good selection of snacks and meals.

Close to Shin-kyō Bridge is a great little *Yakitori-ya* bar – look for the recommendations written in English near the entrance. Countless travellers have been·won over by the charm of the lady who runs it and by the great food she prepares. There's an English menu, and meals start at an economical ¥300 – try the yaki-udon for only ¥500. It closes early (around 7 pm).

In the shrine area, some shops sell inexpensive food and have English menus. For a more upmarket lunch or dinner, the restaurant at *Nikkō Kanaya Hotel* is recommended both for its atmosphere and for its meals, which cost from ¥2000 to ¥5000.

Getting There & Away

The best way to visit Nikkō is via the Tōbu Nikkō line from Asakusa station in Tokyo. The station, which is separate from Asakusa subway station, is in the basement of Tōbu department store, but it is well signposted and easy to find from the subway. Limited express trains take one hour 55 minutes (¥2690). They require a reservation (on a quiet day you'll probably be able to organise this before boarding the train) and run every 30 minutes or so from 7.30 to 10 am; after 10 am they run hourly. Rapid trains don't require reservations, take 15 minutes longer and cost ¥1300. They run once an hour from 6.20 am to 4.30 pm. Buy tickets from a vending machine or the ticket office.

As usual, travelling by JR trains is more time-consuming and more expensive; it is only of interest to those on a Japan Rail Pass. The quickest way is by shinkansen from Tokyo or Ueno to Utsunomiya (53 minutes, ¥4510), changing there for an ordinary train (no other options) for the 45 minute, ¥720 trip to Nikkō. Trains from Utsunomiya to Nikkō leave about once every 30 minutes. Not all trains go all the way to Nikkō – unless you checked beforehand, you may have to get off part way and wait for a train that makes the whole journey.

MASHIKO   益子

Mashiko, a centre for country-style pottery, has about 50 potters, some of whom you can see working at their kilns. The town achieved fame when Hamada Shōji settled there and, from 1930, produced his Mashiko pottery. Today he is designated as a 'Living National Treasure' and has been joined by a legion of potters. The noted English potter Bernard Leach also worked here for several years.

Mashiko's kilns are spread out over a wide area; getting to them requires a lot of footwork. Get a copy of the *Tourist Map of Mashiko* from the information counter at Utsunomiya station (see the following Getting There & Away section) or the Tokyo TIC. **Hamada House** and **Tsukamoto Kiln** (☎ 0285-72-3223) are recommended, but there are some 300 kilns in the area, and you could spend weeks seeking them out.

Hamada House has both wood-fired kilns and modern automated ones, and visitors can play around with the machinery. One-hour introductory courses at the Tsukamoto Kiln cost ¥3570, but a reservation is required. The **Mashikoyaki Kyōhan Centre** (☎ 0285-72-4444) also has a one hour course, but firing the items produced takes a month.

Getting There & Away

It is possible to combine Mashiko with a visit to Nikkō if you set off from Tokyo very early and use the JR route. See the earlier Nikkō Getting There & Away section for travel details to Utsunomiya. From Utsunomiya, buses run regularly during the day to Mashiko (one hour, ¥1150).

Ask at the tourist information counter outside Utsunomiya for instructions for getting to the bus stop and for bus times.

HIKING AROUND TOKYO

Those interested in hiking in the Tokyo area should visit the TIC and pick up a copy of its excellent *One Day Hiking Courses From Central Tokyo* pamphlet. See the Guidebooks entry under Books in the Facts for the Visitor chapter for more resources.

ONSEN (HOT SPRING BATHS)

If you have a yen for a Japanese hot springs diversion, pick up the TIC's *Japanese Hot Springs* pamphlet, which lists onsen in Hakone, Nikkō, and Shimoda and Itō on Izu-hantō, as well as three onsen in Tokyo itself. See also the Public Baths & Onsen entry in the Entertainment chapter.

FURTHER AFIELD

Domestic travel in Japan is a painless affair. You can hop on the shinkansen at Tokyo station in the morning and be sightseeing in some of the county's most famous cities by early afternoon. There is no doubt, however, that extensive use of trains of any kind in Japan can eat through a travel budget in little time. Those who plan extensive sightseeing would be well advised to get a Japan Rail Pass before coming to Japan.

For most visitors, Kyoto is the single most rewarding destination in Japan. With more than 2000 temples and shrines, and endless reminders of traditional Japan, Kyoto is the perfect counterpoint to the restless hyper-modernity of Tokyo. Those with the time (three hours on the shinkansen) and money (about ¥25,000 for a round trip) should make every effort to visit, even if it's just a quick two day trip.

An hour from Kyoto by local train, Nara is the second of Japan's great cultural meccas, boasting several splendid temples and shrines. Moreover, the pleasant layout of the city makes it perfect for aimless strolling and temple hopping.

An hour west of Kyoto by local train (17 minutes by shinkansen), Osaka is Japan's second largest city and a rival to Tokyo for sheer bustling urban energy. While Tokyo citizens pride themselves on their sophisticated manners, Osakans are a down-to-earth lot who enjoy hearty food and rough humour. Its casual atmosphere and warm people make Osaka an worthwhile day trip if you're in the Kansai area.

Heading west from Osaka, the shinkansen and regular JR trains continue to Kōbe, Himeji, Hiroshima and on into the southern island of Kyūshū, with its wonderful hot springs and natural sights.

North and north-west of Tokyo are deep mountains and traditional villages to lure the adventurous traveller. Further north, the island of Hokkaidō has some of Japan's most unspoiled nature as well as the city of Sapporo, with its friendly locals and excellent seafood. For more information on these and many other places, see Lonely Planet's comprehensive *Japan* guidebook.

Glossary

aka-chōchin – red-lantern bar; working-class pub with snack food like *yakitori*
anime – animated films
annai-jo – information office
arubaito – from the German 'arbeit', meaning 'to work', adapted into Japanese to mean part-time work

bashi – bridge
basho – *sumō* wrestling tournament
bentō – boxed lunch or dinner, usually of rice, fish or meat and vegetables
bijutsukan – art museum
biru – building
bodhisattva – Sanskrit term; Buddhist monks who have postponed enlightenment in order to help others along the same path; *Kannon* and *Jizō* are popular examples
bonkei – art of miniaturising whole landscapes
bonsai – art of cultivating miniature trees by careful pruning of the branches and roots
bottle keep – system that allows you to buy a bottle of liquor and leave it at the bar for subsequent visits
bugaku – dance pieces played by court orchestras in ancient Japan
bunraku – classical puppet theatre using life-size puppets to enact dramas similar to those of *kabuki*
bushidō – literally, way of the warrior; esoteric ethos of the *samurai* class
butsu – Buddha statue (as in Kamakura's Daibutsu, or Great Buddha)

carp – see *koi*
chaniwa – tea garden
chanoyu – tea ceremony
chizu – map
chō – city area between a ward (*ku*) and *chōme* in size
chōme – city area of a few blocks

dai – great; large
daifuku – literally, great happiness; sticky rice cakes filled with red bean paste and eaten on festive occasions
daimyō – regional lords under the *shōgun*
deguchi – exit, as at a railway station
densha – train
depāto – department store
dōri – avenue or street (also *dōro*)

Edo – pre-Meiji Restoration name for Tokyo
eki – railway station
ekiben – *bentō* lunch boxes sold at railway stations
ema – small votive plaques hung in shrine sanctuaries as petitions to resident deities
en – garden (also *teien* or *niwa*)
enka – often referred to as Japanese country and western; ballads about love and loss that are popular with the older generation

fugu – poisonous blowfish or pufferfish, elevated to haute cuisine with a bite
furigana – Japanese syllabic script (*hiragana*) used as an aid to pronouncing *kanji*
furii kippu – all-day open ticket
futon – cushion-like mattress that is rolled up and stored away during the day
futsū – literally, ordinary; a basic stopping-at-all-stations train service

gagaku – music of the imperial court
gaijin – literally, outside person; the usual term for a foreigner; contracted form of *gaikokujin* (outside country person)
gawa – river
geisha – not a prostitute but a 'refined person'; a woman versed in the arts and other cultivated pursuits who entertains guests
genkan – foyer area where your shoes are exchanged for slippers before entering the interior of a building
geta – traditional wooden sandals
gochisō-sama – after-meals expression of thanks

haiden – hall of worship in a shrine
haiku – 17 syllable poem
hakubutsukan – museum
hanami – cherry blossom viewing
hanko – personal stamp or seal used to authenticate documents; carries the same weight as a signature in the west
hantō – peninsula
hashi – chopsticks
higashi – east
hiragana – phonetic syllabary used to write Japanese words
honden – main building of a shrine
hondō – main building of a temple

ichiba – market
ike – pond
ikebana – art of flower arranging
itadakimasu – literally, I will receive; before-meals expression
izakaya – Japanese version of a pub; beer, sake and lots of snacks available in a rustic, boisterous setting

ji – temple; see also *tera*
jikokuhyō – book of timetables; usually for trains
jinja – shrine (also *jingū* or *gū*)
jitensha – bicycle
Jizō – *bodhisattva* whose special charges are travellers and children

kabuki – form of Japanese theatre drawing on popular tales and characterised by elaborate costumes, stylised acting and the use of male actors for all roles
kaikan – literally, meeting hall; hotel-style accommodation sponsored by government
kaiseki – Japanese banquet cuisine in which every small detail of the repast are carefully controlled
kaisha – a company or firm
kaisoku – rapid train
kami – Shintō gods or spirits associated with natural phenomena
kamikaze – literally, wind of the gods; the typhoon that sank Kublai Khan's 13th century invasion fleet and the name adopted by Japanese suicide bombers in the waning days of WWII

kampai – 'cheers', as in a drinking toast
kan – building/hall
kana – the two Japanese syllabaries (*hiragana* and *katakana*) used to supplement *kanji* in the Japanese writing system
kanji – literally, Chinese writing; Chinese ideographic script used for writing Japanese
Kannon – Buddhist goddess of mercy (Guanyin in Chinese, Avalokiteshvara in Sanskrit and a camera company in Japanese)
karaoke – a famous export where revellers sing along to taped music minus the vocals
katakana – phonetic syllabary used to write foreign loan words, among other things
katamichi – one way ticket
katana – Japanese sword
keigo – honorific language used in formal situations and to show respect to elders
ken – prefecture
kendō – 'the way of the sword'; fencing technique based on the two-handed samurai sword
kimono – robe-like outer garment, traditionally made of bast fibres or fine silk
kissaten – coffee shop
kita – north
ko – lake
kōban – local police box; a common sight in urban Japan
kōen – park
koi – carp; considered a brave, tenacious fish; *koinobori* windsocks are flown in honour of sons whom it is hoped will inherit these virtues
kokuminshukusha – 'peoples' lodges'; an inexpensive form of accommodation found in rural Japan
kokutetsu – Japan Railways (JR); literally, national line
kotatsu – heated table with quilt or cover over it to keep the lower body warm in the winter
koto – 13-stringed zither-like instrument
kyūkō – ordinary express train (faster than *futsū*, stopping only at certain stations)

live house – nightclub or bar with performances of modern music by bands and solo performers

machi – town; the city area between a *ku* (ward) and *chōme* (a few blocks)

mama-san – Occupation-era term that has survived: a woman who manages a snack or hostess bar; otherwise a matronly proprietor of a bar

manga – Japanese comic books or magazines

matsuri – festival

meishi – business card; very important in Japan

miko – shrine maidens

mikoshi – portable shrines carried around by phalanxes of sweaty half-naked salarymen during festivals

minami – south

minshuku – Japanese equivalent of a B&B; family-run budget accommodation usually found in rural Japan

mizu-shōbai – see *water trade*

mochi – pounded rice made into cakes and eaten on festive occasions

mon – gate, as at a shrine or temple

morning service – *mōningu sābisu*; a light breakfast served by coffee shops until around 10 am; usually a doorstep slice of bread, a boiled egg, and jam and butter

Nihon or **Nippon** – Japanese word for Japan; literally, Source of the Sun

ningyō – Japanese doll

niō – temple guardians

nishi – west

nō – classical Japanese mask drama performed on a bare stage

nomiya – traditional Japanese pub; see also *izakaya*

noren – door curtain for restaurants, usually with the name of the establishment

noriba – bus stop/boarding point

o- – prefix used to show respect, eg o-tōsan (father); see also *san*

obi – sash or belt worn with *kimono*

o-cha – Japanese tea

ofuku – return ticket

o-furo – traditional Japanese bath

OL – common term which stands for office lady; female employee of a large firm; usually a clerical worker

o-miyage – souvenir; an obligatory purchase on any trip for Japanese

onsen – mineral hot spring with bathing areas and accommodation

origami – art of paper folding

pachinko – vertical pinball game which is a Japanese craze (estimated to take in ¥6 trillion a year) and a major source of tax evasion, yakuza funds and noise

pink salon – seedy hostess bars; pink is the Japanese equivalent of blue, as in pornography and the like

prepaid card – *puriipeido kādo*; magnetically coded card for a given sum of money which can then be spent on telephone calls, railway tickets and so on

rakugo – performances of stand-up comedy or long tales; a traditional art that is dying out

robotayaki – *yakitori* and the like, served in a boisterous, homey, rustic atmosphere; see also *izakaya*

romaji – roman script, as used in English

ryokan – traditional Japanese inn

sakura – cherry blossoms

salaryman – male employee of a large firm

sama – even more respectful than *san* (see below)

samurai – Japan's traditional warrior class; largely employed as Customs officials at Narita airport nowadays

san – a respectful suffix applied to personal names; similar to Mr, Mrs or Ms, but more widely used

sanshō – Japanese three-spice powder

sembei – soy-flavoured crispy rice crackers often sold in tourist areas

sen – line, usually railway line

sensei – teacher, but also anyone worthy of respect

sentō – public bath

setto – set meal; see also *teishoku*

shakuhachi – wooden flute-like instrument

shamisen – three-stringed banjo-like instrument

shi – city

shichimi – Japanese seven-spice powder

shin – new, as in *shinkansen* (new trunk line)

shinjinrui – literally, new person type; basically Japanese yuppies or young Japanese in general
shinkansen – bullet train
Shitamachi – low-lying plebeian quarters of old Edo, centred around Ueno and Asakusa
shodō – Japanese calligraphy; literally, the way of writing
shōgun – military ruler of pre-Meiji Japan
shokudō – Japanese-style cafeteria/cheap restaurant
soba – traditional buckwheat noodles
sumi-e – black ink-brush paintings
sumō – Shintō-derived sport where two immovable objects in ritual diapers collide in a ring

tabi – split-toed socks used when wearing *geta*
tako – traditional Japanese kite
tanka – poem of 32 syllables
tatami – tightly woven floor matting on which shoes should not be worn
teiki-ken – discount commuter tickets between two designated stops
teishoku – a set meal in a restaurant (usually lunch)
tera – temple (also *o-tera*, *dera* and *ji*)
to – metropolis, as in Tokyo-to
tokkyū – limited express train; faster than ordinary express *(kyūkō)*
torii – entrance gate to a Shintō shrine
tsunami – huge 'tidal' waves caused by an earthquake

ukiyo-e – wood-block prints; literally, pictures of the floating world
uyoku – right-wing groups that yearn for the good old imperial days

wafuku – Japanese-style clothing
waka – 31 syllable poem
warikan – custom of sharing the bill (among good friends)
washi – Japanese paper
water trade – the world of bars, entertainment and sex for sale

yakitori – grilled chicken on a stick
yakuza – Japanese mafia
Yamanote – historically refers to the high city region of old Edo
yamato – a term of much debated origins that refers to the Japanese world, particularly in contrast to things Chinese
yatai – festival floats
yōfuku – western-style clothing
yukata – like a dressing gown, worn for lounging after a bath; standard issue at ryokan and some budget business hotels

ACRONYMS
IDC – International Digital Communication
ITJ – International Telecom Japan
JETRO – Japan External Trade Organization
JNTO – Japan National Tourist Organization
JR – Japan Railways
JTB – Japan Travel Bureau
KDD – Kokusai Denshin Denwa
MIPRO – Manufactured Imports Promotion Organization
MITI – Ministry of International Trade & Industry
N'EX – Narita Express
NHK – Japan Broadcasting Corporation
NTT – Nippon Telegraph & Telephone Corporation
TCAT – Tokyo City Air Terminal
TIC – Tourist Information Center
YCAT – Yokohama City Air Terminal

富士山 富士山 富士山 富士山 富士山 富士
富士山 富士山 富士山 富士山 富士山 富士
富士山 富士山 富士山 富士山 富士山 富士

Index

Maps

Text

Tokyo

MAP 1

MAP 2

To
Tokyo Dome
(Big Egg)

Namboku Line

Suidōbashi Ⓜ

Iidabashi Ⓜ

Iidabashi

3

Iidabashi Ⓜ

Suidōbashi

Sotobori-dōri

Chūō & Sōbu Lines

Toei Line

Sarugakuchō

2

Nihon
University

Hakusan-dōri

4

Kudan-Kita

Bookshop
Neighbourhood

5
Meiji
Universit

Jimbōchō Ⓜ

36 ● 34 ● 32 ● 31

Jimbōchō Ⓜ

35 ☑ ☑33

Yasukuni-dōri

Ⓜ Kudanshita

Jimbōchō

Toei Shinjuku Line

40
Ⓐ

37

39

Kiyomizu Moat

38

Kitanomaru-kōen
Park

Sanbanchō

45

Hanzōmon Line

41

43

47

Ⓜ Takebashi

44

48

46

To Hanzōmon
Station

Fukiage
Imperial
Gardens

Area not open
to public

Imperial Palace
East Garden
(Higashi Gyoen)

42

78 ●

77

Area not open
to public

Shinjuku-dōri

Hanzo Moat

Uchibori-dōri

Sakurada
Moat

Shimo-dōkan
Moat

79

Wadak
Squar

Wadak
Squar

Shinjuku-dōri

83

80

Area not open
to public

Kami-dōkan
Moat

Imperial Palace
Outer Garden

Nijūbashi-ma

82

MAP 3

81 ●

Imperial Palace
Plaza

MAP 2

PLACES TO STAY

3 Tokyo International Youth
  Hostel
  東京国際湯ユース
  ホステル
4 YMCA Asia Youth Center
  ＹＭＣＡアジア青少年
  センター
5 Hilltop Hotel
  山の上ホテル
11 Akihabara Washington
  Hotel
  秋葉原ワシントン
  ホテル
15 New Central Hotel
  ニューセントラル
  ホテル
16 Central Hotel
  セントラルホテル
17 Grand Central Hotel
  グランドセントラル
  ホテル
21 Tokyo Green Hotel
  Awajichō
  東京グリーンホテル
23 Hotel New Kanda
  ホテルニュー神田
25 Hotel Juraku
  ホテルじゅらく
30 Tokyo Family Hotel
  東京ファミリーホテル
62 Yaesu Terminal Hotel
  八重洲ターミナル
  ホテル
70 Tokyo Station Hotel
  東京ステーション
  ホテル
73 Hotel Kokusai Kankō
  ホテル国際観光
75 Marunouchi Hotel
  丸ノ内ホテル
76 Palace Hotel
  パレスホテル

PLACES TO EAT

6 Pronto Coffee
  プロントコーヒー
14 Doutor Coffee
  ドトールコーヒー
18 Taiwan Yatai
  台湾屋台

19 Botan
  ぼたん
20 Ichi-no-chaya
  一ノ茶屋
22 Kanda Yabu Soba
  神田やぶそば
29 Hisago
  ひさご
35 Mandala
  マンダラ
36 Muang Thai Nabe; Muito
  Bom; Menam no Hotori
  ムアンタイなべ；
  ムイトボン
63 Nanban-tei
  南蛮亭
64 Banya
  番屋

OTHER

1 Institute Franco-Japanais
  du Tokyo
  日仏学院
2 British Council
7 Yushima Seidō
  湯島聖堂
8 LOAX Electronics Store
  ラオックス電化店
9 Akihabara Eki-mae
  Commons
  秋葉原駅前広場
10 Akihabara Department
  Store
  秋葉原デパート
12 Mansei-bashi Bridge
  万世橋
13 Transportation Museum
  交通博物館
24 Kanda Post Office
  神田郵便局
26 Hitachi Building
  日立製作所
27 Nikolai Cathedral
  ニコライ堂
28 Mitsui Kaijō Insurance
  Building
  三井海上ビル
31 Tuttle Bookshop
  タトル書店
32 Issei-dō Bookshop
  一誠堂書店

33 Jimbōchō Post Office
  神保町郵便局
34 Wonderland Books
  ワンダーランドブック
37 Tayasu-mon Gate
  田安門
38 Nihon Budōkan Hall
  日本武道館
39 India Embassy
  インド大使館
40 Yasukuni-jinja Shrine
  靖国神社
41 Ireland Embassy
  アイルランド大使館
42 Britain Embassy
  イギリス大使館
43 Chidorigafuchi Water Park
  千鳥ヶ淵水上公園
44 Craft Museum
  工芸館
45 Science Museum
  科学技術館
46 Kitahanebashi Bridge/Gate
  北桔橋門
47 Tokyo National Museum of
  Modern Art
  国立近代美術館
48 Hirakawa-mon Gate
  平川門
49 Tokyo Immigration Bureau
  東京入国管理局
50 Federation of Economic
  Organisations
  経団連
51 Nippon Keizai Shimbun
  (Nikkei) Head Office
  日本経済新聞
52 Tokyo International Post
  Office
  東京国際郵便局
53 Bank of Japan
  日本銀行
54 Bank of Tokyo-Mitsubishi
  東京三菱銀行
55 Mitsukoshi Department
  Store
  三越百貨店
56 Nihombashi Bridge
  日本橋

CHRIS ROWTHORN

Kanda's Akihabara district is the technophile's version of heaven – it's the biggest real-time array of electro-gadgetry on the planet. Myriad stalls specialising in obscure software, cyber toys and peripherals spill onto the streets leading to massive discount shops, where everything from Global Positioning Systems (GPS) customised for Tokyo travellers to corporate televisual networks is available under one roof.

MAP 3

MAP 2

Imperial Plaza

41

40

42

Tōkaidō & Other
South-bound Lines

Keihin Line

Kyōbashi

Kyōbashi-kōen
Park

Hatchōbori

H a t c h ō b o r i

Tōkyō

South-bound Shinkansen

Yamanote & Keihin Tōhoku Lines

Hibiya

Yūrakuchō

36

37

38

39

Ginza-Sakura-dōri

43

Shuto Expressway Loop Line

48 47

45

44

Hibiya Park
Building

Hibiya

49

50

Yūrakuchō

46

Ginza-Ichōme

55

56

Ginza

57

58

59 60

Ginza Marume-dōri

65

61

Shinfumicho

K y ō b a s h i

Yūrakuchō

74

75

77

76

73

78

79 80

81

82

83

84

85

86 87

88 89

Ginza

Ginza

Azuma-dōri

Matsuya-dōri

Higashi Ginza

93

94

95

64

62

63

Shuto Expressway No 1

Tsukiji

chisaiwaichō

113

114

112

115

110

111

109

Sony-dōri

Namiki-dōri

Suzuran-dōri

Chūō-dōri

108

90

91

92

Miyuki-dōri

96

97

98

99

126

127

122

123

124

116

117

121 120

118

119

125

Shimbashi

106

107

Higashi Ginza

Harumi-dōri

100

Tsukiji

Tsukiji
Hongan-ji
Temple

Shimbashi

Shimbashi

Hamabashi-dōri

Nishi-Gōbangai-dōri

Sukiyabashi-dōri

Sotobori-dōri

Ginza

Sotobori-dōri

Ginza Sakura-dōri

Harada-ōri

51

52

53 54

70

72

71

67

68

69

66

Kyōbashi

Takarachō

Hatchōbori

Shuto Expressway Loop Line

Tōkaidō & Other
South-bound Lines

Shimbashi

Shidome

105

103

104

Tsukiji
External
Market

101

102

Tsukiji
Produce
Market

Tsukiji Central
Fish Market

Kachidōki-bashi
Bridge

Hama Rikyū Detached
Palace Garden

Tsukiji-gawa River

Water
Bus
Pier

Sumida-gawa River

To Harumi &
Tōkyō International
Trade Center

Tsukiji-gawa
River Gate

Yūrakuchō Line

Shidome

Hamamatsuchō

Kyū-Shibarikyū
Garden

Tōkyō Monorail

To Shiba &
Shinagawa

Yamanote & Keihin Tōhoku

Shinkansen Lines

K a c h i d ō k i

MAP 4

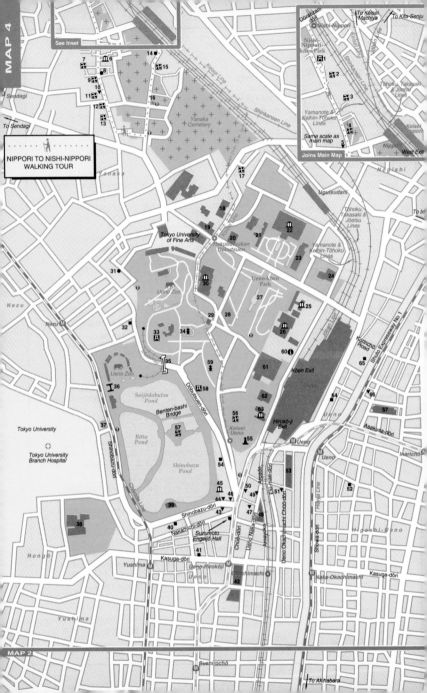

See Inset

7
6
8
14
15
9
10
11
12
13
16

Keisei Line

Yanaka Cemetery

Shinkansen Line

To Sendagi

Sendagi

NIPPORI TO NISHI-NIPPORI
WALKING TOUR

Yanaka

Dōkanzan-dōri
Nishi-Nippori
Nishi-Nippori-kōen Park
1
2
3
Yamanote &
Keihin-Tōhoku
Lines
4
Same scale as
main map
Joins Main Map

To Keisei
Machiya
To Kita-Senju

Keisei Line
Shinkansen Line

Tōhoku, Takasaki
& Jōetsu
Lines

Keisei
Nippori

West Exit

Negishi

17

Uguisudani

To Iri

Tōhoku,
Takasaki &
Jōetsu
Lines

18
19
20
21
22
23
24

Tokyo University
of Fine Arts

Hakubutsukan-
Dōbutsuen

Ueno-kōen
Park

Yamanote &
Keihin-Tōhoku
Lines

31
30
27
25
26
60

Ueno Zoo

Nezu

32
33
34
28
29

Nezu

35
59
51
62
63
55
56

Ueno Zoo

36

Suijōdōbutsu
Pond

58

Benten-bashi
Bridge

37

Bōto
Pond

57

Shinobazu
Pond

Tokyo University

Tokyo University
Branch Hospital

Chiyoda Line

Shinobazu-dōri

39
45
44
46

38

40
43

Nakamachi-dōri

Surumoto
Engeijō Hall

41

Kasuga-dōri

Yushima

Ueno-Hirokōji

42

Kōen Exit

Ueno

Hirokō-ji
Exit

53
52

Asakusa-dōri

Inaricho

Ueno

Ueno

Kōhinata
Road
Shuto Expressway No 1

65
64
66
67

Jōban Line

Keisei
Ueno

Ekimae-dōri
Arcade
Ueno Naka-dōri
Chūō-dōri
Ameyoko
Ueno Okachimachi Chūō-dōri

50
49
51
47
48

Ueno

Hibiya Line

Shōwa-dōri

Higashi-Ueno

Kasuga-dōri

Naka-Okachimachi

Naka-Okachimachi

Yushima

Okachimachi

Hongō

Yushima

54

Suehirocho

To Akihabara

MAP 2

continued on next page

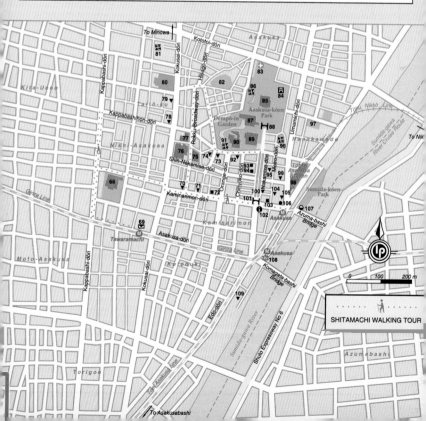

continued from previous page

78 Asakusa Imahan
浅草今半
79 Akiyoshi Yakitori
秋吉やきとり
92 Daikokuya
大黒屋
95 Capricciosa
カプリオーサ
99 McDonald's
100 Tonkyu
とんきゅ
104 Real Italian Gelato
105 K F C
109 Komagata Dōjō
駒形どじょう

OTHER

1 Suwa-jinja Shrine
諏訪神社
2 Senkō-ji Temple
浄光寺
3 Yōfuku-ji Temple
養福寺
4 Keiō-ji Temple
経王寺
6 Asakura Chōso Museum
朝倉彫塑館
7 Ryūsen-ji Temple
龍泉寺
8 Sandara Kōgei Basket
Store
さんだら工芸屋
9 Kaizō-in Temple
海蔵院
11 Kannon-ji Temple
観音寺
12 Chōan-ji Temple
長安寺
13 Jōzai-ji Temple
常在寺
15 Tenno-ji Temple
天王寺
16 Police Box
17 Kanei-ji Temple
寛永寺
18 National Diet Branch
Library/Ueno Library
国立国会図書館
19 Tokyo National Cultural
Property Research Center
東京国立文化財研究所
20 Gallery of Horyū-ji Treasures
法隆寺宝物館
21 Hyōkeikan Hall
表慶館

22 Tokyo National Museum
東京国立博物館
23 Gallery of Eastern Antiquities
東洋館
24 Rinnō-ji Temple
輪王寺
25 National Science Museum
国立科学博物館
26 National Museum of
Western Art
国立西洋美術館
27 Great Fountain
28 Children's Playground
こども広場
29 Ueno Zoo Main Entrance
上野動物園表門
30 Tokyo Metropolitan
Museum of Art
東京都美術館
31 Rokuryū Onsen
六竜温泉
33 Tōshō-gū Shrine
上野東照宮
34 Five Storey Pagoda
35 Aesop-bashi Bridge
いそっぷ橋
36 Hanazonomon Gate
花園門
38 Tokyo Regional Court
東京地方裁判所
39 Suijō Music Hall
水上音楽堂
42 Matsuzakaya Department
Store
松坂屋百貨店
45 Shitamachi History Museum
下町風俗資料館
48 Ameyoko Centre Building
アメ横センタービル
53 Marui Department Store
丸井百貨店
55 Saigō Takamori Statue
西郷隆盛像
56 Kiyōmizu Kannon-dō Temple
清水観音堂
57 Benten-dō Temple (Ueno)
弁天堂
58 Gojō-jinja Shrine
五條神社
59 Daibutsu Pagoda
大仏パゴタ
60 Ueno Park Information
上野公園案内所
61 Tokyo Metropolitan
Festival Hall
東京文化会館

62 Japan Art Academy
日本芸術院会館
63 Ueno-no-mori Art Museum
上野の森美術館
67 Taitō-ku Ward Office
台東区役所
68 Tokyo Hongan-ji Temple
東京本願寺
69 Asakusa Post Office
浅草郵便局
75 Rox 3 Building
ロックス3ビル
76 Rox Building
ロックスビル
77 Asakusa Engei Hall
浅草演芸ホール
81 Banryū-ji Temple
萬隆寺
82 Hanayashiki Amusement
Park
花やしき遊園地
83 Sensō-ji Hospital
浅草寺病院
84 Asakusa-jinja Shrine
浅草神社
85 Sensō-ji Temple
浅草寺
86 Asakusa Eikō-dō Temple
浅草寺影向堂
87 Five Storey Pagoda
88 Hōzō-mon Gate
宝蔵門
89 Sensō-ji Kindergarten
浅草寺幼稚園
90 Dempō-in Temple
伝法寺
91 Chingo-dō Temple
鎮護寺
96 Benten-dō Temple
弁天堂
97 Hanakawado-kōen Park
花川戸公園
98 Matsuya Department Store
松屋百貨店
101 Kaminari-mon Gate
雷門
102 Tourist Information Center
観光案内センター
106 Kamiya
神谷
107 Sumida-gawa River Cruise
(Suijō Bus) Pier
隅田川水上バス発着所
108 Komagata-kōen Park
駒形公園

MARTIN MOOS

Cruise boats offer glimpses of Asakusa's old Edo culture along the Sumida-gawa River.

MAP 5

PLACES TO STAY

2 Kimi Ryokan
貴美旅館

4 Hotel Castle
ホテルキャッスル

6 Ikebukuro Royal Hotel
池袋ロイヤルホテル

9 Hotel Star Plaza Ikebukuro
ホテルスタープラザ
池袋

25 Hotel Metropolitan
ホテルメトロポリタン

30 Business Hotel Ikebukuro
Park
ビジネスホテル池袋
パーク

38 Hotel Sun City Ikebukuro
ホテルサンシティ池袋

41 Hotel Sunroute Ikebukuro
ホテルサンルート池袋

47 Hotel Grand City
ホテルグランド
シティー

48 Ark Hotel
アークホテル

51 Sun City Prince Hotel
サンシャインシティ
プリンスホテル

PLACES TO EAT

1 Ryūjō
龍城

3 Taiwan Hsiao Tiao
台湾小調

8 Sushi Kazu
寿司和

10 Sasashu
笹周

11 Subway
サブウェイ

12 Doutor Coffee
ドトールコーヒー

16 Mekong
メコン

17 Capricciosa
カプリチョーサ

18 Akiyoshi
秋吉

19 Malaychan
マレーチャン

20 Chez Kibeau
シェ・キーボウ

21 Tonbo
とんぼ

24 Yōrōnotaki
養老乃瀧

32 Beijing-tei
北京亭

33 McDonald's
マクドナルド

36 Toneria
舎人庵

37 Doutor Coffee
ドトールコーヒー

44 Komazushi
こま寿司

45 Oriental Kitchen
オリエンタルキッチン

53 McDonald's
マクドナルド

54 Cambodia
カンボジア

55 Sumika Rāmen
純香ラーメン

57 KFC
ケンタッキーフライド
チキン

59 McDonald's
マクドナルド

60 Yeti
イエティ

61 Kao Thai
カオ・タイ

63 Wendy's
ウエンディーズ

64 Capricciosa
カプリチョーサ

OTHER

5 Kimi Information Center
貴美インフォメー
ションセンター

7 Ikebukuro Post Office
池袋郵便局

13 Police
警察署

14 Marui Department Store
丸井デパート

15 Virgin Megastore
バージンメガストア

22 Tokyo Metropolitan Art
Space
東京芸術劇場

23 The Dubliners
ザ・ダブリナーズ

26 Metropolitan Plaza
メトロポリタンプラザ

27 Sezon Art Museum
セゾン美術館

28 Seibu Department Store
西武百貨店

29 Tōbu Department Store
東武百貨店

31 Marui Field Sports Store
丸井フィールド
スポーツ館

34 Persona
ペルソナ

35 Cinema Rosa
シネマロサ

39 Parco Department Store
パルコ

40 Bic Camera (main store)
ビックカメラ本店

42 Mitsukoshi Department
Store
三越百貨店

43 Bic Camera
ビッグカメラ

46 Toshima-ku Ward Office
豊島区役所

49 Tōkyū Hands
東急ハンズ

50 Toyota Amlux
トヨタアムラックス

52 Toshima Post Office
豊島郵便局

56 Biblos Bookshop
洋書ビブロス

58 Daimaru Peacock
Department Store
大丸ピーコック

62 Mickey House
ミッキーハウス

65 Billy Barew's Beer Bar
ビリー・バリューズ・
ビア・バー

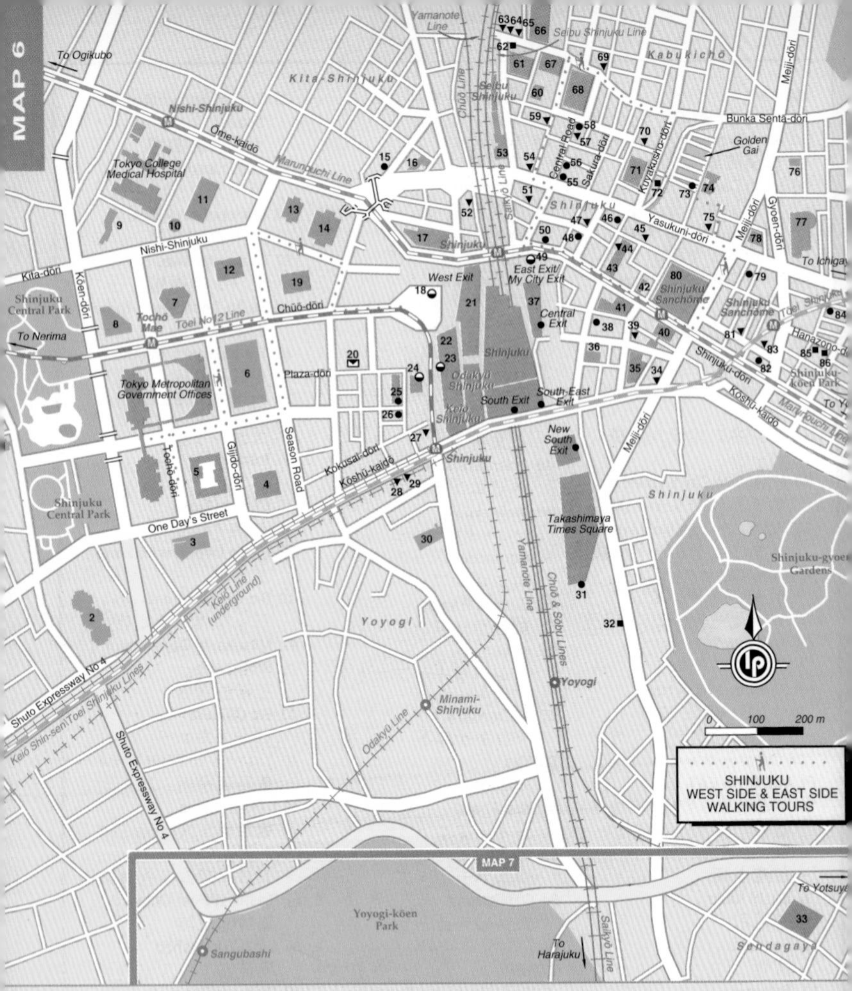

MAP 6

Map labels:

To Ogikubo · Kita-Shinjuku · Yamanote Line · Seibu Shinjuku Line · Kabukichō · Meiji-dōri · Bunka Sentā-dōri · Golden Gai · Nishi-Shinjuku · Seibu Shinjuku Line · Ōme-kaidō · Marunouchi Line · Central Road · Shinjuku · Kōshū-dōri · Yasukuni-dōri · To Ichiga · Tokyo College Medical Hospital · Nishi-Shinjuku · Kita-dōri · Kōen-dōri · To Nerima · Shinjuku Central Park · Tōchō Mae · Tōei No 2 Line · Chūō-dōri · West Exit · Shinjuku · Plaza-dōri · Tokyo Metropolitan Government Offices · Odakyū Shinjuku · Shinjuku · East Exit/My City Exit · Shinjuku-Sanchōme · Shinjuku-Sanchōme · Shinjuku-gyoen · Hana-zono · Central Exit · South Exit · South-East Exit · Shinjuku-dōri · Tōchō-dōri · Shinjuku Central Park · Kōdō-dōri · Season Road · Kōkūsai-dōri · Kōshū-kaidō · Shinjuku · New South Exit · Kōshū-kaidō · To Tokyo · One Day's Street · Kōei Line (underground) · Takashimaya Times Square · Shinjuku · Shinjuku-gyoen Garden · Shutō Expressway No 4 · Yoyogi · Chūō & Sōbu Lines · LP · Shutō Expressway No 4 · Keiō Shin-sen/Tōei Line · Yoyogi · Minami-Shinjuku · Odakyū Line · Yamanote Line · Shinjuku · 0 100 200 m · SHINJUKU WEST SIDE & EAST SIDE WALKING TOURS · MAP 7 · To Yotsuya · Yoyogi-kōen Park · To Hanajuku · Shibuya Line · Sendagaya · Sangubashi

MAP 6
PLACES TO STAY

1 Shinjuku New City Hotel
新宿ニューシティー
ホテル

2 Park Hyatt Tokyo; New York
Grill/Bar; Sky Bar
パークハイアット
東京；ニューヨーク
グリル／バー；
スカイバー

3 Shinjuku Washington Hotel
新宿ワシントンホテル

6 Keio Plaza Intercontinental;
Aurora Lounge; New York Bar
京王プラザインター
コンチネンタル；
オーロララウンジ；
ニューヨークバー

8 Hotel Century Hyatt
ホテルセンチュリー
ハイアット

9 Tokyo Hilton International
東京ヒルトンインター
ナショナルホテル

16 Star Hotel Tokyo
スターホテル東京

30 Hotel Sun Route Tokyo
ホテルサンルート東京

32 Shinjuku Park Hotel
新宿パークホテル

36 Central Hotel
セントラルホテル

53 Shinjuku Prince Hotel
新宿プリンスホテル

62 Green Plaza Shinjuku
グリーンプラザ新宿

72 Shinjuku-ku Capsule Hotel
新宿カプセルホテル

76 Hotel Sun Light Shinjuku
ホテルサンライト新宿

85 City Hotel Lornstar
シティーホテル
ロンスター
86 Winning Inn Shinjuku
ウィニングイン新宿

PLACES TO EAT
27 Laobian Gyozakan
老辺餃子館
28 Rose de Sahara
ローズデサハラ
29 Court Lodge
34 Daikokuya
大黒屋
39 Tsunahachi Tsunohazuan
つな八
44 El Borracho
エルブラッチョ
45 Irohanihoheto
いろにほへと
47 Kurumaya
車屋
51 Ibuki
いぶき
52 Omoide Yokochō Street
思い出横丁
54 Suzuya
すずや
57 Tenkaippin
天下一品
59 Doutor Coffee
63 Beijing
北京
64 Shinjuku Negishi
新宿ねぎし
65 Tainan Taami
台南担仔麺
69 Tokyo Kaisen Ichiba
東京海鮮市場
70 Yatai Mura
屋台村
75 Tokyo Dai Hanten
東京大飯店
81 Keika Kumamoto Rāmen
桂花熊本ラーメン
83 Istanbul
イスタンブール

OTHER
4 KDD Building
ＫＤＤビル
5 Shinjuku NS Building
新宿ＮＳビル
7 Shinjuku Sumitomo Building
新宿住友ビル
10 Island Hall
アイスランドホール

11 Shinjuku Island Tower
新宿アイスランド
タワー
12 Mitsui Building
三井ビル
13 Shinjuku Nomura Building
新宿野村ビル
14 Yasuda Kasai Building
安田火災ビル
15 T Zone Computers
ティゾーン
コンピューター
17 Odakyū Department Store
小田急百貨店
18 Shinjuku Main City Bus Stop
新宿西口バス
ターミナル
19 Shinjuku Center Building
新宿センタービル
20 Shinjuku Main Post Office
新宿中央郵便局
21 Odakyū Department Store
(main store)
小田急百貨店
22 Keiō Department Store
京王百貨店
23 Narita Limousine Bus Stop
成田リムジンバス
乗り場
24 Shinjuku Highway Bus
Terminal; Haneda
Limousine Bus Stop
新宿高速バス
ターミナル;羽田
リムジンバス乗り場
25 Yodobashi Camera
ヨドバシカメラ
26 Sakuraya Camera
サクラヤカメラ
31 Kinokuniya Bookshop
紀伊国屋書店
33 National Nō Theatre
国立能学堂
35 Mitsukoshi Department
Store (main store)
三越百貨店（本店）
37 My City
マイシティー
38 The Dubliners Irish Pub
ザダブリナーズ
40 Marui Fashion A Building;
Virgin Megastore
丸井ファッション
館Ａ館；バージンメガ
ストアー
41 Mitsukoshi Department
Store (south building)
三越百貨店

42 Sakuraya Camera
サクラヤカメラ
43 Kinokuniya Bookshop
(main store)
紀伊国屋書店
46 Top's Bar
48 Kirin City
キリンシティー
49 Hato Bus Stop
はとバス乗り場
50 Studio Alta
スタジオアルタ
55 No 1 Travel
ナンバーワントラベル
56 Pole Star Building;
Catalyst; Garam
ポールスタービル；
カタリスト；ガラム
58 Blue; Kingston Club
ブルー；
キングストンクラブ
60 Joy Cinemas
ジョイシネマ
61 Shinjuku Tokyū Bunka
Kaikan Building
新宿東急文化会館
66 Tokyo Kenkō Plaza Hygia
Building; LL Bean
東京康健プラザ
ハイジヤ
67 Grand Odeon Building;
Cinemas; Liquid Room
グランドオデンビル
シネマ；リキッド
ルーム
68 Shinjuku Koma Theatre; Code
新宿コマ劇場
71 Shinjuku Ward Office
新宿区役所
73 Bon's
74 Hanazono-jinja Shrine
花園神社
77 Park City Isetan 1
Department Store
パークシティー
伊勢丹１百貨店
78 Marui Interior Building
丸井インテリアビル
79 Yamagoya
山小屋
80 Isetan Department Store;
Isetan Museum
伊勢丹百貨店；
伊勢丹美術館
82 Rolling Stone
ローリングストーン
84 Arty Farty
アーティファーティ

MAP 7

MAP 6

North Gate

Meiji-jingū Treasure Museum

1

Olympic Memorial Building

Meiji-jingū Shrine

Yoyogi-kōen Park

South Pond

Meiji-jingū Kaikan Building

Shrine Office

Southern Rest House

To Shinjuku

Sendagaya

Meiji-dōri

Yamanote Line

Sōbu Line

Meiji P.

13

3

Jingūmae

34

Kitan-dōri

Harajuku

2
Takeshita-dōri

Meiji-jingūmae

4
5 6 7
11
12

8
9

10

14

16
17 18
15

Omote-sandō

19

20
21

33

31

Jingūmae

29

22

30

Omote-sandō

National Gymnasium

To Yoyogi

Jinnan

Kōen-dōri

Inokashira-dōri

NHK Studio Park Building

Jingū-dōri-kōen Park

Jingūmae

23

28
27

25

26

24

Kamiyamachō

117

123
122

121

120

124

125

119
118

126

Shibuya

Mitake-kōen Park

Children's Castle

Hanzōmon Line

Ginza Line

Dōgenzakachō

127

128

Shōtō

133
134 135

132

139

136

137

Seibu-zaka

Jingū-dōri

Meiji-dōri

Aoyama-dōri

131

143
142
140
141

116

175

174

112

129
130

144
145 146

147

149

148

150

Dōgenzaka

Dōgen-zaka-dōri

Miyamasu-zaka-dōri

Shibuya

Hachikō Shibuya Exit

East Exit

113

Shuto Expressway No 3

Sakae-dōri

Shibuya

Keiō Inokashira Line

To Shimokitazawa (underground)

151

153

154

Tōkyū Shibuya

Shibuya

South Exit

152

155
156 157

158

159

Tamagawa-dōri

Shuto Expressway No 3

Yamanote Line

Saikyō Line

Tōkyū Tōyoko Line

Shibuya-gawa River

Shibuya

To Ebisu & Shinagawa

To Daikanyama

Inset (enlargement, top)

Mikawadai-kōen Park

Roppongi

To Akasaka
Detached
Palace

Roppongi-nishi-kōen Park

Roppongi-dōri

Roppongi
Crossing

Gaien-higashi-dōri

Hibiya Line

Roppongi Cemetery

Roi
Building

To
Axis
Building

0   100   200 m

54
53 55
56
51
52 57 58
60 59
61 70 73
69 72 74 75
71 76 77
68
62 65 67 88 89
66 85 90
64 84 86 87
63 78 80 83
79 81
82

43

42

44
45
46
47

Main map

To Akasaka
Detached
Palace

Renter-bori Moat

Hitotsugi-dōri

Aoyama-dōri

Akasaka

Akasaka

MAP 3

Meiji-jingū
Baseball
Diamond

Prince Chichibu
Memorial
Rugby Stadium

Jingū Gaien
Gardens

41

Aoyama
Ichōme 39

Akasaka

Tokyo
Broadcasting
Station (TBS)

Akasaka-dōri

Hanzomon Line

Ginza Line

Gaien-mae

38

37
36

Gaien-nishi-dōri

Gaien-higashi-dōri

40

Aoyama
Cemetery

Nōgizaka

50 49

48

Roppongi

To
Ark Hills

Chiyoda Line

Minami-Aoyama

Aoyama
Cemetery

Aoyama-kōen
Park

Roppongi

109

106 103

Roppongi

100

Roppongi-dōri

See Enlargement

105

104 102

101

Roppongi-dōri

10

107

Shuto Expressway No 3

99

TV Asahi

Roppongi

108

98

Nishi-Azabu
Crossing

Nishi-Azabu

Moto-Azabu

91

97 96

92

93

95

94

To Hiroo

0   100   200 m

MAP 7

PLACES TO STAY
1 Yoyogi Youth Hostel
代々木ユース
ホステル
40 Asia Center of Japan
アジア会館
42 Hotel New Ōtani
ホテルニュウ
オータニ
46 Capsule Hotel Fontaine
Akasaka
カプセルホテル
フォーンテーン赤坂
57 Hotel Ibis
ホテルアイビス
91 International House of
Japan
国際文化会館
112 Shanpia Hotel Aoyama
シャンピアホテル
青山
115 Shibuya Business Hotel
渋谷ビジネスホテル
116 Shibuya Tōkyū Inn
渋谷東急イン
124 Shinjuku Tōbu Hotel
新宿東武ホテル
159 Hotel Sun Route Shibuya
ホテルサンルート
渋谷

PLACES TO EAT
2 McDonald's
4 Doutor Coffee
5 Stage Y2
ステージＹ２
8 Studio V
スタジオＶ
12 Son of the Dragon
(Ryunoko)
龍子
13 Ghee
ギー
14 Tacos Del Amigo
タコス・デル・アミゴ
16 Cafe de Rope
カフェ・ド・ロペ
19 Bamboo
バンブー
20 Apetito
アペティート
21 Brasserie Flo
ＦＬＯ表参道
23 Aux Sept Bonheurs
オー・セ・ボヌール
24 Las Chicas
ラス・チカス

25 Kinokuniya International
Supermarket
紀ノ国屋
27 Pita Shop Atena
ピタショップアテナ
29 Cafe des Pres
カフェ・デ・プレ
30 Subway
33 L'Amphore
アンフォーレ
36 Tony Roma's;
Doutor Coffee
44 Ten-Ichi
天一
45 Fisherman's Wharf
47 Tendon Tenya
49 Inakaya
田舎屋
50 Gokoku
五穀
54 Havana Cafe
ハバナカフェ
58 Shōjikiya
正直屋
64 Moti
モティ
68 Almond
アーモンド
69 Johnny Rockets; Cerveza
ジョニーロケッツ；
セルベザ
70 Tainan Taami
台南担仔麺
76 Seryna
瀬里奈
77 Moti Darbar
モティダールバリ
78 Paco's Cafe
パコス・カフェ
80 McDonald's
81 Tony Roma's;
Hard Rock Cafe
トニーロマーズ；
ハードロックカフェ
82 Spago; Fukuzushi
スパゴ；福寿司
84 Bellini's Pizza Kitchen
ベリーニズピザ
キッチン
86 Bikkuri Sushi
びっくり寿司
87 Hamburger Inn
ハンバーガーイン
96 Bistro de la Cite
ビストロ・ド・ラ・
シテ
97 Casa Monnon
カサ・モンノン

99 Maenam
メナム
100 Bengawan Solo
ブンガワンソロ
103 El Mocambo
エル・モカンボ
104 Hokkaien
北海園
105 Monsoon Cafe
モンスーンカフェ
106 Rice Terrace
ライステラス
108 Bindi
ビンデ
119 Tenmi
天味
122 Charlie House
141 Samrat
サムラート
144 Sakana-tei
酒菜亭
145 Bougainvillea
ブーゲンビリア
146 Reikyō
麗郷
151 Tainan Taami
台南担仔麺
154 Shizenkan
自然館
156 Kanitipur
カンティプール
157 Court Lodge
158 Akiyoshi
秋吉

OTHER
3 Tōgo-jinja Shrine
東郷神社
6 Do! Family Art Museum
ドゥファミリー
美術館
7 Ota Memorial Art Museum
大田記念美術館
9 Chicago Thrift Shop
シカゴスリフト
ショップ
10 Condomania
コンドーマニア
11 Laforet Building
ラフォーレビル
15 Oh God; Zest
17 Vivre 21
ビブレ２１
18 Oriental Bazaar
オリエンタル
バザール

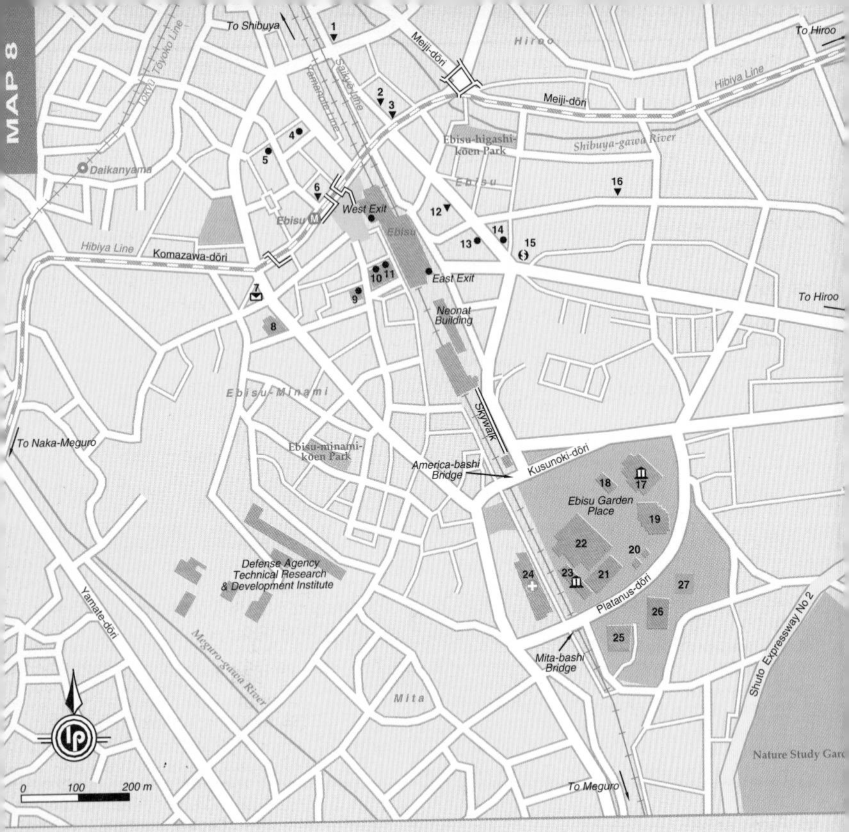
MAP 8
To Shibuya
Tōkyū Tōyoko Line
Yamanote Line
Saikyō Line
Meiji-dōri
Hiroo
To Hiroo
Hibiya Line
Meiji-dōri
Ebisu-higashi-kōen Park
Shibuya-gawa River
Daikanyama
Ebisu
West Exit
Ebisu
Hibiya Line
Komazawa-dōri
East Exit
To Hiroo
Neonat Building
Ebisu-Minami
Skywalk
To Naka-Meguro
Ebisu-minami-kōen Park
America-bashi Bridge
Kusunoki-dōri
Ebisu Garden Place
Defense Agency Technical Research & Development Institute
Platanus-dōri
Shuto Expressway No 2
Yamate-dōri
Meguro-gawa River
Mita-bashi Bridge
Mita
Nature Study Garc
0
100
200 m
To Meguro

MAP 8

PLACES TO STAY

27 Westin Hotel Tokyo
ウエスティンホテル東京

PLACES TO EAT

1 An An
杏庵

2 Fujii
藤井

3 KFC

6 Wendy's

12 Subway

16 Mai-Thai

20 Taillevent Robuchon

OTHER

4 Daimaru Peacock Department Store
大丸ピーコック

5 What the Dickens; Milk

7 Ebisu Eki-mae Post Office
恵比寿駅前 郵便局

8 Matsuzakaya Department Store
松坂屋デパート

9 Piga Piga
ピガピガ

10 Bodeguita
ボデギータ

11 Shanghai
上海

13 Wonderland Books

14 Zona Rosa
ゾナ・ロサ

15 Fuji Bank
富士銀行

17 Sapporo Breweries HQ; Beer Museum Yebisu
サッポロビール本社；
恵比寿麦酒記念館

18 Mitsukoshi Department Store
三越デパート

19 Ebisu Garden Terrace Niban-kan Building
ガーデンテラス弐番館

21 Garden Hall
ガーデンホール

22 Ebisu Garden Place Tower
ガーデンパレスタワー

23 Tokyo Metropolitan Museum of Photography
東京都写真美術館

24 Kōseichūō Hospital
厚生中央病院

25 Ebisu View Tower
恵比寿ビュータワー

26 Garden Terrace Ichiban-kan Building
ガーデンテラス壱番館

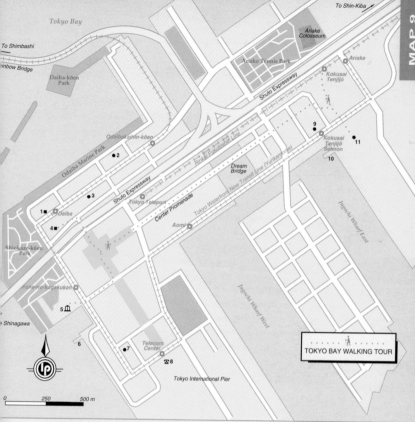

MAP 9

MAP 9

PLACES TO STAY
1 Hotel Nikkō Tokyo
  ホテル日航東京
4 Hotel Grand Pacific Tokyo
  ホテルグランド
  パシフィック東京

OTHER
2 Decks Tokyo Beach
  デックス東京ビーチ
3 Fuji Television Japan
  Broadcast Centre
  フジテレビ日本放送センター
5 Museum of Maritime Science
  船の科学館

6 Suijō Bus Aomi Pier
  水上バス青海発着所
7 Time 24 Building
  タイム２４ビル
8 Telecom Center
  テレコムセンター
9 Tokyo Fashion Town
  東京ファッション
  タウン
10 Suijō Bus Ariake Pier
  水上バス有明発着所
11 Tokyo 'Big Sight'
  International
  Exhibition Center
  東京ビッグサイト
  （東京国際展示場）

Map Legend

BOUNDARIES

International Boundary

Provincial Boundary

ROUTES

Freeway, with Route Number   A25

Major Road

Minor Road

Minor Road - Unsealed

City Road

City Street

City Lane

JR Train Line, with Station

Shinkansen Train Line

Private Train Line, with Station

Subway Route, with Station

Cable Car or Chairlift

Ferry Route

Walking Tour

AREA FEATURES

Building

Cemetery

Hotel

Market

Park, Gardens

Pedestrian Mall

Urban Area

HYDROGRAPHIC FEATURES

Canal

Coastline

River

Creek

Lake

Intermittent Lake

Rapids, Waterfalls

Salt Lake

Swamp

SYMBOLS

CAPITAL .... National Capital

CAPITAL .... Provincial Capital

CITY .... City

Town .... Town

Village .... Village

Place to Stay

Place to Eat

Pub or Bar

Airport

Ancient or City Wall

Archaeological Site

Bank

Castle or Fort

Cliff or Escarpment

Embassy

Gate

Hindu Temple

Hospital

Monument

Museum

One Way Street

Pagoda

Parking

Police Station

Post Office

Shrine

Stately Home

Swimming Pool

Telephone

Temple

Tomb

Tourist Information

Transport

Zoo

Note: not all symbols displayed above appear in this book